THE ONE YEAR®
Salt & Light Devotional

THE ONE YEAR®

Salt
&
Light

DEVOTIONAL

{ 365 inspirations
to equip & encourage you to live
out your calling in the world }

Chris Tiegreen

TYNDALE
MOMENTUM®

The nonfiction imprint of
Tyndale House Publishers, Inc.

Visit Tyndale online at www.tyndale.com.

Visit Tyndale Momentum online at www.tyndalemomentum.com.

TYNDALE, Tyndale Momentum, Tyndale's quill logo, and *The One Year* are registered trademarks of Tyndale House Publishers, Inc. The Tyndale Momentum logo, *One Year,* and The One Year logo are trademarks of Tyndale House Publishers, Inc. Tyndale Momentum is the nonfiction imprint of Tyndale House Publishers, Inc., Carol Stream, Illinois.

The One Year Salt and Light Devotional: 365 Inspirations to Equip and Encourage You to Live Out Your Calling in the World

Designed by Eva M. Winters

For information about special discounts for bulk purchases, please contact Tyndale House Publishers at csresponse@tyndale.com, or call 1-800-323-9400.

ISBN 978-1-4964-3005-2

Printed in the United States of America

25	24	23	22	21	
7	6	5	4	3	2

{ Introduction }

We live in an age when some people believe religion in general or Christianity in particular is one of the most corrosive elements of society, while others believe it is one of the most constructive. We hear absurdly indefensible claims like, "Religion is the cause of almost all wars," as well as overly confident claims that virtually all hospitals, homeless shelters, educational norms, traditional values, work ethics, democratic principles, and economic successes spring from Christian ideals. The reality is somewhere in between, but of course we as believers want to make the most of our influence and increase it. Scripture calls us to be the salt of the earth and lights in the world—preserving, flavoring, brightening, and warming both society as a whole and the lives of those around us. The Kingdom of God is exceedingly good, and we are to personify it and offer glimpses of it everywhere we go.

Some Christians seem to know how to do that naturally, winsomely, and effectively, while others act out of past wounds, get triggered by conflict, fight fire with fire, and try to win people to the Kingdom by vilifying them. In between, most Christians treasure their beliefs on Sunday but have no idea how to translate their private spirituality into their public interactions. And with good reason: Secular society constantly tries to marginalize faith. People want to cross this divide and make a difference but don't know how. This devotional will suggest creative, nonthreatening, unembarrassing, and (most importantly) effective ways to make a difference.

In our efforts to be a positive force for the Kingdom, we may notice a frequent tension. On the one hand, God has set his people apart to be dedicated to him and conformed to his image. On the other hand, he sends us into the world to be involved and influential. We are "in the world but not of the world," and emphasizing one of those truths at the expense of the other leads to imbalance and irrelevance. If we are only set apart to God, we are in no position to make a difference; if we just blend in, we have nothing distinctive about us to make a difference with.

Much of this devotional is about maintaining that balance—keeping our "saltiness" flavorful and our light bright. This is much more than a matter of sharing our faith. Our goal is a lifestyle that begins deep inside and works its way out. The message of God's Kingdom flourishes best in a climate in which Kingdom truths and values are present. The environment surrounding it matters. On many occasions, we as believers in Jesus will have to take the lead in establishing that environment. We will never establish the Kingdom in its fullness before Jesus returns—Kingdom fullness comes with the King—but we are nevertheless called to work toward it, to expand it, to partner with him to help it grow.

Throughout this devotional, you will see some of the same themes coming up again and again: the long view versus a short-term approach; a lifestyle that goes well beyond words; the need to embody the truths of God's Kingdom and the character of the King; what it means to live in the true image of God; and how to serve as an agent or catalyst for God's blessings. You will also find a prayer at the end of each day's reading. These are simple prayers, and some of them may not seem very profound. But they don't need to be profound for God to answer them; they just need to be prayed. If you will express them consistently or use them as prompts to pray deeper, longer prayers, you will find him answering them, sometimes in surprising ways.

That's my prayer for you as you go through these readings—that God will encourage you, move you, and use you in surprising ways to bless this world with his wisdom, power, and love. You carry those blessings with you already, and your world is desperately longing to see them. May they overflow in your life in increasing measure each day.

The Rising Light

The LORD is God, shining upon us. (Psalm 118:27)

FROM THE OPENING SCENE AT Creation to the eternal daytime of Revelation, Scripture is full of glimpses of light. We know the source of all light, of course: the Father of lights (James 1:17, ESV), who loves to bless his people with his goodness. Often this true light is reflected in the people who recognize it. After all, Isaiah called God's people to rise and shine with his glory (Isaiah 60:1-3), and Jesus told his followers not only that he was the light of the world (John 8:12), but that they were too (Matthew 5:14). In the darkness that surrounds us every day, God draws people to himself through human agents who shine with his brilliance.

But you already know we don't shine perfectly; that is painfully obvious. A quick look at history and the culture around us reveals that God's people have only made a mark on this world when we have demonstrated unusual wisdom, power, or love. These are core attributes of God, and our impact as agents of salt and light will necessarily involve at least one of these three. They make up the foundation of our faith and demonstrate something of who God is to those around us.

This is a high calling—higher than our natural abilities. But that's by design. Few people are impressed when we show ourselves to be as wise, empowered, and loving as average people. But when these divine resources flow through us from beyond ourselves, wonderful things happen. Others notice. We become testimonies to a larger truth than even our own finite eyes can see and minds can grasp.

Make this your mission. Seek the gifts that come from beyond yourself. Resolve to live in the light, to reflect the glory of your Father in ways that differ from typical human interaction. Getting there will be a process, but the journey comes with a promise—that God's light, shining in you and through you, will change this world.

Father, fill me with the wisdom, power, and love of your presence. In the same ways I've received your light, let me reflect it for others to see. May the dawn of your glory rise in me and shine through me each day. Amen.

Be Fruitful

Go and make disciples of all the nations. (Matthew 28:19)

JESUS SENT HIS FOLLOWERS OUT INTO the world with a message, and both the sending and the message remain nonnegotiable today. No matter how much our society relativizes its versions of truth, how often people tell us to keep our beliefs to ourselves, or how skeptical others are of our faith, the imperative is still there. We should have no problem complying with the formal and informal rules of society and respecting the diversity of our culture and the people who compose it—but we still have a responsibility to be influential somewhere, somehow, in someone's life.

So how do we go about this? Some of us are bold in our conversations, while others' strengths are seen in examples of love and faith. Some of us emphasize apologetics and debate while others focus on works of mercy and compassion. And some of us seek demonstrations of spiritual power. Of all the many ways of reaching people with the truth and love of God, which are right?

Probably all of them, and some we haven't even thought of yet. The point is not which method is right—God created diverse personalities and distributed varying spiritual gifts—but whether we are intentional about our mission in the first place. People who rely exclusively on principles develop a relationship with principles rather than with God. As Jesus showed throughout his ministry, he works in different ways at different times. His character is not situational, but his ways are. And we are called to follow them attentively.

In the earliest pages of Genesis, God told the first couple to be fruitful and multiply, to fill the earth and influence it (Genesis 1:28). Jesus' words to his followers are the spiritual version of that mission. How each of us goes out into the world will depend on Jesus' leading, but the imperative of going applies to all. Every believer is called to pursue a life of fruitfulness, whether we ever see the fruit or not. Set your heart on that mission in full confidence that he is with you and will lead, strengthen, and bless you wherever you go.

Jesus, how do I fit into your purposes? Which corner of the world am I called to influence? How do you want me to represent you and your message? Show me, lead me, fill me. I say "yes" to your calling today and forever. Amen.

Foreigners and Nomads

All these people died still believing what God had promised them. . . .
They agreed that they were foreigners and nomads here on earth.
(Hebrews 11:13)

FOR THE FIRST THREE HUNDRED YEARS of Christian history, followers of Jesus were keenly aware of their alien status in this world. Our spiritual forebears lived in often-hostile territory among people who ignored or dismissed them and sometimes actively persecuted them. As believers in Jesus, they were no longer strangers and foreigners to God and his promises (Ephesians 2:19), but they were strangers and foreigners to the world and its ways. The citizens of heaven lived as exiles on earth.

That's not a new twist in the history of God's people. Exile is one of the first scenes in our story—fallen humanity driven out of Eden. The story line of redemption is a cycle of exiles and remnants: captives in Egypt and Babylon, wanderers looking for a place to live, returnees trying to rebuild the broken walls of their existence, hearts longing for their true home. Even today, we are told we are in the world but not of it—an ever-expanding righteous remnant growing into a vast, eternal Kingdom. As citizens of heaven living in occupied territory, we know that our story is not at its end.

That means we are living in two extremely important processes: (1) growing into the environment of heaven and learning God's ways; and (2) learning how to relate to and influence the world we live in. The two complement each other, but there is also tension between them. Will our spiritual growth separate us from our culture or engage it? Are we being sent into the world or delivered from it? Are we, as the saying goes, becoming so heavenly minded that we are no earthly good? Or, as it really should be, are we seeking heaven-mindedness in order to benefit those around us? These are questions foreigners and nomads have to ask. We have been loved, chosen, and called—and everything in our lives should be pointed toward demonstrating why.

Father, teach me how to relate to your world and mine. Help me fulfill my calling. As long as I am a stranger in this world, make me an ambassador of your Kingdom. Amen.

Salt and Light

You are the salt of the earth. . . . You are the light of the world.
(Matthew 5:13-14)

JESUS NEVER MINIMIZED THE ROLES of his followers. He never told them to have modest aspirations; never reminded them they were only human; never limited their potential as Spirit-filled, divinely aided beings. No, he called them salt and light—agents of seasoning, preservation, growth, and brilliance—sent not just to tell a story to the world but to help it flourish. John Chrysostom, a church father from the fourth century, understood these words as an elevation of Jesus' disciples over the prophets of old. Followers of Jesus are meant to preserve the new life given to them, Chrysostom preached, halting the world's corruption and shining divine light into every dark corner. To be salt and light is a high calling indeed.

But this calling comes with warnings. Jesus suggests the possibility of salt losing its flavor or potency and light being hidden and rendered ineffective. Salt is meant to be salty; light is meant to shine—not so they can be glorified, but because the world desperately needs what salt and light provide. Each believer in Jesus is designed, gifted, and called to meet needs. We are meant to be present and active without being ostentatious, effective without being overbearing, and influential without seeking power. That means that in some measure or another, you are on display.

As someone who claims the name of Jesus, you are called to season the world with your salt and shine your light into it. You may not want a prominent role, and you may not even desire the responsibility of bearing his name, for fear that you won't live up to it. But his name is given to you anyway, and for better or worse, you will shape his reputation in the eyes of others. Jesus' words to his disciples unapologetically commission them as agents of his Kingdom. They signal a high calling for all his followers—then and now—to be exactly what the world needs.

Jesus, how can I ever live up to your standard? How can someone like me represent who you really are? Still, you have called me and equipped me. May I serve you well by serving the world you love. Fill me with power and light today and every day. Amen.

Knowing Who You Are

We love each other because he loved us first. (1 John 4:19)

YOU ARE CALLED TO LOVE. It's one of the fundamental truths of the gospel—God is love (1 John 4:8, 16); God sent his Son to us because of his love (John 3:16); and the Son sends us into the world in the same spirit (John 20:21). If we are to represent our Father well, we must know how to love, and we must demonstrate that love to those around us. Words, miracles, and knowledge are not enough; if we get everything right but forget to fill our works with love, we are nothing but noisemakers (1 Corinthians 13:1-3). Loving others is a fruit of the Spirit and the core of the message we believe.

Even so, many Christians become so focused on trying to love others (and failing) that they forget where love comes from in the first place. We cannot reflect God's true and deep love without having fully received it first. If we try to, we'll only burn out. If our efforts to be selfless cause us to neglect our self, we'll have nothing to give. Before we ever know how to love, we have to know how to *be* loved.

Your ability to love the world depends entirely on the degree to which you see yourself as loved by the Father. Maybe you have thought it selfish to dwell on the Father's delight in you, but you have little to offer the world until you grasp this. We love because he first loved us. That's how it works. You can only share what you already have. If you haven't received supernatural love, you can't give it away. If you don't know how he delights in you, you can't delight in others in any way that transforms them. The best thing you can do for those around you is to bathe in the Father's love yourself. Only then will it flow out of you and draw others into his open arms.

Father, let me see myself the way you see me. Open my heart to perceive the height, depth, width, and breadth of your love. Bathe me in your delight so I can delight in others with your love. Amen.

Where You Fit

*God has given each of you a gift from his great variety of
spiritual gifts. Use them well to serve one another. (1 Peter 4:10)*

EVERY CHRISTIAN HAS BEEN called to love, serve, bless, and exercise his or her gifts. This is not news to us; believers talk a lot about calling and ministry within the church and beyond it. But how do we apply this general calling individually? How do we know where God wants us to be and what he wants us to do? Where do we fit in?

Writer and preacher Frederick Buechner addresses these questions: "The place God calls you to is the place where your deep gladness and the world's deep hunger meet."[1] In other words, there is an intersection between your sense of purpose and the world's places of need. Wherever that intersection is, you will find fruitfulness and satisfaction there. This calling may not always be easy, and the fruit may not always be evident—in fact, you almost certainly will face hardships and dry seasons—but you will be secure in your service. It will fit your gifts and desires.

The beauty of this balance between "your deep gladness" and "the world's deep hunger" is that it remedies two spiritual distortions: the idea that serving God must always *feel* sacrificial and painful; and the idea that if you are satisfied, you are selfishly neglecting others. God's will and yours converge to fulfill his purposes and satisfy your heart. Yes, his calling involves sacrifice, but it leads to joy, just as it did with Jesus (Hebrews 12:2). And though it is possible to spend one's life seeking self, that does not mean *all* satisfaction is selfish. As so many psalms remind us, God is a fulfiller of hearts and a satisfier of desires. Where you fit in this world is the place where your heart was created to fit—in him, and for his glory. Find a need that you are delighted to fulfill, and you will discover your calling there.

Lord, I will follow you wherever you lead. But in my service, lead me into joy. In my sacrifice, fulfill me. You have made me for a purpose; may my eyes always be open to see it. Amen.

In His Image

Imitate God, therefore, in everything you do, because you are his dear children. Live a life filled with love, following the example of Christ.
(Ephesians 5:1-2)

"I LIKE YOUR CHRIST. I do not like your Christians. Your Christians are so unlike your Christ." This quote, often attributed (probably mistakenly) to Gandhi, reflects a common objection about Christianity—that the behavior and attitudes of Christians are a poor reflection of Jesus. It's an easy complaint to make, of course, but it isn't the real issue. The big question about Jesus is whether *he* expressed the truth, not whether his followers do. If Jesus is admirable and praiseworthy in comparison to his followers, then why not believe in him? It makes no sense to reject him based on historical examples of Christians behaving badly. But many skeptics prefer to focus on Christian faults and avoid the Jesus question altogether.

Still, the criticism makes a point. Throughout the ages, far too many believers have represented a Father of compassion in a spirit of judgment or a Father of patience in a spirit of anger. We have turned the gospel into words and doctrines rather than attitudes of the heart. We have become so focused on teaching the truth that we've forgotten to live it.

This misplaced focus has hindered the spread of the Good News. Historically, the church has begun with evangelism and indoctrination, and then tried to demonstrate love, compassion, mercy, and grace. Jesus' example turns the process around—demonstrating the *nature* of God before teaching about him. We were made in the Father's image and are being restored into that very same image through Jesus—the exact image of God (Hebrews 1:3)—by the power of the Spirit. That means our primary objective above all else is to reflect the Father's heart—to till the soil of God's Kingdom long before we try to plant the seeds of our words into it. If you want your world to know your Father, be like him. Represent him well, and let your words follow.

Father, it is often said that apples don't fall far from the tree, and I want to be one of the closest—to reflect who you really are. Transform me in my deepest depths to exude your Spirit. Amen.

Your First Objective

Jesus said to her, "I who speak to you am he." (John 4:26, ESV)

WHEN JESUS ENCOUNTERED A Samaritan woman at Jacob's well, he didn't share the gospel with her—at least not in the way most evangelicals today would describe "the gospel." He didn't lay out the plan of salvation, a set of spiritual laws, or a sinner's prayer. He didn't explain the fall of humanity, the gap between us and God, or the way he planned to bridge that gap with the Cross. Hints of those elements are in their dialogue, of course, but today's spiritual watchdogs would blast Jesus for using such subtleties and mishandling a perfect opportunity to share the truth.

We could learn a lot from this conversation, though. Jesus modeled what we often forget—that truth is relational. For Christians, truth is not an object; it's a Person. Everything in Jesus' conversation with the Samaritan woman led back to him. Faith always comes first; understanding comes later. He brought her into a relationship with the Source of all truth.

In trying to share the transforming power of the gospel with others, many Christians today focus first on dissuading people from their worldviews—perspectives on politics, evolution, or abortion, for example. This approach may fuel conversation, but it is rarely fruitful and usually polarizing. The first objective of Christians is not to win people to a worldview; it's to invite them into a relationship with Jesus. From there, we can trust God to take them wherever he wants them to go intellectually, emotionally, and spiritually. The doctrine-first approach is almost impossible, while the Jesus-first approach sets the foundation for everything else to come in God's time and in his way. Our agenda for other people is often misguided; his is completely trustworthy and will get them exactly where they need to be.

Holy Spirit, you have a way into every human heart and a language for every mind. Help me remember that it is not my responsibility to convince hearts and minds of my views but to introduce them to my Savior. Open doors for me to point to Jesus. Amen.

Learning the Language

*I try to find common ground with everyone, doing
everything I can to save some. (1 Corinthians 9:22)*

IN THE AGE OF DISCOVERY, when Europeans were getting acquainted with Asia and exploring the Americas, the Jesuits developed a reputation as master language learners. They admirably navigated the challenges of many of the world's most widely spoken languages, as well as many lesser known ones, and they spread the gospel in native tongues. But when they ventured into the Amazon basin, they encountered a dizzying variety of previously unknown languages. Many African languages coming into the Brazil colony from the slave trade compounded that challenge. The linguistic landscape was far more overwhelming than anyone had thought.

Some young Jesuits were daunted by the multitude of newly discovered tongues and preferred to teach Portuguese and Spanish to Amazonians and Africans in order to preach their message. But António Vieira, a Jesuit priest, orator, and writer, challenged them with a sermon on the Spirit's work at Pentecost and urged them to continue reaching people in native languages. The missionaries would have to be creative and industrious, and they would have to expand their vision because the mission was clear: Messengers of the gospel are called to reach people on their terms and in their own culture.

And that's what God did with us. He clothed himself in flesh and left the throne of heaven to reach us in our own context. He sends us into the world on the same terms. If we want to have any influence in the worlds of business, arts, academia, or any other cultural sphere, we have to (1) be willing to be influenced by and learn from others and (2) humbly enter into other cultures and languages, both literally and figuratively. Speaking church language, expecting "Christian" behavior, and limiting ideas from those who do not believe as we do accomplish little. God speaks our language, understands our issues, and opens his arms. And we are called to live in this world with the same accommodation and heart.

Father, you are Lord of the common ground, and you always know how to find it. Bridge the gaps between me and my peers; give me an agreeable heart; and make connections that build healthy relationships for the good of your Kingdom. Amen.

Embracing the Culture

*Even though I am a free man with no master, I have become a slave
to all people to bring many to Christ. (1 Corinthians 9:19)*

HUDSON TAYLOR, the well-known missionary to China in the late nineteenth century, ruffled feathers among his fellow British expats when he wore Chinese clothes and grew his hair to match Chinese styles. Some of them found his behavior scandalous and scolded his attempts to fit in. They assured him he would never be seen as Chinese because his fair complexion and facial features would always mark him as a European. Even so, knowing the limitations, Taylor did everything he could to connect with Chinese people culturally. Why? Because the gospel is enough of a spiritual stumbling block on its own. Removing cultural stumbling blocks goes a long way toward opening hearts to its message.

Taylor was only following the lead of the apostle Paul, who had become "all things to all people" so many centuries earlier in order to win the hearts of some (1 Corinthians 9:22, ESV). Paul, in turn, was only following the lead of the Father, who became an insider in the culture of his own creation to reach those who had ears to hear his voice. God made quite a few major statements with the Incarnation, one of them being the lengths he would go to in pursuing the love of human beings. Jesus was God's strategy for removing cultural stumbling blocks between heaven and earth—for overcoming barriers and making the message heard. The prophets had spoken truth and been rejected; Jesus embodied it and, though rejected by many, was embraced by others. Some people are drawn to truth only when it is dressed in familiar clothes.

In being light, recognize the value in whatever connections you have with the world's ways. Don't adapt to its philosophies, but understand the opportunities of being an insider. Remove as many unnecessary obstacles as you can. The most transforming cultural influences are often those that come from within.

Father, you have set me in my context for a reason. Help me use my similarities with others in order to make a difference in their lives. Clothe me spiritually in Jesus and culturally in the places that need your love. Amen.

Which Christianity?

*You must have the qualities of salt among yourselves and
live in peace with each other. (Mark 9:50)*

A LOT OF PEOPLE REJECT Christianity without knowing exactly which Christianity they are rejecting. The problem is perception—seeing the enormous variety of Christian beliefs and practices as essentially the same. People reach back into the depths of history to blame the entire faith for the misbehaviors of certain representatives from the past: "Look at the wars Christians have started." "See how corrupt the church has been." "Haven't Christians always opposed advances in knowledge?" And on and on.

The problem is bigger than painting all of Christianity with blame for exceptional mistakes. The non-Christian world tends to equate the nominal Christianity of the powerful with the undercurrent of true Christianity based on the spiritual— i.e., they confuse the institutional church with the devout church, or, as some academics express it, the Church of Power vs. the Church of Piety.[2] Christian structures have long been exploited by the powerful, who often rise in position without holding true Christian beliefs. The result is a distorted faith that often turns people away from Jesus.

Your job in this world is to demonstrate the difference. Your kind of Christianity did not instigate the violence of the Crusades, come up with the devastation of colonialism, or perpetuate slavery. The two major streams of Christianity running throughout history—the power-hungry and the pious—are not the same thing. You have an opportunity to prove that to the people around you. Political commentary, a sense of superiority, and anger toward opposing opinions will not accomplish that goal. A life full of love and peace will. Know the difference, and even in expressing your opinions, remember the heart of God. His Spirit seeks not to compete with people but to draw them in.

Holy Spirit, make me as winsome as you are. Give me the love of the Father and the favor of Jesus. May my heart, my words, and my life draw people to you. Amen.

Spreading Joy

Always be full of joy in the Lord. I say it again — rejoice!
(Philippians 4:4)

JOY IS CONTAGIOUS. Unfortunately, so is discouragement. In fact, almost all of our attitudes are. Studies have shown that the emotions of one person can affect the emotions of everyone else in the room—even when no words have been spoken. One agitated person spreads agitation; one angry person spreads anger; one peaceful person spreads peace; and for better or worse, each emotional contagion moves on. Patterns are established not by which emotion is best but by which is strongest. The one who carries the stronger attitude or emotion influences those in his or her path.

On the surface, that research confronts us with all the times we have been swayed by people with dominant personalities. But it also presents us with enormous opportunities. Think about it: If the peace inside you is strong, you can walk into an unsettled room and pacify it. If the joy you carry is greater than the disappointment of those around you, you can lift them up out of their discouragement without even saying a word. Or to put it in an often-used metaphor, you have the opportunity not just to be a thermometer that measures temperature but a thermostat that sets it.

You have much greater influence than you may have believed. And you have a biblical mandate to use that influence for good. Scripture commands joy, and though your circumstances may not be joyful, you have the opportunity to enjoy God and the climate of his Kingdom to its fullest. Not only do you benefit from the truth of God's joy, but the people around you will too. In fact, your joy may be the first true glimpse of the Kingdom they have experienced—and their gateway into deeper experiences of it. Living in the fullness of the Kingdom—its joy, peace, love, satisfaction, and more—is the greatest testimony of its reality you can offer.

Lord, I have to confess that my bad moods and bitter attitudes have misrepresented your Kingdom and distracted people from your truth. Renovate my heart. Fill me with peace, joy, and love. Create the climate of your Kingdom in me so I can create it for those around me. Amen.

Be Real

*I pray that God, the source of hope, will fill you completely with joy
and peace because you trust in him. Then you will overflow with
confident hope through the power of the Holy Spirit. (Romans 15:13)*

"JUST BEING REAL." These are the words we say whenever we want to separate ourselves from pie-in-the-sky thinking and confess the messiness of real-life experience.
They reflect an admirable desire for authenticity, express an honest admission that
life is not always as it should be, show a real vulnerability to the struggles we are
facing, and open up conversations with others. They are the opposite of hypocrisy.

But does our desire to "just be real" actually reflect reality? In terms of what
we are humanly experiencing, maybe so. But in terms of how God sees things—by
definition, he is the realest reality—probably not. In fact, our authenticity about our
own thoughts and feelings is very often an expression of discouragement or disappointment that shifts our eyes away from the reality of God's Kingdom.

There's no shame in experiencing or expressing disappointment. The issue is how
we can get from point A to point B—from the false reality of our experience to the
true reality of God's Kingdom. No measure of faking it till we make it or putting
on a good show will get us there. These are the hypocrisies we need to avoid. No,
the only path into the greater reality of hope and joy and confidence is to experience inner transformation, a specialty of the Spirit sent by the God of all hope. It's a
process, to be sure, and not always a comfortable one. But it's authentic. Ultimately,
we should be able to tell people that our hope, joy, and peace—our experience of
God's *shalom*—is the greatest truth we have experienced and a testimony of how he
redeems and restores the human heart. Only then will "just being real" mean something entirely refreshing and new.

*Lord, you already know my struggles and how I've shared them openly with others. But
don't leave me in them; use them to transform me and demonstrate your transforming
power to those who need it. Bring me into the ultimate realities of hope and fulfillment.
Amen.*

A Fence or a Gate?

They crush people with unbearable religious demands and
never lift a finger to ease the burden. (Matthew 23:4)

THE PHARISAICAL SPIRIT, regardless of which religion or denomination it has shown up in, has always sought limits. Its highest priority is discovering and enforcing the restrictions God has placed on us. Rather than asking what is permitted, it focuses on what is forbidden. The result is a constant emphasis on sin and failure.

Unfortunately, this is one of the most common takeaway points many people have seen in Christianity throughout history—that it is a legal code of unpermitted thoughts and behaviors given by God to help us avoid hell. In part, our religious instinct interprets everything in legal terms, and the church has played into that mind-set far too well. Throughout the ages, plenty of Christian teachers have expounded on religious demands and tried to enforce them. And even today, it's often said that Christians are known for what we are against more than what we are for.

This attitude highlights a profound dividing line between true and false spirituality. It's true that God forbids some things; he wants us to reflect his image and conform to his character. But his emphasis is on freedom, not restriction. He loves his children and gave us his Word not to put a fence around our lives but to open a gateway into an eternal adventure with him. The entrance into the Kingdom is as narrow as a single Savior, but the fields within are vast and open. Of all the messages the world needs to hear, this is the most important. God is not the giver of false burdens; he is the liberator.

That does not mean you can live without responsibility, of course. It means, however, that your responsibilities will bring rest and freedom to you and others. When you read Scripture, you are to see it as an invitation into unexplored realms. Carry that openness into the world, and invite others in. God does not quench the human heart. He sets it free.

Father, forgive us for focusing on limitations. Lift our eyes to see your opportunities. Take us on adventures with you and draw many—even multitudes—into your delights. Amen.

A New Testament Church

Dear friends, don't be surprised at the fiery trials you are going through, as if something strange were happening to you. (1 Peter 4:12)

"WE WANT TO BE LIKE the New Testament church." That desire has been expressed countless times in recent decades by Christians and church leaders hoping to recapture the excitement and power of the earliest believers shown in the book of Acts. We want to pierce through all the layers of tradition and reenter the simplicity of those first days after Pentecost, when the apostles ministered with signs and wonders and believers selflessly committed to truth and each other. We want to get back to the original faith.

Or do we? Our hearts may long for spiritual simplicity and the power of the Spirit, but our behavior suggests otherwise. The New Testament church was quite familiar with laws, politics, and culture that went against their practices and beliefs. They understood adversity, prayed boldly through trials, and persevered through persecution. They willingly suffered abuses and ignored insults without complaining about being pushed to the margins and misrepresented by society. They did not fight against the grain of the culture; instead, they became shining lights within it.

That's the sort of New Testament spirit we should aim to have. Many Christians waste much of their relational capital complaining about lost values and social ills rather than living in the power of the gospel, but spiritual power is never dependent on political conditions or social trends. In fact, it is best lived in the midst of them. The New Testament church thrived in adverse conditions, demonstrating the goodness of God in the context of a contentious world. It was not fazed by secularization or paganism or immoral surroundings. It simply became a lighthouse unmovable by tumultuous seas.

If you want to influence your world, this is how you will need to approach it. If the New Testament church is a God-given model, today's Christians have a lot to learn about distractions and perseverance. An adverse culture is not a cause for lament. It is not a personal attack. It's an opportunity to demonstrate the nature of God.

Lord, open my eyes to see what you are doing in the world. Turn my focus to the opportunities ahead. Help me persevere, not with complaint or discouragement but with confidence and faith. You have given me everything I need to thrive. Amen.

Set Apart

Daniel was determined not to defile himself by eating the food and
wine given to them by the king. (Daniel 1:8)

WHEN GOD'S PEOPLE LIVED IN the kingdoms of Israel and Judah, they knew what was expected of them and established their own spiritual and social culture. But when they were dispersed into other kingdoms by Assyrians and Babylonians, they were suddenly confronted with diverse rituals and lifestyles that went against their own. God's people were given pagan names and forced to work for idolatrous masters. They often could not choose their own food or customs. And they certainly could not worship at their own Temple, which was in their distant homeland and eventually destroyed. They had to live as people of God among people who did not know him.

The book of Daniel refers to how Daniel and his friends did this by remaining faithful in prayer and dietary restrictions. Books like Ezra, Nehemiah, and Malachi suggest different ways Jews struggled with issues related to the laws of Moses and intermarriage with foreigners. The book of Esther makes no mention of any of these issues (or even of God), though a new feast, Purim, is inaugurated that is still celebrated today. In other words, Jews seem to have navigated life in foreign lands in a variety of ways, maintaining customs, cultural traditions, and God-given laws in extenuating circumstances.

The point is that diaspora Jews had to figure out how to live as a minority within a majority culture, just as Christians today have to do in many parts of the world. Some Christians encourage extreme separation and standing firm against the currents of cultures, while others adapt to their surroundings. In every case, biblical and modern, the issue is not the degree to which believers accommodate; it's the spirit in which they do so. Is it for influence or compromise? Faithfulness or apathy? Love for God or legalistic adherence to rules? As you live in this world, know the difference. In whatever ways you distinguish yourself, do it for the right reasons: love, faithfulness, and impact. Wherever you are, choose to be who God made and called you to be.

Father, you have set me apart from the world but also placed me within it. Give me the willingness to compromise what isn't important, stand for what is, and clearly discern the difference. Amen.

A Generous Spirit

Who are you to condemn someone else's servants? Their own master will judge whether they stand or fall. And with the Lord's help, they will stand and receive his approval. (Romans 14:4)

THERE HAVE BEEN ERAS WHEN the most dedicated Christians considered any participation or interest in sports as acceptance of an entire host of ungodly influences: gambling, drinking, materialism, pride, and more. There have been times when the church outlawed any interest on a loan as usury. And there are places in the world today where cosmetics are scandalous among Christians because they hint at immorality. In other words, what is commonly accepted in one place or time may be forbidden in another; what for one person is a passion may be to another person an idol. Though all true believers are born of the same Spirit, we have had widely differing views on cultural practices and have lived out our faith in different ways.

Does morality change across continents or times? Of course not. But our perceptions of morality do. We have a hard time drawing clear lines between outward direction and inward conviction, or cultural norms and spiritual compromise. The picture gets more complicated when we realize that God deals with his children individually, addressing what might be a deep heart issue in one person and a peripheral distraction in another. His priorities for his children are not uniform; he knows what each of us needs to work on and in which order we need to do it. Those of us who like evenly applied principles become poor judges of the behavior of others.

That's why we are told not to judge. God and Scripture urge us to have a generous spirit toward other believers, and our attitude toward non-Christians should be even more generous. The world is full of critical people; we are not to be among them. We have been invited into a culture of grace, and we are called to extend it to others.

Father, you have demonstrated a generous heart toward me; my path into your arms has been filled with many misperceptions and mistakes. Thank you for your grace. Fill my heart with the same generosity toward those around me. Amen.

A Pattern of Mercy

Forgive us our sins, as we have forgiven those who sin against us.
(Matthew 6:12)

ON THE SURFACE, Matthew 6:12 seems like an ordinary request—a petition to be forgiven paired with an understanding that we should do likewise for others. But what if the prayer is more loaded than that? What if, instead of acknowledging forgiveness from God and for others as two separate but similar mercies, this prayer actually links the two together? What if it's a prayer to be forgiven by God *in the same way* we forgive those who have offended us, as if God's forgiveness is contingent on our forgiveness of others?

In fact, this is what Jesus implies a few verses later (14-15) and then again in his parable of the forgiven debtor (Matthew 18:23-35). Somehow, our ability to receive God's mercy is directly related to our willingness to show mercy to those who have sinned against us. The insinuation is clear: If we don't forgive others, we will not be forgiven. That puts a lot of weight on our ability to demonstrate grace.

Jesus' point, of course, is that we cannot live in a culture of grace in our relationship with God but step out of that culture in our relationships with others. If we are not very forgiving, it is unlikely that we have ever really received or understood the forgiveness we have been given. Those who have been washed in the mercy of God instinctively share it with others. Or, as Jesus said on another occasion, "Give as freely as you have received!" (Matthew 10:8). Those who understand the weight of the debts that have been removed from them through Christ will hardly go out and weigh others down with the same burdens.

Choose to live in a culture of grace, not just in your relationship with God, but also in your relationship with the world around you. For one thing, the two cannot be separated; for another, there is no other way for the world to experience the generous, forgiving heart of the Father than to experience it in those who love him. In his mercy, you have been given a vision of the Kingdom. Let others see it in you.

Father, I have received so much from you, and I want to become an expression of your mercy. I let go of the offenses I have experienced just as you have let go of mine. Amen.

The Image in the World

God created human beings in his own image. (Genesis 1:27)

IN ANCIENT ROME, the images of emperors on coins and statues represented their authority and presence throughout the empire. At first, this honor was given by the subjects to the ruler; they sought to win their sovereign's favor and elevate his prestige by creating statues and currency in his likeness. By the third century AD, this distribution of the imperial image began moving from the empire's center outward as emperors tested their reception in each corner of their realm. The many representations of the emperor's face were meant to remind the people of the beneficence of their ruler.

God did something similar in Creation but with much greater depth and authenticity. He made human beings in his image and urged them to fill the world as his representatives. As we know, that image shattered in the Fall, and we became poor reflections of our sovereign. But he sent his exact image into this world (Hebrews 1:3, NIV) and set about conforming us to that image by the power of his Spirit (Romans 8:26-30). Now we are sent out as representatives of his authority and presence in every corner of his realm. Jesus' face on us and in us is meant to remind people everywhere of the goodness of their King.

That has huge implications for how we live, and on the surface, it may seem like a lot of pressure. We know we don't represent him perfectly. But representing him as an object of his mercy is important, and all believers qualify as objects of mercy. Even more important are those occasions when we reflect the heart of our Father's compassion, patience, and kindness to those around us. We may forget to do so in the course of our normal activities, but from heaven's perspective, this is what our normal activities should be about. Beyond our to-do lists, all of our relationships are, first and foremost, opportunities to demonstrate the nature of our Father. We were created, reborn, and restored in the image of a very good King.

Father, only you can remake me into your true image, and I pray you will. Give me opportunities to express your nature; remind me at critical moments whom I represent. Love your world through me. Amen.

Freedom and Fulfillment

The letter kills, but the Spirit gives life. (2 Corinthians 3:6, ESV)

ERIC LIDDELL WAS ALL SET to run the 100-meter race for Great Britain at the 1924 Paris Olympics until he found out the qualifying heat for the race was on a Sunday. Participating would violate his dedication to resting on the Sabbath, while not participating would violate the trust of his teammates and the hopes of his country. Many thought his refusal to run was an act of legalism, while others saw it as an admirable sign of devotion. It came across as either an insult or a beautiful testimony.

That's often how devotion looks to the outside world—it mystifies some and earns respect from others. It also sparks debate among Christians, some of whom see adherence to principles as legalism and some of whom see it as uncompromising commitment. The real question, from any point of view, is the motive. Was the action done out of love or obligation? Commitment to God or captivity to law? Personal devotion or the expectations of others? If inspired by the Spirit, it gives life. If done for the sake of a law, it kills. And in most cases, the motives behind our acts of devotion are eventually revealed by how much joy and fulfillment we receive from them.

Your life will create a testimony in some form or another, positively or negatively, whether that testimony is about God, the power of his Spirit, an image you've created for yourself, a lifestyle, a philosophy, or anything else. If your testimony is to point to your love for God, it will need to include some sense of separation from the world in general—some noticeable convictions and commitments that mark you as his. But if those convictions and commitments are done out of obligation, they will produce a different testimony: one that points to the confining, restricting aspects of religion. Liddell's testimony was honored in the film *Chariots of Fire* for a reason—it came from genuine devotion and in the context of a free and fulfilling life. If your commitments come from that kind of love, they will reflect the freedom of God's Kingdom well.

Lord, I want to be bound to you by love and nothing else—captive to your love, free in all else. Your Spirit gives me life. May my convictions produce fulfillment and a testimony of your goodness. Amen.

Changing the Atmosphere

The Spirit who lives in you is greater than
the spirit who lives in the world. (1 John 4:4)

YOU ARE CALLED TO CHANGE the environment wherever you go. The Spirit within you does not conform to negative attitudes, restless crowds, toxic cultures, or any other contrary situations you might find yourself in as you carry out your daily activities. His desire is to work in and through you to change the atmosphere around you—to bring a glimpse of his Kingdom, a taste of *shalom*, to those you encounter. Your attitudes, words, and actions are powerful transformers of the world.

You cannot affect the environment of the world, however, unless you have been immersed in the environment of heaven. First and foremost, that means being in deep and intimate fellowship with God. As you begin to understand and experience the culture of the Trinity—the selflessness, mutual admiration and love, full openness and vulnerability, and complete absence of evil among the Father, Son, and Spirit—you begin to take on God's nature. As you take on his nature, you begin to impart it to those in relationship with you. They may not be able to articulate why they feel different around you, but they will—simply because they are getting a glimpse of heaven. Your immersion in God's Kingdom empowers you to carry it everywhere you go.

That means that the greatest gift you can give to the world begins in a very personal place—your fellowship with the Father, Son, and Spirit and the holy environment of their love. You will not become perfect in the divine attributes and culture of heaven, but you must continue to grow in them. Why? Because you can't impart what you don't have. The stronger you grow in the Spirit, the more powerfully he influences your world through you. If you allow him to dramatically change the atmosphere within you, he will then dramatically change the atmosphere around you. And your influence as salt and light in this world will open hearts to the Spirit who fills you.

Spirit of God, saturate me in the character of the Kingdom, the culture of heaven, the
fullness of your love and power. Make me an outpost of the heavenly environment. As I
carry your presence into this world, give others a taste of who you really are. Amen.

The World

When you love the world, you do not have the love
of the Father in you. (1 John 2:15)

ONLY JOHN RECORDS JESUS' well-known statement about God's great love for the world that compelled him to send his only Son so that we might have everlasting life (John 3:16). Years after Jesus spoke those comforting words, this same John warned us not to love the world. If we do, he wrote, the love of the Father is not in us. On the one hand, God loves the world; on the other, loving the world is a sign that we don't love God. How can this be?

For one thing, God is in no danger of turning his love for the world into an idol. We are. There is a substantial difference between God's sacrificial love for the world and the pull of the world's ways on the affections of our hearts. But it should be clear that "world" means different things in the varying contexts of Scripture. God certainly loves his creation and longs to redeem it. But the world's systems—its deeply imbedded corruptions; its enticements to sin; its power structures that oppress the poor and exclude the pure-hearted; its self-serving economic, political, and cultural networks—stand in opposition to God's nature and the ultimate direction of history. We're called to the kind of sacrificial love God has for the people of the world, but we are called away from the pride and corrupt desires that fill this fallen realm that is passing away.

Go into the world with the same kind of love God has for his creation and all who are made in his image. Aligning your heart with the words of John 3:16 will make you like your Father. And beware of the competition in your own heart. Choose carefully which love to indulge. A self-serving attachment to the world's ways will pull you away from the love of the Father and his love for the world. Instead, let the Father send you with the same love that sent his Son to give his life.

Father, help me love the world as you love the world. Send me as you sent your Son. Redeem every inch of my life from its false loves, and use me as an instrument of redemption. Amen.

Your Mission Statement

The Son of Man came to seek and save those who are lost.
(Luke 19:10)

JESUS MADE SEVERAL STATEMENTS that reflected his mission. He came to seek and save the lost (Luke 19:10). He came not to be served but to serve (Mark 10:45). He came to offer abundant life (John 10:10), to preach the Kingdom of God (Luke 4:43), and to testify to the truth (John 18:37). He quoted a messianic passage from Isaiah to declare that he was the fulfillment of long-awaited promises (Luke 4:16-21). He knew why he had come into this world.

Paul had a similar sense of mission. He knew he was called as an apostle to Gentiles (Acts 9:15; 22:21; Romans 11:13), an ambassador of God and minister of reconciliation (2 Corinthians 5:19-20), and a bondservant of Jesus (Romans 1:1; Philippians 1:1). His ministry took various turns and carried him to unexpected places at times, but he never lost his focus. He knew what he was sent to do.

Not all of us will live with that degree of clarity, but having a sense of mission is important. And articulating that sense of mission—developing a personal mission statement, deciding what is really important in life, discerning how our gifts best intersect with the world's needs—will help us keep moving toward it without getting distracted. Though God orchestrates our circumstances and directs our paths, and though his Spirit may change our direction as mysteriously as the wind shifts (John 3:8), far too many Christians live passively, knowing what they were saved *from* without knowing what they were saved *for*. Prayerful assessment of life, location, career, relationships, habits, and all other relevant components of a calling will help you fulfill your God-given mission.

Spend some time asking God what your mission is in this world. What is he calling you to do? For what purposes did he create you, design you, redeem you, and restore you into his Kingdom? Write out a personal mission statement that will keep you on track, even if it needs to be adjusted in later seasons. Live intentionally, knowing why you are here.

Lord, you are the director, the renovator, the orchestrator of my life. What purpose do you want me to fulfill? How do you want me to use my gifts? How are you sending me into the world? Give me clear direction and help me follow it faithfully. Amen.

See with New Eyes

"The time has come," he said. "The kingdom of God has come near.
Repent and believe the good news!" (Mark 1:15, NIV)

"REPENT AND BELIEVE." On the surface, these instructions seem simple enough. But *repentance* is a word freighted with centuries of baggage, and *belief* has come to mean a variety of things—from mild opinion to zealous conviction. The Hebraic interpretations of these words[3] would have emphasized behavioral change, while the Greek interpretations would have emphasized a transformation of the mind. So which did Jesus and the Spirit really mean? What should repenting and believing look like in our lives?

Repentance and belief certainly have behavioral implications, but the gospel would never begin with an instruction to behave better. As seen in the Old Testament and our own experience, laws and standards of behavior are not enough to transform our lives; that's why Jesus came. But if we learn to see differently—if our vision of God, ourselves, our world, and our situation changes—then our lives begin to change from the inside out. Outward transformation does not last unless it is the natural consequence of a genuine inner transformation. When Jesus told his hearers to repent and believe because the Kingdom was coming, he surely meant to imply a complete reorientation in every area of life. But most fundamental in that reorientation is a new set of eyes and ears, a new way of perceiving, a different sense of expectation, and a vision for what God is doing in the world. For the Kingdom to be received, people need to have a Kingdom mind-set.

If you want to change the world, you will have to change the way you see—to lift your vision beyond the personal focus with which so many Christians limit themselves. His Kingdom includes immeasurable vistas of love and restoration, full of unexpected mercies and creative strategies for entering people's hearts. You are becoming a partner in his mission. Let your mind be stretched, your heart be opened, and your faith be expanded. Reorient yourself and step into the newness of his Kingdom.

Jesus, help me make whatever adjustments I need to make to see your Kingdom come in my life and in the lives of those around me. Give me new eyes to see and new ears to hear. Amen.

In His Presence

*You will show me the way of life, granting me the joy of your presence
and the pleasures of living with you forever. (Psalm 16:11)*

IT'S POSSIBLE TO READ PASSAGES of Scripture like the Psalms with an eye toward your own needs. Many were written in that same spirit—psalmists often began writing with a desperate personal plea—and there is nothing wrong with finding personal encouragement in them. But it is also possible, and sometimes necessary, to read them with an eye to what other people need from you. Words of Scripture do not just fill you up; they fill you up in order to make you overflow. And one of the things you are designed to overflow with is the joy of God's Kingdom. Your satisfaction and fulfillment are a divine calling.

It's okay if you go through discouraging times; that's normal. Some Christians have long-term bouts of depression, whether from brain chemistry, negative thought patterns, or tragic life events. But God's plan for you, as a believer, is to be able to overcome, to see the far greater realities above the hard reality you are facing, to lift your vision to a higher perspective. This elevation of perspective, this abiding joy, really is possible. It's part of your inheritance as a child of God.

Everything you need to make an impact for the Kingdom of God is found in his presence, and you can't get it anywhere else. Other translations of Psalm 16:11 describe "eternal pleasures" (NIV) and "fullness of joy" (ESV) as the result of being in the presence of God. It is not possible for a child of God to sit in the presence of his or her Father—to experience the warmth of his embrace and the encouragement of his promises—and come away with hopelessness. If the world needs anything today, it needs evidence of hope. It needs the testimony of people who are filled with joy. It needs you to saturate yourself in the life-giving, heartwarming, hope-instilling environment of your Father's presence.

Father, fill me with joy. Satisfy the promise of your Son in me—that I would experience abundant life as you intended. Make my heart glad, for my sake and for the sake of those around me who desperately need to know that fulfillment and joy are possible. May the light of your everlasting pleasures shine in me. Amen.

The Key to Change

God knew his people in advance, and he chose them
to become like his Son, so that his Son would be the
firstborn among many brothers and sisters. (Romans 8:29)

"LEOPARDS DON'T CHANGE THEIR SPOTS." Such pessimism may be widely accepted, but it doesn't fit the message of Jesus or the hope of our calling. Transformation is at the heart of the gospel. If people don't change, something is tragically insufficient in the work Jesus did on our behalf. But, of course, there is no insufficiency in Christ. We have been given the key to radical change in our hearts, minds, and spirits.

How does this change happen? There is no short answer, but we can be sure of one thing: It begins in the presence of God. An encounter with him is transforming. How could it not be? When human beings experience an unimaginably powerful, radiant, pure God, we cannot remain the same. Scripture shows us plenty of examples in the lives of Jacob, Isaiah, Ezekiel, Peter, Paul, and others. Paul wrote of this phenomenon in one of his letters to the Corinthians: By beholding the glory of the Lord, we become like him (2 Corinthians 3:18). John even tells us this is our ultimate destiny: We will be like the Lord when he appears (1 John 3:2). If we are ever going to be salt and light in this world, it will be because we got a glimpse of our Lord.

The world needs a revelation of real change. Creation longs for it (Romans 8:19). You have an opportunity to be that revelation, or at least one example of it. But your transformation won't happen merely by self-discipline, willpower, renewed zeal and commitment, or any other human decision—though all of these play their part. No, real change will come by spending time in the presence of someone completely other than ourselves who calls us to be like him. We will grow into the vision that fills our hearts and minds. Let your vision of him be the power that transforms you from within.

Lord, show me your glory. Moses made that request, and you answered. You revealed your glory to prophets and disciples, and they were forever changed. I want that to be my story too. Envelop me in your presence and transform me into your image. Amen.

Vessels of Truth

It was the Lord's Day, and I was worshiping in the Spirit. Suddenly,
I heard behind me a loud voice like a trumpet blast. (Revelation 1:10)

WE LIVE IN A POST-TRUTH WORLD. Truth hasn't gone away, by any means; it is just as absolute as it always has been. But in terms of perception, of modern philosophies and discourse, the idea of absolute truth has fallen out of fashion. In many ways, society's openness to diverse understandings and perspectives is a welcome trend; the absolutism of the past has not always served us well and has driven many people, even (or especially) in the church, to harsh judgments, presumptuous biases, and atrocious persecutions and inquisitions. Even so, though a variety of perspectives often strengthens our own views, some issues really are nonnegotiable. The truth is out there. And the world desperately needs it.

People are hungry for real revelation and insight, whether they realize it or not, and there's only one place to get it: in God's presence. His revealed Word is reliable, of course, but our interpretations of it are not. We do not obtain real understanding simply by reading the Bible and trying to figure out how it all fits together. That approach has led to tens of thousands of denominations, all of them certain they are closest to the truth. Meanwhile, the people with real spiritual influence have gotten their insights by sitting in God's presence, conversing with him, and opening their hearts and minds to the depths of his words and his Word. Like John on Patmos, we get unusual insights when we are worshiping in the Spirit and encountering God ourselves.

If you want to grow in understanding, put more of your focus on relating to God and less on trying to figure everything out. In response to your faith, he will show you things in the depths of your heart that you could not have understood otherwise. You will see his purposes and other people in new ways. You will know things in your spirit that don't come naturally. And you will be prepared to offer life-giving wisdom and revelation to your world.

Holy Spirit, fill me with your presence and show me truths of the Kingdom, just as Jesus promised. Give me insights that become a blessing to the people around me. May I not just know truth but embody it. Amen.

The Promise of Power

You will receive power when the Holy Spirit comes upon you.
(Acts 1:8)

EARLY CHRISTIANS WENT around their cities, regions, and beyond telling people about Jesus and demonstrating a new way of life and power for living. They still had problems and conflicts of their own, to be sure—they didn't stop being human—but they nevertheless became committed to a gospel of salvation and restoration. After all, that's the context for the promise Jesus gave his disciples when they asked about the timing of his restoration of the Kingdom. Instead of telling them they were thinking along the wrong lines, he told them they didn't need to know such things. Meanwhile, they would receive power for the Kingdom work he had assigned them.

Nothing in the New Testament suggests that the power of the Holy Spirit wanes or ceases, though God may move in different ways in different seasons. He has certain emphases that fit specific times and places, and sometimes we are led to cry out for a fresh move. And he does move. The power is still there. The world needs people who are filled with the Spirit and energized by him. And, as with everything else of lasting significance, there's only one way to receive his power: by being in his presence.

We know God is always with us; his presence is not in question. But his *manifest* presence—that's another story. We aren't empowered by the Holy Spirit by default; we have to be in relationship and conversation with God and available for his purposes, just as the first believers were on the Day of Pentecost. In fact, we have an open invitation to press in to his promises with faith and persistence. When we do—and when we cultivate the kind of relationship that makes us aware of and receptive to his power—things happen. Doors open. Opportunities to be ministers of restoration come up. And we have the means to step into them with power.

Holy Spirit, I make myself available to you. I lay down my agendas and embrace yours. I lay aside my strength and choose to lean into yours. I open myself to whatever opportunities you place before me to cultivate your Kingdom, restore lives, and express the message of salvation in every area of life. Amen.

Real Change

When you are directed by the Spirit, you are not under
obligation to the law of Moses. (Galatians 5:18)

THERE ARE TWO WAYS TO try to live a godly life, and only one that actually works. The first is to apply cultural or religious standards to our behavior, inner thoughts, and motivations. We call this "legalism," usually implying adherence to Old Testament law, but this really includes any effort to live up to outward norms—even the words of the New Testament or Jesus himself—by an act of the will. As multitudes can testify, this approach is futile. It offers enough successes to keep us working at it, but it's ultimately a losing battle.

The other approach is to be transformed through fellowship and intimacy with God. Our vision of him and interactions with him change us so that we don't have to willfully apply godly standards. Instead, we just live them. Transformed by his love, we do what comes naturally, letting his nature flow out of us because it has become part of us. This is a process, of course, and there may be moments when the transformation seems incomplete. We may have to fill in the gaps with self-discipline. But the goal is a steady inward renovation, a life of just being who we are as new creatures.

History is full of the first approach, and the world is weary and extremely suspicious of it. Almost all religions rely on external constraints, which have usually proven powerless to change the human heart. The gospel is different. It's not a matter of living up to a standard; it's a matter of getting in sync with God. Change that is only external will convince no one that the Good News of God's Kingdom is any different than any other belief system. Real inward change, however, is another story. If the nature of the human heart can be radically transformed, there's hope. That's what the world is looking for, and it needs to see it in you. Your fellowship with the Spirit is one of the greatest gifts you can give to the people around you. It offers hope and changes lives—including yours.

Holy Spirit, may I never have to fake the transforming influence of the gospel. Change me from within. Make me a testimony of your power. Amen.

The Transforming Gaze

We all, with unveiled face, beholding the glory of the Lord,
are being transformed into the same image from one degree
of glory to another. (2 Corinthians 3:18, ESV)

ONE FORM OF CHRISTIANITY IN the late Middle Ages emphasized the importance of church structures and doctrines. Men who were educated in theology and appointed to ecclesiastical positions often considered themselves holier and more dedicated than anyone else—even when their beliefs became highly political and personally ineffective. Other forms of Christianity—more informal and democratic forms whose followers included peasants, women, and mystics who might not have all their theology perfectly in order—emphasized personal interaction with God. The hierarchical, authoritative approaches insisted on precise theology and priestly rule; the unsanctioned approaches ventured into divine experiences with God himself.

Which approach changed more lives? The experiential one, of course. In reality, these various forms overlapped quite a bit. But in every place and in every age, those who spend time allowing their souls to gaze at God are transformed, while those who invest themselves in structures and programs often find their hearts disappointingly stuck in the ways of the world. The soul busy with activities may accomplish a lot and receive accolades, but the soul at rest in the love of the Father, Son, and Spirit experiences an altogether different and more satisfying kind of power. Transformation comes not by methods and achievements but by beholding the Lord's glory.

Scripture always points us in this direction. Each of our lives—and history itself—will culminate in a great transformation based on our spiritual gaze: "We do know that we will be like him, for we will see him as he really is" (1 John 3:2). Principles and disciplines may help us from time to time, but the primary shaper of our hearts and lives is the vision we have. If our vision is filled with the nature of God, we become like him. If it isn't, we don't. Casting our eyes on the nature and glory of God changes us—and through us, it changes the world.

Lord, fix my gaze on you. May I hold your glories, your nature, and your truth in my heart at all times. Transform me with visions of who you really are. Amen.

As He Is

As he is so also are we in this world. (1 John 4:17, ESV)

IN THE EARLY YEARS OF THE CHURCH, *Christian* was not a very complimentary term. It was often spoken with contempt about those who went around like "little Christs." Believers were known not just as people who believed in Jesus as the Messiah; they were known as people who strangely emulated him too.

We have a high calling, and it's bigger than just doing what Christians do or preaching what Christians preach. It's even bigger than obeying what Jesus said. Our calling is to become like him in every way: embracing his nature, having his mind, and expressing his love. As we've seen, John presented this picture in the context of loving others with the same love we have received from the Father, and other places in Scripture apply this likeness even more broadly. The invitation to follow Jesus was never only about a belief system or a social group. It was a calling to conform to the image of God in Christ, to become who we were originally designed to be, to reflect the glory we were given at Creation. That includes doing the works Jesus did (and even greater ones, according to his words in John 14:12), having his thoughts (1 Corinthians 2:16), and being sent into the world in the same way he was sent (John 20:21). It's a comprehensive mission that involves not just what we do but who we are.

Always remember that Jesus is the image we are growing into. Aim for everything that image entails—even his purity of heart and mind, the miraculous works he did, and the wisdom and revelation he received. Never settle for the fallacy uttered by so many that "I'm only human," as if all we can expect is mediocrity. Jesus came as a human, and there was nothing mediocre about him. He set a high standard, to be sure, but then he called us to follow him. Let one of your most persistent daily prayers be "More, Lord." Know the glory of your purpose, and never settle for anything less.

Lord, what does Jesus look like in me? Whatever that image is, I ask for it in its fullness— more today, more tomorrow, and even more every day until my life is complete and my mission fulfilled. Amen.

Of a Different Spirit

Put on your new nature, created to be like God—
truly righteous and holy. (Ephesians 4:24)

THE WORLD IS FULL OF CONFORMISTS: idealists whose disillusionment turns them into cynical realists; honest politicians who eventually embrace the culture of dishonesty so common in their profession; ministers whose spiritual vision gets lost beneath the business model of their churches; lovers of eternal truth who eventually buy into the lies of immediate gratification. The issue is bigger than weak wills and a tendency to compromise. It's an inability to overcome the prevailing spirit or ethos of a culture.

The truth is that we are all called to be conformists, but of a different sort—not those armed only with strong willpower and determination, though those character traits certainly help, but those who carry a Spirit who is greater than any contrary spirit of the age. In an environment of hate, we are to demonstrate love. In an atmosphere of lust and greed, we are to keep our hearts and minds pure. In a climate of fear, we are to insist on being completely at rest. We are, after all, created to be like God. If we're going to conform to something or someone other than ourselves, we might as well set our sights on the best.

You are a carrier of a different kind of spirit and an example of a different way. Go into your world today with the nature of God and refuse to adapt to any other nature. You will encounter pride, greed, judgment, fear, and more, but you must not adapt to them. In subtle ways, you will be tempted by the culture of the workplace or marketplace to become cynical, anxious, selfish, or manipulative, but these no longer fit your nature. You bear the essence of God, and it is stronger than any of your former ways. Greater is the one who is in you than anything or anyone else in the world (1 John 4:4). In every situation, resist the pressure and live out the truth of your new nature.

Father, you have put your own power and promise within me, and I'm tired of settling for less. May the unyielding light of heaven never be obscured by the circumstances and people around me. Remind me constantly of who I really am. Amen.

The Opposite Way

To you who are willing to listen, I say, love your enemies!
Do good to those who hate you. Bless those who curse you.
Pray for those who hurt you. (Luke 6:27-28)

THE AMERICAN CIVIL RIGHTS MOVEMENT provoked many emotions and prompted wildly differing responses. Some of those responses were nonviolent, while others were downright militant. But woven throughout the entire era, and continuing into today, are occasional examples of unexpected love—stories of black leaders expressing love toward a KKK member or former racists embracing their neighbors of any color or belief. Past militants tell stories of how their hatred was overcome by the love of their enemy. Why? Because the nature of God changes the brokenness of the human condition.

You will find this dynamic to be true not only in cases of love versus hate, but also in any other showdown between the nature of God and the ways of the world. When we enter an environment of greed, we can strip it of power with a spirit of generosity. When we find ourselves in a climate of pride, we can defuse it with a spirit of humility. Where there is despair, we can undo it with hope; where there is fear, we can overcome it with faith. We break the power of the world by living out its opposite.

While the world surrounds us with its distortions, you will find that those distortions are almost always the antithesis of something good, beautiful, and true. And when you choose the good, beautiful, and true counterpoints to the world's ways, you will begin to unravel them. We are told that we can "conquer evil by doing good" (Romans 12:21), and it's true—if we will put it into practice. The culture of heaven always overcomes the culture of earth if we learn to see ourselves as carriers of heaven's ways.

Father, the reality of your nature is far greater than the counterfeits and distortions of this fallen world. So why do I so easily conform to them rather than to you? May the power of your Spirit overcome every adversity in me and around me. Amen.

A Mission of Joy

Always be joyful. (1 Thessalonians 5:16)

"JOY IS THE SERIOUS BUSINESS OF HEAVEN," C. S. Lewis once wrote, suggesting that the delights of God's Kingdom are not just an option for us but actually an imperative. Most of us can imagine the atmosphere around God being one of joy, although some of us may have trouble seeing anything but judgment or the seriousness of the mission. And most of us can appreciate the invitation into God's joy as a wonderful opportunity—that is, if we can get past the responsibilities and to-do lists of this day, or this week, or this year. But joy as an expectation? A mandate? An all-important necessity? That seems unrealistic. Some might even see it as an excuse to be irresponsible.

But joy is high on God's list of priorities for us. Anything we do that does not include joy, or at least lead to it, misrepresents his nature. He is not sitting in heaven sweating over our financial difficulties, our relational problems, or our desperate need for fulfillment. Never has he looked at our problems and said, "Oh no! What am I going to do? How can I possibly fix this one?" No, he sees the end of things from the beginning (Isaiah 46:10) and is not in suspense about what is to come. He is already relaxed about the outcome. You can be too.

One of your primary assignments in life—before paying the bills, before accomplishing your tasks or dreams, and instead of stressing out your friends and family with all of your worries—is to carry the simple joy of heaven everywhere, even into the dense, dark places of the world. To do so, you will have to be rooted in that other realm, which is untouched by the stresses and conflicts of the world. Insist on your joy, your peace, your simplicity being unflappable and unflagging. Represent the heart of your Father by reflecting his delight and his assurance that all will be well.

Father, I lose sight of your joy in the midst of my problems, even when I know it to be true. Let me not be deceived by my circumstances. Lift my eyes above the fray and out of the moment to see—and embody—the joy of your Kingdom. Amen.

Don't Stop

Never stop praying. (1 Thessalonians 5:17)

Brother Lawrence excelled at constantly being aware of the presence of God and maintaining long conversations with him through the mundane tasks of his day. Of course, as a kitchen worker in a monastery, his mind could afford to wander into eternal realities while he scrubbed dishes. Even so, he did what many others have not had the discipline to do. He prayed with almost every breath.

We all have opportunities to fill downtime and mundane tasks with prayer. We might not be able to pray constantly—most of us have jobs and responsibilities that require focus on the matters at hand—but we can pray more than we do. In 1 Thessalonians 5:17, Paul is not necessarily instructing his readers to pray continuously. Instead, he is urging them not to give up on the prayers they are praying because their petitions are vital.

How is this so? God gave agency to human beings as partners with him in the work of this world. The keys of the Kingdom seem to have been ours at the beginning (Genesis 1:28), and we lost them in the Fall. Jesus won them back and gave them again to his followers (Matthew 16:19). He looks for those who will intercede (Isaiah 59:16) and reveals his plans to those who will hear them (Amos 3:7) so they will declare and pray his will into this realm. For whatever reason, God has chosen not to work *around* humanity but to work *through* us. Our prayers are critical to his intervention against evil on earth.

If you really want to be salt and light in this world, pray and don't give up. Let your requests be reshaped by God's Spirit, if needed, but don't just drop them. Things are happening behind the scenes. Hearts are opening. Lives are changing. Your petitions, along with your persistence in them, are critical to the process. In the spiritual realm, you are an agent at the front lines, and your prayers are the means to advance. Don't give up the fight.

Spirit of God, fill my heart and my mouth with petitions you want to hear. Overcome the evils of this world, change the headlines I read, through my intercession. May the prayers of your people prepare a highway into the hearts and minds of many. Amen.

God's Will

*Be thankful in all circumstances, for this is God's will for you who
belong to Christ Jesus. (1 Thessalonians 5:18)*

IF YOU'RE LIKE MOST CHRISTIANS, you've prayed to understand God's will for your life. It's a reasonable prayer, and one he is sure to answer—in time. God promises to give wisdom and specific direction to all who seek him. Of course, that means seeking *him* first and foremost, rather than seeking information. But when we grow in our relationship with him, we grow in our understanding of what he wants us to do. Our calling becomes clearer in his presence.

One often-quoted principle about discovering God's will is that he will not reveal more until we are following what he has already revealed. If that's the case, Paul's words in 1 Thessalonians become vitally relevant. Before we embark on the next phase in our lives, before we know which decision to make about when, where, and what we are supposed to do, we can be certain that God's will for us is to be thankful in all circumstances. We cannot move forward until gratitude has become central in our hearts and minds. We can only advance with the right attitude.

That theme comes up often in Scripture. Our minds are preoccupied with what we are supposed to do, while God is far more focused on who we are. Religion emphasizes doing; the gospel emphasizes being. Why? Because your heart is the wellspring of your life (Proverbs 4:23). Unless you want to live your life acting a part, everything you do flows out of who you really are. God is much more interested in your ability to represent him than your ability to check off instructions.

Gratitude is a profound reflection of your relationship with God, and it sets the tone for everything you will do in his name. As you listen for his direction, embrace what he has already revealed. Regardless of circumstances, live in thankfulness, and your heart will align with his.

Father, synchronize my heart with yours. Open my eyes to see how enormously your blessings outweigh my problems. May words of gratitude pour from my mouth in all things, at all times. Amen.

The Moment to Shine

You will shine among them like stars in the sky as you hold
firmly to the word of life. (Philippians 2:15-16, NIV)

IT HAS BEEN SAID THAT THE ONLY eternal thing we can do on earth that we can't do in heaven is win souls for Christ. This appeals to the evangelists among us; after all, the turning of hearts toward the Savior is a beautiful thing. But this maxim reduces our life's mission to words of persuasion. Is that really all God intends for us? Are we meant to live as escapists waiting to be rescued from a sinking ship? Are there really no other eternal investments we can make?

In fact, there are plenty. We can live as a reflection of our Father and glorify him in places where glory is hard to see. We can worship God in the midst of adversity, which we will no longer face in heaven but which makes for a startling testimony in the here and now. We can do the works of Jesus by his power (John 14:12), like feeding the hungry and healing the sick, allowing others to experience God's touch long before heaven. We can pray for the Kingdom of God and against the evils infecting this world (Matthew 6:9-13). We can comfort people with the comfort of God (2 Corinthians 1:3-4). We can forgive people of their sins as representatives of Jesus (John 20:23). We can do the kinds of good works that prove we are God's handiwork (Ephesians 2:10). In short, we can shine in the dark—an opportunity that we will not be able to fulfill in the Kingdom of light. We are invited into a robust, comprehensive mission.

Your lifetime, however long it lasts, is your moment to shine with eternal truth in the midst of a fallen, broken creation. Never minimize that opportunity; it will become visible to men and angels as a reflection of who God is and what he has done. Your light becomes an eternal testimony to the glory of God—now and forever.

Father, I will face no adversity in heaven, no obstacles in giving you my praise. But here,
may my praise flow as a testimony of your light in the midst of darkness. Let my life be
filled with eternal wonders that make you known. Amen.

Seasoned Words

*Let your conversation be always full of grace, seasoned with salt, so
that you may know how to answer everyone. (Colossians 4:6, NIV)*

READ THE COMMENTS AT the end of news articles, on Facebook posts, and in blogs—
if you dare. You'll find that regardless of the topic, they often descend quickly into
tangential arguments and vicious name-calling. We might suspect that the abrasive
words come only from those who make no claim to follow Jesus, but that simply
isn't true. Self-professed Christians are at times among the worst offenders. Far too
easily, we speak and write words that are seasoned with poison.

This is especially true on social media, where no one needs a real face or name to
participate, but it also happens in live conversations too. Sometimes Christians get
sucked into a toxic environment, and other times we create it. Instead of changing
the atmosphere with the Spirit of Christ, we accommodate it in a spirit of contentiousness. We miss an enormous opportunity to season our surroundings with grace.

Open your eyes to the opportunities all around you to impart the peace and
patience of God. That doesn't mean you need to load up your conversations with
sugar and nauseate people with your sweetness. It does, however, mean that if you
season your words with the right amount of salt—if you choose the right words and
avoid the wrong ones, calmly speaking grace and understanding into others' lives—
you give every conversation a more beautiful and enjoyable flavor. Be strong enough
to endure hostility; be mature enough to hold your tongue; and be wise enough to
defuse volatile situations with well-chosen words. God's Kingdom is full of lively
conversation but never of demeaning or biting commentary. He is interested in winning hearts, not arguments. He knows how to make a point without injuring, and
he wants us to do the same. Bless and do not curse (Romans 12:14); build up and
do not tear down; encourage and comfort wherever you can. Give people a taste of
the Kingdom through your words.

*Father, your words are powerful, and you've given us a taste of the same power. Forgive
me for every careless word I've spoken, and use my tongue to strengthen and build. May
my words always reflect your heart. Amen.*

A Gentle Spirit

Let your gentleness be evident to all. (Philippians 4:5, NIV)

SOME OF PAUL'S CONTEMPORARIES might have thought him a bit prickly. His words could be cutting, and the misperceptions and barbs of his critics sometimes offended him. Most sympathetic observers, however, would have understood the intensity of his language to be a product of his passion and energy. He was zealous for the message God had given him and sensitive to anything that opposed it.

But how did the apostle see himself? Gentle and unassuming, "like a mother feeding and caring for her own children," he wrote to one church (1 Thessalonians 2:7). In fact, this characteristic of gentleness comes up often in his writings, probably because it was so evident in the ministry of Jesus. Neither Jesus nor Paul was weak, but both understood the imperative of expressing the patience and kindness of God's heart. They knew how to harvest fruit without bruising it.

Regardless of whatever offenses we've experienced from the callousness of others, we need to embrace the gentleness of God. He has handled us with great care, and he calls us to comfort and care for others with the same tenderness. Eighteenth-century theologian Jonathan Edwards, never reluctant to preach a bold sermon, emphasized the gentleness of the Christian spirit as a mark of true discipleship. Edwards was well familiar with the dynamics of religious controversy and knew what a lack of gentleness could produce. A quick glance at the social and political climate today reinforces the point a thousand times over. The world is not in need of more contentious spirits. It is in desperate need of people with gentle hearts. In the name of Jesus, be one of them. Let your gentleness be evident to all. Defuse the combustible relationships around you with the *shalom* of God's Kingdom. Let the Prince of Peace bring peace through you.

Jesus, you were gentle in even the most bitter and hostile circumstances. I get drawn into the world's tension far too easily. Lift me up, fill me with peace, remind me of my security in you, and let me demonstrate your gentleness to all. Amen.

A Greater Life

I pray that from his glorious, unlimited resources he will empower
you with inner strength through his Spirit. (Ephesians 3:16)

THE MERCHANTS OF EPHESUS PRIDED themselves on the wealth of the city, much of which had been amassed through the manufacture and sale of religious artifacts and imagery of the Greek goddess Artemis. That's why in Acts 19 they had rioted against Paul and his teaching of the gospel; conversions were bad for business. Also problematic were Christians who refused to engage in the emperor cult. Neglecting sacrifices in the name of Rome's ruler—sometimes called the "father of the fatherland"—might cause imperial repercussions or bring divine misfortune on the city. So when Paul invoked the "Father from whom every family on earth is named" (Ephesians 3:14-15, in literal translations) and made an appeal according to his riches and glory, Paul was intentionally contradicting the local culture. He was suggesting that the Kingdom of God offered much greater benefits than any believer or nonbeliever had ever experienced.

He was right. While Ephesian culture offered wealth, good standing with a powerful empire, and spiritually potent amulets and spells, God's Kingdom provides unlimited resources that connect us with the most powerful Spirit in the universe and give us glimpses of ultimate glory. The "energy" at work within us—one of the words often translated as "power" in Paul's writings—empowers us to live not in our own strength but in the strength of Jesus himself. As we follow him, our roots grow down into his love, and he makes his home in our hearts. The result is an altogether different kind of life than we have known.

As you relate to the world around you, be aware of where you are drawing your life and getting your energy. Your natural soul will want to feed on the perks and promises of a fallen culture. Your reborn spirit can only be satisfied with the life of Jesus within. One gives you temporary enjoyment, the other overwhelming joy. For your sake, and for the sake of the world, let the Spirit of Christ fill you with the light of his power and love.

Father, Paul's prayer is mine—that I would tap into the unlimited wealth of your glory, be empowered by the life of Jesus, and be filled with supernatural love. Amen.

Knowing the Unknowable

May you experience the love of Christ, though it is
too great to understand fully. (Ephesians 3:19)

JOHN WESLEY ONCE SAID he felt his heart "strangely warmed" as he listened to some-one at a prayer meeting read an excerpt from Luther's commentary on Romans. He couldn't put his finger on what was happening; he just knew the Spirit was at work, and faith was growing in him. That's often the case in our encounters with the truths of God. We know what we do not yet understand and believe what we cannot yet explain. It isn't that God's truth is irrational, only that it often works in us before our rational minds catch up to it. We experience him in extra-rational ways.

Paul must have understood this dynamic well, since he prayed for the Ephesians to *know* the kind of love that surpasses knowledge. Though we can certainly grasp the incongruity of such a request, we're also aware that the Holy Spirit can help us know what cannot be known, to experience what cannot be fully explained. His gifts for us, including his love, are infinite. Our hearts and minds are not. If we are ever going to grow in our relationship with God, we will have to get comfortable with the idea of knowing things that are beyond us. Our brains will have to be content tasting divine truths they cannot fully hold.

Many people call such knowledge superstition because they cannot map it out, put it in a test tube, or prove it in a formula. Even so, they crave it. Every human heart longs for transcendence. A hardened skeptic still feels overwhelmed by the vast-ness of space and the majesty of mountains and seas. Whispers of divine creativity and wisdom move everyone, even if they don't recognize them as divine. But anyone who has experienced the transcendent truth of God's nature knows things that no mind can grasp. And that love—that divine experience—can pass through barriers no words can ever pierce.

Jesus, may I know the fullness of your love even beyond my understanding, and may others see it in my eyes, hear it in my voice, and feel it in my heartbeat. Amen.

The Power Within

*All glory to God, who is able, through his mighty power at work
within us, to accomplish infinitely more than we might ask or think.*
(Ephesians 3:20)

WHEN PAUL TELLS US THAT God is able to do beyond what we can ask or imagine, we might begin to wonder, *Have I asked too little of him? Are my prayers too small? After all, I can imagine a lot.* If our minds can conceive of great things and God's ability exceeds them all, then the sky's the limit. Actually, there is no limit. Not even the sky.

Our next questions bring us down to earth. *I know God can do anything, but will he? Does he want to answer my prayers?* He has given us plenty of promises, assuring us that he is the kind of God who answers. And our own experiences remind us that he does, often in remarkable ways. But those requests for the deep desires of our hearts may still lie on the table. We don't know whether to hold out hope for them. We know God is exceedingly able, and he is exceedingly good, but is he exceedingly able and good on our behalf?

He is, of course, and he pledges not only to shape the desires of our hearts but to fulfill them too. Paul's letter to the Ephesians addresses how we are rooted in Christ's love, how Christ is rooted in our hearts, and how fully we are meant to experience the heights and depths of that relationship. So when Paul praises God's surpassing abilities, he has a certain focus in mind: God is able to transform his people and the world through his incomprehensible love *according to the power at work within us.* There may be times when he works independently of his people, but God's normal modus operandi is to work through us. While we look for him to demonstrate his exceeding power out in the world, he is looking to demonstrate it in and through those who have experienced his love. Our former futility has been replaced with resurrection power—and the promise of answers to really big prayers.

Father, what big prayers do you want to answer through me? What kind of power do you want to demonstrate in me? You are able; I am willing. Demonstrate your love in amazing ways. Amen.

Where the Spirit Falls

*How wonderful and pleasant it is when brothers
live together in harmony! (Psalm 133:1)*

IN EARLY 1726, the young Moravian community at Herrnhut was small, growing, and completely at peace. The religious refugees gathering there were grateful for the safety and security of the fellowship. But later in the year, when a couple of malcontents began sowing seeds of discord, the fellowship ruptured. People took sides. The sense of unity experienced in the early days was completely gone.

As leader of the community and lord of the manor, Count Zinzendorf exercised his authority and established conditions for living on the land and guidelines for relating to other members. He patiently won the hearts of those who had turned against him. People expressed forgiveness toward one another. And after a few months of peace, something happened. Zinzendorf led a prayer of confession, and others joined in. Hearts were opened. According to those present, the Spirit fell with the same power the first disciples experienced at Pentecost. People who formerly only tolerated others were now crying in their arms. Even members of the community who were traveling great distances at the time felt a shift in the Spirit and remembered the moment. The fellowship was radically transformed.

The Moravians are known today for their century-long prayer commitment and their missionary efforts that helped spark the modern missions movement. But those fruits came from a deeper root of unity. Jesus told his followers that the world would know them by their love for one another (John 13:35). When hearts are united in love, amazing things happen.

Never assume you will be able to fulfill your mission as a believer on your own. Your wisdom, power, and love are given by God in the context of fellowship. As the unity of your fellowship increases, so do the wisdom, power, and love—and every other fruit that comes as the body exercises spiritual gifts together. When God enters into the bonds of spiritual union with his people (John 17:21), we are empowered, and lives and worlds are changed.

Father, forgive my judgments and divisive attitudes. Open my heart to those around me. Give me—give us—life-changing, world-changing love. Amen.

Diversity United

He makes the whole body fit together perfectly . . . so that the whole
body is healthy and growing and full of love. (Ephesians 4:16)

NOT LONG AGO IN MADABA, JORDAN, not far from where Moses died, a museum invited visitors to help create a mosaic of at least two million pieces. Each visitor would paint a ceramic fragment, and the museum artisans placed it appropriately into an enormous image of the King's Highway. No two fragments were alike, but each one served the larger purpose of the image. Two million pieces created a beautiful, coherent whole.

What if your life is like that—one piece in an enormous mosaic of God? He is infinite, of course; many more than two million pieces would be necessary, and the range of colors would have to be dazzling. But in light of Creation and our being made in God's image, the idea of stunning diversity serving one coherent whole makes sense. All of God's creatures, each one different, unite to form a beautiful picture of their Creator.

Many people resist such an image, insisting that unity implies uniformity and that every piece should be the same size, shape, and color. But God did not create such a boring picture, and any attempt to refine his work severely misreads his purposes. His people vary in age, race, gender, nationality, language, background, and experience. Our life stories emphasize various aspects of his nature—we all have unique perspectives and preferences; we all are given different gifts and contexts in which to exercise them; and our doctrines emphasize the importance of different truths, even when they serve a coherent whole. We belong to the same Lord and must fit his image, but within that unity, our differences are essential.

Embrace your uniqueness. While many Christians ask God to bless their corner of Christianity and praise their own distinctives, spend your time blessing others— and yourself—as important and necessary expressions of God's nature. You can reflect God in a way no one else can, and if you don't fulfill your purpose, no one else will. Learn to see yourself as a vital expression of who God is. Then with all your heart, live it out for the world to see.

Lord, I want to conform to your image, but you have created me to conform as no one
else does. Let the world see what Jesus looks like uniquely in me. Amen.

Whole Redemption

*"LORD, help!" they cried in their trouble, and he saved
them from their distress. (Psalm 107:13, 19, 28)*

THROUGHOUT THE OLD TESTAMENT, God demonstrates a pattern of delivering his people from their distress. The most notable of these occasions is the Exodus, when Moses leads the Israelites out of slavery in Egypt and eventually to the Promised Land. This real-time, physical deliverance is reinterpreted in the New Testament as a picture of the spiritual salvation we receive in Christ, who leads us out of captivity to sin and death into everlasting life with him. Together, these two rescues give us a complete picture of salvation that includes fulfilling all our needs, both in this world and in the age to come.

It's important to interpret these two events together. If we separate them and look at the Old Testament only as a material picture of a real deliverance—if the Exodus is just an allegory of greater, future things—we risk seeing our salvation as only spiritual. But when we read both stories as parts of a greater whole, it becomes clear that God is concerned not only for our souls, but our bodies, our social conditions, our injustices, our relationships, our finances—our entire lives. God freely gives us a spiritual salvation *and* significant restoration in this world. He doesn't offer a wonderful future while leaving us trapped in the present. His mercies apply to today.

It's true that we may still contend with illness, debt, and all sorts of captivities after our salvation experience, just as it's true that we also struggle with sin after salvation. But the message of the Kingdom is comprehensive, not promising immediate freedom from all trouble (as the Israelites discovered after fleeing Egypt), but surely promising help in every situation. Like the people of Israel, we are transferred from one master to another, and our new Master is vitally interested in all of our needs.

Always represent the gospel as fully as you can. Salvation is not some sort of magic trick that makes life trouble-free, but neither is God limited to an invisible realm that makes no difference in the here and now. God enters into our lives to deliver, heal, repair, and restore. His pattern of meeting us in our distress is for all times.

Lord, you are merciful in every area of life. Your promises are true in every situation. You fix our eyes on eternity, but train us for eternity even now. May I always present the truth of your Kingdom in all its fullness. Amen.

The Renewal

Don't copy the behavior and customs of this world, but let God
transform you into a new person by changing the way you think.
(Romans 12:2)

ONE OF THE MOST COMMON complaints against Christianity is its historical record. Catholics are blamed for atrocities during the Crusades, inquisitions during the Counter-Reformation, and forced conversions in the settling of the New World. Protestants are blamed for violence in the Thirty Years' War, the Nazi movement, and the Ku Klux Klan. Jesus was responsible for none of these events, of course, and neither were Christians who followed his teachings closely. But the distortions stand out, and the entire faith is colored by them.

How were professing Christians able to commit such un-Christian acts? Their hearts were not transformed. They claimed a set of beliefs and were culturally Christian but didn't resemble Christ. Regardless of what their mouths confessed, they followed the ways of the world.

Doctrine and beliefs are not in themselves transforming. If we want to be like Jesus and follow him, we will need to have our minds renewed. The gospel is much more than a behavior-modification program; it's an inward renovation so dramatic that it is best described as a death and rebirth. Anything less leads to the same frustrations all religious people feel when they fall short of their high standards.

The transforming power of the gospel changes the way we see and think. It changes our perceptions of God, ourselves, other believers, nonbelievers, and even our enemies. It undoes our old agendas and gives us a new purpose. It erodes our old nature and fills our hearts with the nature of God. It rearranges our relationships in the most satisfying ways possible. But only if we let it.

So let it. Surrender your will daily to the power of the Spirit. Let God be salt and light to your soul so you can be salt and light to your world. Let go of the old, and live in the newness God promises.

Father, transform me. You promise newness; take me on an adventure that makes all things in my life, including me, entirely new. Renovate my heart and mind to think, feel, and see in new ways. Amen.

A New View of God

*I plead with you to give your bodies to God because of all he
has done for you. Let them be a living and holy sacrifice—
the kind he will find acceptable. (Romans 12:1)*

JESUS TOLD A PARABLE ABOUT three servants who were given a portion of their master's
money to steward. Two invested the money and earned increases, but one hid it away
to preserve it, arguing that he knew the master to be "a hard man" (Luke 19:21). Of
the parable's many messages, one is that our perception of God determines whether
we live with hope or fear, whether we will feel free in his presence or captive to his
demands. How we see him affects our entire lives.

Many people have jaundiced views of God. They understand him to be a judge
or hard master, the relative who always gives you what you need for your birthday
but never what you want, the parent always pushing vegetables without ever offering dessert. Whether from bad experience, bad theology, or a little of both, these
people live with the expectation that God will disappoint them. Even if they remain
religious, they don't remain devoted. They have lost their joy.

Scripture shows us a different picture of God—the winsome kindness of Jesus,
the jealous lover in passionate pursuit of his beloved, the delighted parent singing
over his child. This is the extravagant love that compels us to offer ourselves as a living and holy sacrifice. Every time we think we have a handle on God, he turns and
shows a new face—not one inconsistent with what he has already revealed, but one
that shines on another facet of his nature. And it's always beautiful.

The world does not know this God. You do, or at least you are growing in your
knowledge of him. Do you see the gap that needs to be filled? God is not going to
fill it unilaterally. He is going to move his people—including you—into it through
the power that works within you. Offer yourself to this God and show the world his
welcoming expression. Unravel the myth of the hard master. Live as a worshiper for
all the world to see.

*Father, I offer you myself because of all you have done for me. Let me be a living
sacrifice, acceptable to you, a reflection of your true nature. Amen.*

A New Self-Image

*Don't think you are better than you really are. Be honest
in your evaluation of yourselves, measuring yourselves
by the faith God has given us. (Romans 12:3)*

THE ROMAN CHURCH SEEMS to have been divided. Jewish believers who had led the church but were exiled from Rome around AD 49 (Acts 18:2) returned to find their leadership unwelcomed. Gentile Christians, who led the church in their absence, may have seen themselves as the new chosen people, while Jewish believers prided themselves on their long history as God's original chosen ones. When Paul warned the congregation's members not to see themselves as better than they really were, he was likely addressing this sense of superiority as well as their tendency to rank spiritual gifts in a hierarchy of importance. In any case, Paul says, their true worship of God—as living sacrifices offered in gratitude—should lead them to honest self-perception.

We can take Paul's instructions in the other direction to address another problem many of us have: seeing ourselves through eyes of guilt and shame, listening to voices from the past that remind us of how we've messed up, or believing voices about the future that hint at the inevitability of disappointment. Just as we should never exaggerate our own self-image, neither should we minimize it. One attitude offends those around us; the other fails to share the extravagant love of God with them. We are to measure ourselves with God-given faith because we are to see ourselves as God sees us.

That's the bottom line. Any self-image that is more or less than who we really are is essentially disagreement with God. On one hand, you are only one of many people extravagantly loved by God, which gives you no basis for elevating yourself above them. On the other hand, you are loved beyond your wildest imagination, which gives you no basis for minimizing your own gifts and value. Those around you need to see the love of God for you, and they need to see it coming through you. A true self-perception enables you to embody both.

Father, it is much easier for me to believe in your love for others than to believe in your love for me. Show me how you see me. Then show me how you see others. Enlighten me to live in a way that treasures all of us the way you do. Amen.

A New Community

*In his grace, God has given us different gifts for
doing certain things well. (Romans 12:6)*

AT EVERY LEVEL, the human body is a highly complex machine. Proteins and ribosomes within cells are remarkably intricate structures that work together to accomplish a wide range of functions; organs are made up of billions of cells all working together for one purpose; and the body itself is a highly organized system of interdependent organs and components that function as one coordinated unit. As the psalmist wrote, we are "fearfully and wonderfully made" (Psalm 139:14, ESV).

It's no wonder, then, that believers in Jesus are described in the New Testament as the body of Christ. Our wide variety of differences actually serves a purpose. There are some aspects of God you will never see unless you experience them through other believers; and there are some aspects of him other believers will never see unless they experience them through you. We each relate to God individually and can worship him on our own—to a point. But solo spirituality is always limited. No one has every gift, every story to tell, or every perspective. Unless we experience God in fellowship with others, we will never experience him as fully as he wants us to.

That has huge implications for our testimony in society. If we continue to see ourselves as divided personalities all trying to convince others of the right or normal way to be a Christian, we will have limited impact on the world we live in. If, however, we are able to see each other as vital assets in the functioning of one large unit, we may learn to maximize each other's gifts, build each other up, and form a coordinated representation of the image of God. One approach points to Christianity as a highly debatable idea and fragmented religion; the other points to Jesus as the head of a spiritual body. The divided approach fits within human explanations; the latter is unexplainable apart from supernatural power. The church has an ever-open opportunity to choose which kind of organism it will be, and the world is always watching.

Holy Spirit, unite us. As diverse and scattered as we are, we are one in you. Coordinate our gifts; weave together our stories of your grace; give us one emphatic testimony of who you are. Amen.

A New Love

Don't just pretend to love others. Really love them. (Romans 12:9)

MANY CHRISTIAN MOVEMENTS throughout history and today have emphasized the importance of demonstrating love, both within the fellowship and beyond it. This is not surprising; Jesus told his followers to love one another because that love would mark our identity in him. In response, Christians consciously try to be an example to the world so it will see the gospel within them. The motive is good—to follow Jesus' instructions and offer a meaningful testimony—and the outcome is sometimes effective. But the entire focus leads to one big, unsettling question: Why?

Why do Christians love others out of obligation? Why don't we love because we are loving? Why, when all secular eyes are on us, do we have to remind ourselves that people are watching? Why doesn't love pour out of us whether people are watching or not? In fact, it can. That's the goal. Some of Jesus' instructions focus on how we should behave, but the essence of his teaching was not behavioral. It was directed at the heart, our inner condition, the fallenness that gets us out of sync with God and must be remedied by a supernatural act. When we are born of the Spirit of the God who is love, love ought to come naturally. In our newness, it's who we are. If God is love and we are becoming like him, then we are love.

This issue highlights the difference between religion and relationship, between regulating behavior and living from the new nature. The gospel of "do" monitors our actions; the gospel of "be" doesn't have to. The path from one to the other is a process, and we may find ourselves reverting to the former when necessary. But the goal is transformation—or, as Paul puts it, really loving people without hypocrisy. Our renewal changes the way we see people. Love becomes our natural bent toward believers, along with those who do not believe as we do. The change in us does not end with us. Only real love can flow into others' lives.

Jesus, I choose to love others as you commanded. But far better for me to "be" love than to simply act the part. Fill my heart and soul with your love, and let it flow freely toward those around me. Amen.

A New Mercy

Bless those who persecute you. Don't curse them;
pray that God will bless them. (Romans 12:14)

SCRIPTURE TELLS US THAT THE spoken word is concrete. It sets things in motion. That's why the blessing Isaac mistakenly gave to Jacob instead of Esau couldn't just be taken back (Genesis 27); the mercenary prophecies of Balaam that so confounded his patron, King Balak, could not be erased with a "never mind" (Numbers 22–23); and the words of prophets actually effected things in spiritual and material realms (Ezekiel 37:1-14). God gave Aaron and his priestly successors a blessing to speak over the people because it actually accomplished something (Numbers 6:22-27). Words sent into the world have the potential to transform it.

That's a lot of power to have, and the temptations to use it selfishly are great— especially in the matter of blessing and cursing the people around us. Clearly, we would want to bless our friends and family, and maybe a few strangers we meet along the way. But our enemies? Our old way of seeing things might tempt us to cast curses on them. But our new vision fills our hearts with a new mercy. Jesus said that loving our enemies and praying for our persecutors makes us like our Father (Matthew 5:44-45), and our transformation into his image will include an entirely new perspective on them. The urge to curse must be overcome by the desire to bless.

In your renewed vision, how do you see your enemies? As adversaries? Or as wounded people acting out of past hurts and abuses, who don't yet know the promise or completeness of God's restoration? Though everyone is responsible for their malicious words and actions, the conditions behind them are usually pitiful. God sees an opportunity to bless and transform. So must we.

Take advantage of that opportunity. Your words of blessing invite God to pursue hearts and change lives. They set in motion profound spiritual effects that may or may not ever be visible to human eyes. Most of all, they reflect the heart of your Father and further his mission in this world.

Father, in every contentious relationship, lift my eyes to see as you see—to look beyond the surface and see the pain and the wounds of resistant hearts. Fill my mouth with words of blessing, and respond to them with your transforming grace. Amen.

A New Peace

Do all that you can to live in peace with everyone. (Romans 12:18)

FEW OF THE EARLY LEADERS OF the Reformation had any intention of breaking with the Catholic Church. Their intention, as the name of the historical period suggests, was to reform, not to divide. They had strong convictions about the way things ought to be and voiced them—usually respectfully, at least in the early years—with the hopes of maintaining the integrity of their existing relationships.

That tension of being who we are and believing what we believe without turning our beliefs into a battlefield is also a common experience today. We feel the pressure to choose between peace and war. Some among us relish the opportunity to provoke a fight, while others feel they cannot be at peace with the world without compromising their values. Somewhere in between is a biblical response—a Jesus response—that puts the initiative for peace in our hands without requiring us to conform to others' expectations. As some translations of Romans 12:18 put it, "If possible, so far as it depends on you, live peaceably with all" (ESV). In other words, we have to do our part to create an atmosphere of peace.

But try as we might, sometimes we can't. Many people were not at peace with Jesus because he would not compromise his message. These conflicts, however, were never from any lack in Jesus' desire to bless and restore. He spoke words of forgiveness even to his fiercest persecutors. He welcomed all who came to him. He spoke "the truth in love" (Ephesians 4:15).

That's the balance we seek—the wisdom to speak truth while expressing love, as well as the humility to receive truth from others, whether it's expressed in love or not. Winning hearts is far more important than winning arguments, and when relationships become our focus, speaking the truth as we understand it becomes a lot more effective. In your renewed vision of the people around you, create an atmosphere of peace without compromising who you are. Do all that you can to bring into every relationship the culture of the Kingdom of God.

Holy Spirit, my prayer is that you would so fill my heart with peace that I exude it and impart it to others. Make my life, my attitude, my demeanor a safe place for everyone, even when we are discussing hard truths. Give me an inviting temperament. Amen.

The Critical Spirit

Do everything without complaining and arguing, so that no one can criticize you. Live clean, innocent lives as children of God, shining like bright lights in a world full of crooked and perverse people.
(Philippians 2:14-15)

ONE OF MOSES' GREATEST CHALLENGES in the entire story of the Exodus was the constant complaints he received from his critics. They blamed him for their increasing difficulties in Egypt, for leading them toward certain doom at the edge of the Red Sea, and for practically every moment of hunger, thirst, and hardship in the wilderness. Ultimately, the complainers caused the whole nation to delay its entry into the Promised Land by an entire generation—forty years. God was very displeased with the critical spirit among them.

You are probably well aware that complaining is not a gift of the Spirit. Neither is criticism, cynicism, or contentiousness. Yet in spite of that knowledge, Christians can be remarkably similar to the Israelites and the general population in their ability to criticize and harp on the faults seen in those around them, blame their own circumstances on the decisions of others, and vilify those who don't agree with them. Pastors and other church leaders often lament the amount of criticism directed at them, as if their job is to please everyone; families are divided by the disapproval of a parent, a child, or a sibling; and colleagues avoid coworkers who know only how to complain without offering any solutions. A negative attitude is rarely of benefit to ourselves or anyone around us. In fact, it is not at all a reflection of the God of hope and peace.

Don't get caught up in the spirit of the world, which speaks the language of criticism and complaint far too fluently. You are called to a different way—a different attitude expressed by different words coming from a different heart. People are drawn to a hopeful, encouraging spirit; their insecurities need reassurance from the Spirit of God. You are the vessel for that reassurance. Do everything without criticizing or complaining so others can see the hope—the light of truth—within you.

Holy Spirit, fill me with the fruit of your presence to such a degree that there is no more room for the fruit of my own insecurities and frustrations. Let my heart overflow with hope, encouragement, and a willingness to serve. Amen.

Agents of Growth

Salt is good, but if salt has lost its taste, how shall its
saltiness be restored? It is of no use either for the soil or for
the manure pile. It is thrown away. (Luke 14:34-35, ESV)

JESUS' WORDS TO HIS DISCIPLES about salt have historically been interpreted in terms of flavor and preservation—seasoning society and slowing the corruption of the world. But the fertilizing powers of salt were well-known in the ancient world and have been in many cultures since; the right kind of salt in the right measure enhances the soil and makes things grow. When Jesus called his followers "the salt of the earth," he was not only hinting at taste and preservation. Even more so, he seems to have been envisioning his followers as agents of increase. Where traditional interpretations of Jesus' warnings have emphasized the possibility of salt losing taste or flavor, the original language more accurately implies losing potency or effectiveness, or even more literally, being made foolish or becoming nonsensical. Only then does "salt for the soil or for the manure pile" make sense.[4] If believers are the world's fertilizer, we are meant to be spread throughout the land. We help those around us bear fruit.

You may think your mission in this world is to bear fruit for God's Kingdom, and it is. One of the most significant ways to do that is not to accumulate your own achievements but to enhance the lives of those around you—to seek their fruit more than your own. Too much salt corrodes and destroys; too little accomplishes nothing. But the right amount of you—or, more specifically, the right amount of what God has filled you with and empowered you to do—helps the world flourish. It blows wind in the sails of those around you. It turns you from being one fruitful plant to being the catalyst for a fruitful landscape.

Too many Christians are focused on fulfilling their own little mission, never realizing that their mission is to enhance the mission of their brothers and sisters. Broaden your vision and seek to fertilize the land around you. Serve others by helping them grow.

Lord, I've seen too many people walk through the world leaving a wasteland behind them. May a garden grow in every footprint I've left behind me. Help me as I help those around me flourish. Amen.

The Heart's True Love

*Don't you realize that friendship with the world
makes you an enemy of God? (James 4:4)*

ONE OF THE BIG DEBATES OF the late Middle Ages and early Renaissance periods was whether Christians were to renounce society or engage with it. They asked, *Is it better to withdraw into prayer and meditation or get involved in social life, creative activities, business, and politics? Should we have our own parallel institutions and governments or influence the ones that already exist? Is the Kingdom shaped more by contemplatives or activists?*

Though none of these is an either/or question, a person's theology inevitably sent him or her in one direction or the other, and this dynamic continues to play out today. Those who are waiting to escape the world through death or rapture will tend to draw near to God by pulling away from the mess of society. Those who envision the return of Jesus and his rule over the nations on earth will tend to prepare for his coming by getting involved. Each kind of believer finds plenty of biblical support, and each views his or her own focus as the essence of true spirituality.

The idea of being salt and light in the world suggests that we are to be engaged with it, of course. So why does James come down so hard on "friendship with the world"? Because there is a difference between being fully engaged with the world as a compassionate member of society and being ensnared as a lover of its idols. The heart is designed first to love God, then to love other people and the gifts God has given. The issue is whether we receive fulfillment from him or from mundane, temporary experiences and things. Human beings are called to a singular passion for him.

God sets all of his people apart for his purposes, and he guides most of us into occasional seasons of disengagement from outside influences so we can focus on him. But these are usually seasons rather than ongoing lifestyles. Follow the pattern of Jesus in being a friend of sinners (Matthew 11:19; Luke 15:2). Love the world as he does and influence it without adapting to its demands. Be fully engaged—and fully his.

Lord, I love the gifts you have given, and I love the experiences you provide. Let me love your world without being influenced by unworthy attachments. May I never have a love that draws me into the world if it does not also draw me closer to you. Amen.

Silver and Gold

Store your treasures in heaven, where moths and rust cannot destroy,
and thieves do not break in and steal. (Matthew 6:20)

SILVER AND GOLD MADE the Spanish empire rich. Considered valuable because of their relative scarcity and ability to resist decay, these precious metals were also symbolic of several ideals: elegance, status, longevity, even eternity. They were the noble metals, signs of regal abundance. So in the age of discovery and exploration, when new passageways to Europe's east and west were established and Spain was rapidly conquering much of the Americas, silver and gold became its ultimate goal. The wealth of the empire became paramount.

Of course, nothing in this world lasts forever—not kingdoms and empires, nor eras of abundance, nor silver and gold themselves. Even so, citizens of this world are easily captivated by its precious substances: wealth, status, power, influence, pleasure, and more. These may be given to us by our Creator to enjoy—in measure—but not to compete for or hoard in some desperate effort to exalt ourselves and maximize our experiences. In fact, these riches are usually given as pictures of something greater or as tastes of promises more real. But our hearts tend to cling to lesser realties that our eyes can see rather than the greater ones seen only by eyes of faith. We tend to go after whatever looks like the sure thing.

We need to reconsider what "the sure thing" is. When we find more joy in concrete but momentary pleasures than we do in a relationship that lasts forever, we make a disappointing statement to the people around us, many of whom are looking for a more fulfilling life. On the other hand, when we find more joy in God and his Kingdom than we do in the fleeting treasures of this world, the statement we make is even more profound. We point to eternal realities that are truer than silver and gold—and far more lasting.

Lord, inspire me to set my sights on the realities of heaven and my mind on things above, just as your Word tells me to do. Anchor my heart in your Kingdom, and let my satisfaction in you be evident to all. Amen.

Drawing In, Pouring Out

If you try to hang on to your life, you will lose it. But if you give up
your life for my sake, you will save it. (Matthew 16:25)

ONE OF THE MOST COLORFUL characters in literature is Ebenezer Scrooge, a miser whose epiphany—aided by the ghosts of Christmas past, present, and future—changed his outlook on life and his behavior toward everyone around him. Scrooge had not always been so stern and cold, as readers discover in his vision of Christmas past. He suffered wounds as a young man that hardened his heart and turned him inward as a stingy moneylender. But after his experience one Christmas Eve, he would never be so stern and cold again. In one night, he learned something most of us take a lifetime to understand.

All human beings, including you, are on a desperate search for fulfillment. Our instinct is to seek fulfillment by building ourselves up and gathering into our hearts as much pleasure, experience, people, and things as we can. It's a fatal instinct, one that will only end in frustration and emptiness—perhaps like that of Scrooge, though we hope not in such extremes. The antidote to this instinct is turning outward, focusing on the needs of others. We seek their fulfillment instead of our own, with discernment and full awareness of who we are as God's beloved children. Luke 6:38 tells us that whatever we give out, we receive back in greater abundance.

This shift from taking in to giving out not only opens the way to your own fulfillment. It also profoundly changes your relationship with those around you and increases your influence in their lives—not for the sake of your own agenda but in representing the compassion and generosity of the Father. Hanging on to your life leaves them and you empty; giving up your life pours into them and lets your heart be filled. The dynamic is a paradox; the fruit is the growth of God's Kingdom in this world. And the opportunity, once you learn to walk in it, is hard to resist.

Jesus, you poured yourself out for me because of the joy set before you. I pour myself out for you and others for the same reason. Fill my heart with the pleasure of seeing others fulfilled. Let my life overflow with the abundance of your love. Amen.

Obscure Invitations

The LORD gave this message to Jonah son of Amittai: "Get up and go
to the great city of Nineveh." . . . But Jonah got up and went in the
opposite direction to get away from the LORD. (Jonah 1:1-3)

JONAH WAS GIVEN AN INVITATION to partner with God in his work—literally an offer he couldn't refuse—but Jonah was terrified of the prospect. We can hardly blame him; most of us today would flee from an opportunity to preach the gospel in the streets of Mecca or to have declared the virtues of democratic liberalism in the Red Square at the height of the Cold War. Jonah's calling had similar connotations, so he ran the other way. He saw God's invitation as a responsibility too overwhelming to follow.

Most of God's invitations aren't quite that extreme, but they do tend to appear disorienting at times. After all, Jesus' invitation in Luke 9:23 to take up our cross and die daily carries some pretty radical implications for us. We shouldn't be surprised if God's calling sometimes comes disguised as something we might not like. But even when we don't understand his directions, we have to learn to trust him, knowing his nature is not to harm us but to bless us. We see this often in Scripture. Naaman the Syrian didn't understand Elisha's directions to wash in the Jordan River, but his healing came with obedience (2 Kings 5:9-14). Paul didn't understand why the doors of Asia had closed on him to spread God's message, but Europe was in full view once he turned around (Acts 16:6-10). The first steps of a calling can be difficult, but the last ones are always worth the cost of pressing through the confusion and fear.

Don't make the mistake of assuming God's instructions will always come with a clear view of the end. The fruitfulness and rewards may be hidden from natural eyes, especially at first, and the invitation may not look very appealing at all. But clarity comes along the way, and eventually so do satisfaction and fulfillment. Move toward his instructions, and he will make things clearer as you go. He knows how to lead. Press ahead and expect him to open doors along the way.

Lord, help me discern the difference between conviction that keeps me from going down the wrong road and fear that keeps me from going down the right one. Give me wisdom when your instructions are disorienting and confidence that I've heard you well. Lead me wherever you will. Amen.

God in the Flesh

The Word became human and made his home among us. (John 1:14)

WHEN PIONEER MISSIONARY Hudson Taylor began to "turn Chinese"—in dress, language, and mannerisms—he was doing much more than attempting gimmicks. Many of his fellow missionaries looked down on his efforts, but Taylor's approach was not unlike the one taken by the incarnate Word many centuries ago. God clothed himself in flesh (1 Timothy 3:16), divested himself of divine privilege by taking the form of a man (Philippians 2:7), and entered into our world born of a woman (Galatians 4:4). Why? Because words had not been enough to portray the Father accurately or to change our nature. The Son, the perfect image of the Father and the carrier of the Spirit, was. Humanity didn't need another sermon or moral lesson. We needed a picture we could relate to. We needed to know what the divine life looks like in a human being.

Taylor took Christianity into inland China in a form Chinese people could relate to, not only by preaching in their language, but by demonstrating a devoted life in their culture. In some areas of the country, he was the first to do so and was a rare example of the wisdom, power, and love of the Spirit. Today, he is an example of what is called "incarnational missions"—the method initiated by God himself in sending his Son.

This method is not limited to God and missionaries. It is actually the kind of influence he calls all of us to have. When Jesus told his followers to go into the world in the same way his Father had sent him (John 20:21), this is what he meant. The gospel that begins with God in the flesh of his Son ends with the Spirit in the flesh of those who believe in the Son. It's an amazing opportunity to take the presence of God with you into every corner of your world—to make your home in the world because God has made his home in you.

Father, your love compelled you to send your Son; Jesus, you send me as the Father sent you; Holy Spirit, you now make your home in me. Thank you for welcoming me into this fellowship. Use it to bring others in too. Amen.

A Heart like God's

God knows how much I love you and long for you with the
tender compassion of Christ Jesus. (Philippians 1:8)

DUTCH SCIENTIST CHRISTIAAN HUYGENS, the seventeenth-century inventor of the pendulum clock, noticed something in his workshop one day. Despite their different origins, the pendulums of two clocks were swinging in perfect unison. Huygens intentionally staggered the oscillation between the two by resetting one, and when he checked on the clocks later, they had again synchronized themselves. His observation led to the discovery of "entrainment" or "coupled oscillators"—a phenomenon found throughout the natural world whenever two or more oscillating mechanisms or organisms are found in proximity with each other. Simply put, nearness can cause different rhythms to conform to the same beat.

That principle applies not only to the natural realm but also to the spiritual. When our hearts spend time in God's presence, they begin to align with his heartbeat. We begin to feel his feelings, to love what he loves and hate what he hates. We develop the same motives and will. We conform to his image through gazing at him and enjoying his fellowship. In other words, we think, feel, and move in rhythm with him.

Think about what that means for your relationship with others and your ability to represent God's nature. For one thing, you begin to see the world as he sees it, to love with his compassion, and to long for people to know their Creator the way you have experienced him. For another, you begin to look like him, to carry something of the divine nature within yourself (2 Peter 1:4), to embody the wisdom, power, and love of your Father (Ephesians 3:17-19). On both counts—your relationship with the world and its perceptions of you—you begin to step into the image of God with which you were first endowed and in which you are now being renewed. Your intimacy with the Father has a profound impact on the picture others have of him. And your own heartbeat can lead them into an encounter with him.

Father, synchronize my heart with yours. Let my spirit flow with the same love that your Spirit does. Daily conform me to your image so others see Jesus in me. Amen.

The Grief of God

My heart is torn within me, and my compassion overflows.
(Hosea 11:8)

IN SPITE OF OUR PERCEPTIONS and theologies, God is not cold, sterile, and unmovable. In fact, the prophets and apostolic writers describe him in very emotional terms, fully capable of being grieved or provoked to jealousy. His essence and character never change, but his attitudes fit our situations. He is compassionate, joyful, affectionate, zealous, and much, much more.

If your heart aligns with God's, you begin to see yourself and others with his overwhelming love and affection. You know who you are—completely adored. And you know who others are—the objects of his enormous affection. But you also know his grief for those who don't enter into his love and his anger over whatever gets in the way. His favor can be exhilarating, but his disfavor can be frightening. We don't realize how every attitude and emotion of God is somehow a reflection of his great love.

Think about it. In Scripture, God's jealousy, grief, anger, and hate—what we would call negative emotions—are never what we take them for at face value. They are deeper reflections of his love. He hates the kind of hypocrisy that obscures his true face; he gets angry at the sin that has marred his beautiful children and disrupted our fellowship with him; he is jealous for our love and wants exclusive commitment; and he grieves over the fallenness of creation and the brokenness that blocks our vision of his goodness. He is neither petty nor capricious in any of these ways, but his responses are nevertheless real.

If you enter into this synchronization with God—and you should—you will not only feel his affection for those around you, but you will also feel the longings and grief of his Spirit. This is not an easy or comfortable calling, but it does carry the Father's heartbeat. Embody it well, and carry it into every relationship you have.

Father, your heart is infinite, and it can handle the enormity of this world's sorrows. Mine cannot. Even so, give me a taste of your compassion, a hint of your heartbeat, a longing that reflects yours. Let me love as you love. Amen.

Full Discipleship

*Is there . . . any fellowship together in the Spirit? Are your
hearts tender and compassionate? (Philippians 2:1)*

SOMEHOW MODERN CHRISTIANITY has developed a kind of discipleship that is
reduced to knowing God's Word and doing it—the mind and the will. We read or
hear Scripture and apply it. We learn what the Bible says and live it out. The two
sides of this approach are both vital, and we would never want to neglect them. But
are the mind and the will the only components of our personality? Or are we missing something?

We are, and it's the reason so many followers of Jesus say they have done what
they are supposed to do but still feel distant from God. They have left out the heart.
Salvation for them was a one-time event, much like a couple who stares at their
marriage certificate to remind themselves of their relationship. But God has called
us into a heart-to-heart mutual pursuit that involves his love, hate, joy, anger, zeal,
jealousy, delight, grief, and affection. It's the kind of discipleship Paul explores in
Philippians 2:1-2, among other places, where he suggests that since the believers
share common feelings for one another, they should line up their minds with one
another too. Just as aligning our hearts with those we love is the way we grow closer,
so is aligning our hearts with God the way we draw near to him. We bring every
aspect of our personality to him, and our hearts begin to beat with his.

This holistic discipleship transforms our lives and relationships, and it has positive effects on the people around us. When we are moved by the ethos, mood, emotion, and energy of the Spirit, others get to see real people inhabited by Jesus, not
Christian automatons controlled by a system of principles. They see God's compassion, grief, and joy in the flesh, fully expressed in the lives of his image-bearers. In
other words, they get a taste of his heart—the winsome, compelling side of his nature
by which all human beings can know and grow closer to him.

*Father, may I never stop learning your Word and doing it. But add to my mind and will
the fullness of your feelings and attitudes. Put your heartbeat within me, and let it shape
my passions daily. Amen.*

The Joy of Heaven

*There is joy in the presence of God's angels when
even one sinner repents. (Luke 15:10)*

A LONG LINE OF ORTHODOX, Catholic, and Protestant leaders and thinkers have remarked that joy is the defining characteristic of a Christian. They have emphasized the depth of satisfaction and fulfillment that comes from knowing God and living in his presence. Our heart connection with God may lead us to experience all kinds of sentiments that reflect his nature, but perhaps the most significant for us to understand is the joy and affection he has for his people and his celebration of love. If any single mood captures the culture and climate of his Kingdom, it's joy.

We know from the prophets that God delights in his people and rejoices over them with singing (Zephaniah 3:17). We see Jesus tell his disciples of the joy in heaven over wayward souls that return to God (Luke 15:10). We hear the words of Paul reminding us to rejoice at all times (Philippians 4:4; 1 Thessalonians 5:16). And we are given a glimpse of the multitudes gathered around God's throne, worshiping him with exhilaration and singing new songs about his goodness and love (Revelation 5:11-14). In all our efforts and desire to become like the Father and do what is pleasing to him, it should be very clear from Scripture that letting ourselves be joyful will go a long way toward aligning our hearts with his. Our emphasis on doing the right thing must always come in the context of picking up on his joyful mood. Otherwise our doing becomes hard and unfruitful.

Remember this as you live out your role as salt and light in this world. Joy is captivating. Arduous obedience is not. The heart of God is winsome. Discouragement is not. The true nature of God will win hearts and minds even when words will not convince. One of our highest priorities as believers is to join in his celebration, overflow with gladness, rejoice when wayward souls find their true home, and reflect the culture and climate of the Kingdom everywhere we go.

Father, may I embody the mood of heaven in everything I do. Even if I were to do everything right according to the teaching of your Word, without joy I would be out of sync with you. Let my heart burst with your goodness always. Amen.

Truth and Love

We will speak the truth in love, growing in every
way more and more like Christ. (Ephesians 4:15)

MANY GREEKS FOUND THE beliefs of the early church absurd because the idea of a resurrection did not fit their philosophical traditions. Romans found their beliefs offensive because they could not accommodate sacrifices to pagan deities and the emperor. Regardless of the reason—the gospel's emphasis on our fallenness and insistence that we need a Savior, its mandate to deny self and live for Christ, or the seeming absurdity of an incarnate deity who would die by execution—Scripture warned us about this. The cornerstone would be rejected (Luke 20:17-18), and the rock of offense would make doubters stumble (1 Peter 2:8). The pride of humanity is offended by the truth.

The gospel and all its applications are offensive enough on their own without our adding any barriers to them. Even so, many believers become militant in their conversations. They speak the truth out of fear or woundedness; lavish it on others with extra doses of guilt and shame; or add a dash of anger, a hint of bitterness, or a touch of resentment to make sure their point is made. Perhaps we respond this way to build up walls around our hearts, to protect us from whatever backlash we might receive in a difficult conversation. Whatever the situation, and whatever our idiosyncrasies, we have to be able to speak truth from no other motive but love, and to make that love evident in the way we speak.

That will require a change in perspective. Most people have a personal agenda in their conversations about truth—to win an argument, defuse a situation, get relief from a dysfunctional relationship, save themselves from heartache . . . The needs and desires are many. But a heart in sync with God's is motivated by love and the other person's well-being. In every conversation, ask God for his perspective on the other person. Let his perspective become yours. And speak the truth—even when it hurts—with no other motive than love.

Lord, you lovingly, patiently, and persistently spoke truth into my life; may I have the same attitude as I talk with others. Fill my words with grace and peace. Amen.

Serve with Excellence

God gave these four young men an unusual aptitude for
understanding every aspect of literature and wisdom. (Daniel 1:17)

IN SERVICE OF SECULAR Chinese authorities, Jesuit missionaries in the seventeenth century used their knowledge of science, technology, math, linguistics, and geography in exchange for missionary activity within the realm. Their benefits to society led to official tolerance of and, at times, appreciation for their religious views. The missionaries were allowed to stay because they made significant contributions and offered solutions to real problems. They leveraged their capital in this age to influence its inhabitants for the one to come.

We still see this phenomenon today, especially in countries that are otherwise closed to missionaries. Those who teach English or offer practical training in some other skill, for example, are highly valued. Providing a useful service—not to manipulate a system but to genuinely meet needs—gives messengers of faith room to work in restricted places. The believer who wants to "serve" only by declaring his or her own message and opinions will not be effective in any context; but the believer who has a servant's heart will be widely welcomed.

This is why marketplace ministries are as important as church ministries, if not more so. They keep us from being marginalized into "religious" areas of influence. When you serve, your message is heard. When you don't, doors remain shut. And if your service is excellent, of the highest quality, the doors that open to you are far greater and more significant than when you serve with mediocrity.

Like Daniel and his friends, serve with excellence. Pray for God's solutions to practical problems, and offer them in businesses, schools, government, or wherever else you have access. God is in favor of healthy societies, families, communities, and organizations. In every way you can, demonstrate that you are too.

Lord, you do show up in the broken places of this world, often through the service of your people. You meet needs, offer solutions, and fill hearts. Let me be one who serves well in these things, brings value to those around me, and demonstrates your creativity, wisdom, and favor. Amen.

Society's Assets

*Upright citizens are good for a city and make it prosper, but
the talk of the wicked tears it apart. (Proverbs 11:11)*

EVERY CITY HAS A MOOD. Or perhaps an ethos, an attitude, or a culture. Whatever environment it has created for itself has enormous potential to shape the lives of its residents and form their perspectives. As much as we like to think we are independent individuals unaffected by the attitudes and decisions of the people around us, we are all part of a community. Our lives are interconnected.

That's why Scripture tells us that upright citizens are good for a city and that negative talk can rip it apart. Our cities may not have the same dynamics as those in the ancient world when this proverb was written, but they are still built on relationships. A society filled with people who are invested, positive, constructive, and dedicated to God's ways will prosper, even when its citizens don't understand why. A society filled with people who are apathetic, negative, destructive, and amoral will never have a shortage of problems. The differences between the two may not be readily apparent on the surface—prosperity takes different forms—but the long-term health of a culture stands or falls not on its majorities but on the level of involvement of its godly remnants. A little salt and light can have a huge effect on their surroundings.

As conventional as it sounds, God has called his people to be upright citizens. Society needs us to contribute our ethics and gifts to its well-being. Doing so puts us in positions of service and influence and seasons the whole culture. It's one of the ways God extends his grace to this world and creates avenues for reaching others' hearts and lives.

Never underestimate your significance as a godly member of society. You may think your contributions are unnoticeable, and you may never see any tangible effects of your influence. But you are part of God's Kingdom on earth, and that is never unimportant. Your city—or town or region—has its own atmosphere, and you have a hand in shaping it.

Lord, you use all sorts of building blocks to construct your Kingdom, and you specialize in turning the raw material of our lives into the finest material. Make me a prime example of your handiwork. Use me to bless my society. Amen.

A Cause for Rejoicing

When the righteous prosper, the city rejoices. (Proverbs 11:10, NIV)

THROUGHOUT THE TWENTIETH CENTURY, doctrines of prosperity and wealth grew strong in some sectors of Christianity and spread to much of the world—not only to prosperous countries, but also those where people desperately sought a way out of their poverty. Reactions against the "prosperity gospel," as we have come to call it, have rightly pointed out the extremely influential people in Scripture who were not at all prosperous but were nevertheless walking in God's power and love. But many Christians have taken the opposite extreme in insisting that we should shun wealth and comfort. They believe those who do prosper are somehow less spiritual—forgetting, of course, that there are many examples of biblical figures who had quite a bit of money and were also walking in God's power and love. Somewhere in between these extremes is the truth that it is possible and even desirable for believers to earn wealth and use it not for selfish purposes but to bless others. Success is *not* a bad thing.

The prosperity of the selfish helps no one. But Proverbs tells us that the prosperity of the righteous—those who do not live selfishly but have a Kingdom-oriented heart and seek God's will—is an enormous blessing to the community. Why? Because a Kingdom mind-set will look for ways to demonstrate and expand the Kingdom, and prosperity has a way of multiplying opportunities to do so. When the righteous prosper, everyone benefits.

Do not seek prosperity as so many others do, with greed and a focus on getting everything you want. Do, however, seek it as a Kingdom calling. See your job as a platform for expanding Kingdom ways. Being successful in business, industry, law, education, government, or any other sector of society in order to serve and influence systems is a sacred calling. It promotes a Kingdom in which injustices, abuses, poverty, and brokenness cannot continue. Live in such a way that whatever prosperity you experience gives those around you a reason to rejoice.

Lord, you have given to me out of your abundance. I open my arms to receive as much as you want to give so that I may give out of what I receive. Make me a blessing in my job, my activities, my networks of relationships—everything. Amen.

Agents of Blessing

Through the blessing of the upright a city is exalted.
(Proverbs 11:11, NIV)

YOU ARE STRATEGICALLY PLACED in this world to make a difference. You probably know this by now, even if at times you struggle to see how. Perhaps you spend much of your mental energy focusing on the problems you face, or on the people who created those problems, and the ways you wish you could fix them. Or maybe you've had seasons of seeing your life as your own, wondering how to find fulfillment or manage the tasks at hand. Perhaps there are times when you just exist—moment by moment, day by day. Even so, you're aware of bigger things. You recognize a calling from the Spirit within you. You want to live with a sense of destiny.

On the one hand, we can sometimes be so focused on the big picture that we miss the opportunities in front of us. On the other, we can become so focused on the details of daily life that we miss pursuing the more significant relationships we have already been given. In between those two points of focus, the macro and the micro, we live and work among people who could be influenced in one way or another by a godly attitude. We have many opportunities to pray blessings on those around us— people at the office, in a classroom, standing in line, commenting on social media, passing by on the street—all of whom need, as we do, regular touches from God. We have platforms from which to improve lives, encourage hearts, and demonstrate Kingdom values and ways. We are called to impart grace, and we have open doors to do so—through prayers, words, favors, and acts of kindness and compassion. We are living, breathing, walking agents of blessing.

Listen to the voice that reminds you of all the people placed in your path who need a priestly touch from a son or daughter of God. Be an advocate before God's throne on their behalf. Ask him to meet their needs. Let your city—or office or neighborhood or school—be exalted through the blessings you bring.

Lord, show me my potential. How can I bless the lives that cross my path? What words can I speak and pray? What deeds can I do? May every circle of my relationships be lifted up by whatever blessings I bring. Amen.

Enjoy Your Gifts

Whatever you do or say, do it as a representative of the Lord Jesus,
giving thanks through him to God the Father. (Colossians 3:17)

GERARD OF FRACHET, a thirteenth-century Dominican writer, told many stories in which certain deceased members of the order were consigned to suffering in purgatory for various sins. Among those sins of his brothers were being too passionate about architecture, too interested in manuscripts, and too enthusiastic about the construction of new monasteries. Aside from reflecting a bizarre definition of sin and a glaring absence of grace (which was not unusual for the time), his stories also illustrate an extreme form of a more subtle assumption many Christians still hold: that if we enjoy something too much, it must be wrong. Or, as Gerard might have put it, pleasure is the enemy of true spirituality.

This belief is far from the truth, of course. It contradicts the portrayal of God as revealed in Scripture, who is supremely satisfied in his work and takes great pleasure in his children and his Kingdom. If Scripture can speak of "the zeal of the Lord," and we are called to be like him, then zeal is entirely appropriate. In fact, our unique combination of interests and passions may be given to us specifically to accomplish his purposes. He wants us to be enthusiastic about our work, whether or not others see it as "spiritual." The world is in desperate need of people who love God and are passionate about what they do.

Finding satisfaction in your work and interests reflects the Creator who, at every step of the creation process, looked at his handiwork and saw that it was good. Though life may place demands on you to do whatever needs to be done, regardless of whether you enjoy it, God's intention is ultimately for you to find your sweet spot. When you get there, give him thanks and represent him well. Make the most of the gifts he has given you, and enjoy them. Let the world see the satisfaction of the Creator—and a taste of his glory—in you.

Lord, may I never dishonor the interests and dreams you have placed in my heart. Give me discernment about which ones are yours and let me pursue those wholeheartedly. Make me fruitful in satisfying places. Amen.

Kingdom Investments

The purses of heaven never get old or develop holes. Your treasure will
be safe; no thief can steal it and no moth can destroy it. (Luke 12:33)

FOR CENTURIES, alchemists sought ways to turn everyday materials—dirt, clay, stone, and base metals—into precious metals and gems. Some studied the processes and reactions of nature, while others looked for divine illumination that would reveal the key to transforming substances. These alchemists believed the properties of treasure were embedded in elemental forms and that the right knowledge or power could bring them out. They wanted to turn what was common into something priceless.

Their techniques never worked, for reasons we now understand. But their desire touched on something innate in human experience—some longing for the eternal that has echoed in our souls from long ago. And in a sense, we can do what alchemists never learned to do. Jesus referred to it in his teachings, and Paul elaborated on it later. We can take the material substance of this world and leverage it for eternal gain. We can invest our money, time, talents, and much more in God's Kingdom and receive something of everlasting value in return.

Have you considered what a privilege that is? Investors in this age marvel at 20, 50, or even 100 percent returns. But Jesus promised something much greater. Our gifts in this material world can be sown into the soil of God's Kingdom and bear fruit that lasts. We can hardly imagine what compounded interest looks like throughout all of eternity, but that's the promise of Kingdom investments. When we give to God, we receive back from him—both in this age and the one to come.

Don't miss that investment opportunity. You will never encounter a better one. The things we accumulate in this age can be destroyed by moth, rust, decay, or a bad economy. But the Kingdom economy is never bad, and no investment in it fails to have some sort of influence that will echo forever. Leverage the temporary resources of your life for eternal purposes, and see how God transforms them. They will become more valuable than you could imagine.

Lord, you can turn trinkets into gold when they are given in faith. Give me a generous heart that offers my all to you in love and faithfulness, and use it for eternal glory. Bear fruit in me that lasts forever. Amen.

Defending the Defenseless

*Speak up for those who cannot speak for themselves; ensure
justice for those being crushed. (Proverbs 31:8)*

WHEN COLONIALISTS IN South Africa were threatening to take over the land of an indigenous people group in the late nineteenth century, missionary John Mackenzie and some of his colleagues intervened. They helped Khama III, chief of the Bamangwato people in the area now known as Botswana, rally resistance and get a hearing with Queen Victoria. The eventual result was a land protection agreement that served the interests of the indigenous people well for years to come. Mackenzie was one of many Protestants who defied the unfortunate and misinformed stereotype of missionaries as tools of exploitation. In fact, missionaries very often advocated for local people and became a thorn in the side of the powerful. They set political affiliations aside and took a stand for justice.[5]

Many people don't have the courage or the insight to do that. Instead, they have adopted a set of principles they believe are based on God's Word and then live according to those principles rather than the movements of his Spirit or the character he has clearly revealed in Jesus. Scripture tells us quite plainly that God is on the side of justice for the oppressed and defends their interests, regardless of the political platforms of the players on the stage. He calls his people to have the same outlook and sensitivity. He pulls us out of the stereotypes and aligns us with his heart.

Have the courage to speak out for those who cannot speak for themselves, not because it's the trendy thing to do—it may or may not be, depending on the situation—but because it is God's nature to do so. Sometimes your voice will follow the political, cultural, and religious lines you normally follow; sometimes it won't. In any case, your primary affiliation in this world is the Kingdom of God, and you are to be known for that above all else. Your heart will be drawn to those in need, your eyes will see injustices, and your soul will be unsettled about them. Praying, speaking, and taking action align you with the mission of God.

Father, your desire to lift up the oppressed and seek justice on their behalf is one of the most prominent themes in your Word. Make it a prominent theme in my life. Give me eyes to see and courage to intervene wherever I can make a difference. Amen.

Life in Open Spaces

You strain your water so you won't accidentally swallow a gnat,
but you swallow a camel! (Matthew 23:24)

THE PATRIARCH OF THE Russian Orthodox Church in the 1650s wanted to make the rituals of the church consistent with the Greek churches and issued decrees to align them. One of the changes he required was that the sign of the cross be made with three fingers instead of two—a seemingly minor detail from a modern perspective, perhaps, but one that rattled traditionalists and provoked a searing controversy over maintaining the divine harmony between God and those who worship him. For some, the patriarch's reforms were a sign of the last days, a foreboding indication of apocalyptic times ahead.

We live in a more casual age in which few people are so rigidly tied to their rituals, though some still are. But regardless of whether we are nitpicky about outward signs and symbols, many of us are equally narrow in our tolerance of divergent doctrines and practices, even on issues where Scripture is not entirely precise. We invest a lot of belief, emotion, and energy in our pet perspectives. Across the ages, the Christian world has made many of these internal disputes visible. And the watching world looks on with the same bemusement with which some might look at a seventeenth-century controversy in the Russian church.

Should we just loosen up and stop defending our pet standards? On some issues, perhaps; on others, not necessarily. But we should learn to live with perspective, to see ourselves as outsiders see us, and to give a lot of thought to what's really important and what isn't. If God had wanted us to agree with precision on every point of faith, he would have given us a very precise book of systematic theology. He didn't. He gave us stories, testimonies, and experiences of how he has worked in this world and on behalf of his people for millennia. As part of that overarching story, make your life an illustration, not an argument. Live the role of salt and light that seasons and warms the lives around you.

Lord, may I never place higher demands on myself or my fellow believers than you place on me. You have brought me into open spaces; let me share that freedom with others with a welcoming, open heart. Amen.

The Nonconformist in You

Put on your new nature, and be renewed as you learn to know
your Creator and become like him. (Colossians 3:10)

THE CANDIDATE MADE PROMISES before the election, and he was completely sincere. He was a newcomer wanting to make a difference, not a jaded politician. For now, his goals were local; but down the road, they were much bigger. And his fresh, reassuring words made his growing body of supporters hope he would succeed. But once he was in office, something changed. He began to work the system. He made compromises, not because he wanted to break promises but because it seemed like the only way to get things done. He conformed to the culture of his surroundings—the same culture his supporters wanted to change.

Whose story is this? No one's in particular, but almost everyone's who has entered any area of society—government, law, education, church, media, or anywhere else—with an eye toward change. Multitudes of people have embarked upon their life of work with a change-the-world attitude, only to find that *they* are the ones who change. Why? Perhaps it's because the system is inevitably bigger than they are. Or maybe it's because the temptations to compromise are just too great. But it's also true that many have not learned how to carry the character and ways of God into places that contradict his character and ways. We forget the Spirit within us.

Conformity is a social phenomenon. It may also be a spiritual one. Every Kingdom citizen is called to be a conformist toward God and a nonconformist toward the world's systems. We see this displayed in the lives of Joseph and Daniel, who served God powerfully in very ungodly kingdoms because they knew who they were and remained faithful to the one who, in his sovereignty, had allowed them to be there. You have the same ability and, if you're willing, the same godly stubbornness. In the Kingdom of God, salt is not meant to lose its flavor, and light is not meant to dim. Let the Spirit change the environment within you; then trust the power within you to change the world around you.

Holy Spirit, you are not a compromiser. Neither do you want me to be a casualty of the system. Show me the third way—the way of innovation, of breakthrough, of power to change. Open doors for your transforming ways. Amen.

Shalom

He will be called: Wonderful Counselor, Mighty God, Everlasting
Father, Prince of Peace. His government and its peace will never end.
(Isaiah 9:6-7)

THE HEBREW WORD *SHALOM* IS well-known as a greeting and a blessing. We translate it as *peace*, which is certainly accurate, but it means so much more. *Shalom* includes fullness, completeness, wholeness, satisfaction, and well-being—peace in every sense, in every area of life. It's that sense of fulfillment we long for when we think about the perfect vacation, the end of our to-do list, the enjoyment of life, and relief from all our fears and insecurities. We know we will get to experience it in heaven, but we want God to give us tastes of it now. We know he can; we see it in Scripture when God gave Solomon—the king whose name comes from *shalom*—*shalom* on every side (1 Kings 4:24; 1 Chronicles 22:9). We see it in Jesus' calming of the storm (Mark 4:39) and his blessing of peace over his disciples (John 14:27). And as we read in Isaiah, the promise of the coming Messiah identified Jesus as the Prince of *Shalom* whose government would never be without it.

Shalom is an appealing, magnetic quality of life, and God's people are to embody it just as Jesus did. Unfortunately, many of us are still filled with worries, anxieties, insecurities, doubts, nerves, bitterness, or some other form of anti-*shalom*, but it nevertheless remains a promise and an opportunity for us. Perhaps that's why Paul was so insistent on telling people to rejoice always and be thankful in every circumstance, and why the most common command in Scripture is not to be afraid. *Shalom* is our inheritance, and far too many of us are missing out on it. As a result, far too many people in the world are missing out on demonstrations of what it can look like.

Learn to live in *shalom*, and notice how people respond to you differently. The human heart longs for peace and is drawn to it but rarely encounters people who live and breathe it. Be one of them. Rest in the presence and power of Christ. Let the fullness of the Kingdom thrive within you.

Jesus, you are the Prince of Shalom, *and you promise to fill me with your Spirit. Settle my heart, fill me with joy, and let me model the fullness of your Kingdom for all to see. Make me whole. Amen.*

Deference That Defuses Competition

*Those who exalt themselves will be humbled, and those who
humble themselves will be exalted. (Luke 14:11)*

JESUS NOTICED HOW ALL THE attendees at a dinner party tried to sit in places of honor at the table—trying to navigate the complex social pecking order in ways that served *their own* best interests. His advice to them exemplifies the wisdom of humility and self-awareness, as well as one of the most effective ways we can change the atmosphere around us by defying it. Deference may seem out of place in a highly competitive environment, but it defuses and undermines the spirit of one-upmanship. The problem for many of us, however, is that a deferential attitude may cost us some opportunities in the short run.

But not in the long run. God knows how to take care of his own. Ultimately the question is, Who do you see as the orchestrator of your life—yourself or God? If you're relying on yourself, you will likely do everything you can to work out your own advances and promotions, and you will constantly be under pressure. If you allow God to order your life, you can rest in his wisdom and timing. You'll learn to take steps toward a goal or position in his way at the right moment. The initiative is his; you are only responding. It's a much more peaceful way to live.

While you are waiting for God to open doors and direct your paths, you are able to represent his nature to others. No longer will you experience a cutthroat zeal to be exalted; instead, you'll demonstrate a patient confidence that you are right where you need to be at every moment. Those who rest in the flow of God's Spirit and entrust the course of their lives to him stand out as exceptional, demonstrating not only the mature character that tends to open opportunities but also the nature of their Father, who is not stressed about anything. Submission and trust make a beautiful testimony, and ultimately a fruitful one—for you and for those who need a glimpse of the sovereign God.

Father, empower my faith in your sovereignty over my life. Enable me to strip the competitive atmosphere around me of power by submitting to you. Help me to serve others well, as I trust you to lift me up at the proper time. Amen.

Humility That Disarms Pride

"God opposes the proud but gives grace to the humble."
So humble yourselves under the mighty power of God, and
at the right time he will lift you up in honor. (1 Peter 5:5-6)

MACHIAVELLI'S *THE PRINCE* DESCRIBES all the ideal characteristics of a ruler for undermining opposition, stabilizing his realm, and optimizing his own power. Humility does not make the list, except as a quality a ruler might wish to *appear* to have. And it's true, in terms of achieving status and power in a proud world; humility has little utilitarian value. Those who make the most visible marks on history are rarely known for their self-effacing attitudes.

The Kingdom of God is another matter, however, and it lasts much longer than history. Those who shape its story and make their mark are those who know who they are in God's sight and defer to him. Hebrew sages and prophets, with a discerning eye on Israel's history and a sensitive ear to God's voice, kept coming back to this remarkable theme: God's affinity for the humble. He mocks the proud but gives grace to the humble (Proverbs 3:34). The high and lofty one lives with those who are lowly and contrite (Isaiah 57:15). The Lord has required only that we do right, love mercy, and walk humbly with him (Micah 6:8). Jesus emphasized this truth in his teachings, and the New Testament writers pointed to it frequently. While the world talks about being "on the right side of history," we would rather be on the right side of God. And we will find humility a valued commodity there.

If you want to disarm the power of pride in the environment around you, enter into it with great humility. Cultivate a humble heart, and cling to it stubbornly. The temptations to conform to an atmosphere of self-importance will be great, but genuine, confident humility is ultimately more influential than the masks the vain wear. Many of the proud will ignore you; others will be confounded. Either way, you will position yourself to transform the spiritual culture and represent the heart of your Father well.

Jesus, as great as you are, you clothed yourself in humility and took the form of a human being. So why are we human beings so eager to clothe ourselves in pride? May I never be one who does. May the immense value you've placed on my life lead to humble worship. Amen.

Peace That Unravels Chaos

He awoke and rebuked the wind and said to the sea, "Peace! Be still!"
And the wind ceased, and there was a great calm. (Mark 4:39, ESV)

THE GOSPELS OF MATTHEW, MARK, and Luke tell a remarkable story of Jesus sleeping in the back of a boat as a storm rages on the Sea of Galilee. The disciples panic and even accuse Jesus of not caring whether they drown. Jesus calmly gets up, rebukes the wind and the waves, and stills the storm. The disciples are amazed at his authority, but Jesus points the responsibility back toward them. Why did they have such little faith? The question suggests that they could have spoken to the storm with the same authority themselves—or at least been confident that Jesus' presence would have calmed it for them.

We live in the midst of storms too; they rage around us daily. Like the disciples, we ask God to wake from his slumber, demonstrate that he cares, and do something about the situation. Meanwhile, God turns the responsibility back toward us, reminding us of the authority we have in Christ, the promises he has given us for prayer, and even the assurance that we can do the works Jesus did (John 14:12). So we wonder, *What do we have to learn in order to speak peace into our circumstances? How can we sleep calmly as life rages around us? Why was Jesus able to calm storms and we aren't?*

Jesus could change the environment around him because the peace inside him was greater than the storm outside. In his situation and in ours, a crisis represents a conflict of two opposing forces: the Kingdom of God and the turmoil of the world. Which will win? The one that doesn't back down. If you really want to unravel the chaos in your life, cultivate the peace within. Let it rule in your heart (Colossians 3:15). Enter disruptive situations with the assurance that the peace inside of you is greater, and speak words of peace around you. Storms will calm. Chaos will bow to the *shalom* of God's Kingdom, and others will get a taste of its glory.

Jesus, you came not as the great exception but as the great example. Teach me to be like you. Fill me with the peace that calms storms. And may my words demonstrate the power of your presence. Amen.

Service That Trumps Control

Among you it will be different. Whoever wants to be a
leader among you must be your servant. (Mark 10:43)

JOSEPH STALIN WAS OBSESSIVE about his image and hypersensitive to criticism—not only for the threat of subversion it might represent, but also for the offense to his ego. Stalin is certainly not history's only authoritarian ruler to quash all hints of dissent. Many rulers of this world have focused on their own authority and image in the eyes of those who serve under them. Few have focused on the needs of others simply to help meet those needs. Rather they meet needs for the sake of reinforcing their image as benevolent rulers, acting out of self-interest rather than compassion. Those who "serve the people" almost always seem to give in to the temptation to serve themselves instead.

There are exceptions, of course, but there should be more. Jesus insisted that his followers are never to enter into the dynamics of domination, and he gave us a startling picture of what true leadership looks like. The King of the universe came to serve and to give up his own life for the benefit of others. He knew how to issue commands, but never for any reason other than meeting the needs of others and serving the higher interests of those who follow him. He demonstrated that leaders first and foremost are not those who rule well but those who submit well—to God and to the ultimate good. He established servant leadership as the Kingdom norm.

As in every other attitude, Christians are meant to be agents of the alternate way. Having a servant's heart will change the atmosphere, make a profound impression on the people around you, and open their hearts to the reality of God's nature. You may at times feel (and be treated as if) you are giving up too much or being a doormat, but do not grow weary in doing well (Galatians 6:9). You do not have to become a doormat to demonstrate the deference and humility of God's Kingdom. An attitude of service disarms powers no one else sees and sets the stage for the Spirit of love.

Holy Spirit, your power is always captivating, never enslaving; always inviting, never enforcing; and always giving, never demanding. May I serve with the same power in order to open hearts to your generous love. Amen.

Patience That Calms Impatience

Be still in the presence of the LORD, and wait patiently for him to act.
(Psalm 37:7)

THOUSANDS OF PHILISTINE WARRIORS were gathering to take revenge on Israel, and Saul's army began to panic (1 Samuel 13). A battle was inescapable, but the Israelites were greatly outnumbered. Saul waited for the prophet Samuel to come make an offering and ask for God's favor. The longer Saul waited, the larger the Philistine army grew and the more afraid his own men became. Finally, after seven days, Saul took matters into his own hands and made the offering himself. Then Samuel arrived, informed Saul that he had acted rashly, and declared that Saul's reign would not last much longer because of his impatience.

Patience is an attribute of God, a fruit of his Spirit, and a common characteristic of his Kingdom. Those who enter into relationship with him will have to learn it well. That presents a huge problem for us. As technology advances, human beings are becoming more and more conditioned to be impatient. We're accustomed to microwave cooking, drive-thru windows, and ATMs, and we even get agitated when a web page takes more than a few seconds to load. From our perspective, time is precious, and we don't want to waste it. We forget the big picture of God's Kingdom, which he has been cultivating for millennia. He sees the entire timeline of history at once and asks us to see it with the same certainty. He wants us to live with a sense of his timing.

When we really learn how to do that, we become the antidote to a restless society, an urgent situation, or even a room full of impatient people. The calm patience within us can defuse the impatience in those around us and reassure them that God has all things in his hands. When we reflect and represent the God who does not panic about anything, we prepare hearts to open to his ways and see from a different perspective. Being still in the presence of the Lord makes his presence much more known.

Lord, I confess that I struggle with impatience. I know you are ageless, but I am not, and I want to make the most of my time. Help me see the big picture so others will see it too. Let me rest in your presence so it becomes all the more visible to those around me. Amen.

Giving That Overcomes Greed

*One gives freely, yet grows all the richer; another withholds what
he should give, and only suffers want. (Proverbs 11:24, ESV)*

EYES GROW BIGGER IN an age of consumerism. They have to. Expectations rise, the standard of living grows, Christmas lists get longer, and the income and space we need to keep up continue to expand. Almost imperceptibly, an eye for acquisition turns into a penchant for greed. We hardly know where to draw the line between needs, wants, and excess.

Those who work in the business world often face greater temptations to conform to a culture of greed, though hardly anyone would label it as such. The God-given need and desire to earn income can easily morph into a never-enough approach to gaining more, and this attitude is considered normal. But the "culture of more" is certainly not confined to commerce; we all participate, even when our means are limited. Our hearts are becoming conditioned to being extremely liberal with our own wants and extremely tight with what we give away.

How do we cope with such a strong trend? As always, if we want to change the environment around us, we need to carry a very strong environment within us and refuse to compromise it. In this case, we carry the Kingdom attribute of giving into a surrounding culture of getting. We become generous in places where generosity makes no sense to the bottom line. We combat the spirit of greed with a spirit of open hands and open hearts. We flip the switch on society's bad habits.

God offers wonderful promises for those who do. If we pour out where others know only how to take in, we actually experience the blessing others seek. The way to true wealth in God's Kingdom is to give, not to acquire. Whether that looks like prosperity, sufficiency, or even just a very content heart, our generosity makes a statement. It points to a very generous Father who knows how to provide for his people out of the abundance of his supply.

Father, why do we feel that we need to "get what's ours" when you've already promised to give what is yours? Why do we assume we have no access to the riches of your Kingdom? Refocus my eyes, give me faith in the certainty of your provision, and make me a testimony of your generosity. Amen.

Contentment That Conquers Coveting

Every good and perfect gift is from above, coming down from the Father of the heavenly lights. (James 1:17, NIV)

MOST PEOPLE ARE DRIVEN by discontent and unaware of that fact. But if we analyzed our motives, we would realize that they generally come from a focus on whatever is missing in our lives—the void we want to fill, the problems we want to fix, the glass that is half empty. We rarely recognize the things that are going well in our lives or make strides to do so. No, we aim for the unfinished items on a never-ending to-do list of trying to make our lives complete. In the process, we keep our gifts and successes in the back of our minds and miss out on the gratitude and satisfaction we could have.

The problem-solving side of our nature has its benefits, but it also contributes to one of the many cultural antitheses to the Kingdom of God: discontentment. Scripture frames this issue more broadly as covetousness—the perpetual desire for what we don't have, whether it is material, relational, emotional, or anything else. In fact, it is the subject of one of the Ten Commandments, possibly the "thou shalt not" we tend to ignore the most. Encompassing much more than greed, covetousness leads to constant dissatisfaction and steals gratitude from our hearts. It causes us to fit seamlessly into our culture.

A heart full of gratitude and contentment not only transforms our lives, it also undermines a culture of covetousness and points to the Father of blessings. The world around you needs to know this Father. Its citizens are looking for something to fill the empty places in their hearts, not realizing that every good and perfect gift comes from the Father who has made all things. A mood of discontentment—in another heart, in a room, in any social environment—can be broken by the quiet songs of gratitude echoing in a content believer's heart. Be that mood-breaker. Change the culture. Point to the Kingdom of blessings already given.

Father, open my eyes to the blessings you have poured into my life. Give me supreme satisfaction in the gifts you have given, the love you have shown, and the fullness of my relationship with you. May others see your goodness in me. Amen.

Philippians 2:3-4

Love That Is Greater than Self

*Don't be selfish; don't try to impress others. Be humble,
thinking of others as better than yourselves. (Philippians 2:3)*

THE HOSTILITY WAS PALPABLE, the contentiousness at boiling point, the atmosphere tense. Factions in the church had recently polarized, each holding their own positions as divine and any others as an attack from the forces of evil. Sadly, differences of opinion in the body of Christ often take on such extremes. But at one prayer meeting, when most participants were far more focused on conflict than on prayer, one woman stood up in tears and confessed her judgments against the others. A suddenly softened heart from another faction joined in, and soon the confessions flowed and hugs were exchanged. Opinions had not changed, but the environment had. And people began working together toward a solution.

That story is a composite of many such experiences witnessed by believers around the world. It happens again and again. Unfortunately, sometimes conflict reaches its final result of splitting a fellowship forever. But the dynamic of a divisive atmosphere being broken by one humble confession or contrite heart is common and powerful—not only in churches but in organizations, institutions, or informal groups of people. When the church at Philippi was in the midst of conflict, Paul urged selflessness. Why? Because it embodies God's love. It breaks the power of pride. It pulls down walls and opens hearts to the *shalom* of God's Kingdom.

You don't need to preach to change the world around you. The power of God's presence within you can alter your environment and open people's eyes to God's ways. Attitudes are contagious, and if yours is strong, it will spread—even before you have said a word. An attitude of selflessness is powerful because it follows the model of Jesus. If you live selflessly, lives will change. You will need to be persistent, but you can be because you know whose you are. As an agent of the Spirit of God, carry his selflessness into selfish places and watch closed hearts unfold.

Jesus, your selflessness changed the world forever. You call me into the world with the same attitude—serving, giving, yielding to the interests of others whenever it serves the greater good. May my attitude melt the hearts around me and open them to your love. Amen.

The Spirit of Truth

If I could speak all the languages of earth and of angels, but
didn't love others, I would only be a noisy gong or a clanging cymbal.
(1 Corinthians 13:1)

YEARS AFTER CATHERINE THE Great became empress of Russia, she recalled her early religious training as a young girl in Germany. Along with other fields of study deemed necessary to prepare her for her future, she had been steeped in Bible instruction. Her tutor had taught her plenty of verses on the love of God and justification by grace through faith. But he drilled them into her with such harshness that she always had difficulty separating in her mind the message from the means of instruction. He taught her the message of grace without demonstrating it at all—words without heart. She had learned the gospel, but it didn't come across as very good news. And it certainly didn't seem to follow her throughout her life.

Millions of people share similar experiences of hearing the words of God's truth in some spirit other than that in which it was first given. This phenomenon is nothing new; Jesus rebuked the religious experts for such hypocrisies. Somehow along the way, Christians got the impression that the truth of God's love and grace can be conveyed in a spirit that doesn't reflect him. It can't. It isn't the words themselves that have power; it's the spirit behind the words. Or to put it another way, messengers of the gospel need to actually reflect it.

That should be a sobering thought for anyone who wants to share the love of God with others. His love is not a series of Bible verses to memorize, a doctrine to impart, or a set of teachings to obey. It can only be imparted to others as a demonstration. It's a lifestyle. Only when the spirit behind our words reflects who God really is do people begin to see him. Otherwise, our words may not have any positive effect at all. Far more important than what we say is how we say it. When a message of love and mercy comes from a heart of love and mercy, lives will be changed.

Father, you wrapped your love in flesh when you sent Jesus, and I'm asking that I would embody your love in the same way. In my words, actions, attitudes, and every other expression, help me reflect who you really are. Amen.

Better Questions

The creation waits with eager longing for the revealing
of the sons of God. (Romans 8:19, ESV)

"WHY IS THIS HAPPENING, Lord? And why is it happening to *me?*" Countless people have asked these questions in various forms in the midst of their trials, and rarely have they received clear answers. We can certainly understand the sentiment; the human heart wants to understand the mystery behind painful circumstances and how we fit into them. In times of crisis, a sense of guilt may provoke thoughts of divine punishment or discipline, while a sense of privilege or entitlement may provoke indignation over the injustice experienced. We long for some sort of emotional resolution to our hardships.

God rarely answers these questions because they are misdirected toward self and not toward the work he is doing. Every crisis creates an opportunity for him to show something of himself—his power, his provision, his protection, his comfort, his mercy, or any other characteristics of his that intersect with our experience. Our lives, especially the unresolved areas of them, are a platform for his work. Scripture is not entirely a collection of theological musings; more to the point, it's a collection of stories showing how people experienced their God. Our lives are to write similar stories. We are to showcase who he is.

That's why the better questions to ask in a difficult season are, "Lord what are you doing in this situation? How do you want to reveal yourself?" Those questions are answered much more often. In the meantime, we need to understand that God is far more interested in our faith than in our understanding. When we believe and God responds to our faith, we become a catalyst for the display of his nature—a foretaste of the revelation of the children of God. History is headed toward a final unveiling, but as with all things in the Kingdom, we have opportunities to bring future things into present experience. The world wants to see the God of power, provision, protection, comfort, mercy, and love in you. In every circumstance, let it.

Father, you know how easily I become focused on my own situations. Lift my eyes to see beyond them to the work you are doing in my life. Let me be a demonstration of your glory, even—or especially—in my most difficult times. Amen.

Living the Big Picture

*The creation was subjected to futility, not willingly, but because
of him who subjected it, in hope that the creation itself will be
set free from its bondage to corruption and obtain the freedom of
the glory of the children of God. (Romans 8:20-21, ESV)*

ONE OF THE CORE TENETS OF existential philosophy is that we live in an irrational universe and are therefore responsible for creating our own sense of meaning—or rejecting meaning altogether. For many centuries, great thinkers have felt the frustration of being bound in darkened understanding. Every human being has tasted and seen the futility of the human experience—no government has fully succeeded; no family has completely avoided dysfunction; no individual has figured out how to avoid sickness, pain, and death. The entire human experience should either send us in search of a Savior or cause us to throw up our hands in surrender.

The existentialists and many others have thrown up their hands in surrender, but we who believe in the message of Jesus and the Good News of his Kingdom have tasted freedom. None of us has fully escaped the futility, of course—we still live in a fallen world and experience its frustrations—but we have seen the light of truth and are drawn further into it. We let the fruitlessness of our existence drive us into the arms of a Deliverer. We have found a better way.

As messengers of the better way, our job now is to live lives of meaning in the presence of those who are searching for it. There is nothing arrogant about that; as D. T. Niles said, Christianity is one hungry beggar telling another where he found bread. We have all been captives to the futility of earth, but now we see beyond it. Our lives are visibly, noticeably redirected toward eternity. Whatever that looks like in your experience, make the most of it. Don't get frustrated. See the bigger picture and live in it for others to see as well.

Lord of heaven and earth, anchor me well in your Kingdom and make the peace of eternity visible in my eyes. May my words reflect eternal hope and my smile welcome others into it. May the assurance of my hope be contagious. Amen.

Unveiling the Treasure

We now have this light shining in our hearts, but we ourselves are like fragile clay jars containing this great treasure. This makes it clear that our great power is from God, not from ourselves. (2 Corinthians 4:7)

ONE OF THE MORE DISTURBING religious trends in the last few decades is a dramatic decrease in the number of people who believe that the Bible is a reliable expression of truth. This isn't the case in every part of the world, but it is in many countries that were once considered to be Christian societies. Along with that trend is the predictable result that fewer people know what the Bible says or can even discuss it intelligently. In fact, alarming misperceptions about the Bible have grown, such that many perceive it as completely fictitious—the arbitrary creation of a few storytellers or religious conspirators.

If people were interested in sitting down and talking about these things, we could reeducate them about the historical foundations of our faith. Apologetics might be our best strategy. But as important as coherent explanations are, they don't go very far in an age when people determine what they believe viscerally rather than rationally. Most choose sides and then try to justify their position afterward, which explains why almost everyone believes their side wins in a debate. Apologetics supports the understanding of those who have chosen to believe; it less often prompts faith in the first place.

The solution is to let Jesus be visibly attractive in us, just as he was to his first hearers and followers. That means living unexplainable lives. We are people who carry supernatural treasures in fragile clay jars, and somehow those around us need to see the treasure. They are hungry not for arguments or good marketing but for whatever is true, authentic, and transcendent. Not everyone will be drawn to the Jesus in us, just as not everyone was drawn to him two millennia ago. But many will. If people are reading the Bible less, we will have to demonstrate it more. It's the most effective way to get the truth of God into a world that doesn't know him.

Jesus, you are the treasure hidden in a field, the glory the world is looking for. It is not too bold to ask you to become more visible in me. You promised you would. Even if you have to break the jar, make this treasure seen. Amen.

A Reason for Hope

If someone asks about your hope as a believer,
always be ready to explain it. (1 Peter 3:15)

PETER WROTE TO CHRISTIANS IN the first century who were experiencing a local wave of persecution. The fact that he urged his readers to avoid persecution by doing good suggests that some of them may have been causing unnecessary trouble. But he assured the believers who were making positive contributions to society and still suffering that they would be rewarded. God does not let the sacrifices of his people go to waste in his Kingdom.

In the midst of this encouragement—to avoid trouble but to suffer well when trouble is unavoidable—Peter made a remarkable statement. He urged his readers to be ready to answer whenever someone asks why they have such hope. The clear implications of this statement are that hope is visible in those who believe, and when having such an attitude doesn't seem to fit the circumstances, it is worth asking about. In other words, he expected his readers to be noticeably hopeful in the face of adversity and for others to be baffled by what they saw. That way, whenever that curious situation provoked a conversation, Christians would be able to explain where their lives were truly anchored.

In the Bible, hope is never just wishful thinking, as so many understand it when using the word today. It is the expectation of a certainty—something that hasn't happened on the timeline of history yet but undoubtedly will. That confidence in God's future plan will anchor our lives in the reality of his Kingdom, but it will mystify those around us. When they ask—and they will when adverse circumstances throw our hope into stark relief—we need to have an answer. We may never need to explain the gifts God has given us, the skills we have, or the knowledge we have, but we will need to explain our hope. It points to another realm, and some of the people God has put in our lives are eager to see it.

Lord, I do want my hope to be visible in every situation—especially the hard times. Make my attitude so striking to others that they ask why I have it. Then give me words that point clearly to the reality of your Kingdom. Amen.

A Clear Conscience

Keep your conscience clear. Then if people speak against you,
they will be ashamed when they see what a good life you live
because you belong to Christ. (1 Peter 3:16)

WHEN MARTIN LUTHER STOOD before Holy Roman Emperor Charles V in 1521 to defend his views rather than recant them, he calmly appealed to reason, the testimony of Scripture, and the certainty of his own convictions. "Here I stand," he allegedly said. "I can do no other." He refused to act against his own conscience.

Luther wasn't perfect, of course. Some of his habits and prejudices seem awfully out of place, especially to modern eyes. But no one can argue that he didn't live out his convictions. Even his detractors, then and now, have admired his resolute insistence on the truths he believed. A clear conscience is a powerful testimony, even when people disagree with one's position.

Peter urged his readers not only to have strong convictions, but also to back up their stance with an admirable way of life. He knew the kinds of accusations people threw at followers of Jesus. Sometimes those accusations were absurd: that the Christians' love feasts were actually orgies where cannibalism (consuming the "body" and "blood" of the Lord's Supper) was routinely practiced. Other accusations were more realistic from a pagan point of view: that Christians' refusal to make sacrifices for the emperor would put the community under divine and temporal judgment. In any case, Peter's antidote to disfavor was to live favorably—to make the accusations incongruent by living so blamelessly that people would have a hard time thinking negatively about them. Dirt doesn't stick to smooth surfaces very well.

Make your life a smooth surface. You won't be able to live flawlessly—no one can—but you can live with an attitude and lifestyle that wins the favor of those around you. If you are still mistreated, you will know it's because of the gospel's offensiveness, not yours. And many others will know it too. Your life will reflect the goodness of a mistreated Savior and open eyes to who Jesus really is.

Jesus, you demonstrated the power of a spotless life—and also the reactions it can entail.
Give me a clean conscience, the courage to live by my convictions, and the strength to
endure any backlash. Let me live with integrity and grace. Amen.

A Ministry of Beauty

The heavens proclaim the glory of God.
The skies display his craftsmanship. (Psalm 19:1)

IN THE EARLY 1800s, the French novelist Stendhal visited Florence, Italy, where the Italian Renaissance had flourished and many of the world's greatest works of art were produced. He was overwhelmed by the magnificence of his surroundings, especially when he visited the Basilica of Santa Croce and saw Giotto's frescoes at the tombs of Michelangelo and Galileo. He became dizzy, felt that life was draining from him, feared that he would fall, and later wrote about the sublime beauty of celestial sensations. He was overcome with awe.

This physical response to beauty was later named after him: Stendhal syndrome, a condition well-known in Florence and at other sites of transcendent grandeur. Tourists have even been treated at local hospitals and psychiatric wards for the response. The human mind and body can only absorb so much at one time; an overload of glory short-circuits our senses.

God is the author of truth, beauty, and love—a trinity of divine gifts that come from his nature. For centuries, Christians have emphasized ministries of truth and love, focusing on doctrine and works of charity. Far fewer have emphasized a ministry of beauty. In spite of the fact that many nonreligious people say they come closer to believing in God after experiencing an awe-inspiring view than at any other time, and in spite of the many glimpses of transcendent beauty and glory we are given in Scripture, many believers today assume that truth and love are essential to God's nature while beauty is an unnecessary luxury. We minimize its power.

In an age when hearts are hardened to claims of truth and jaded to expressions of love, beauty may be one of the most effective ways to reflect the nature of God in this world. It can draw people toward the glory of God before they even realize who he is. Seek beauty wherever you can, preserve it whenever you can, and create it however you can. Because you were made in the image of a Creator, your creativity is a compelling statement of who he is.

Father, you are the creator of a magnificent universe that is gorgeous from any perspective. Fill me with your creativity. Let me reflect your beauty in the things I do. Persuade hearts with the power of your artistry. Amen.

Creation's Applause

*Their voice is never heard. Yet their message has
gone throughout the earth. (Psalm 19:3-4)*

NICOLAS HERMAN WAS powerfully changed by a tree. The tree itself didn't change him, of course, but Nicolas's perspective of it did. He saw its barrenness in the dead of winter, and it suddenly dawned on him that the tree would be resurrected into beautiful greenery in a matter of a few short weeks. From that realization he became persuaded of the reality of God's grace, providence, and promises of new life. No arguments or sermons were needed in that moment. He was transformed by a scene. Today we know Nicolas Herman for the fruit he bore as a monk and writer called Brother Lawrence.

Beauty carries powerful messages, whether we can articulate those messages or not. The only explanation for that power is that it reflects the nature of the Creator. It is inspirational and persuasive because that is the essence of God's work. He is an artist, and no artist creates a masterpiece for it to be hidden behind a veil. He wants to share his expression, and he does—"day after day," Psalm 19:2 tells us. There is deep fellowship between the Creator and the person who looks at his artistry with wonder and awe.

Tragically, multitudes of people carry out their daily lives without noticing the transcendent beauty of God's work. They walk around in the universe's most magnificent museum without recognizing the masterpieces that surround them. Created in God's image to see his glory and carry it within us, we instead become absorbed in the mundane trivialities of our own obligations and responsibilities. Meanwhile, the heavens proclaim his glory relentlessly.

Don't be one of the billions who go through life without noticing the power of God's artistry. Taste and see that he is good—and brilliantly creative, from the intricacies seen through the microscopes of molecular biologists to the majesty seen through the telescopes of astrophysicists, from the mysteries of quantum physics to the complexities of space and time. Enter into a conversation with the Artist, and draw others into it too. Let your life and words join creation's applause.

Father, the world marvels at your creation without knowing their Creator. This cannot be. How can my life point to your artistry? What can I say to bring you applause? Help me see, and help me help others see. Amen.

A Visible Revelation

Ever since the world was created, people have seen the earth and sky.
Through everything God made, they can clearly see his invisible
qualities—his eternal power and divine nature. (Romans 1:20)

CHARLES DARWIN WAS CAUGHT between two competing beliefs: (1) that nature seems randomly filled with cruelty and pain and (2) that the brute forces of nature alone could not account for the intricacies of its design. He fluctuated between these two beliefs—randomness versus design—for much of his career, claiming at most points to be agnostic about them. Even in light of his theories, he had trouble conceiving of such order coming out of pure chance.

We are told that the world is in a fallen condition, a distorted picture of what it once was. Science cannot explore such theological claims, nor can it marvel over the artistry of the Creator, but it can make observations about the order and complexities of life. These are still an unsolvable mystery to all but those with eyes of faith. They defy the natural processes we observe today. They point to an intelligence from outside the natural world.

Paul did not write about nature as poetically as the psalmists did, but he did point clearly to the purpose of God embedded in this world. However much God's creativity is displayed for our admiration, it is given for another reason too: to reveal who he is. He wants us to get a glimpse of his personality. For the same reason we were created in his image, we are given eyes to see his handiwork. He wants to be known.

Paul argues that the rebellious human race has glimpsed the glory of God and has been casual about it. What should have sent us in search of the Creator—the beauty and design of nature, the stunning miracle of a newborn, the joy of simple pleasures—became instead an idol or even just a happy accident. We have to learn to see the world in a new way. More than that, we have to help others see it too. Yes, it is a fallen world, full of imperfections, but it's also a shadow of things to come. Most people don't want to leave the Creator's beauty behind. Remind them they don't have to.

Lord, the beauty of this age pales in comparison to what you have in store for those who love you. May I live with that anticipation always, and may it provoke the imagination of those around me and point them to you. Amen.

Beyond Mediocrity

I have filled him with the Spirit of God, giving him great wisdom,
ability, and expertise in all kinds of crafts. (Exodus 31:3)

ISRAEL HAD ITS SHARE OF CRAFTSMEN. Every ancient culture did. But when it came time to construct the Tabernacle and its articles of worship, run-of-the-mill craftsmanship would not suffice. So God called Bezalel to the task and filled him with his Spirit, assigning Oholiab and other craftsmen to help. It is the first time Scripture mentions someone being filled with the Spirit, and the privilege was given to an artist. Apparently, God is interested in excellence.

But Christians haven't always thought so. There have been times in Christian history when patrons and artisans of the church produced many of the world's finest masterpieces. And today, the world's standards dictate that success comes from seeking excellence in whatever craft you pursue. But for decades, perhaps even longer, many in the church have grown comfortable with mediocrity. They think devotion is all that matters and that excellence is either a worldly demand or an exclusive luxury that snubs their heartfelt creations. Some unwritten rule seems to have convinced us that whatever we do in the name of the Lord is good enough, even when it isn't our best.

That isn't true of all Christians, of course, and the evangelical community has begun producing outstanding works of music, film, literature, and art again. We must hold on to the truth that no one needs to excel in order to gain God's approval, but grace should never undo our desire to excel for his glory. If we are to represent our Creator well, we will need to be known for cutting-edge creativity. Adapting secular creativity for our own purposes is not enough. We are filled with the Spirit to do excellent work.

Many are finding that divinely inspired and motivated excellence and creativity do wonders for our reputation and draw hearts toward God. We serve a King who is worthy of our highest offerings. When we give them, he fills them with power and glorifies his name.

Lord, you are worthy of my best. May I and every other believer seek excellence in all we do—even if it seems to be a mundane task. Let me never forget that anything done with excellence in your name can glorify you. Amen.

A Spiritual Labor

Devote yourselves to prayer with an alert mind and a thankful heart.
(Colossians 4:2)

JOHN HYDE, AN AMERICAN MISSIONARY to India in the early 1900s, constantly had profound prayers weighing on his heart. He prayed for the people he ministered to and the cities he ministered in. He prayed for fellow missionaries and for God to raise up more workers to send into the harvest. Those who knew him told stories of his bedroom light coming on at 2 a.m., 4 a.m., and 5 a.m.—every night's sleep punctuated by intercession for others. His evangelical outlook prompted far-reaching evangelical prayers, and God answered them. Because of his persistence in prayer, he became known as "Praying Hyde."

We might wonder, *Is that kind of inconvenience really necessary when talking to a God who is available all the time and who answers many prayers before we even voice them?* But God has historically responded in power to people like Hyde who pray with tears and persistence. Paul wrote of Epaphras praying earnestly for the Colossians, describing his intensity with a wrestling term from which we get the word "agonize" (Colossians 4:12). He told the church he agonized for them and the Laodiceans as well (Colossians 2:1). He made it clear in words and by example that no matter how familiar and intimate we are with the Father, Son, and Spirit, our prayers are more than a casual matter and can accomplish a lot in the spiritual realm. Some might think us strange to spend a night on our knees. God welcomes the fellowship and the petitions.

Press through in your prayers to God. You may not always see what he does with them, but the world is in desperate need of many of the things you will pray. In the age of the Internet, we are used to making transactions with a click. In the spiritual realm, a battle is raging, and clicks are not enough. Fill heaven with the sounds of your faith and perseverance, and expect answers to come. God changes the world through the requests of those who intercede on its behalf.

Father, forgive me for neglecting the one thing this world needs most: the prayers of your people. Fill my heart with zeal for coming to the throne of grace. Teach me to plead your promises. Align my prayers with your heart and answer in power. Amen.

A Wide-Open Prayer

Open your mouth wide, and I will fill it with good things.
(Psalm 81:10)

ONE OF THE PERSISTENT PLEAS OF "Praying Hyde" was for God to answer the promise of Psalm 81:10 by responding to the mouth wide open and filling it with answers to its requests. Hyde was thinking beyond food, of course. One year he prayed for at least one soul to be saved a day, and by the end of the year more than four hundred people had come to Christ through his ministry. The next year he doubled the request, and God answered; the year after, he doubled it again, and God answered again. Hyde saw no limit to his prayer. The wider a saint opens his or her mouth, the more God is able to fill it.

Sadly, too many of God's people live with closed mouths, closed hands, and limited expectations. God is good to us anyway; he meets our needs and fulfills many of our personal requests. But when we open our hearts and expectations to fit the wideness of his mercy and the abundance of his Kingdom, we find extraordinary responses to our persistent faith. We become agents of a divine overflow, with heaven's graces pouring into the world through our prayers. The irreligious people of the world do not know such agents exist and will probably never recognize us as such, but recognition is never the point. We serve God and respond to his ways. And his way is to reveal himself through the petitions of those who love him.

One of the greatest things you can do for this world, and one of the greatest marks on history you can make, is to devote yourself to the divine discourse in which we appeal to God and he accomplishes his will through our appeals. We cannot do that with small expectations because we serve a big God. His agenda is enormous. But so are our prayers if we get a glimpse of his purposes. Open your mouth wide, and see how God responds. Be persistent, and don't lose heart. The most effective place to be a world-changer is on your knees.

Lord, forgive me for praying too small and for praying only for my own interests. My heart is yours; fill it with your desires. Then fill my mouth with the petitions that meet those desires, and respond with power. Change the world through my prayers. Amen.

Unearthly Battles

*If two of you agree here on earth concerning anything you ask, my
Father in heaven will do it for you. For where two or three gather
together as my followers, I am there among them. (Matthew 18:19-20)*

REES HOWELLS WAS KNOWN FOR his remarkable intercession, and the stories of how
God responded to his requests are powerful and captivating. But later in life, after
Howells had learned the secrets of intercession, seen individual lives changed, served
as a missionary, and developed a college in Wales for ministry training, he turned
his attention to international affairs and the events of World War II. "The world
became our parish and we were led to be responsible to intercede for countries and
nations," he wrote of his small band of intercessors who committed to pray with
him.[6] The correlations between the prayers of his group and the headlines of the day
are remarkable—some of Hitler's inexplicable decisions make more sense in light of
a divine hand—and though historians are compelled to explain each turn of events
in natural terms of cause and result, a spiritual battle was taking place that dramatically paralleled the earthly battles in the great global war. The prayers of God's people
turned the tide of history.

Not many Christians really understand that. We tend to rationalize our unanswered prayers and lose our focus when we don't see immediate results, as if God's
workings would always be visible to our eyes or answered within our time frames. Yet
history is full of examples of prayers that made a difference decades later or even in
future generations. If Scripture teaches us anything, it's that God is a master builder
who layers his work year after year, generation after generation, and era after era.
Sometimes we see what he is doing in "real time," but often we don't. We have to have
faith like the saints of old, who saw the promises and plans of his Kingdom from a
distance through spiritual eyes (Hebrews 11:13).

Live with that perspective, and pray your heart out. The workings of this world
depend on the divine hand, which is moved by the prayers and faith of God's people.
You have the capacity to effect tomorrow's world today, and one day the fruitfulness
of your prayers will be revealed.

*Lord, lift my vision to see beyond my own immediate needs and interests. Call me to a
lifestyle of world-changing prayer. Let the headlines serve as my prayer list, and let my
prayers prompt victories I may never see. Amen.*

Agents of Change

We are Christ's ambassadors; God is making his appeal through us.
(2 Corinthians 5:20)

IN THE MID-1970S, two well-known ministry founders—Bill Bright of Campus Crusade for Christ (now known as Cru) and Loren Cunningham of Youth With A Mission—met for lunch, each feeling strongly that he had a message for the other. As they discovered, they each had the same message: that for a nation to be transformed by God's Kingdom, God's people would need to influence seven spheres of society: government, business, education, media, arts and entertainment, family, and religion. The principle has been taken up by a variety of groups over the years and has often been tweaked into different forms. But the idea of influencing these arenas has remained largely intact. Many have embarked on a battle to win the culture not by force but by blessing and influence.

Whatever you think of that specific paradigm, the purpose behind it is good and true. Christians do not belong to this world (John 17:16), but we are definitely in it (John 17:15). We live distinct lives, set apart for his service, but few of us are called to retreat to separate places that confine our influence only to prayer. We are called into culture, not away from it. We are agents of reconciliation, ambassadors of the better way, and we are designed not only to voice God's appeal but also to demonstrate it.

Many Christians don't know how to do that. Large segments of entire generations have abandoned Washington, Hollywood, and Wall Street to worldly influences and then complained about how ungodly those culture-shapers are—completely missing the importance of being agents of change and reconciliation in places of influence. As much as a resistant world needs preachers of God's Kingdom, it needs even more those who will embody it in all of its graces and blessings. The world needs to see a God who is for them in the faces of those who are called by his name. Your mission, should you choose to accept it, is to go in that spirit. Be an ambassador of the extremely good will of the Father, and influence your culture with his creativity, wisdom, and love.

Father, I hardly know where to begin. My culture is bigger than I am—but never bigger than you. Make me a small catalyst for big change on the mountaintops of your world. Amen.

The New You

My old self has been crucified with Christ. It is no longer I who live,
but Christ lives in me. (Galatians 2:20)

MUCH OF THE NON-CHRISTIAN WORLD thinks it hates Christianity. It hates the narrow-mindedness and bigotries of people who call themselves Christians. It hates the corruption it has seen in churches past and present. It hates the militant attitude evident in crusading pilgrims, colonial expansion, and even suburban cliques. It is weary of religious conflicts, intellectual misrepresentations, political manipulations, and hypocritical behaviors. Of course, none of this is the essence of Christianity. What the world *really* hates is the distortions of the real thing.

Those distortions are numerous. History is full of "Christian" kingdoms, societies, organizations, and individuals who did not exactly behave in Christian ways. In fact, we are all distortions of the real thing to some degree; none of us has conformed to the template of Jesus perfectly. So when people throw up superficial arguments against Christianity—like "What about the Crusades?" or "What about all the religious wars that have been fought?" or "Haven't you seen the corruption in the church?"—we have only two legitimate responses: "Yes, Christians both true and false have done a lot of bad things" and "Jesus didn't."

The counterpoint to our admission that Christians have failed is that we claim to be born of and filled with his Spirit, yet we look very little like him at times. But the real issue is that Jesus' words, miracles, and sacrifice are not undone by our flaws. Rather, our flaws are why he came to save us. We are forgiven of them once and for all, and we are being cleansed of them as we live now. In the meantime, we are new creations. We have a genuinely different quality of life than we once had, a transformation that has begun in seed even if it is not yet in full flourish. As believers, we are rooted in the Kingdom.

Don't get distracted by accusations of unchristian behavior, from this age or ages past. Confess your own faults in humility, but then point to Jesus. He has not failed and never will. He came to save this world from the things it hates.

Jesus, you made me new in the Spirit. Continue to make me new in experience. Let my transformation be evident to all and honor your name. Amen.

The Healing Turn

*He comforts us in all our troubles so that we can comfort
others. When they are troubled, we will be able to give them
the same comfort God has given us. (2 Corinthians 1:4)*

"To take pity on people in distress is a human quality which every man and woman should possess, but it is especially requisite in those who have once needed comfort, and found it in others." So begins the *Decameron* by Giovanni Boccaccio, who addresses his own heartbreak but in the context of a much larger one: the Black Death that plagued Europe in the mid-1300s. In periods of tragic loss, words of mutual comfort are especially powerful to frightened survivors. But they are true at any time. Whatever compassion and comfort we have received from others and from God equips us to offer the same compassion and comfort to those around us.

This dynamic has been repeated often throughout the ages. Many have turned their traumas into ministries over time. Those who have been imprisoned find themselves stepping back into prisons to minister to others. Those who have experienced abuse are best able to help the abused heal. Victims of unfaithfulness provide support for those going through it now. War veterans talk with those returning from a battlefront. God has worked the "pay it forward" instinct into our psyches. We give out of our own experiences.

That means that you are somehow equipped by your own past to serve others going through similar experiences. For no other reason than that you have lived for a while and experienced pain, you have something the world needs. You may not think you navigated your traumas well the first time around, but you at least learned something from them. You can relate to those in need.

Your greatest effectiveness in this world will be in the place of your deepest wounds. Let God speak healing into your traumas; then turn his comfort outward as you speak healing into others' lives. Wounded hearts will connect with God through the divine touch you have received and now give.

Lord, connect me with those who need what I have to offer. Let my conversations lead to those who need your touch in the ways I have received it. May your ministry to me heal others too. Amen.

Behind Your Faith

*Heal the sick, raise the dead, cure those with leprosy, and cast out
demons. Give as freely as you have received! (Matthew 10:8)*

As FAR AS WE KNOW, none of the disciples had been raised from the dead, cured of
leprosy, or rescued from demon possession. Some may have been healed of sickness;
a relative of Peter's had been (Mark 1:30-31), and it would not have been unusual for
Jesus to heal common ailments throughout his ministry. But the disciples certainly
saw Jesus perform miracles, and he sent them all out on a mission to do likewise,
urging them to give as freely as they had received. They had lived in an environment
of supernatural occurrences, and they were to share them with others.

The gospel writers don't tell us the disciples' reactions to being handed such an
extravagant ministry, implying only that they went out and did as they were told.
They might have balked at the enormity of it all—on another occasion they had
trouble casting out a violent spirit (Mark 9:14-29). They might have asked for a
how-to manual on supernatural ministry, but Jesus would have referred them only
to himself and the power they had observed as they followed him. In other words,
they had every reason to question whether they were up to the task, but Jesus seems
to have given them no opportunity. He sent them. That's all the qualification they
needed.

That is all the qualification you need too. You have been called to impossibilities.
You are armed with nothing but promises from God, the name of Jesus, and whatever degree of faith you will receive and embrace. And that's enough—perhaps not
to see a miracle with every prayer or declaration, but to keep at it until you do. The
issue is not whether you can duplicate Jesus' miracles but whether you will follow
his heart into a needy world. Do that, and behind your faith you will see his supply.

*Jesus, I have received so much from you. I am called to give even more, far beyond my
own resources and abilities. Lord, I believe; back me up with your provision. Care for
people powerfully through me. Amen.*

Sheep among Wolves

I am sending you out as sheep among wolves. So be as shrewd as
snakes and harmless as doves. (Matthew 10:16)

DURING A BRIEF PERSECUTION that included Stephen's martyrdom, many early believers fled Jerusalem and settled in towns in Judea, Samaria, and the regions beyond (Acts 8:1-2). Other first-century Christians went willingly so they could spread the message of their faith. In their new environments, believers encountered both eager listeners and hostile resisters, and they had to learn how to handle controversy. Would they get into heated verbal exchanges? Appeal to higher authorities for protection? Take on the character of their surroundings? Attack the faith of others? Focus on the virtues of their own? The answers to some of these questions were obvious. Other responses were more uncertain. They had to embody the *shalom* of God's Kingdom without getting killed or run out of town.

Jesus had warned of such encounters, and he gave clear instructions: Be as harmless as sheep even though you are surrounded by wolves, but don't be as ignorant as sheep. In your mind, understand the manipulations and strategies of human adversaries without engaging in them. Think like a snake to protect yourself; live like a dove to protect the message you carry. One requires street smarts that will keep you from being deceived or exploited; the other requires an innocence that will keep you from being accused of deceiving or exploiting. Know that harm might be done to you, but never do it to others.

That is not an easy balance to achieve, but it is necessary for carrying the Kingdom message into this world. Jesus knew the hearts of those who criticized and conspired against him and did not entrust himself to them. But he never stooped to their level. He saw political maneuvers without engaging in them; he responded to hate with love; he escaped plots without pulling any strings. Your mission in this world has the same character. You are a sheep among wolves, with no protection other than your insights and his promises. And that is enough.

Jesus, may I never take on the character of those who oppose my faith and your message. You have called me to be like you—even when it hurts. Direct my steps, protect my heart, and multiply my fruit. Amen.

A Revelation of God

Call on me when you are in trouble, and I will rescue you,
and you will give me glory. (Psalm 50:15)

THE STORY OF REBELLION AND EVIL isn't completely clear, but over the course of the Bible's pages, a coherent picture emerges. Apparently a rebellion in heaven turned many of its beings away from God and then infected the inhabitants of earth. As believers, we can hardly imagine any adversity in heaven's environment; God's presence precludes sin, pain, heartache, disease, and lack. But in rebellious realms of spirits and flesh, we all know the trauma of fallenness. Sickness, grief, poverty, injustice, unfaithfulness, and many more afflictions are pervasive. We experience trouble often.

It had to be this way if God was going to reveal himself in fullness. In a perfect environment of heaven, he could be worshiped for his greatness, glory, love, power, and wisdom. But who would know of his mercy, healing, comfort, compassion, provision, and justice? How would these beautiful characteristics of God ever become visible unless someone needed them?

So without creating evil, God allowed a world in which our need would reveal his character. That means that whenever you cry out to God for help, it is not just about you. Your need is a platform for him to demonstrate something of himself. Whenever you experience a crisis, it is not because something is dreadfully wrong but because an opportunity is arising. The rescuer God becomes visible to those surrounding someone who needs rescuing. Keep looking to him in faith and see what he does.

However long it takes, your story will be a good one. No one is thrilled by a movie in which the hero faces a few minor setbacks. The most satisfying endings are those that come together after the darkest moments of impossible adversity. If your life seems to be following that trajectory, refuse to judge God in the middle of the story. The resolution is coming, and it will be good for you, a reflection of him, and a testimony to those around you.

Lord, your promise is much clearer in Scripture than in the middle of my circumstances. Give me eyes to see beyond the moment, to look for your rescue, and to praise you even before it comes. Reveal yourself not only to me but through me. Amen.

The Direction of Influence

Jesus reached out and touched him. "I am willing," he said.
"Be healed!" And instantly the leprosy disappeared. (Luke 5:13)

ANCIENT HEBREW LAWS WERE aimed at protecting God's people from harmful influences, both spiritual and physical. Lepers, for example, were marginalized so their disease would not infect others (Leviticus 13:45-46). Proverbs instructs those who want to be wise to hang out with the wise rather than risk being affected by the contagion of fools (13:20). The direction of influence in both cases suggested that the pure could be corrupted by the impure and that the negative influence was stronger than the positive. To remain good, pure, wise, healthy, and clean, one had to stay away from corrupting agents.

But Jesus reversed that trend. Rather than avoiding lepers, he touched them. Rather than avoiding sinners, he spent time with them, even allowing himself to be accused of impurity and corruption. Why? Because the cleanness in him was stronger than the uncleanness in anyone else. Instead of his purity being tainted, the impurity of others was undone by his presence. The negative suddenly became less powerful and less influential than the positive. He flipped the narrative in favor of the new, incorruptible nature God has given his people.

"Bad company corrupts good character," a well-known saying from the Greek poet Menander, still applies for those who are not secure in their own identity. Paul even used it as a warning for an immature church (1 Corinthians 15:33). But for those who know their God, know their identity, and are secure in the cleansing Jesus has given us, the narrative changes. We can go into the world without fear of being corrupted, be exposed to lies without wavering in truth, and befriend those who lack convictions without worrying about losing our own. We can be more confident in the positive influence we have than in any negative influence others have over us.

Know who you are, live with conviction, and do not fear the world. You can change the atmosphere of a room just by being in it. You can influence those around you just by having unshakable trust in God. His power inside you is greater than the pressures outside of you. Live with unwavering faith.

Lord, make me like Jesus. Let me mature in him so thoroughly that the power inside of me overcomes the powers outside of me. Give me holy influence over all that is unholy in this world. Amen.

The Royal Priesthood

You are royal priests, a holy nation, God's very own possession.
As a result, you can show others the goodness of God, for he called
you out of the darkness into his wonderful light. (1 Peter 2:9)

LONG AGO, GOD DESIGNATED one tribe of Israel to serve as the nation's priests and, in a larger sense, created Israel to be a priestly nation for others (Exodus 19:6). In each case, his purpose was to establish relational connections and lines of communication between himself and a fallen world. Priests stood at the vertical axis between heaven and earth to represent human beings to God and God to human beings. They voiced the confessions and requests of the people to God, and they voiced God's desires and instructions to the people. They bridged the gap between human and divine.

God also appointed kings to serve the public good—to stand at the horizontal axis of human institutions to protect, provide for, and preserve the nation's welfare. People looked to the king to govern, mediate relationships with others, and bridge any gaps needed to be bridged.

The New Testament covenant grafts all Jesus followers into the royal priesthood of Israel, which means that every believer becomes a king and a priest in the service of others (Revelation 1:6; 5:10). We are filled with the holy presence to hear confessions (James 5:16), declare forgiveness (John 20:23), and intercede for each other (Ephesians 6:18). Jesus is our high priest and eternal King; we represent him on earth in both roles. We have a royal responsibility to serve the greater good.

That responsibility is not confined to fellow believers. Just as Israel served as a priestly nation for the world, so do we. No one outside the church, and probably few within, will recognize us as priests or kings. But our effectiveness does not depend on being recognized. Encourage, heal, bridge gaps, confess sins on behalf of your city and nation and world, and speak God's life into your surroundings. Stand attentively at the intersection of heaven and earth to serve the interests of God and those who need him.

Lord, impress upon me the importance of my position as a dual citizen of heaven and earth. May I represent you well to this broken world, and may I represent it compassionately and earnestly to you. Bridge any gaps you desire to bridge with me. Amen.

Engaging the World

*We know that we are children of God and that the world
around us is under the control of the evil one. (1 John 5:19)*

MANY OF THE EARLY REFORMERS caught up in the political and religious conflicts of
the sixteenth century were convinced that Satan had thoroughly infiltrated all human
systems and institutions. Governments, universities, church structures, everything—
it was all under the sway of evil. That didn't prevent them from soliciting the support
of governments or starting new universities and church structures, but their belief
that everything had been irreparably corrupted quickly made them give up on the
goal of reforming the old. Instead, they aimed at starting something new.

The reformers may or may not have exaggerated the darkness they faced, but they
did point to a biblical truth: that the fallenness of this world has led to the corruption
of virtually every system and institution human beings construct. That doesn't mean
this world is as depraved as it could be, but it does mean its entirety has been touched
by depravity. Many governments and institutions have served as agents of blessing,
although imperfectly; and many have served as agents of horrific evil. In every case,
the potential for neglecting God's ways and furthering human rebellion is enormous.

Some Christians have taken that as justification for completely avoiding human
institutions, as if abandoning them and their potential influence offers any sort
of solution. The New Testament is much more optimistic about our involvement
in normal life. Early Christians came from every walk of life. Paul seemed to connect with commercial circles, and he certainly never shied away from religious institutions. He realized that even governments that don't recognize God's authority
have been allowed or instituted by God to preserve public order (Romans 13:1-5).
We have nothing to gain by creating a separate subculture. Salt and light have no
impact in isolation. Instead of corruption making Jesus unclean, his purity overcame
corruption. Follow his lead and bring the freshness of your gifts and skills into a
decaying world.

*Jesus, your holiness makes things pure; your freedom releases captives; your life overcomes
death and decay. Transform any fear of being negatively influenced into confidence of
influencing positively. Make me an agent of change. Amen.*

Your Source

*Dear friends, I warn you as "temporary residents and foreigners"
to keep away from worldly desires that wage war against your very
souls. Be careful to live properly among your unbelieving neighbors.*
(1 Peter 2:11-12)

ONE OF THE GREATEST FEARS OF the English government and church during England's early colonial period was that their travelers might be seduced by foreign cultures and religions. It was not an unfounded fear; some explorers in the Pacific "went native" and never returned home, while some adventurers, traders, and occasionally even ministers in the Middle East adopted Islam as their new religion. Exotic lifestyles often had more appeal than familiar traditions did, and loyalties became confused. It was not unusual for temporary visitors to invest their hearts in their new surroundings and choose permanent residency there.

You are a temporary resident still living among the ways of the world while subscribing to the ways of God's Kingdom. For many people throughout history, that kind of expat existence has proven tempting, whether in the field of diplomacy, missionary service, business, or any other long-term cross-cultural experience. Peter warned his readers not to disengage from the world but to remain detached from its influences. He wanted their loyalties to remain clear.

The question is not whether you avoid certain things, as if legal prohibitions governed your spiritual life. They don't (Colossians 2:20-23). The issue is the source from which you draw your life. How do you feed your soul? Is it with the temporary substances and pleasures of this world or the eternal truths of God? Are you trying to soak in all you can from your surroundings, or are you being fed through your spiritual roots? As Paul wrote, all things are lawful for you, but not all things are helpful (1 Corinthians 6:12). Where does your nourishment come from?

As you live as a royal priest in this world, remember the source of your life. Don't live in fear of corruption, but don't immerse yourself in old ways that are now foreign to you. Your neighbors need to see the life of God flourishing within you. Live with clarity, and they will.

Lord, my life is yours, and you are my life. May I never become confused by my dual citizenship in heaven and on earth. Let me walk in the ways of your Kingdom and invite others into them wherever I am. Amen.

Blessings of Priests

Tell Aaron and his sons to bless the people of Israel
with this special blessing. (Numbers 6:23)

IMAGINE A SCHOOL WHERE, in addition to their teaching responsibilities, instructors were given a secret assignment: to look for students who would be good candidates to receive a scholarship at year's end. These students would not necessarily have the highest grades or test scores, though they'd likely score very well. The real criteria would be more subjective. Which ones were most eager to learn? Which ones needed things to go their way for once? Which ones had shown signs of honesty, integrity, and sincerity? Any identified by their teachers would be eligible to receive the benefit of a scholarship at the end of the year.

That resembles the picture of God's assignment to Aaron and the Levitical priests in Numbers 6. God said that if Aaron and his sons blessed the Israelites with the words of a particular prayer—"May the LORD bless you and protect you . . . smile on you and be gracious to you . . . show you his favor and give you his peace" (Numbers 6:24-26)—he would make the blessing manifest. We are given no explanation for why God did not bless his people directly, though it may be because of his agreement to work through human agency in this world (as with prayer, forgiveness, and the promise he gives his followers of binding and loosing things on earth). Regardless of the reason, his deal with Israel's priests was for them to mediate the words of blessing and for him to honor them.

As royal priests of the Kingdom of God, we carry the same assignment (Romans 12:14; 2 Corinthians 1:11; James 3:10; 1 Peter 3:9). Our assignment is a little different than that of the schoolteachers; God's blessings are unlimited. Everyone needs one, and we can afford to declare them indiscriminately. Even so, we are sent as scouts into the world to mark the people around us with blessing, which we can fully expect God to honor. Few people take advantage of this enormous opportunity, but we should—whether privately, out loud, or however we choose. God will manifest many of the blessings we speak.

Lord, I don't know your specific will for people's lives, but I do know you want to bless them, to draw them close, to reveal who you are and demonstrate your love. If my words are a catalyst for that ministry, may they be plentiful. Amen.

Words of Grace

God sent his Son into the world not to judge the world,
but to save the world through him. (John 3:17)

AS THE MODERN MISSIONS MOVEMENT began to swell in the nineteenth century, most missionaries personified the message of Isaiah 52:7—"How beautiful on the mountains are the feet of the messenger who brings good news, the good news of peace and salvation, the news that the God of Israel reigns!" A few, however, carried only bad news: a message of condemnation for the horrific sins "the heathens" practiced. They spent most of their time deconstructing local religions and hardly any proclaiming the gospel of redemption and restoration. Like street-corner preachers on a global stage, they were messengers of judgment.

There are times when the law of God needs to be declared in order to convince hearts that their righteousness is insufficient and they are thus in need of him. But judgment is never the end of the message, and it usually isn't the beginning, either. The kindness of God is a much better catalyst for repentance than his severity is (Romans 2:4). Likewise, the message of our universal depravity is usually fruitless unless it is sandwiched between a clear affirmation of each human being's immense value in God's eyes and each human being's vast potential as his beloved and restored child. The gospel is above all a message of love and hope. That's the message Jesus delivered.

Jesus made it clear that an age of judgment is coming, but this is not it. This is an age of rescue, of blessing, of restoration and the favor of God (Luke 4:19). If our message does not line up with that truth, something is wrong. If it does, we will find that many hearts that had once turned away from him are drawn to him—slowly, perhaps, and sometimes suspiciously, but eventually in confidence and hope. The Kingdom of God is far more spacious than many of us have imagined, and his grace reaches farther than many of us are willing to concede. Yes, the gate is narrow, but the land inside is abundant, fruitful, and wide. Let your words be filled with the grace that makes that clear.

Jesus, may my voice harmonize with yours in every way in declaring the time of God's favor, restoration, and mercies as wide as his Kingdom. Let the Father's love and the Spirit's power fill my words. Amen.

The Greatest Testimony

Get rid of all bitterness, rage, anger, harsh words, and slander,
as well as all types of evil behavior. Instead, be kind to each
other, tenderhearted, forgiving one another, just as God
through Christ has forgiven you. (Ephesians 4:31-32)

THE PROTESTANT REFORMATION broke the Roman church's monopoly on sanctioned truth in western Christendom. It also opened up a complex, chaotic argument about how to interpret Scripture. Sometimes the Reformers disagreed respectfully, but many times they turned caustic and cruel in their slander of others, even calling their opponents liars and tools of the devil. With the eternal destiny of souls at stake, they put all emotions and strategies into the ongoing argument. The acrimonious, savage environment that followed for more than a century turned many hearts and minds away from the idea of absolute truth altogether. If so many voices disagree, they reasoned, how can anyone really know who is right? The seeds of secularism were sown in a culture in which many thinkers decided they had had enough.

Many of us have the same tendency today—to argue for the truth of the gospel with attitudes that do not reflect it at all. The New Testament is emphatic in its promotion of peace, unity, kindness, encouragement, compassion, understanding, forgiveness, and love, yet some of its most ardent defenders continue to go after each other with rancor, bitterness, slander, and insults. All the while, the seeds of secularism continue to grow, largely for the same reason they did four and five centuries ago: The many voices water each other down and rip each other apart, convincing onlookers that if anyone happens to be right, no one could possibly know who it is.

Christians' greatest testimony has never been our ability to win an argument but rather our ability to demonstrate love. When we focus on the former, we lose points in any cultural conflict that happens to be raging. When we focus on the latter, we become messengers of the better way, ministers of reconciliation, and agents of Kingdom growth. In all your efforts to bear fruit in this world, remember the true seeds of the Kingdom. Love with all your heart.

Lord, forgive us all for falling short of your demonstration of love. You never ask us to compromise truth, but you emphatically command us to love those who do. May I never get so lost in my own words that I forget to do so. Amen.

Christ and Culture

I saw a vast crowd, too great to count, from every nation and tribe and people and language, standing in front of the throne and before the Lamb. (Revelation 7:9)

ONE OF THE MOST SIGNIFICANT theological works of the twentieth century was *Christ and Culture*, a 1951 book by H. Richard Niebuhr that explores the relationship between Jesus and human culture—whether he is at odds with it, is above it, works within it, works against it, or enters into it to transform it. Wherever a Christian's opinion falls will shape his or her relationship with the surrounding world. How we envision the Kingdom of God will determine how we affect society.

That's the view from within Christian theology, but what about outsiders' views? One of the big questions in the humanities and social sciences in recent decades has been whether it is ever ethical for someone to "impose" his or her beliefs on another culture. The Christian mission, whether in a radically non-Christian culture or in one's own neighborhood, is an effort to affect the beliefs of another. In an age of cultural relativism, many see that as a problem. They forget that Christianity was once foreign to all non-Hebraic cultures (as other religions were foreign beyond their sources), and that every teacher, conversationalist, politician, and philosopher is engaged in changing the thoughts of others. But they also assume that the gospel will undermine a culture and destroy its distinctiveness. And that was not Jesus' mission.

Jesus came not to make the world uniform but to make it new, and it is clear from Revelation's scenes of heaven that people of every tribe and tongue—still very distinguishable—will worship before his throne. Remember that in your interactions with those from different backgrounds. Focus on the gospel's power to change hearts toward God. God enjoys radical diversity within the unity of his Kingdom. So should you.

Lord, I believe my concepts of you and your Word are true. But I also know that my understanding is limited and that many believers see you in different ways. I want to stir up love for you in others; I trust you to bring about change—or not—in your way and your time. Amen.

Heralds of Invitation

Go out into the country lanes and behind the hedges and urge anyone
you find to come, so that the house will be full. (Luke 14:23)

ONE OF SOCIETY'S MORE unsympathetic perceptions of missionaries and other religious people is that they shove their faith down people's throats—a sentiment expressed candidly in the vicious online commentary that often follows news articles and blog posts but is also communicated more subtly in university classrooms and mainstream media. It's historically true that conversions sometimes came through heavy-handed tactics, even at the point of a sword. But those were exceptions to our calling and, in spite of accusations of economic coercion or cultural imperialism, it's not how things normally happen today. In fact, most missionaries are ambassadors of reconciliation and hope, which all can agree are much needed in this world. Jesus sent his followers out with good news.

There's nothing wrong with having conversations about spiritual topics. Many accusations against Christians are scare tactics from people who don't want to be bothered with other people's beliefs while freely expressing their own. But every conversation is filled with opinions that may or may not change the mind of someone else. The desire to influence is embedded in the human heart, and our society overflows with settings where influence is the primary goal: classrooms, political and philosophical debates, newspaper columns, television ads, blogs, social media, and so much more. The problem for some isn't that we talk about faith; it's that we talk about a particular kind of faith—one that comes with a lot of cultural baggage and stereotypes. Many people are done with the idea of Christianity even before fully understanding what it is.

That's a challenge to overcome, and it begins with defying the stereotypes. We want to be heralds of invitation rather than coercion, conversationalists who talk about eternal truth and explore its implications. Whether we are imploring people to be reconciled to God, as Paul did (2 Corinthians 5:20), or showing other hungry beggars where we found bread, as D. T. Niles famously said, we have no reason to be intimidated into silence. Jesus warmly invited all to feast at the Father's table. We are called to do the same.

Jesus, there had to have been something extremely appealing about your nature, even when your words were polarizing, to draw so many to you. Conform me to that nature. May many come with me to your feast. Amen.

The Humble Commission

Go into all the world and preach the Good News to everyone.
(Mark 16:15)

THEY WERE ONLY FOLLOWING INSTRUCTIONS. The many missionaries and conversationalists of the Kingdom who have gone into the world with the gospel of truth were doing what Jesus said to do. The Great Commission in its various expressions (Matthew 28 and Mark 16 contain two of the clearest) compels followers of Jesus to carry claims of truth with them wherever they go and urge others to believe them. This is an integral, inseparable part of the Christian faith.

It's also an offensive one. Many have taken these claims to be arrogant. The idea of one group professing to have the one eternal truth and taking it to others, implying that all other perspectives are false, seems pompous. And in an age of relativism and hyper-tolerance, "pompous" doesn't go over very well. The Great Commission becomes a great annoyance to everyone around.

Is it arrogant to see yourself on a mission to the world? It depends on your attitude. Everyone thinks that what they believe is true, which is why they believe it. And they think those who disagree with them have false beliefs. That's what disagreeing implies, always and without exception. So believing in the gospel is no more arrogant than anyone else's beliefs. The problem is when we become insensitive to the reality that many nonbelievers gain genuine wisdom from other meaningful experiences. Our goal is not to deny this or shame them for it; instead we should find where God has already been working in their lives and draw that treasure out into its ultimate conclusions. In the process, we might learn a lot from those around us without fear of compromising our own beliefs.

In your efforts to fulfill Jesus' instructions, make sure your conversations are two-way exchanges. The Great Commission doesn't tell you to watch your attitude, but the rest of the New Testament does. You do not have the corner on truth; you only know its source. Point to him in humility.

Jesus, your message can be offensive, but I don't want my attitude to add to the offense. Give me a genuine love for people and an inquisitive heart for what they have learned. May my influence come through mutual respect. Amen.

Deuteronomy 10:15-19

Unchanging Love

He shows love to the foreigners living among you and gives
them food and clothing. (Deuteronomy 10:18)

MANY RELIGIOUS GROUPS, including Christians, have been known throughout history to be kind and hospitable in places where they are the minority, and exclusive and intolerant in places where they are the majority. In a Christian context, that sadly reflects nothing about having a changed heart. Instead, it communicates a need to accommodate in minority situations and assumes cultural superiority in majority situations. The dynamic doesn't apply to every individual believer, of course, but it does apply to society as a whole. We have not always been loving to the strangers among us.

We lament no losses when this is the case with other religious groups; we have no stake in their image. But we have to wonder how history might have been different if Christians had always been the exception to this dynamic. Rather than pushing for state- or culture-enforced compliance with Christian morals and doctrines, what if we were known for voluntary love and hospitality? What if the "strangers" among us always got the same compassion and support from us, regardless of our demographic status? Or to put it more pointedly, what if we looked like Jesus rather than the scribes and Pharisees who shunned him?

We are clearly told to be hospitable (Romans 12:13), but the theme goes back much further than Christian times. God chose the Israelites "as the objects of his love" yet showed no partiality, telling his people to love the alien among them because the Israelites themselves had once been aliens in Egypt (Deuteronomy 10:15-19). He commanded them to leave enough food for outsiders and the poor (Leviticus 19:10). The prophets repeated the message often. God's people are to demonstrate not his severity but his kindness. We are to be revelations of his heart.

Live with that purpose. You may live in a Christian-majority neighborhood or town, or you may be vastly outnumbered. Either way, your love must be the same. You are called to reflect not the trends of your culture but the image of your God.

Lord, on behalf of Christians throughout history, I join in confessing and repenting for tragic misrepresentations of your name. May you restore the true image of your nature in your people today, and may we reflect it widely and clearly. Amen.

A Life of Honor

*Peter and John replied, "Do you think God wants us
to obey you rather than him?" (Acts 4:19)*

PETER AND JOHN HEALED a crippled beggar, took advantage of the occasion to preach, and were arrested for creating a stir. The next day they were released, but with a warning not to spread their "propaganda any further" (Acts 4:17). Of course, they were compelled by the Spirit and their own convictions to keep declaring the message they had received and the works God was doing. So they and other apostles were arrested again, miraculously released, and then brought before the authorities. In each case, their response to the council was that God was a higher authority than human beings, and they had to obey him above all (see 5:29).

In one sense, the apostles clearly defied human authorities by violating their instructions. In another, they submitted to those authorities, recognizing that their violations would result in punishments they were willing to pay. They attempted no overthrows, encouraged no riots, and intended no disrespect. They simply did what God told them to do and accepted the consequences.

You have likely discovered in your walk with God a tension between his will for your life and the social, cultural, and legal constraints placed upon you. In every situation in which that tension is evident, you have had a choice to make: to follow God or human expectations. In most cases, you have probably been able to do both; we are called to serve God the best we can within the parameters set by civil authorities (Romans 13:1-5). But there are times when respectful defiance is necessary, with the understanding that we may have to endure unwanted consequences. Our ultimate allegiance is always and forever to God.

Never live with a flippant attitude toward the civil authorities of your society and the social order. There is a significant difference between defying authority because you dislike it and defying authority because you are following a higher one. The latter points to God; the former merely points to self and dishonors God, self, and others. Honor him above all else, while honoring others wherever and whenever you can.

Lord, may I live up to the calling you have given me in every situation, even when I have to go against society's wishes. But help me to remember that part of your calling is a lifestyle of honor. Help me give honor wherever and however I can. Amen.

A Material Witness

They felt that what they owned was not their own,
so they shared everything they had. (Acts 4:32)

MONASTIC ORDERS IN THE Middle Ages faced a paradox. Many had seen the dangers of greed, not only from a growing merchant class but also in the ruling clergy. So they fled the temptations of money by devoting themselves to lives of prayer and the simplicity of owning nothing. But in doing so, they drew the admiration of donors as well as the interest of those who wanted to make a contribution to their order in return for personal prayers. The money they ran from now flowed into their communities. One of their biggest conundrums was how to manage the excesses of worldly wealth.

For different reasons, we face that conundrum too. We live in an age of capitalist consumerism, an entirely different economy with far greater temptations. Many Christians are so immersed in their lifestyle that they are not even aware of the conundrum—or of the centuries of teaching from Jewish and Christian writings, and especially of Jesus, about stewardship, greed, and money's corrupting influences. Money isn't evil, of course—even the monks knew that—but the desire for it easily becomes so. The more we insist that the real issue is idolatry and attachment, even while clinging tightly to our wealth, the more we imply we might have a problem.

One of the signs of the Spirit's presence after Pentecost was a willingness to share generously with those who had come to Jerusalem for the feast. Many Jewish pilgrims who saw what the Holy Spirit was doing could not bring themselves to leave the city. The local believers freely used their possessions for exceptional hospitality in an extraordinary time. While most of us have learned that it is possible to be extremely godly and generous with material prosperity, many of us have not yet found the balance or realized that the way we use money makes a statement to those around us. But it does. More than our words, it preaches a message about our values, our priorities, and our compassion. It points to our sense of union with others and our relationship with God. It reveals how we invest in his Kingdom.

Jesus, you made it clear that for such a material good, money has huge spiritual implications. I cannot serve two masters; may I always serve you with the things I have and demonstrate with them my values and loves. Amen.

Heartily Willing

*The apostles left the high council rejoicing that God had counted
them worthy to suffer disgrace for the name of Jesus. (Acts 5:41)*

ONE OF THE STORIES OF THE execution of John Brown, a Scottish Covenanter in the seventeenth century, describes the scene of a group of soldiers arriving at Brown's house one morning with an ultimatum for him to recant his beliefs and swear allegiance to the king or be killed. Brown refused to recant. He turned to his young wife and asked if she was willing for him to part. "Heartily willing," she replied, understanding the times and the implications of his stance. Brown was shot in front of his wife and children, and before the soldiers marched off, the executioner asked her what she thought of her husband now. "I have always thought well of him," she said, "but now more than ever."[7]

Few Christians in developed Western countries face such oppression today, though many in other parts of the world do. But from the start of the first-century church, it has been clear that human rulers often feel threatened by the higher loyalties of those who are committed to God. At the beginning of the first wave of persecution against Jerusalem's Christians—a relatively short but intense period—the presence of the Spirit was so powerful that, as with John Brown and his widow, the choice was clear and even desirable. Considering the one in whose name they suffered, suffering was a privilege. The benefits of serving him were well worth the costs.

At any moment of our lives, that truth is worth keeping at the forefront of our minds. Many modern cultures have grown soft with the comforts and conveniences so common to us, and most people think something has gone terribly wrong when life gets difficult. But we know better. In the Kingdom of God, at least for now, we can be certain of difficulties. We will need to persevere. The rewards are immensely worthwhile, but the costs are real. Wherever you are facing them in your life today, let your high calling and the name of Jesus make you "heartily willing" to go on.

Jesus, your name is above all names; your Kingdom is greater and more lasting than any other. May I never sacrifice eternal glories for the conveniences of the moment. Amen.

Every Calling Is Significant

*We apostles should spend our time teaching the word of God, not
running a food program. Select seven men who are well respected and
are full of the Spirit and wisdom. We will give them this responsibility.*
(Acts 6:2-3)

"THERE WERE RUMBLINGS OF DISCONTENT," Acts 6:1 tells us, as the number of believers in Jerusalem began to grow. Apparently the Greek-speaking Jews—those whose recent roots lay outside of Jerusalem among Jews of the diaspora in Asia Minor, Babylon, Persia, Europe, or North Africa—felt that their widows were not receiving the same amount of food and level of ministry as the native Hebrew-speaking widows were. The apostles were too preoccupied with their high-level teaching ministry to get involved in administrative details, so they prayerfully appointed seven men, all with Greek names, to oversee this duty.

If you're familiar with the book of Acts, you know where the story turns next: away from the apostles and toward the deacons. The following chapters are all about the remarkable works of Stephen and Philip, who had been appointed to serve tables for widows and were declaring the gospel and demonstrating its miraculous ways. They were not second-rate workers in the Kingdom of God or support staff for those with a "real" ministry. They, too, were filled with the Spirit and wisdom of God. Their calling was just as significant, if not as prominent, as that of the apostles.

Far too many Christians throughout history have equated a calling to serve God with church ministry. But every believer is in full-time service. There is no real dividing line between sacred and secular work in God's eyes, if that work is done for him. Every inch of this planet is a venue in which his name can be glorified and his message made known.

What does this mean for those who are not teachers or preachers? For one thing, there are a lot of ways to "teach and preach," and not all of them are verbal. But the real implication for each of us is that whatever work we engage in, there is something in it—some angle, some network of relationships, some expression of attitudes and values—that becomes a greater focus than the work itself. Every activity offers a platform to love, serve, trust, encourage, comfort, pray, and do the works of God.

*Father, I'm not nearly as interested in status or position as I am in impact. Make my life
fruitful wherever I am—in the church or outside its walls, in wisdom and power—for the
glory of your name. Amen.*

The Next Step

*The Lord said, "Go, for Saul is my chosen instrument
to take my message to the Gentiles and to kings,
as well as to the people of Israel." (Acts 9:15)*

"WHAT IS MY PURPOSE IN LIFE?" Multitudes of people have asked that question. Anyone who believes there is any design in creation wants to know where he or she fits into it. And in his timing, God can give quite specific direction. God told Abraham to move—but gave no clear direction on where until Abraham was on his way. Joseph was given a dream of being an influential ruler but went through years of seemingly senseless hardships before he finally saw that dream fulfilled. Moses waited years before being told step by step where to go and what to do. These men and many others saw pieces of God's purpose for their lives. None, however, got the full blueprint.

Paul's mission was made clear first to Ananias and then to him—that this Jew of Jews (Philippians 3:4-5) would minister to Gentiles. But that was a destination point, not a plan. Along the way, Paul would influence apostles, preach in synagogues, and create a stir among Temple crowds. Even with his strong sense of purpose, he had to be led step by step, at times being turned in directions he did not expect to go. His divinely directed mission in this world was only revealed to him at critical moments.

God gives destination points to some people. To a few, he gives specific routes. But to most of us, he gives a lifetime of next steps, many of which are not completely clear in the moment. But whatever degree of guidance he gives—and he will give some, though sometimes it may not seem like much—you can be certain of his calling for your life today: to represent him, reflecting his heart and his image, in every relationship you have, regardless of the job you have or the tasks on your to-do list. If you look for meaning, you will see it in every moment. That *is* the big picture of your life—even if the destination is not yet clear.

Lord, I would love to see your road map for my life. Encourage me with glimpses of it. But even more, help me see purpose in knowing you and loving others. There is no bigger picture than being your child today. Amen.

Changing History

One day as these men were worshiping the Lord and fasting,
the Holy Spirit said, "Appoint Barnabas and Saul for the
special work to which I have called them." (Acts 13:2)

THE MORAVIANS BEGAN A prayer movement in the 1720s that lasted more than a century. Out of their dedication to corporate prayer came some of the first drops of the gushing stream we now know as the modern missions movement. God prompted some of the Moravians to go to the Caribbean islands to minister to slaves, and though the work was difficult and many died, a sense of responsibility for the unevangelized world began to spread within Protestant circles. Over the next two centuries and beyond, many Christians would dedicate their lives sacrificially for all to hear the Good News of the Kingdom.

Things happen when we come to God with no agenda other than worshiping him. That's what the leaders of the church in Antioch seemed to be doing when Barnabas and Saul were appointed for their work; the literal sense of Acts 13:2 is that they were ministering to the Lord rather than asking him to minister to them. When we focus on worship, we are entering into the environment of heaven, where worship fills the atmosphere all the time. We cannot help being changed in that environment. God's voice and his purposes become clearer. Divine thoughts begin to flow. The Holy Spirit speaks. And in the case of Saul (also called Paul), Barnabas, the Moravians, and many other people and groups who have encountered God in worship, things change. Plans unfold. World history takes a different turn.

One of the greatest things you can do for this world is to enter into the environment of heaven by worshiping God. It might be tempting to worship him out of self-interest—to prompt answers to prayer, for example— but that isn't worship. Come to him without any agenda other than loving him and anticipating his goodness. The more you immerse yourself in his praises, the more you will carry the aroma of heaven with you. In his timing, you may hear his voice or sense his purpose. And this world will undoubtedly be the better for it.

Lord, may my adoration rise to your throne and bless your heart. May my voice join in with the praises of heaven. And may heaven so fill my heart that the course of history— at least my corner of it—changes. Amen.

A Place of Revelation

Paul shouted to him, "Stop! Don't kill yourself! We are all here!"
(Acts 16:28)

ON THE SURFACE, Paul and Silas's time in Philippi had not gone as expected. They had found no synagogue. They had cast a spirit out of a fortune-telling girl and were imprisoned when her owners stirred up a protest. Beaten with thick Roman rods and put in stocks designed to create discomfort, they sang hymns of praise until an earthquake broke their shackles and opened the prison doors. They were free—or could have been, if they had left. Instead, Paul took advantage of the critical moment to minister to the jailer who would have suffered dire consequences for letting the prisoners escape.

Kingdom citizens understand that one of their roles is to see what God is doing in the midst of a crisis and position themselves in it as a catalyst of his revelation. Most of us would have assumed that the miraculous jailbreak was a divinely orchestrated occasion to flee. But Paul saw something else: a divinely orchestrated occasion to point to God. So Paul remained in his cell, out of concern for the jailer's life and need for salvation—both the immediate kind in saving his skin from certain execution, and the ultimate kind in putting his faith in Jesus. Paul and Silas could have left again the next morning, yet Paul insisted that the magistrates face up to the injustice they had committed in beating and imprisoning two Roman citizens—and in the process, admit that these alleged troublemakers had the integrity to see the problem through to the end.

Those who want to be catalysts for a revelation of God's nature learn not to flee a crisis discreetly. Instead, they position themselves in the middle of it. Why? Because that's where God is most likely to reveal himself. It's the best place to see answers to prayer, offer solutions to problems, and meet the needs of those experiencing the weight of the crisis. His Kingdom comes when rival kingdoms are shaken. And when they are, we are very often called to be there.

Lord, transform my instincts from avoiding trouble to seeing your face in the midst of it. Give me eyes to look for your revelation—and how I can be a part of it. Amen.

A Subversive Message

"Paul and Silas have caused trouble all over the world," they shouted,
"and now they are here disturbing our city, too." (Acts 17:6)

PAUL AND SILAS WERE TRAVELING through the Hellenistic world to persuade both Jews and Gentiles of the truth of Jesus. This divisive message often split synagogues, which in turn sparked waves of outrage and protest. The real agitators were the protestors, not the messengers, but as agitators often do, they blamed others for their violence. Paul and Silas were accused of causing trouble wherever they went—literally of trying to stir up revolts. As a result, their opponents painted the life-changing message of Jesus as a subversive one.

In many ways, it is. It subverts a false kingdom. As much as possible, Paul tried to become all things to all people in order to remove barriers to the gospel (1 Corinthians 9:19-23), but God's message cannot be accommodated to everyone's tastes. It still upsets the world's systems and reorders their values. It calls for a decision that may strain relationships and divide groups. It insists on a different way of thinking and relating to others. It seeks to win hearts, not appease them.

If at all possible, do nothing to create controversy. Your life's message does enough of that on its own. There are some places in this world where the gospel will not make many waves; perhaps those around you have believed in it or heard it enough for it not to make a stir. But you will likely find yourself in some places where your beliefs are challenging to those around you. You may be seen as a troublemaker simply for standing up for your convictions. Jesus said to be as shrewd as snakes and harmless as doves in those places (Matthew 10:16); Peter urged maintaining a clear conscience (1 Peter 3:13-17). Be gracious to those around you, but be prepared to endure. The controversy surrounding Jesus and his followers is normal. In some measure or other, you are destined to turn your world upside down.

Jesus, you are no stranger to turmoil. I would prefer to avoid it, but may I never compromise my beliefs to do so. Fill my mouth with words of grace and peace but also with timely words of truth—whatever the cost. Amen.

An Image of Grace

The people of Berea were more open-minded than those in
Thessalonica, and they listened eagerly to Paul's message.
They searched the Scriptures day after day to see if Paul
and Silas were teaching the truth. (Acts 17:11)

CHRISTIANS HAVE AN IMAGE PROBLEM, and much of it is deserved. In our efforts to uphold standards of morality and social values—an understandable goal fueled by admirable motives—we sometimes come across as critical, narrow-minded, and negative to those around us. Perhaps that is unavoidable; absolutes, however true, are not popular in our relativistic age. Even so, our attempts to apply Christian values to non-Christian lives are often misguided. The result, as many have noted, is that we're known more for what we're against than what we're for.

Unfortunately, that attitude is often applied even within our own circles. Self-appointed watchdogs and discernment ministries blast anything that doesn't look and smell like their narrowly defined gospel. They don't consider the possibility that God might be trying to help them grow. Many appeal to the example of the Bereans in Acts, who searched the Scriptures to discern the truth of Paul and Silas's message. The difference is that the Bereans searched the Scriptures to see if the teaching was true, not to see if it was false—a subtle but decidedly different approach. They were excited about the possibility of learning something new, and they wanted to verify it. They looked at Scripture with an open mind.

Many believers today need to take that same approach with other believers—to live with an open mind like the Bereans, or at least recognize that genuine Christians have different perspectives and understandings. But we also need to apply that attitude outward—not to embrace whatever the world teaches indiscriminately, but to realize we can learn a lot from those around us. Willing hearts and open minds are winsome and appealing in their own right; they also give us connections, understanding, and a voice when we need to make a stand. And they go a long way toward changing a bad image.

Lord, you are the author of all truth, but you share it widely. Help me recognize it in
unexpected places, commend and connect with its unlikely advocates, and voice it always
with grace. Amen.

A Cultural Kinship

In him we live and move and exist. As some of your own
poets have said, "We are his offspring." (Acts 17:28)

MATTEO RICCI, a Jesuit missionary to China in the late 1500s and early 1600s, saw a lot of truth in Confucian teaching and suggested that God had used that philosophy throughout the centuries to prepare the Chinese for the gospel. Other missionaries criticized Ricci for syncretism, arguing that he was corrupting the purity of the gospel with foreign teaching. But this case, like many others, leads to an age-old question—to what extent does God work through the wisdom gained by sages living outside of his covenant? We know God gives pure revelation, but many of the most effective and inspired teachers of his Word have found connecting points with secular philosophy, just as Paul and other New Testament figures did with Greek and Roman cultural influences. Somewhere between isolating and accommodating these teachings is an enticing open door.

In Paul's day, Athens was known for being a source of shrines, a hodgepodge of common and unusual beliefs, and, according to the ancient geographer Pausanias, the city that surpassed all others in its worship of various gods. No wonder Paul was "deeply troubled" by all the idols he saw as he walked along Athens's streets (Acts 17:16). The city was perhaps the premier hub in the production of pagan artifacts and monuments. So it may be surprising that Paul, who was clearly not shy of conflict, did not begin his message to the Areopagus—"the high council of the city" (17:19)—with a blistering critique of the city's paganism. Instead, his first approach was to commend the city leaders for their religious nature, to affirm that their search for truth was worthwhile. He offered something of an endorsement for their monument to an unknown god. In other words, he found a connecting point with them.

That wasn't the end of Paul's message, of course. He went on to explain the good news of Jesus, getting specific about what God had done in Christ and what it meant for our salvation. But he established whatever affinities he could before stretching them in favor of truth, giving us a model of interfaith discourse. He understood the fruitlessness of frontal attacks, and so should we. Generous words open conversations—and hearts—for God to enter in.

Father, you have prepared cultures, kingdoms, and hearts for your truth. Give me eyes to
see the connecting points in every situation and build relationships through them. Amen.

Find the Connection

*One of your altars had this inscription on it: "To an Unknown
God." This God, whom you worship without knowing, is
the one I'm telling you about. (Acts 17:23)*

MISSIONARY DON RICHARDSON was perplexed in his attempts to share the gospel
with the remote Sawi people of Indonesia. They considered Judas the conniving hero
of the gospel story and Jesus the fool who was duped by him. But when Richardson
realized that rival villages sometimes settled their hostilities with a ceremony in which
families exchanged a child with their enemies—a "peace child"—he saw an immediate connection with God's sacrifice of his Son. This "redemptive analogy" became
the key to connecting gospel truth with Sawi culture.

Likewise, Paul connected with the local culture in Athens by building his sermon
around the statue dedicated "to an Unknown God," which became a launching point
toward the God of Israel. Instead of criticizing the idolatrous culture that had grieved
him days before, he made an effort to find something in common with it and begin
conversations based on that point. His desire to make his message understandable
was greater than his desire to establish differences.

The lesson we learn from Paul and other missionaries about building bridges
applies not only to other cultures. It shows us how to relate to the culture we live in.
We may see all sorts of differences between our own beliefs and lifestyles compared
to those of others, but God hasn't sent his followers out on a mission of establishing
differences. We are to live distinctively, of course, but we are also to create links—to
relate to others through whatever commonalities we can find. Our ability to share our
lives, as well as to learn from those around us, depends on our willingness to connect.

Instead of criticizing others' faiths and perspectives for how wrong they are, look
for ways they might be right. Then build on those connecting points. You will be
enriched by the experience, becoming more knowledgeable about other views and
more fruitful in your efforts to share your own. And better yet, you will build bridges
that God can use to reveal his truth.

*Jesus, you clothed yourself in flesh to make the Father known in ways we could
understand. Open my eyes to opportunities to express your truth too. May I find
connections to your Word everywhere I look and know how to share them well. Amen.*

Rhythms of Redemption

When they opposed and insulted him, Paul shook the dust from
his clothes and said, "Your blood is upon your own heads—I am
innocent. From now on I will go preach to the Gentiles." (Acts 18:6)

HARVESTS COME IN DIFFERENT CYCLES. Growing seasons vary by crop, climate, and terrain, and no one argues with the schedule. No one demands that grapes and olives mature when barley and wheat do. Nature has its course, and human beings adapt to its rhythms.

Redemption has its rhythms too. In 1500, about one in every ten people in the world identified themselves as Christian. In 1900, the number had risen to one in five. Today, nearly one third of all people on this planet consider themselves to be Christian, and the percentage is rising. But the growth of Christianity has not been steady or uniform. Centuries ago, Christianity spread through much of Asia, across Europe, and then to the Americas soon after they were discovered. In modern times, we've seen waves of growth in Asia and Africa and now the beginnings of movement in the Islamic world. God has moved in different places at different times. That's how he works.

Throughout history, some places have seemed particularly ripe for harvest while others have not. Paul found some fruitfulness among the Jews of his generation but much more among the Gentiles. As he later wrote, God had ordained specific times for Israel to resist, for the Gentiles to be grafted into Israel's covenant, and for Israel to be drawn back in (Romans 11:25). We see this dynamic both on a global scale and in the smaller communities of our own families and cities. The Kingdom citizen is discerning about seasons—how different demographic groups respond at different times. There is something to be said for tilling hard ground for years and preparing it for future fruitfulness, as some are called to do. But there's also something to be said for going where the fruit is ripe for harvesting, as Paul did. Be observant, be sensitive to what you observe, and tend to open hearts. It is always harvest season somewhere.

Father, Jesus called you the Lord of the harvest and sent his followers into the fields.
Open fields before me and direct my steps. Open my eyes to the ready fruit around me.
Amen.

Beyond the Status Quo

About that time, serious trouble developed in
Ephesus concerning the Way. (Acts 19:23)

AFTER MORE THAN TWO YEARS OF Paul's preaching and teaching and performing unusual miracles, Ephesus experienced a spiritual breakthrough. Many new believers burned their old books and articles of magic—the merchandise that supported the economy of this religiously diverse city—to demonstrate their turning to the true God. As the narrative in Acts 19 makes clear, this caused "serious trouble." The manufacturers of these religious artifacts—protectors of the temple of Artemis and, more urgently, their own bottom lines—met to discuss their declining sales. Anger boiled. A riot ensued.

This pivotal scene captures a common tension between God's Kingdom and the world's cultures and systems. When Kingdom values subvert the economic structures and social dynamics already set in place, people get rattled. We can understand that; the status quo supports family incomes and certain ways of life. Big changes create insecurity—especially if those changes point to an invisible deity with an unfamiliar track record. When beliefs are fully integrated with a social system, those beliefs are slow to change.

Your mission as salt and light in this world may involve deconstructing false ways of life and social structures—a mission requiring thick skin and enough endurance to last a lifetime. But the goal is really bigger than that. It involves offering solutions in place of whatever was there. However dysfunctional the status quo may have been, it was working for some. They need a viable alternative. Your lifestyle, your words, and your assistance need to provide one.

Make no mistake: The gospel is more than words. The Good News of the Kingdom includes a demonstration of Kingdom ways and intervention into the world's systems. Paul left Ephesus in the midst of controversy, but the newly established church was there to help restructure the city's economy. We don't know if they did, or to what degree. But we do know God offered a better way for Ephesus through his people. Your world needs a better way too. Live it, talk it, and most importantly, help establish it.

Lord, make me a messenger of the better way. Give your people visions for restructuring society with Kingdom solutions. May our influence in this world become a testimony to your wisdom and goodness. Amen.

Worth Everything

*My life is worth nothing to me unless I use it for finishing
the work assigned me by the Lord Jesus. (Acts 20:24)*

PÁDRAIG—LATER KNOWN as Saint Patrick—was captured by Irish pirates and held in bondage for six years in the late 400s. After his escape and return to Britain, he had a vision that would send him back to Ireland as a missionary. He followed his assignment, persevered against opposition and hardships, baptized thousands of people, and formed new Christian communities. Many Irish today consider him to be their patron saint and foremost apostle.

Paul spoke often of his assignment as an apostle of the message of Jesus, and no one could accuse him of not taking it seriously. He had received clear instructions from the Lord in a dramatic encounter with Jesus, and it shaped the rest of his life. He was relentless in his pursuit of his calling and very aware of his need to fulfill it. He persevered through numerous trials and much opposition to finish his assignment because the task was bigger than his life. He was determined to complete it or die trying.

Paul, Patrick, and many others throughout history have been given a specific assignment to fulfill, while countless others have been given a general assignment. The pattern we observe among Christian believers is that those who have a strong and specific sense of calling work zealously and endure a lot, while those who are aware of a general calling are usually less motivated. If we consider only the calling, this pattern is understandable. If we consider the caller, it doesn't make sense.

Most of us admire people like Paul and Patrick for their unique roles in history. But we tend to minimize the importance of our own roles as God's children, as if that were any less of a calling. It isn't. Every moment matters. Every believer is sent into the world as salt and light. Every relationship is an opportunity to reflect God's nature. And every calling—specific or general—is bigger than our own lives. Why? Because of the one who calls. Serve him wholeheartedly in every situation.

Father, there are no small callings in your Kingdom. You are worthy of my life, however you choose to use it. May I fulfill any assignment you give me, specific or not, with all my heart every moment of every day. Amen.

Places of Influence

If I am innocent, no one has a right to turn me over to
these men to kill me. I appeal to Caesar! (Acts 25:11)

THE LAST THIRD OF THE BOOK of Acts is dedicated to one lengthy, twisting-and-turning saga: Paul's arrest in Jerusalem, his numerous appearances before Jewish and Roman authorities, and his eventual journey as a prisoner to Rome. The accusations against him were false; he even tried to preempt them by demonstrating that he was still loyal to Jewish customs and laws. But the Roman authorities, who could find no basis for the charges against him, were concerned with his polarizing message and whatever unrest might result from his release. So they dragged out his hearings, suggested changes of venue, and tried to appease all interests. Paul, however, refused to become subject to the political whims of his adversaries and, as a Roman citizen had the right to do, appealed to Caesar's jurisdiction. He followed God's unexpected path to the high courts of Rome.

God has a way of putting his people in strategic places for influential audiences to see and hear—although they may not always be comfortable. Paul had planned to go to Rome on his own, as his earlier letter to the Romans makes clear. But would he have gained an audience with Rome's highest authorities on his own? Probably not. As Joseph and Daniel experienced centuries before, the entryway into a king's courts was traumatic. But the fruit was influential, and the benefits in reaching places of power exceeded the costs of getting there.

Learn to use the avenues of this world to create highways for God's Kingdom. Paul leveraged his Roman citizenship not only to avoid injustice in Jerusalem and Caesarea but also to enter an open door in Rome. Do not resist the orchestrations of God; let them propel you into the boardrooms, classrooms, courtrooms, meeting halls, and marketplaces of society as he wills. You do not have to be as overt as Paul in your message—he was a forerunner in a world that had never heard the gospel—but don't waste the opportunity to represent God somehow. Use the background you have been given to shape the future God has planned.

Father, you are sovereign over every circumstance of my past, every situation in my present, and every purpose for my future. May I see the open doors and represent you well everywhere you position me. Amen.

Kingdom Promotions

For the next two years, Paul lived in Rome at his own expense.
He welcomed all who visited him, boldly proclaiming
the Kingdom of God. (Acts 28:30-31)

WHEN JOSEPH WAS A YOUNG MAN, God gave him dreams of his future and the influence he would have (Genesis 37). Almost immediately, the circumstances of his life seemed to turn in the opposite direction. He was sold by his brothers into slavery in Egypt, falsely accused while there and imprisoned, and forgotten by the one person who might have been able to help him gain his freedom. But every step of the way, Joseph rose in favor among those with influence. And every step of the way, what looked to be a setback was really a step closer to the purpose God had given him. Joseph's disappointments were really his promotions.

The same was true for Paul, though Paul was likely more aware of God's work in his circumstances. His arrest was the means to an end, which ultimately involved a trip to Rome and a hearing in high places. But even in captivity, Paul was not deterred. He wrote letters. He preached to members of the Praetorian Guard (Philippians 1:12-14). He encouraged Christians and churches. He became an example in his days of hiddenness. His circumstances never detracted from his message; in fact, they served to enhance it.

You may not find yourself in this world's halls of power, but you can be certain that God will orchestrate events in your life to put you in places of influence—even when you aren't aware of the influence you have. Earthly setbacks may be promotions from God's perspective and opportunities in disguise. That was true of Joseph, Paul, and many other biblical characters, each of whom could have lamented their losses every step of the way. But laments do not fit the Kingdom well, at least not with regard to circumstances orchestrated by our sovereign God. Never be discouraged by limiting situations; God is not limited in them at all. In reality, neither are you.

Lord, forgive my limited vision. I see hardships and setbacks; you see opportunities and promotions. May I never waste a circumstance you have given me. Give me Kingdom influence, even when I don't see it. Amen.

Living from Heaven

We are citizens of heaven, where the Lord Jesus Christ lives.
(Philippians 3:20)

THE PEVENSIE CHILDREN SPENT a lifetime in Narnia as kings and queens, almost completely forgetting their former life in England until they returned to it through a wardrobe. While in England, their memories of Narnia faded until they were thrust back into it at a time of need. The way C. S. Lewis portrayed the memories of his characters throughout The Chronicles of Narnia series makes a profound statement about the way we live: Whatever realm our minds are immersed in shapes the decisions we make and the influence we have.

That's important for us as believers because we are told that we are already citizens of heaven, seated with Christ there in his position of power. For people in such a high state, we live awfully powerless lives sometimes. Why? Not because we lack power—the power of the Resurrection itself works within us (Ephesians 1:19-20; 3:20)—but because we forget who we are. We live as citizens of earth trying to draw on heaven's resources rather than as citizens of heaven pouring its resources into earth. We need constant reminders of our position.

Immerse your mind in the things of heaven (Colossians 3:1-2). When you live as a citizen of earth trying to draw on heaven's resources, your starting assumption is one of lack and poverty. But that isn't God's description of who you are or where you sit. You can be energized by the thought that you are an overcomer (Romans 8:37); everything, even your losses, will work out for your good (Romans 8:28); you have access to the mind of Christ (1 Corinthians 2:16); God himself is at work within you (Philippians 2:13); and much, much more. In other words, you are called to be an outpost of heaven on earth, a connecting point between the two realms. Anchor yourself there, and live, pray, and speak with that power. It will make a world of difference in your life and the lives of others.

Father, forgive me for pleading like an orphan and outcast of your Kingdom. Give me a throne-room mentality as your child and royal heir. Energize me with the power of the Resurrection. Immerse me in the heavenly realm so that I may live from there toward earth. Amen.

Where We Sit

He raised us from the dead along with Christ and seated us with
him in the heavenly realms because we are united with Christ Jesus.
(Ephesians 2:6)

JACOB HAD A DREAM OF angels ascending and descending from the spiritual to the material realm and back again (Genesis 28:10-19). Elisha was surrounded by a hostile army but could clearly see that heaven's armies far outnumbered his enemies (2 Kings 6:8-23). Jesus was transfigured into a glorious environment that revealed a heavenly conversation between him, Moses, and Elijah (Luke 9:28-36). In each case—and in many others shown in the books of Ezekiel, Daniel, Revelation, and more—the invisible world became visible. The spiritual invaded and overshadowed the material. The place of our true citizenship was made manifest to someone with eyes to see it.

What does this other reality have to do with our daily existence? As we've seen, if we live by sight rather than by faith, we will see ourselves as earthbound, finite, limited, and in bondage to circumstances. But if we live by faith and not by sight (2 Corinthians 5:7)—not only aware of our true citizenship but anchored in it fully—we will pray differently, speak differently, and live differently. We will grow into the identity we really have and assume God's victory, provision, and protection over us, rather than pleading as struggling sinners trying to attain them. We will live a resurrected life that sheds disappointment easily. Why? Because we understand that heaven is not lamenting losses. The always-increasing Kingdom (Isaiah 9:7) is continually celebrating gains.

Many Christians are living with a defeatist perspective, not realizing that the perspective of heaven is available to them and is not defeatist at all. Meanwhile, one of the world's greatest needs is people with access to heaven's resources—its wisdom, power, love, revelation, provision, and mercies. For those who are seated with Christ, these things are never out of reach. We may need to persevere in our understanding and experience of them, but they are there. Assume them, grow in them, and give them freely to the citizens of earth. From where you sit, all things are possible.

Jesus, what does it mean to be seated with you? What will my eyes be privileged to see?
How do I access the power of your resurrection and the wonders of your love? Show me.
Pour out your provision to the world through me. Amen.

Rightside Down

When you produce much fruit, you are my true disciples.
This brings great glory to my Father. (John 15:8)

IMAGINE A DEEPLY ROOTED TREE firmly planted in the ground—and then a hand
from heaven reaching down, grabbing the trunk, pulling the tree and its roots out
of the ground, turning it upside down, and planting it firmly in heaven. From there,
the tree's roots grow upward and its fruit hangs down, available to all who will take
of it. The transition process may have been quite traumatic, but the result is good.
Earth is fed by a tree rooted in heaven.

That's a picture of what God does with his people if we will let him. The process
can be extremely disorienting; not many people enjoy having their roots ripped out
of this world. But the result is a truer, deeper orientation. As we have seen, Scripture
tells us we are to be rooted and grounded in the love of God (Ephesians 3:17); that
our citizenship is in heaven (Philippians 3:20); that we are seated there with Christ
(Ephesians 2:6); and that we are branches of the true vine, Jesus, who is seated at the
right hand of the Father (John 15:1-5; Ephesians 2:6). Our position is secure. All
that remains is for us to recognize it and live from it.

This Kingdom citizenship is more than a psychological trick or a matter of
semantics. It is not a matter of talking yourself into something that isn't true. No, it
is really an issue of convincing yourself of what God already says of you—that you are
one with Christ (John 15:4; 17:21) and risen with him (Romans 6:5; Colossians 3:1;
Galatians 2:20). It falls in the category of considering yourself dead to sin and alive
to Christ (Romans 6), not because you want it to be true but because it is. And it
makes the difference between feeling burned out and being energized as you give the
fruit of heaven to people around you. Apart from him, you can do nothing of eternal
value. With him? Not even the sky is the limit.

*Jesus, you are my life, and you are unlimited. Give me the faith to see where I am truly
rooted. Bear immeasurable fruit in me and through me. Fill me with the power and
presence of eternal realities. Amen.*

As He Was Sent

As the Father has sent me, so I am sending you. (John 20:21)

WHEN JESUS CAME DOWN from heaven (John 3:13), he came as a human, not a divine being. Philippians 2 describes him as having left the heavenly abode and the privileges of deity; taking the form of a man; living as a servant, even to the point of death; and being exalted into heaven again. While on earth, Jesus often interacted with his Father in heaven (Luke 5:16), saw and heard heavenly things (John 5:19-20; 12:49-50), received the ministry of heaven's angels (Matthew 4:11), and had experiences of heavenly glory (Luke 9:28-36). The implication is that even as a human being Jesus had access to heaven's resources. God sent him—in his image, in his power—for a purpose.

Part of that purpose was for Jesus to send his followers out in the same way he had been sent. We can imagine that commissioning from many angles: having the same agenda, the same methods, the same character, the same power, and the same relational dynamics. We can even imagine encountering the same kinds of opposition that Jesus experienced and, in some parts of the world, the same suffering.

Jesus made this sending specific with two examples of what the mission would include: the same Holy Spirit and the same focus on forgiveness. In short, he commissioned us to represent him and work in his name with more freedom and license than we normally are willing to take upon ourselves.

Perhaps we don't want to be presumptuous, or assume divine privileges, or equate ourselves too closely with the unique Son of God. But while it's true that Jesus is exceptional, he is also our example, and he invites us into his fruitfulness, his inheritance, and even his authority. Our reluctance to claim too much may come from humility, but it amounts to a denial of God's gifts and calling on our lives. He has created us to be Kingdom influencers and world changers.

Your ministry may never be as dramatic as that of Jesus or the early apostles. But don't limit your vision. Learn to draw from heaven's resources—whatever it takes. Ask the Father for guidance and the Spirit for power. Live to carry the Son's mission forward.

Jesus, thank you for the privilege of bearing your name, though I can hardly imagine bearing your fruit. Teach me. Empower me. Send me wherever and however you choose. Let your Kingdom flourish in me and through me. Amen.

On Earth as in Heaven

Your kingdom come, your will be done, on earth as it is in heaven.
(Matthew 6:10, ESV)

As ROMAN TERRITORY EXPANDED into Africa, Gaul, and the Greek east in the centuries before and after Christ, many cultures experienced what some historians call "Romanization"—a tendency to take on Roman ways and norms. The same dynamic had occurred when Alexander the Great's expanding territory "Hellenized" cultures only a couple of centuries earlier. Sometimes societies adapted willingly, sometimes grudgingly, sometimes unconsciously, and sometimes only in superficial ways. In any case, some degree of adaptation occurred, which is common whenever one kingdom inherits another. Cultures have influence, shaping and adapting to each other.

We pray often for God's Kingdom to come, just as Jesus instructed. In the minds of many, this is a far-off request for Jesus to return one day and establish his Kingdom, which he surely will. But doesn't it also have some here-and-now implications? Is there any indication that we should pray "your will be done" for now and "your kingdom come" for later? Or might there be some process of heaven-ization that influences this world today?

In fact, there is. The question is what that should look like. Clearly we want God's Kingdom to come in our hearts and in our families. But salt and light are not content to remain in saltshakers and under lampshades. We want to spread our influence everywhere. Jesus invites us to pray for his ways to influence the marketplace, the workplace, and other public spaces too—just as they are followed in heaven.

Pray this request not as a line in a ritual prayer but as a battle cry over the kingdoms of this world. Before Jesus ever comes back *for* us, he will certainly come *to* us and *through* us. Let the future realities of his Kingdom spill over into the visible realities of our day. Let him empower you to make progress toward his ultimate goal. Pray for his will to be done—right now, in our age, on earth, just as it is in heaven.

Lord, with enthusiasm I pray: Your Kingdom come, your will be done, on earth—in my life, my family, my church, my workplace, my city, my nation, my world—just as it is in heaven. Show me what that looks like and help me step into it daily. Amen.

2 Corinthians 4:1-4

Declaring Light

Satan, who is the god of this world, has blinded the minds of
those who don't believe. They are unable to see the glorious
light of the Good News. (2 Corinthians 4:4)

Princess Aurora lay in a deep sleep, and the entire kingdom, surrounded by darkness and dense forest, slept with her. Only the kiss of the virtuous prince from afar could break the spell cast on her, and he was imprisoned, apparently conquered by forces of evil. Armed with the sword of truth and the shield of virtue, the prince eventually escaped to kiss the princess and rescue the kingdom. The darkness lifted, and all joined in the royal couple's wedding banquet.

Disney's rendition of Charles Perrault's seventeenth-century *Sleeping Beauty* not only makes for a great movie; it also paints a pretty good picture of the gospel. Isaiah wrote of all nations being shrouded with the darkness of night as the glory of God rose and appeared over his people (Isaiah 60:1-3). Paul wrote of the minds of the human race being blinded by evil forces so they cannot see God's glorious light but also of the Good News being unveiled. From images like these, we know that our prayer for God's Kingdom to come is not an innocuous request. Whenever we pray for one kingdom to come, we are implying that another needs to go. We are entering into a menacing spiritual fray.

Enter in with the confidence that you are shielded with Jesus' virtue and armed with his sword of truth. You likely already have a list of things you are praying for; with care, add to it the things you are praying against. In the Spirit, oppose the agenda of evil and pray that it would be replaced by the agenda of God's goodness. The world needs plenty of spiritual advocates. Be one.

That role will usually play out behind the scenes, but it is nevertheless a vital one. Identify those who are bound in spiritual confusion and pray for their liberation. Go to battle in prayer for those who have been wounded by all sorts of abuses and threats. Construct prayers that shine the light of God's Kingdom into dark corners. Wherever you look, become the fighting prince of your King.

Father, you have enlisted us as unusual soldiers to influence the world behind the scenes. Raise us up in power to destroy darkness and declare the light of your Kingdom. Unveil your glory in this world. Amen.

Radiant

All nations will come to your light; mighty kings
will come to see your radiance. (Isaiah 60:3)

WHATEVER BROTHER LAWRENCE HAD, it drew the attention of bishops and dignitaries from far away. Many who visited the monastery in Paris went out of their way to meet the kitchen worker who exuded the presence of God. The low-ranking brother had learned the art of worshiping in high places, and it showed. His gentleness of spirit, simple wisdom, and heavenly attitude were noticeable, even though he served in a hardly notable position.

Brother Lawrence is an example of what it means to live as a "Kingdom outpost" in a foreign land—a carrier of the light of God in dark times. Isaiah had prophesied such radiance, declaring that all nations would come to the light of God through his people as they reflected him. The glory of the Lord rises on his people, and they become the image that draws others in. As carriers of his presence, we have the remarkable privilege of shining in dark places. We live in a world that needs his radiance. As much as we defer to him to show it, he turns the responsibility back to us.

Does that seem overwhelming? It should; it is beyond our ability. But it is not beyond his. Jesus informed his disciples that without him, they could do nothing (John 15:5). That implies that with him, they could do quite a bit—"everything," as Paul would later write (Philippians 4:13). In fact, we find that in Christ, our responsibility is less about doing than it is about being. His Spirit transforms us from within; what we do always flows from who we are.

Remember that. You are not called to be the light, only to reflect it. Like the glow-in-the-dark toys you once held up to the light to absorb its properties, saturate yourself in the presence of your Lord. Soak up his radiance. When the lights go off, you will shine, not because you try to but because of the person you have become. And those around you will see him.

Lord, shine on me. Let me soak in your goodness and light. May I radiate your presence, even when those around me don't understand what it is. May nations and kings, and even my friends, see who you are. Amen.

The Apologists of Faith

Jesus took them through the writings of Moses and all the prophets,
explaining from all the Scriptures the things concerning himself.
(Luke 24:27)

AFTER HIS RESURRECTION, Jesus met two of his followers on the road to Emmaus and, without disclosing his identity, had a lengthy conversation with them about the events of the crucifixion and resurrection. Mystified by the claims of those who insisted he was alive, these followers marveled at the possibility. Jesus rebuked them for their denseness—playfully, we hope—and went on to explain how thoroughly the Hebrew Scriptures pointed to him. He became the first apologist for the truth of his own identity.

The field of apologetics is much wider today. Few nonbelievers buy into the authority of our Scripture; philosophies have diversified beyond ancient imaginations; science has presented far more challenges than most believers are equipped to deal with; and secularism has produced a vast population that simply does not care what the arguments are. Regardless of how rational our faith is, most who do not believe are convinced that our faith is either irrational or irrelevant. Arguments can only go so far.

Paul opened up the Scriptures on quite a few occasions to demonstrate how Jesus fulfilled Hebrew law and prophecies, but in Athens, he spoke to the people in the language of their philosophies. He adapted. So must we. You will not be able to prove God through the languages of science or philosophy, but you may at least be able to remove objections to his existence. You will not be able to use Scripture effectively in support of your faith among people who do not believe it is inspired, but you may be able to demonstrate that it has more coherence and power than they once thought. Apologetics does not change many minds, but it plays a vital role in supporting the changes hearts have decided to make. With that in mind, arm yourself with truth, but go to battle with demonstrations of wisdom, grace, and love. Live the faith, and then talk about it. Let the resurrection power in you convince those around you that what you say is true.

Lord, my words matter to others only when my life demonstrates who you are. Give me both—powerful words and a persuasive way of life. May everything in me exude authenticity and the reality of your Kingdom. Amen.

The Full Expression

Anyone who does not love does not know God, for God is love.
(1 John 4:8)

ONE OF THE MOST PROMINENT biblical themes is the love of God. Unfortunately, it's also one of the most distorted; people have turned "God is love" into "love is God," which is not at all the same thing. Aside from this, his love can also seem inaccessible. Despite its prevalence shown throughout the Bible, we somehow manage to agree with it emphatically in our minds but question it incessantly in our hearts.

You have most likely experienced a curious phenomenon—that it's much easier to assure someone else of God's love than it is to believe it for yourself. We have lingering questions and deep-down doubts about how God's love applies to us. We assume that his love is part of his job description, something he has to offer to all of his children but not necessarily something he is passionate about, at least with regard to us personally. In other words, we can easily believe God loves us because he has to but not so easily believe that he loves us because he wants to.

But he does. He delights in his love for each of us, not in spite of our unworthiness but even because of it. It's true affection. Like any loving parent, he will not endorse everything we do or affirm our sinful tendencies, but he nevertheless loves us with deep, relentless affection. If we don't know that—if we never feel it and do not believe it deep in our hearts—we will not be able to love others well. And we will not be able to become the "full expression" of the love of God for those around us (1 John 4:12).

That's the direction we are headed, at least in theory. God calls us to be that full expression of his love, which means he first insists that we experience the full expression of his love. Soak in it and relish it without reservation. Doing so frees you to see yourself with the same delight he has for you and then to show that delight to others.

Father, expand the capacity of my heart, my mind, and my spirit to embrace the fullness of your love. Transform me with it. Make me an instrument of your love. Amen.

Relentless Love

Do not repay evil for evil or reviling for reviling, but on the contrary,
bless, for to this you were called, that you may obtain a blessing.
(1 Peter 3:9, ESV)

WATCHMAN NEE ONCE WROTE of a Christian in South China whose rice field was in the middle of a terraced hill. Whenever the rains were insufficient to fill his field, he lifted water into it from an irrigation stream by working a waterwheel with a treadmill. But the man who owned the next lowest field often drained the Christian farmer's water into his own field, creating a lot of extra work. The Christian tried his best not to retaliate but was bothered by the injustice. He prayed and decided that defending his own rights was not a Kingdom approach. Instead, he began pumping water for his neighbor's field first, then filled his own. The neighbor was amazed and eventually became a Christian.[8]

God is a God of justice, but even more he is a God of mercy. To stand out in a hostile culture, we will have to find unexpected ways of responding to offenses. Yes, there are times when we should remove ourselves from abusive situations for the sake of our own protection, but less dangerous situations may call for a different approach. The rice farmer in South China responded with a winsome attitude in an aggravating situation, and God used his response to turn an enemy into a friend and believer. The Kingdom grows when his people adopt his nature.

When we realize how God has approached us, taking the burden of our offenses on himself and focusing instead on what we really need, we begin to develop the same attitude in our relationships with others. We stop returning hostility for hostility, defensiveness for defensiveness, and apathy for apathy. Instead, we embrace relentless love that overcomes the barriers in people's hearts. The only way to live a winsome life in a hostile culture is to choose to respond to it in a different spirit. Eventually, obstacles come down, attitudes change, and many hearts open up to the love of a merciful Father.

Father, fill me with relentless, overcoming love. Let my vision be so focused on others'
needs that I hardly notice their faults. May I show others the same kind of mercy you
have shown me. Amen.

The Whole Kingdom

*"I will prove to you that the Son of Man has the authority on earth
to forgive sins." Then Jesus turned to the paralyzed man and said,
"Stand up, pick up your mat, and go home!" (Mark 2:10-11)*

IN THE LATE 1800S AND EARLY 1900S, after the industrialization and urbanization of North America had manifested both its many benefits and its many devastations, several Protestant movements began to emphasize what we now call the "social gospel." The movement sought to address the social problems and physical needs of those who were suffering from poverty, exploitation, poor living conditions, insufficient health and welfare services, and more. Many Christians saw biblical prophecies and Jesus' commands to care for the poor and oppressed as inescapable responsibilities. They focused on meeting material and physical needs.

By and large, the evangelical response to the social gospel emphasized spiritual salvation over all other concerns. After all, the reasoning went, how is it helpful to feed and clothe people who are on their way to hell? So Christians developed false tensions and split the gospel into fragments. We can be grateful for those who saw the absurdity of both extremes, defied the trend, and maintained a holistic message of the Kingdom. Their numbers are increasing today, and old divisions are fading away.

That's as it should be. Jesus demonstrated God's compassion for both immediate and eternal needs, often in the same event. He healed a cripple and forgave him of his sins. He fed multitudes and preached about the bread from heaven. He washed dirty feet and taught eternal truths. He urged his followers to feed the hungry, visit those in prison, clothe the naked, heal the sick, raise the dead, cast out demons, preach repentance, and declare the good news of the Kingdom. He offered a whole message to the whole person—spirit, mind, emotions, body, everything.

May we never do less. The gospel cannot be unraveled or broken into pieces. God's compassion is demonstrated through ministries of mercy and his ultimate purposes through the message of salvation. We are called to represent him as fully as we can to a world that needs to see him in his fullness.

Jesus, your mercies take many forms, and I will never reflect them completely. But may I never divide them either. Pour out your compassion through me in every way you choose. Let me demonstrate your Kingdom wholly. Amen.

Colossians 3:12-15

Ambassadors of the Kingdom

*Since God chose you to be the holy people he loves, you must
clothe yourselves with tenderhearted mercy, kindness,
humility, gentleness, and patience. (Colossians 3:12)*

IT WAS SAID OF GEORGE MÜLLER, who built and maintained orphanages in nineteenth-century England by faith and remarkable answers to prayer, that hearing him pray was like overhearing a conversation between intimate friends. Müller's familiarity with God not only came through in his prayers; his attitude gave people glimpses of heaven. He was so saturated in his conversations with God that God's character and presence shone through.

The people around you need a taste of heaven. This should come as no surprise; they are immersed in a fallen world day after day, and many don't even know there's a promise of something better. While many Christians are focused on what God wants them to do—an important question, to be sure—a more important focus is on what God wants us to be. Does he want us to behave like those around us or be different? Fit the context or stand out from it? Speak words that are expected or offer words of hope?

It is extremely important to remember that you are in this world as a representative of something beyond it. Your passport is issued by another realm. You carry its papers. As an ambassador of the culture of God's Kingdom, you exude hope, kindness, mercy, gentleness, patience, and several other positive attributes the people around you don't expect. Many are used to hearing Christians speak of God's displeasure, disappointment, and disagreement with the ways of the world. But these people are already aware of their brokenness. What they need is a message of hope and restoration. If you have immersed yourself in the presence of God and the ways of his Kingdom, that's exactly what you will give them.

Live in such a way that people who spend time with you feel as if they have encountered another realm, a place of love, joy, and hope. Saturate yourself in God's presence, and let it flow from you. Your calling to "do" will come sooner or later. Your calling to "be" is for today.

Holy Spirit, fill me with your presence. May I sense your sweetness and personality not only in our quiet conversations but even in the busyness of my daily affairs. Let me soak up your nature like a sponge and, when squeezed, release it freely to others. Amen.

Clothed in Love

*Above all, clothe yourselves with love, which binds us
all together in perfect harmony. (Colossians 3:14)*

DIETRICH BONHOEFFER WROTE IN *Life Together* that the community of Christian believers is first and foremost a "community of love"—that our singular focus on Jesus produces a sort of spiritual chemistry that binds us together and cultivates the attributes of our Lord, with love at the center. That kind of bond is clearly what Jesus had in mind when he told his followers that they would be known by their love (John 13:35). If followers of Jesus are known primarily for something else, we have a problem. The defining nature of our fellowship was always meant to be the love of the Father, Son, and Spirit in our midst.

The fact that Christians are known for so many other things does, in fact, present a problem, but it is not an insurmountable one. It simply requires some shifts in focus—away from each other's faults and onto each other's value; away from our own fulfillment and onto the fulfillment of those around us; away from self and onto Christ. These are not easy shifts, but neither are they complicated. They will require a different perspective, a different mind-set, a different motivation from within. Or as Paul wrote, a different set of clothes.

"Above all," Paul emphasized, we should take care to clothe ourselves in Jesus. We may think of this as important primarily in our relationship with those who do not yet believe, but Scripture's focus is on representing him within the fellowship. Not only is our unity as believers at stake; so is our reputation in this world. Jesus made that clear.

Whatever that looks like for you practically—radical forgiveness (verse 13) or uncommon peace (verse 15)—make it happen. Prioritize it. But don't just play a role; the way to become like Jesus is to immerse yourself in his presence. Soak in his words. Have lengthy conversations with the Father. As with two friends who have spent so much time together that they take on each other's characteristics, let yourself be influenced by his nature. Let his love for people fill you to overflowing.

Jesus, you are the center of my life and the life of every other believer—whether we treat you that way or not. May our focus on you and our experience of your love increase. Let us become known for our love, just as you promised. Amen.

Be Strong

Be strong and courageous! Do not be afraid or discouraged.
For the LORD your God is with you wherever you go. (Joshua 1:9)

THE SEPARATISTS IN CHRISTIAN HISTORY—those who have withdrawn from the world or from the larger body of Christ to live out their own interpretations of faith unhindered—have often added a needed perspective to the Christian community. In many cases, their motives have been inspired. But some formed their own communities or movements out of fear. They feared being influenced by the world, being controlled by the doctrines and policies of others, and losing their focus on the realm of the Spirit. They did not withdraw to devote themselves; they retreated to save themselves.

Fear is an unnecessary attitude in the minds and hearts of believers—and usually a harmful one. Yes, our fallen world is full of obstacles to true faith and a relationship with God, and some of those obstacles can be rather intimidating. Opponents are sometimes aggressive and insulting. But too many Christians withdraw because they fear for their reputation, want to avoid conflict, or hate the stigma that comes with being a believer of an ancient faith. Many do not have the assurance that they can defend what they believe or whether what they believe is even defendable. Their faith may or may not be secure. Their confidence clearly isn't.

The good news is that you don't have to be a bold extrovert to influence the world with your faith. You can go into your daily routines and interactions with the quiet confidence of your true identity, carrying the atmosphere of the Kingdom within you and drawing people into awareness and eventual conversations. But you can't do that from seclusion. You have to go out.

Never fear the giants in the land. You are called to take territory for God's Kingdom. That territory is a Promised Land given by someone who does not fail to keep his word. Trust in him. Go forward. You may not have all the arguments, but you have truth. And God will defend you in it.

Lord, adversaries can be brutal to believers, and sometimes I'd rather avoid them. But you have promised victory. May I walk in it confidently and consistently wherever I go. May I step into every inch of your promises. Amen.

Be Focused

When you see the Levitical priests carrying the Ark of the Covenant of
the LORD your God, move out from your positions and follow them.
(Joshua 3:3)

GOD CHARGED JOSHUA AND ISRAEL with the monumental task of taking possession of the Promised Land and told them to be strong and courageous about it. Though he gave them ample reason for confidence, he did not urge them to run off into it haphazardly. He prepared them and gave them strategies. And the first strategy was to focus on his presence—at that time, on the Ark of the Lord carried by the priests—as their cue for moving forward. They were to prioritize worship, his presence, and his leading. They were to focus first and foremost on him.

That's true of any endeavor in life. Centuries later, Jehoshaphat was surrounded by hostile armies and turned to God for help. God spoke through a prophet, assuring the people of Judah of deliverance. Jehoshaphat then appointed worshipers to lead the army into battle. The songs of praise led to confusion of the enemy and an unusually easy victory (2 Chronicles 20). You'll find that in whatever you do, it will go better when your foundation is worship and your method involves sensitivity to the Spirit's leading. A focus on life will result in futility; a focus on God will result in fruitfulness in life. The Ark of his presence should always precede everything you do.

As you seek to fulfill your calling as salt and light in this world, remember to keep your focus not on the world, not on your life, but on the presence of God. That will mean prioritizing worship, but it will also mean watching him for cues on where and when to proceed. Whatever he is doing and wherever he is moving, get in on it. That doesn't mean you should pick up and move to wherever the latest revival is breaking out (though God may direct some to do that). Instead, trust that he is working around you right now. Ask him for eyes to see where and then ways to meet him there. Let your focus on him empower you and guide you wherever you go.

Lord, may I never lose sight of you. Compared to you, the giants in my life are tiny. My worship reminds me of your power and your purposes. Give me eyes to see where you are opening hearts, minds, and circumstances, and the sensitivity to join you there. Amen.

Be Single-Minded

*Purify yourselves, for tomorrow the LORD will do
great wonders among you. (Joshua 3:5)*

GOD HAD AN ASSIGNMENT FOR HIS PEOPLE. He was about to fulfill a long-ago promise for them, and from his many assurances in the previous years, it was clear that he would be going before them to prepare the way, beside them to give them strength, and behind them to keep them from failing. But there were conditions: They had to go forward in faith, follow his instructions, and maintain their devotion to him. These were hardly onerous burdens; he laid it all out for them. Their biggest obstacles were themselves. He would take care of the rest.

But in order for them to overcome their own insecurities and misperceptions, they would have to purify themselves. God would do wonders among them but only if they could see clearly. He did not demand perfection, only purity—singleness of heart, undivided loyalties, a sense of being set apart for his purposes. They would never be able to enter the Promised Land independently of the Promiser; they would never fail to enter it with him. He was working out his purposes in a people set apart to himself.

That's a powerful illustration of how God is working in his people today. He has called you on an amazing adventure in the building of his promised Kingdom, but you can only enter into it by faithfulness to the Promiser. Divided loyalties will keep you in defeat and undermine your fruitfulness. Single-minded allegiance to him—a life dedicated to his purposes and his ways—will propel you into the fullness you've always longed for. It will be no easier for you than it was for the Israelites, but you are assured of his presence and power. He goes before you to open doors, make pathways straight, and give you the courage and persistence to overcome. You will not be left on the wrong side of the Jordan. The promises of the Kingdom are given to you, for you, and through you.

Lord, I know some of the things you have called me to do. Others look too great or are too distant to be clear. In everything, give me faith, courage, and persistence. May my heart be firmly fixed on your purposes and your ways. Amen.

Be Ready

It was the harvest season, and the Jordan was overflowing its banks.
(Joshua 3:15)

IF YOU TELL THE PEOPLE AROUND YOU that your mission in life is to be salt and light in the world, some may be offended. They might assume you see them as targets, or consider yourself superior, or are trying to change their beliefs. They may not understand that you are only interested in representing your Father, seeking to overcome the evil in this world with his love, giving yourself to the ways of his Kingdom rather than the ways of self, and living in a spirit that openheartedly invites others into his purposes, but never against their will. They may have to be convinced that you love and value them for who they are, regardless of what they believe—which, if you are really reflecting the heart of your Father, you do. You may have some considerable barriers to cross.

That's why the illustration of Joshua and the Israelites crossing the Jordan River is so appropriate to our mission in life. The Jordan, then and now, is hardly an intimidating obstacle most times of year. But the Israelites approached its banks at harvest time, which was flood stage. The waters swelled, and crossing would be difficult. God's people needed him to act on their behalf if all of them were to make it across safely.

Culturally speaking, we live in a "flood stage" of boundaries between Christian and non-Christian perspectives. Crossing them may seem impossible. Perhaps you've even given up. But God's message through Joshua is that flood stage is the perfect time for him to harvest. Miracles happen when we allow him to precede us and then follow where he leads. He is a master of making a way where there is no way, of overcoming barriers and giants and fears. He wants us to be ready even in the most unlikely times.

So be ready. Scan your horizon for impossible barriers and watch for God to part them. When he does, move forward—wisely, respectfully, even subtly at times. Waters subside for those who are willing to wade into them by faith.

Lord, you are the master of miracles in my life. May I never be unprepared for them. Open my heart to where you are working, and give grace to my steps. Make a way for me through the waters that flow against your Kingdom. Amen.

Be Mindful

What do these stones mean? (Joshua 4:6)

GOD HAD JUST ACCOMPLISHED something amazing—he parted waters *again*—and his first command was for Joshua and the leaders of Israel to create a memorial. This miraculous event was not to be forgotten; it was to be a landmark in the nation's history and a constant reminder to the Israelites of the kind of God they served. The significance of these stones was not just to provoke gratitude or to prompt praise, though those responses were certainly important. More so, God knew that the only way Israel could move forward in faith was if its people remembered how he had supported them in the past. Their history was a key to their future. On top of the commands Moses had written and long-ago stories of deliverance, they were to remember that after forty years of wandering in a forbidding wilderness, God had proven he was with them the entire way. That journey toward the Promised Land would be vital information to have in the days, years, and centuries to come.

Your history with God is vital information for your future too. You have likely experienced times when you felt powerless and purposeless and wondered if he was still answering your prayers. Your memories may fail you, but your memorials—if you have written things down or found another way of preserving his work in your life—will encourage you. If you have any history with God at all, you know he has answered prayers, helped you navigate difficult situations, and delivered you from trouble. He has not given you a life of ease, but he has given you his presence and promises. You have experienced them, whether you remember them easily or not.

Find some way of remembering them. You cannot go into your world with the expectation of fruitfulness if you've forgotten how he has made you fruitful in the past. You will not anticipate new victories if old ones have escaped your memory. Make a prayer journal, review your successes, begin building stones. They will become lasting testimonies that mean everything to you in adventures and battles to come.

Lord, forgive me for forgetting all the ways you have blessed, delivered, fulfilled, guided, and prospered me. Bring them to mind, and help me reconstruct your history of faithfulness. May my memorials of your work in my past propel me into my future with faith. Amen.

Be Complete

*The LORD said to Joshua, "Today I have rolled away
the shame of your slavery in Egypt." (Joshua 5:9)*

ONE OF MARTIN LUTHER'S GREAT personal revelations was that he had spent years trying to earn something that had already been granted to him. He was striving to obtain God's favor rather than stepping into the favor Jesus had already earned on his behalf. He had been seeking a position of righteousness rather than living in the righteous position he already had. God had impressed upon him the lasting promises of the gospel of grace in place of the futility of a gospel of works.

Before the Israelites continued into the Promised Land, God gave them a moment to renew the covenant that had been given to their ancestors. This new circumcision was loaded with meanings, one of which was to remind them that they were heirs of a long-ago promise, not conquerors of new land. They would be stepping into an inheritance, not to earn anything but to simply receive it. As God's people, they were not going to be striving for status; they would merely be living out their position.

This is vital for you to remember in your mission in life and relationship with the world around you. If you see yourself on a journey toward stepping out of past shame and striving to become somebody in God's Kingdom, you will miss what has already been given to you and spend years in frustration. As a beloved child of the King, currently in good standing by the righteousness of Jesus, you already are somebody. He has rolled away your shame. You are not under contractual labor to build the Kingdom; you are sent out to inherit it. You live from a place of victory, not a place of struggle—even when the battle rages.

God will give you opportunities to remember the covenant you have entered into and to recommit to it, just as he did with Israel at Gilgal after they crossed the Jordan. Your Jericho battle may be coming, but the family inheritance is sure. Your calling is not to ask for what he has given but to step into it by faith.

Lord, may I never live from a place of poverty, unaware of the blessings you have already given me. I want to step fully into the inheritance you have provided. Let my heart receive your provision completely. Amen.

Be Committed

Take off your sandals, for the place where you are standing is holy.
(Joshua 5:15)

JOSHUA HAD A MYSTIFYING EXPERIENCE with a sword-bearing warrior. The two encountered each other in the plains near Jericho, and Joshua wanted to know if the warrior was for the Israelites or their adversaries. "Neither," the man said. He had not come to take the side of human beings but to call human beings to his side as the commander of the Lord's army. Joshua needed to make a decision between his agenda and God's.

That was not a difficult decision for Joshua; he had committed himself to the Lord and sought him zealously for years. Even so, the choice needed to be made. God is the reference point for our battles, not the other way around. Will we look at his Kingdom through the lens of our own agendas or look at our agendas through the lens of his Kingdom? That momentous question goes a long way toward determining whether we fulfill our purpose in life.

In one sense, God is on your side. Scripture says so—Psalm 124:1-2 asks what would have happened if the Lord had not been on Israel's side, and in Romans 8:31, Paul wonders who could possibly be against us if God is for us. But in an ultimate sense, the only way to move toward a life of fruitfulness is to realize that we are on God's side—and that position is nonnegotiable. While many set their own agenda and try to call God into it, he has set his agenda and called us into it instead. That's how the covenant works. He has lavished an extravagant inheritance on us, but we must step into it on his terms.

As you proceed, remember you are walking on holy ground. You have been set apart for his purposes, so wherever you step is with feet that belong to him and are ordained to take territory. The good news is that the commander of the Lord's army goes before you in whatever battles you are called to fight. If you bow before him, as Joshua did, you are on the side that wins.

Lord, spiritual battles abound—not against flesh and blood, but certainly against evil agendas and false ideas. I commit to your purposes in all of them. Other people may ask you to serve their goals; I ask only to serve yours. Go before me in strength, and I will follow. Amen.

Be Flexible

When you hear the priests give one long blast on the rams' horns,
have all the people shout as loud as they can. Then the walls of the
town will collapse, and the people can charge straight into the town.
(Joshua 6:5)

JESUS SENT HIS FOLLOWERS OUT with a message, but he did not confine them to a method. The earliest apostles stayed in Jerusalem to teach the message of Jesus—until they were driven out by persecution or the Spirit's leading. Paul began his ministry by going to synagogues first and then branching out into Gentile populations, but later went directly to public arenas and general audiences to get his message out. Some Christians have traveled far and wide while others have stayed home. Some have been bold evangelists and others quiet examples. Some have emphasized words of truth in their ministry while others have focused on dramatic healings, deliverance, or works of compassion. And in all the diverse approaches, we find ourselves wondering: Which way is right?

They all are. Jesus had demonstrated the works of the Kingdom throughout his ministry, but his Spirit equipped each believer differently—and even the same believers differently at various times in their lives. The flexibility of method within the message may bother some people who look for formulas and strategies, but while human beings tend to rely on principles, God simply looks for followers. He wants us to adapt to situations as he leads—even when we don't understand why he leads the way he does.

That was the case for Joshua and the Israelites as they entered the Promised Land. The first battle at Jericho was a one-time leading, and if Joshua had tried the same approach at subsequent battles, it probably would not have worked. If we want to influence our world, we will have to rely not on techniques but on spiritual direction—moment by moment, situation by situation, person by person. The God of amazing victories will give us his favor if we give him our attention and follow where he leads.

Holy Spirit, I know your direction will not always make sense to me, and I know it will rarely develop into a pattern to follow. Make me sensitive to your promptings, turns, and strategies. Lead me moment by moment. Break down the walls that keep people captive. Amen.

Be Smart

*Israel has sinned and broken my covenant! They have stolen some
of the things that I commanded must be set apart for me. . . .
That is why the Israelites are running from their enemies in defeat.*
(Joshua 7:11-12)

THE ISRAELITES HAD TASTED SUCCESS. They were entering into the promise given to their ancestors long ago. All the land lay in front of them, and they finally seemed to be convinced that God would give it to them. But then . . . defeat. A humiliating loss at Ai on the heels of an exhilarating victory at Jericho. How could God have abandoned them so quickly? How could he be so fickle?

The problem was not with God, of course. It was with the Israelites—only one family among them, actually. Achan had taken some plunder at Jericho, which might have been allowed in later victories but was meant for destruction there. He had violated an explicit command given by God, and all of Israel paid the price.

We have to be very careful about tying problems to disobedience because our experience and our theology tell us that hardship happens for all sorts of reasons. After all, Jesus and the apostles experienced quite a bit of adversity and losses from no fault of their own. Even so, God is very clear in this story that even if defeat is not always the result of sin, sin will result in defeat. Disobedience undermines his intended blessings.

What's the solution? If we want to step into the promises God has for us—if we want to win victories in earthly and spiritual realms and change the world—we will have to distance ourselves from offensive ways. We will need to separate ourselves from corruption, not because of some legal requirement but because we are called to carry the nature of our God. We will need to walk in sync with the Spirit.

Grace will always cover your sin; there is no condemnation for those in Christ (Romans 8:1). But there is still a need for preparation and maturity if you want to walk in your destiny. Your blessings are freely given; your experience of them comes only by following God faithfully.

Lord, purify my heart. Prepare me for your richest blessings. May my mind be so filled with your promise that no other temptation moves me. Amen.

Be Careful

They did not consult the LORD. Then Joshua made
a peace treaty with them. (Joshua 9:14-15)

THE NIGHT BEFORE HIS CRUCIFIXION, Jesus told the Father he had completed the work he had been sent to do (John 17:4). The flip side of this statement implies that he did *not* do what he had not been sent to do. He did not take on responsibilities that had not been given to him; he did not say yes to every request; and he did not align himself with people who were not aligned with his mission. Instead, he remained focused on the specific assignment God had given him.

Joshua made the mistake of binding himself to a promise that he should not have made and with people he should not have partnered with. We can hardly fault him for doing so; we have done the same thing on many occasions. Like him, we default to our own best judgment rather than consulting with God and listening for his guidance. Like Joshua, we trust our eyes and not the leading of the Spirit. And like him, even with the best intentions, we end up in relationships, commitments, jobs, and other preoccupations that were not part of our calling.

We cannot afford to let a false sense of obligation, faith in our own common sense, or careless agreements divert us from our God-given assignments if we want to live out the purposes he has for us. He expects us to honor our commitments even if they are misguided, and his grace will cover our mistakes. We are not punished or dismissed from his plans; Joshua and Israel remained in the Promised Land after their blunder. But they lost something in the process, and we will too. Unholy alliances will limit our opportunities to serve and be fruitful.

Be careful about your partnerships, commitments, debts, and promises. Other people may have a strong idea of what you should do, but you are under no obligation to follow their lead. Your assignment, like that of Jesus, and of Joshua before him, is to do what God has given you to do—to live with a heart that senses his direction and with feet willing to follow it. Ask, listen, and bind yourself only to his ways.

Lord, protect me from unholy alliances; guide me into strategic relationships and opportunities; and let me live freely. Tune my heart to your voice alone. Amen.

A Climate of Love

"You must love the LORD your God with all your heart, all your soul,
and all your mind." This is the first and greatest commandment.
(Matthew 22:37-38)

HISTORY IS FULL OF ZEALOUS BELIEVERS who tried to teach the gospel of truth without imparting a spirit of love. This approach does not lead to a genuine relationship with God; it results only in religious principles. The heart of the Kingdom is inseparable from the heart of its King. To know him is to love him and be loved. To enter into his life is to enter into an environment of overwhelming affection and intimacy. No one knows the Father in truth who does not also know him in love. Love is the climate of his Kingdom.

That's why Jesus pointed to Deuteronomy 6:5 as the greatest commandment. While other religions emphasize submission to God or knowledge of truth, Jesus teaches us first and foremost about the relationship we have embraced. It is a relationship of deep intimacy, openness, affection, and acceptance. In his presence, we stand completely exposed before him and are embraced anyway. We are completely vulnerable yet welcomed unconditionally.

Many Christians have succeeded at nearly every point of their discipleship except this one—which is to say, they have discovered the tangents but missed the core. Jesus calls us back to the center. As recipients of the Father's love, we cast our entire selves—heart, soul, body, everything—into our relationship with him. We take whatever power he gives us and spend it loving him well.

Unless we learn to live in this environment of love, we cannot experience the fullness of our calling. We never need to fear giving more than we receive in this relationship; God's supply is infinite for those who expend themselves on him. But pouring ourselves out is essential. It is a response to his goodness and a reflection of his nature. We love because he loves. And in this climate, both we and the world around us flourish.

Father, my love falls short of yours, but you call me anyway into this beautiful culture of selfless affection. Expand my heart; increase my capacity for love; embrace me as your own. I pour myself out for you. Amen.

Love In, Love Out

A second is equally important: "Love your neighbor as yourself."
(Matthew 22:39)

PLAGUES IN THE LATE SECOND CENTURY and mid-third century decimated much of the population in many areas of the Roman Empire. Nearly a third of the people in some regions died, and most survivors did whatever they could to save themselves. Many fled the cities for refuge in the countryside, where the disease spread more slowly. But Christians were known for another approach. Many believers remained to care for the sick, not only in their own families but also among the pagans. At the risk of their own lives, believers demonstrated love in ways that astounded observers and turned many to Christ.

How were they able to love so selflessly? They had learned how to be loved. They were secure in their relationship with God and trusted him to care for their souls, whether their bodies survived or not. They loved because they had basked in the greater love of their Father.

In our desire to be selfless, we often forget how vital it is to receive love. But Jesus' quote of the greatest commandments reminds us that we are to love our neighbors *as we love ourselves.* That means if we don't love ourselves—if we don't see ourselves as God sees us, with eyes of perfect affection—we cannot give that kind of love to our neighbors. If we receive love incompletely and then try to love our neighbors in the same way, we fall short of their need. No, our mission is to receive the love of God in all its fullness and then impart it—in all its fullness.

It may feel selfish to bask in the Father's love, but this is exactly what the world needs. It may also feel unrealistic. Most of us have a much easier time believing in God's love for others than in his love for us personally. But if it is to be real for our neighbors, it must be real for us. To freely give, we must have already freely received (Matthew 10:8). The key to loving well is knowing how loved we are.

Holy Spirit, fill my heart with divine love. Saturate my soul in your adoring presence. Show me your affection and teach me to show it to others. Amen.

Truly New

*The Holy Spirit produces this kind of fruit in our lives: love, joy, peace,
patience, kindness, goodness, faithfulness, gentleness, and self-control.*
(Galatians 5:22)

BARTOLOMÉ DE LAS CASAS WAS a Spanish historian in the sixteenth century who chronicled some of the earliest experiences of Spanish settlers of the New World. His description of the indigenous people found on the Caribbean island of Hispaniola is often used as an object lesson in history courses: "Of all the infinite universe of humanity, these people are the most guileless, the most devoid of wickedness and duplicity, the most obedient and faithful to their native masters and to the Spanish Christians whom they serve. They are by nature the most humble, patient, and peaceable, holding no grudges, free from embroilments, neither excitable nor quarrelsome . . . the most devoid of rancors, hatreds, or desire for vengeance of any people in the world."[9]

Stories like this are not unusual. Indigenous people who had never heard the gospel were often portrayed as being more kind and content than the "Christians" who conquered or colonized them. This isn't always the case, of course; plenty of pre-Christian cultures were contentious, violent, fractured, and depraved. But if we're looking for evidence that Christian societies are inevitably godlier than those that are non-Christian, we may be disappointed. And in modern conversations about the virtues of Christianity, we may get lumped in with transgressors of any era.

It's easy for us to dismiss those transgressors as nominal Christians who were not really living by faith but were simply power-hungry, fallen humans who never had any real experience with the Spirit. That may or may not be true. What is true, however, is that the Christian gospel either transforms the human heart from within or makes matters worse; it either satisfies or frustrates, it brings either contentment or anger, depending on the response and faith of the believer. It can be a matter of empty words or full hearts. And the watching world can't always discern the differences.

That makes it all the more important to live with a transformed nature. People are hungry for evidence of real change but cynical about the possibility. You are called to be a demonstration of its reality—to be the difference the world needs to see.

*Lord, the world is much too full of self-proclaimed Christians with unchanged hearts.
May I never fall into that pattern. Empower me by your Spirit to defy expectations and
live with your nature always. Amen.*

A Season of Opportunity

We should live in this evil world with wisdom, righteousness,
and devotion to God. (Titus 2:12)

EARLY IN THE SPANISH CONQUEST of the New World, the people of the Caribbean were inquisitive and open to the gospel. Many, in fact, believed—until the conquerors behaved "like ravening beasts, killing, terrorizing, afflicting, torturing, and destroying the native peoples, doing all this with the strangest and most varied new methods of cruelty, never seen or heard of before."[10] The report of Bartolomé de las Casas estimated that a population of about three million was reduced to just two hundred through violence and disease. The "angels" who descended on the islands—how the natives first perceived the Spaniards—were not angelic at all, and the gospel got lost in the devastation.

That is an extreme case of how people who claim to be Christian can taint the Christian message. The example is hardly typical, but it does illustrate two important truths: (1) Christians have a remarkable opportunity to demonstrate the character of God to people who do not know him; and (2) a false representation of God's character makes future attempts at portraying him accurately more difficult. The familiar saying, "You never have a second chance to make a first impression" applies to God and his people too. God can overcome any obstacle, and his Spirit can change any heart, but how we first represent him to others makes a difference.

We are not responsible for the squandered opportunities of past generations. Neither are we responsible for everyone today who claims to represent Christ. But we are responsible for the opportunities in front of us in this generation—not only to take advantage of them ourselves, but to encourage other believers to do so too. Ultimately, the responsibility for changed hearts is on the Spirit of God, who alone can draw human beings to Jesus. But to the degree that we let him change us, we become his illustrations, a divine sampling of grace to a world that needs it.

Holy Spirit, I will always be an imperfect case study in the power of your grace. But let me be a fruitful one. Let many see your power in me. Amen.

Stronger than the Storms

*Of course, your former friends are surprised when you no longer
plunge into the flood of wild and destructive things they do.
So they slander you. (1 Peter 4:4)*

YOU ARE PROBABLY AWARE THAT atrocities committed hundreds of years ago by people claiming to be Christians will be used against you. Their behavior wasn't Jesus' fault and it isn't yours, but blame will be assigned anyway. "Look at what the Crusaders did. Look at what those who carried out the Spanish Inquisition did. Look at what merchants and mercenaries exploring the New World did." And so on. Rarely will a skeptic remind you of all the hospitals, schools, social programs, activist movements, crisis interventions, relief work, linguistic and literary advances, and peace efforts Christians have established throughout history as they followed the teachings of Jesus. No, skeptics will magnify the flaws and counterfeits, and color your entire faith with them.

That is not to say that genuine Christians have not participated in evil or misguided agendas. When the church today admits that fact and repents for the sins of the past, we do a good thing. Confession demonstrates humility and a commitment to truth. But many believers are so alarmed at how we are portrayed that they bend their beliefs and commitments to please people, which can't be done, at least not completely. Jesus will always be a stumbling block, critics will always portray Christians negatively, and even the good things we do will be painted as hypocritical or superficial. For true seekers, our humility and genuineness will make a difference; for confirmed skeptics, it will never be enough. Jesus never tried to please everyone, and neither should we.

Your job is not only to defy the caricatures and be a contrary example; it's to stand firm even when your example is distorted, maligned, and rejected. Be sensitive and responsive, but do not be moved. Acknowledge the misrepresentations without letting them change you. The world actually longs to see people live with conviction, even when they slander those who do. Your life is anchored in God's perfect realm, so remain strong through the storms in this one.

Jesus, you were never acceptable to everyone, yet you remained perfectly committed to truth and love in the face of opposition. You are my model, my example, and my strength. Sustain me in the storms and draw many to you through my convictions. Amen.

Wisdom and Discretion

*When Arioch, the commander of the king's guard, came to kill
them, Daniel handled the situation with wisdom and discretion.*
(Daniel 2:14)

MILLIONS OF JEWISH AND CHRISTIAN believers over the centuries have been displaced from their homelands and brought to foreign countries in which they are the minority and the surrounding culture is indifferent to or even opposes their faith. We can find several examples throughout the Bible of how the people of God have navigated that experience—but no single approach. That's because situations, personalities, and the purposes of God may differ from place to place and time to time. Just as the descendants of the patriarchs had an appointed time as slaves in Egypt and an appointed time to be delivered, so might we need to know how to live under oppression, or in cooperation with, or in opposition to others. God gives us no formulas, only himself and his leadership. Wherever we are, we can follow his direction and timing.

Daniel and his friends did that as captives in Babylon, where Jewish beliefs were marginalized and pagan kings ruled. And when one of those kings threatened the lives of all his advisers, including his Jewish servants, Daniel responded with wisdom and discretion. He knew how to honor hostile authorities while maintaining his religious distinctives. He offered allegiance and duty where it was due, holding his allegiance and duty to God higher. He became a spiritual diplomat between the absolutes of God's Kingdom and the dictates of earthly rulers. He let God teach him how to live in a foreign land.

Many of us will find ourselves in the same position, even when the "foreign land" is our own country and its history is predominantly Christian. In the multiplicity of today's cultures, our beliefs may often be in the minority, and those with opposing beliefs may hold more earthly power. While the response of many is to complain, lament, or feel victimized, we know a better way—to respond with wisdom and discretion, just as Daniel did, honoring authorities, fulfilling our duties, and holding God higher in our hearts. Daniel was no victim; he influenced kings with the reality of a greater Kingdom. We can too.

Lord, give me supernatural wisdom and the sensitivity to live with discretion in an often-hostile environment. May my integrity, loyalty, and discernment demonstrate the reality of your Kingdom and influence all who know me. Amen.

Seek Revelation

The king said to Daniel, "Truly, your God is the greatest of gods,
the Lord over kings, a revealer of mysteries, for you have been
able to reveal this secret." (Daniel 2:47)

GEORGE WASHINGTON CARVER PRAYED each morning that God would reveal to him the secrets of the peanut and other plants, flowers, soils, and weeds. Why? So he might help "put more food in the bellies of the hungry, more clothing on the backs of the naked, and better shelter over the heads of the homeless."[11] He believed these things would never be known unless God revealed the mysteries of his creation. God honored Carver's request by showing him hundreds of unusual uses for the peanut and other crops that changed the face of agriculture in a troubling time. God gave insight in order to demonstrate his goodness to this world.

That's one example of what happens when God's people open their hearts to his wisdom. Daniel sought God through prayer in a time of crisis, and God's answers led to many lives being spared and the Babylonian king being drawn toward him. Likewise, while Joseph was imprisoned in Egypt, he trusted God to interpret Pharaoh's dreams and by doing so prepared both Egyptians and Israelites for a devastating famine. The pattern is clear: When humanity is in trouble, God has solutions, and he often reveals them through his people.

Seek that kind of revelation—not the revelation of some new truth, but the revelation of what God is doing in the moment and how he is applying his Word to the situations going on around you. Offer divine solutions to earthly problems. Spend enough face time with God that you can sense what he is doing, receive inspiration from him, and see how he wants to meet the needs of the world and display his goodness. Let go of limiting thoughts like *God only blesses the godly*. Follow the example of Daniel, who blessed a hostile, pagan king with wisdom from above. Bless the "foreign land" you live in, wherever it is and however hostile it may be. Ask God what he wants you to offer the world, and give it freely.

Lord, there is no problem on earth that you do not already have a solution for. Make me a catalyst for bringing answers into real lives and circumstances. Let my relationship with you bless society in tangible, concrete ways. Amen.

Strategic Moments

*Who knows if perhaps you were made queen for
just such a time as this? (Esther 4:14)*

"IF I HAD A HUNDRED LIVES, I would give them all to . . ." This quote has been said or written by numerous people who felt that they had found their true calling: missionaries who gave their all for the country of their service, pastors who loved the church or city where they ministered, creative or skilled workers who dedicated themselves to one activity their entire lives. The same sentiment could apply to people who devote themselves to a cause or to people who work to understand and make the most of their present times. In fact, understanding your time is a critical part of serving God. You were not born into this world randomly. God chose the seasons of your life and the people and places you intersect with. Whatever time you were born, you were born for "such a time as this."

That famous line from the book of Esther fit the critical timing of Esther's position as queen and as an undisclosed Jew in Persia, where a plot against the Jews had developed. As queen, she had the king's ear—*if* he was open to listening. It was a scary moment but also a strategic one to save God's people. She recognized the importance of her position in this foreign land when her foreignness put her at the intersection of the Jews and a dangerous Persian policy. Though Esther never mentioned God or insisted on following the ways of her people like Daniel did, she submitted herself to the historical moment arranged by the divine hand.

To serve God effectively, you will need to live with that perspective too. Your days may not look very strategic most of the time, but you don't see the whole picture. You can trust the times and places God has given you, the gifts and interests he has blessed you with, and the lives your journey connects you with. You may have to read between the lines of your life to see him at times, just as we have to do with the book of Esther, but he is there. Use the influence you have, wherever you have it, whenever you can.

Lord, I have been born into a strategic time, even when I don't understand the strategy at work. Give me eyes to see, and move me into places of influence at the proper time. May I take full advantage of the critical moments of my life. Amen.

A Time for Opposition

My people and I have been sold to those who would kill, slaughter,
and annihilate us. . . . This wicked Haman is our adversary
and our enemy. (Esther 7:4, 6)

DIETRICH BONHOEFFER WAS an ardent critic of the Nazi party and of its leader from the earliest days of the regime. His homeland had become foreign to him as Nazis imposed their own leadership on the church—sometimes with cooperation from within—and many citizens of the nation slipped into Führer-worship despite his warnings. At a time when huge segments of the church were seduced, Scripture was being ripped apart (with some Christians advocating for the removal of the Old Testament), and God's chosen people were being massacred, the biblical principle of honoring authority took a back seat to resistance. There are times when the salt and light of this world need to be vocal in standing against its evils.

We see hints of this in Scripture: Esther exposing Haman's plot, which led to his execution; the judges of Israel rising up against their overlords (Judges 3:12-30; 4:4-24; and 7:8-25); and David's resistance against Goliath and the Philistines (1 Samuel 17). Most of the time, God has his people comply with earthly authorities as far as possible and contradict them respectfully when needed (Acts 4:19-20). But when his purposes are being opposed, he raises up leaders in defiance and urges his people to overcome evil. He does not insist that we always be passive in the face of injustice. In fact, he urges us to stand for truth and align ourselves with what is right. Sometimes that puts us at the center of conflict.

Don't be afraid to go there. Don't seek it out; many Christians are far too hungry for a fight. But be prepared to resist the ways of this world. Recognize the times, the purposes of God, and the role he wants you to have. You are called to represent his voice and his nature, and you will sometimes find yourself in a position to expose the works of darkness or restrain the tides of culture. Do it honorably and respectfully. Stand strong for justice, truth, and life.

Lord, your Word tells me to respect human authority but also gives examples of standing against it when necessary. Give me discernment to recognize which response is appropriate to each occasion. In the discourses of this world, may my position always reflect yours. Amen.

His Great Compassion

*Nineveh has more than 120,000 people living in spiritual
darkness, not to mention all the animals. Shouldn't
I feel sorry for such a great city? (Jonah 4:11)*

GOD TOLD JONAH TO PREACH TO NINEVEH, and after a failed attempt to escape his instruction, Jonah did what he was called to do. It was a successful mission. The Assyrian city, known in Israel for its brutality, repented and put an end to its evil ways. While most people enjoy their success, Jonah seethed over it. He hadn't wanted God to show mercy to the Assyrians, which is one of the reasons he fled in the first place. Now the city was spared from the judgment he had preached, and Jonah was angry.

After an object lesson with a vine and a worm, God made his point with the prophet. He suggested that Jonah's compassion for a plant was greater than his compassion for people—and that as God, he had every right to show compassion for his creation. The last line of the book reflects its overarching theme: God is concerned even for those who rebel against him, and he wants his people to have the same kind of concern. He is driven by compassion and expects us to align our hearts with his.

You will likely never find yourself in the same situation as Jonah—called to go into the city of an extremely violent, hostile enemy and preach repentance—but you will certainly find yourself in the position of choosing whether to love your enemies or not. You will face every human being with the option of responding to him or her from God's perspective or from your own. You will come face-to-face with your own biases, others' offenses, misunderstandings, and pent-up animosities, and you will have to decide: Will you show compassion or anger, sympathy or hostility, a blessing or a curse? Jonah was filled with the sentiments of rivalry, and he resented God's mercy on people who didn't deserve it. But who does deserve God's mercy? No one, including us. It flows from the compassion of God, which is meant to fill our hearts and drive us into a contentious world. Our hearts are to beat with his.

Lord, give me your heart for people. Help me overcome my biases, to live unoffended, to seek the best of even those who hurt me. Fill me with divine compassion and send me into your world. Amen.

Words of Life

The words of the godly are a life-giving fountain. (Proverbs 10:11)

A LOT OF CHRISTIANS HAVE a negative attitude toward positive thinking. Perhaps that's because self-help advice often suggests that we need *only* positive thoughts, attitudes, and words to be happy—with no solid beliefs or spiritual depth required. But in the context of a relationship with God, discipleship with his Son, and life in his Spirit, positive thinking is a vital aspect of our spiritual growth. Scripture tells us to think good thoughts (Philippians 4:8), to encourage one another (1 Thessalonians 5:11), and to rejoice always (1 Thessalonians 5:16; Philippians 4:4). It gives us numerous examples of seeing challenging situations with a positive perspective (Philippians 1:14, 18, 21-23). In fact, many of the psalms are case studies in how to move from an attitude of anxiety and fear to one of praise and faith. We are actually commanded to think positively.

One of the greatest gifts we can give to those around us is to think positively and put those thoughts on display—not in a forced, artificial way, but as part of a normal, natural conversation. We have reasons for our hope, and sometimes we will be asked about them (1 Peter 3:15). Even when we are not, articulating them helps people see the inner workings of a biblically based worldview and an eternal perspective. Our mind-set can be a blessing to those who are wrestling with doubts, fears, anxieties, and disappointments. Your words can be a life-giving fountain.

Cynicism, pessimism, and negativity are not gifts of the Spirit. They do not reflect how God sees things. They do not accurately represent his Kingdom, which is always growing and making things beautiful. Constructive, positive, life-giving words do, and they build up those who hear them with encouragement, affirmation, and insight. They change the environment and offer a taste of another realm. When you express the realities of God's Kingdom, you invite people into it—even when nothing you say actually issues an invitation. You personify a better way, and many will be inspired to step into it.

Lord, fill my words with hope, encouragement, love, and insight into what you are doing in this world. Align my perspective with yours, make my life a stream in the fountain of truth, and satisfy the thirst of all who need you. Amen.

A Source of Solutions

*Common sense and success belong to me. Insight
and strength are mine. (Proverbs 8:14)*

SOME OF THE PHARISEES, though certainly not all, were experts at pointing out problems. They focused on anomalies, departures from prescribed behaviors, misstatements, and mistakes. When in doubt, they interpreted a person's words or actions in the worst possible light and then condemned their behavior. They assumed malicious intent with Jesus and applied skepticism in every unclear situation.

That isn't hard to do. The world is full of cynics and skeptics who major on people's flaws and neglect their true intentions and gifts. Unfortunately, so is the church. We have our share of Pharisees who focus on problems and interpret things they don't understand in the worst possible light. They are experts at pointing out what's wrong, lamenting what has been lost, talking about how things are getting worse and worse, and anticipating adversity. They may call it "discernment," but it's really just negativity. It is not a spiritual gift and requires very little perceptiveness.

We are called to a better way. Wisdom invites us to enjoy its fruits—to receive the insights of God and experience their benefits. We are told "we have the mind of Christ" (1 Corinthians 2:16), the counsel of the Holy Spirit (John 14:26), and wisdom from the Father (Proverbs 2:6). When we withhold these gifts from those around us and offer only criticism instead, we miss an enormous opportunity to bring God's presence and power into this world. He has a solution for every problem, and he often shares it with those who know how to listen to him. He wants us to connect his wisdom with the world's needs.

Cultivate that gift. Don't be dramatic in your claims, telling everyone you have heard from God. Simply share the insights he gives you. Let go of any preoccupation you have with problems and become entirely focused on divine solutions. Offer the mind of Christ to a world that hungers for his blessing. You may eventually be asked where your insights come from, and your answer will honor him.

Lord, forgive me if I've focused too much on problems, flaws, and mistakes. You are a God of solutions, insights, and restoration. May I become a minister of such things in every situation I face. Amen.

Captive to Hope

Return to your fortress, you prisoners of hope; even now I announce that I will restore twice as much to you. (Zechariah 9:12, NIV)

AFTER CENTURIES OF IDOLATRY and neglect of the revelation they had been given, God's people had been disciplined in numerous ways, including being held captive in a foreign land. Nevertheless, God promised restoration to them with the astounding assurance that they would receive double for their losses—even when those losses were self-inflicted. It's an amazing covenant of mercy, and it demonstrates his nature not only for ancient Israel but for his people in all times. We may go through hard things, but God is always calling us toward hope. He sees the end of every story and assures us it will work out for our good.

Sadly, many people, including Christians, are afraid to hope. We let our experiences with disappointment color our expectations of fulfillment. We are told that "hope deferred makes the heart sick" (Proverbs 13:12), and we nod our heads in painful agreement. We are told in the same verse that "a dream fulfilled is a tree of life," and we long to know what that's like. We want to live with anticipation of the goodness of God in every area of life, but we are reluctant to give our hearts over to it. We cast our hopes far into the future, to the end of the age and the coming of the Kingdom in all its fullness, but temper our expectations for the here and now. After all, we don't want to be disappointed again.

God calls his people to be relentless hopers. Even in the trials and tribulations of harsh discipline, when his prophets warned of devastations to come, he always offered a promise of the restoration that would follow. He encourages us, leads us, and pulls us into a hopeful attitude because that's his nature. He is a God of promise and purpose. He knows the glories to come.

The world needs glimpses of those glories, and we can provide them. We are to be captives to hope, always ambassadors of eternal realities, advocates of the truth behind the scenes. Live with that purpose, in your own life and in your words to others. Refuse to protect your heart by tempering its expectations. Wear the promises of God for all to see.

Lord, let my face shine with the glory of your goodness, my attitude glow with the expectation of blessings, my words resonate with the sound of anticipation. May my hopefulness be contagious to a world that needs it. Amen.

The Right Bias

*The hopes of the godly result in happiness, but the expectations
of the wicked come to nothing. (Proverbs 10:28)*

IMAGINE READING REVIEWS OF a product and noticing three that are negative among hundreds that are positive. Or seeing an A in five classes on your child's report card but a C in another. Or hearing one critical comment about your performance among twenty compliments. Where does your mind focus? Which comments stand out? What does your problem-solving tendency drive you to think about? If you're like most people, you have "negativity bias"—an inclination toward negative events and opinions, even when they are vastly outnumbered by positive ones. Most of us major on the glass-half-empty.

Negativity bias can be explained in psychological and neurological terms, but it has profoundly spiritual implications. It colors our ability to give thanks, to have faith, to hold on to hope, and to express love. It causes us to worry about everything that might go wrong rather than enjoying everything that goes right. It drives us toward our problems and losses, toward unfortunate exceptions rather than helpful examples, toward questions about unanswered prayers rather than a celebration of those answered, toward people's flaws rather than their assets, and on and on. Negativity shapes our lives and attitudes in subconscious ways and undermines our spiritual growth. It's part of our nature.

But it's only part of our fallen nature, not our redeemed and restored nature. It is not a reflection of the image of God within us. We are told instead to rejoice always, give thanks in everything, and to hold on to all that is good (1 Thessalonians 5:16-21). Overcoming our negativity bias is more than good exercise; it's actually a sign of the Kingdom of God growing within us. It's also a witness to others of greater, deeper, truer realities than the ones they're experiencing in the here and now. God knows the negativity embedded in our fallen mind-set, and he gives us the tools to change it. When we do, we become a living testimony to the hope of his Kingdom and the blessings of knowing him.

Father, give me the right bias. Help me flip the switch in my brain that is drawn to the problem areas of life. Fill my heart, mind, and spirit with truth, hope, joy, gratitude, and celebration—and let my bias affect the attitudes of everyone I meet. Amen.

God's Values

The LORD has told you what is good, and this is what
he requires of you: to do what is right, to love mercy,
and to walk humbly with your God. (Micah 6:8)

PEOPLE WHO FIGHT AGAINST INJUSTICE, defend the oppressed, and advocate for the poor have at times been marginalized by evangelicals, who see such activities as part of the "social gospel" and not the main business of the church. Perhaps that's because the social gospel movement often neglected the message of salvation and focused *only* on meeting physical needs. Yet if we're completely honest in our reading of Scripture, we'll recognize that the prophets emphasized justice and mercy far more often than some of the issues we focus on; that Jesus condemned the Pharisees as hypocrites for keeping the letter of the law while neglecting justice and mercy (Matthew 23:23); and that the Bible as a whole is extremely concerned with how we live in this world. It tells us that God is near to the brokenhearted (Psalm 34:18) and defends the poor (Psalm 140:12). When we do not have the same priorities, we are essentially refusing to be like him.

That's a problem. We are made in God's image, restored to his likeness, and called to reflect his nature and pursue his purposes. Somehow we've developed false divides in our culture that pit "conservative" against "liberal" and portray just causes as something "they" do. We sometimes determine our convictions not by whether they are right or wrong but by which groups hold them. We don't want to be on the wrong side.

If demonstrating the fullness of the gospel puts you on the side of people you would not normally agree with politically or philosophically, so be it. Too many Christians have made such an effort to distance themselves from liberalism that they have also distanced themselves from real social concerns. The result is a church that appears as detached, uncaring, and focused on doctrine and behavior as the Pharisees that Jesus railed against. Refuse to fit into a category, and live the gospel as it was given. Express God's heart. Show the world what his values really are.

Lord, if I ever lose sight of your concerns for this world, send me to the prophets and the apostles for a reminder of the balance. Give me a passion for justice and a heart of compassion. I'm on your side alone. Amen.

Everywhere

You will be my witnesses, telling people about me
everywhere — in Jerusalem, throughout Judea, in Samaria,
and to the ends of the earth. (Acts 1:8)

IN THE EARLY YEARS OF ENGLISH expansion into the world of trade, when England was trying to catch up with its colonial rivals, many ministers went along as chaplains, pastors, and scholars to serve those who were involved in the commercial ventures. Most undoubtedly had a sense of calling to vocational ministry, but they could have satisfied that calling in parish work in England. It was often their curiosity about the world and their sense of adventure that drove them beyond borders and beyond convention. They ended up crossing paths with dignitaries in high places, people of other faiths, indigenous populations, and a wide assortment of travelers and tradesmen who would never find their way to a church. Their gifts and skills positioned them for influence in ways their more church-focused colleagues could not have.

All kinds of ministry are needed in God's Kingdom—from the local to the far-flung to everything in between. But history is full of Christians whose longings to serve God were directed back into the church by well-meaning advisers. In times and places where a culture is saturated with Christianity, this type of focus may make sense. But in a pluralistic age, the greatest opportunities for ministry are very often in the least likely settings. The gospel—its words and its demonstrations—will only reach into the corners of the world through the carriers who take it there. God has a place for unconventional adventurers.

Too many people see their earthly interests as competition for their heavenly calling, but God has ordained both. Your passions—commercial, scholarly, frivolous, social, specialized, general, or any other category you can think of—may serve as distractions from your God-given focus at times, but more often they are vehicles that connect you with the rest of the world. The message you carry is absolute; the means by which you carry it can be flexible and multifaceted. The convergence between your desires and the world's needs are useful to God and assets in his Kingdom, and they will fill your heart with purpose.

Holy Spirit, shape my longings, direct my steps, and take me where you want me to go—
no matter how far off the beaten path it is. Amen.

Breaking Through

*A good tree can't produce bad fruit, and a bad tree can't produce
good fruit. A tree is identified by its fruit. (Luke 6:43-44)*

JONATHAN GOFORTH WAS a Canadian missionary to China in the early 1900s, and he was frustrated about the spiritual health of some of his "cold and fruitless" mission stations. He planned to visit them to give them encouragement, a spark, some meaningful challenge that would help them grow. But in his spirit, he was unsettled, as if something unresolved was festering within him. He took his unsettledness to God.

Goforth soon realized that he had been harboring a bad attitude toward another missionary over a fault the man had committed and then tearfully confessed. Goforth had forgiven him already—outwardly. But the Spirit impressed on Goforth's conscience his lack of brotherly love toward his fellow missionary, and the internal pressure began to build.

As Goforth was preaching at the church in his home station, the pressure reached a breaking point. While he was speaking to the congregation, who had no awareness of his struggle, he privately resolved to make things right after the meeting. Immediately, the tone of the service shifted. An unresponsive congregation suddenly became engaged and attentive. People wept in confession and prayer. The years had been marked by fruitless labor, but lives began to be transformed. When Goforth toured the mission stations he had been concerned about, they responded and began to grow. One simple decision to love a brother well had prompted an enormous breakthrough.

The internal life of a Christian is deeply connected to the external fruitfulness he or she experiences. It isn't always an obvious correlation; some people have fruitful ministries for years while wrestling with significant private sins, and some have suffering ministries while living with a clean conscience before God. But over time, the inward life matters. You are already cleansed and qualified to serve Christ, yet the practical outworking of that service sometimes hinges on the ways in which his righteousness is manifesting within you. Resolve whatever issues you have with the Spirit of God. Gifts and blessings flow more freely to the world when he is freely flowing in us.

Holy Spirit, I want nothing to interrupt your flow in and through me. Point out any unresolved issues. Hear my earnest confessions. Heal me from within. Bring me into fruitful breakthroughs. Amen.

Watchmen on the Walls

*O Jerusalem, I have posted watchmen on your walls; they
will pray day and night, continually. . . . Give the LORD
no rest until he completes his work. (Isaiah 62:6-7)*

THE MORAVIANS STARTED a round-the-clock prayer vigil in 1727, and it lasted a hundred years. During that time, they sent out hundreds of missionaries, who influenced hundreds or even thousands more. They were instrumental in the conversion experience of John Wesley, who along with his brother Charles became the founders of Methodism. To this day, groups of Christians around the world can trace something of their founding or influence back to the Moravian movement, which began when a handful of people decided to pray. In other words, prayer can change the world.

Most Christians believe that, but few are convinced enough to devote themselves to the sort of intense intercession that pleads with God, persists in its requests, and holds to his promises. Yet if we're looking to influence our world rather than lament its direction or complain about its faults; if we want to be salt and light the way God intended; if we long for the days when God moved in power; then some spark within us needs to turn into a flame that burns brightly in the prayer closet. We need to see our prayers as vital work in the Kingdom of God.

Two centuries ago, less than one in ten people in the world self-identified as a Christian. Today it's almost one in three. Despite what you've heard about the declining church, Christianity is growing globally. And despite what you've heard about the negative influences of cultural Christianity, it's actually a powerful, behind-the-scenes force for transformed lives and societies. Those trends didn't just happen by accident, and they didn't come arbitrarily from the hand of God. He invites us into his work and listens to our prayers. He sets watchmen on the walls of his Kingdom to pray incessantly and give him no rest because he insists on partnering with human beings. Take him up on it. Invest your life in this. Intercede for your world and know that it will change by your persistence and faith.

Lord, forgive my prayerlessness. May I catch a vision for how you respond to the prayers of your people. Let the petitions I bring to you today—in faith and persistence—transform lives tomorrow on a scale I can scarcely imagine. Amen.

World-Changing Prayer

The moment you began praying, a command was given. And now
I am here to tell you what it was, for you are very precious to God.
(Daniel 9:23)

THE WELSH INTERCESSOR Rees Howells and his circle of prayer partners prayed fervently for the Germans to stop bombing their town in 1941, but he sensed clear instruction from the Lord to expand his prayers to the entire country rather than his own location. So the group spent ten days in near-constant prayer, together sensing the Spirit lead them to pray that God would turn the enemy in other directions. Inexplicably, according to news commentaries, Hitler suddenly turned toward Yugoslavia and Greece and then toward Russia. The immediate crisis for Britain was over; for the world, it would not be over for several more years.

The skeptic would call this turn of events a coincidence and then question the justice of a God who spared Britain at the expense of eastern Europe. Of course, Howells and his group continued to pray for other countries during the war, and battles were eventually won. From outside perspectives, this was a fortunate turn of events. From the perspective of the one who prays, however, the timing was remarkable. The cause-and-effect relationship between specific, Spirit-directed prayers and news headlines was undeniable. Those who pray dare not chalk up the answers to coincidence. The faith that prompts a life of prayer is the faith that gives thanks when answers come.

You have the power to affect world events, whether you realize it or not. That power doesn't come when you try to pull strings yourself and orchestrate events the way you want to see them play out. It does come, however, when you wait for the Spirit's direction and then pray accordingly. God reveals his will to those who are sensitive to his Spirit (Amos 3:7) and then answers those who are willing to pray for his will (1 John 5:14). Enter the prayer room and influence the world's highest places. The God you know is higher still.

Lord, I know the futility of praying for my own agenda. Teach me the power of praying yours. Make me sensitive to the voice of your Spirit and guide my requests. Bless my neighborhood, my city, my country, and my world through my prayers. Amen.

A Lifestyle of Battle

*Upon this rock I will build my church, and all the powers
of hell will not conquer it. (Matthew 16:18)*

SIMON PETER ACKNOWLEDGED Jesus' identity as Messiah, and in response Jesus said he would build his church on Peter, which means "the rock." In fact, he endowed his followers with a surprising degree of authority in this world, assuring them that even the gates of hell—of evil, of the underworld of death and decay, of all that opposes God's Kingdom—would not prevail against them. Since gates are meant for defense, we can assume that Jesus means for his people to be the offense. The city sieges of ancient warfare were intense—picture Homer's portrayal of the battle of Troy, or the final battle in Tolkien's *The Return of the King*—and sometimes they could last for months. But Jesus assures us that our efforts to break through gates of darkness will ultimately be successful. We are to set a siege against evil with the hope and promise that we will win.

Many believers don't yet have that mind-set. Sometimes we just long for survival or for our immediate interests to work out. We want protection, provision, guidance, and everything else included in the *shalom* of God's Kingdom. But to extend God's peace into places where evil currently dominates? We rarely want to go there. It takes time and effort, as well as some kind of plan. It isn't on most of our to-do lists.

But it's on God's to-do list for his people, and he gives us strategies for carrying it out. We are to undo the works of the enemy (Luke 10:19), which Jesus came to destroy (1 John 3:8). We go up against the kingdom of darkness because we can. And the most effective way we can do that begins on our knees. Our prayers are powerful weapons against the forces of evil in this world, even when we don't understand how or why. As with a city siege, a moment of intercession isn't enough, but a lifestyle of battle is. Make prayer part of your days as often as you can. Real life happens behind the scenes, where you have been given stunning authority. Use it often and well.

Father, you oppose evil. I often turn my back to it. That needs to change. I don't always know what to do, but I know how to pray. Fuel my intercession and use it to expand your Kingdom against all opposition. Amen.

Praying the Kingdom

Your kingdom come. (Luke 11:2, NIV)

PETER AND JOHN WENT TO the Temple to pray and saw a lame man at the gate. He was carried there every day to beg for alms. He asked Peter and John for money, but they saw something better for him and declared his healing. The man got up, leaped for joy, and went into the Temple—just in time for what in Jewish practice was called "the standing prayer" at three o'clock (Acts 3:1-8).

Why didn't Peter and John give the beggar money? For one thing, as Peter says, they didn't have any. But more importantly, they were able to envision what the Kingdom of God should look like in that situation, just as Jesus had done when he went from town to town declaring and demonstrating the Kingdom message (Matthew 9:35). The result was something far better than monetary support for a day. A man who had been lame from birth walked for the first time in his life.

If you're ever at a loss for how to pray, a great way to spark your imagination is to ask what the Kingdom of God would look like in the situation you're praying for. It will not only throw into stark relief the aspects that don't look like the Kingdom—though you may already be acutely aware of them—but it will also increase your vision for what God wants to do in this world to demonstrate his nature. It will give you a starting point for praying his goodness into the lives of those around you, and it will sharpen your awareness of what you can and cannot expect him to do. It will turn your attention to the ways he offers his wisdom, power, and love—and the ways he offers them through you.

Make that question a significant part of your intercession. Don't just pray a list of desires; ask him what his desires are. Envision what the Kingdom looks like, then pray that vision. Over time, you will begin to see it increasing around you.

Father, show me your will. Give me a revelation of what your Kingdom looks like in every area of my life. Fill me with the power of vision, and fill my prayers with words that bring it into this world. Amen.

Following His Lead

*The Son can do nothing by himself. He does only what he sees
the Father doing. Whatever the Father does, the Son also does.
(John 5:19)*

MANY OF US RUSH INTO PRAYER with a list of requests. We're pretty clear on what
we want God to do but also careful to add "if it's your will" to the end. But what
if our prayers *began* with a request to know the Father's will? Before itemizing our
requests, what if our conversation with him went deeper to see his intentions for our
lives and circumstances, to get a sense of what he is doing, and to partner with him
in asking that it be done?

That's the model Jesus gave us. He said he only did what he saw the Father doing.
He went away by himself often to talk with his Father, and he lived with an awareness
of how God was working—what his priorities were, and how he wanted to carry
them out. We may think such knowledge is unique to the Son of God, the exact
image of the Father's nature—and to a degree, we might be right. But Jesus is also
our example, the perfect model of what it means to be a child of God in this world,
the template for how to live as someone made in the Father's image. His redemptive
work was unique, but he passed his mission on to his followers and demonstrated the
modus operandi we are to follow. When he said he did only what he saw the Father
doing, he was giving us a pattern to embrace.

Make that the standard for your entire life, and let it begin in your intercession.
Before you spend time asking, spend time listening. Let the Spirit impress on you
his intentions. Let him give you vision, insight, wisdom, and the mind of Christ.
When you have a sense of that—or even when you think you *might* have a sense of
that but aren't sure—proceed with your petitions. You will find them taking a new
shape, and you will see God's answers taking shape around you. Let your prayers
weave his Kingdom into this world.

*Holy Spirit, sharpen my spiritual senses to be like those of Jesus—to see what the Father
is doing, to know his desires, and to pray them and live them well. May your Kingdom
come in my life and my world. Amen.*

Those in Need

*If someone has enough money to live well and sees a brother
or sister in need but shows no compassion—how can
God's love be in that person? (1 John 3:17)*

IN THE YEAR 403, Augustine visited Carthage at the same time that priests of the Roman imperial cult gathered to celebrate their loyalty to the emperor with chariot races, gladiator contests, and public banquets. He preached a series of sermons there, some of which pointed out the misplaced priorities of the culture. The rich, both non-Christian and Christian, were investing their fortunes in entertainers, while the poor remained invisible to them. Even worse, they were investing their souls in superficial pursuits.[12]

John suggested that the love of God within us moves us not only to see the material needs of others but to respond to them with compassion. Of course, in this day and age, we can see around the world through a television or computer screen. The world's needs are always in front of us, and we would soon be overwhelmed trying to contribute to them all. But the point is clear: If we pour out our resources on things that have no eternal value while neglecting those in desperate need, we are missing something vital in our relationship with God. His compassion is not flowing through us as it should. We are not deeply in touch with his Spirit.

God has a heart for the poor. Numerous passages of Scripture make that clear: the law of Moses, the wisdom of Psalms and Proverbs, the judgments of the Prophets, the apostolic writings of the New Testament, and all sorts of stories and references in between. Caring for the poor is one of the more prominent themes of redemptive history, yet it is hardly prominent in the preaching and teaching of modern Christianity in prosperous countries. That has to change. Giving to the poor is not a political philosophy, and it is more than cleaning out our closets and giving away what we don't want anymore. It's a work of God, and it reflects something of who he is to a world skeptical of Christian priorities.

{ *Lord, you are concerned for the poor, and you urge your people again and again to give to them. Sensitize my heart toward the poor. Fill me with compassion. Move me to give what I can. Amen.*

Embracing Humility

Though the LORD is great, he cares for the humble, but
he keeps his distance from the proud. (Psalm 138:6)

IN THE DOMINANT CULTURE OF the Roman Empire, pride was considered a virtue. The humble were seen as weak, and the proud were admired for being assertive and maximizing their self-interests. So when many pagans became Christians, they had quite an adjustment to make. They learned that humility is a virtue in the Kingdom of God and that God resists the proud. His grace comes most easily to those who recognize their pride and do whatever they can to get rid of it.

Pride has made something of a comeback in our culture. Though many of us are turned off by arrogant athletes or performers, others laud them for their honesty—for not feigning humility and for having self-confidence. We've been told that it's not arrogance "if you can back it up," even though arrogance has little to do with truth or falsehood. The real issue is thinking too much of oneself and thinking too little of others. Humility honors others and seeks their interests; pride turns inward and thinks primarily of self. It has become a rather popular attitude, and its acceptability is growing.

Fortunately, God has not given us the mission of cutting down the proud. In fact, many who display arrogance are actually insecure people who are compensating for past wounds. We first need to see through their hardened veneer and minister to their hearts, but we must also demonstrate the power of humility. That's a difficult line to walk, but it can change lives. It puts our Kingdom values on display.

This is one of the ways we have been called to live counter to our culture. Embrace it and refuse to be drawn into the competitive, contentious, self-promoting ways of the world. Let Jesus be your model; though he made extravagant claims about who he was, he came primarily to serve. Your influence in the lives of others depends not on whether you can impress them but on whether you can uplift them. Invite people into the Kingdom culture by seeking their well-being.

Jesus, you laid down your life for me and told me to have the same attitude toward others. Help me live in a spirit of humility, to seek your Kingdom above my own, and to influence lives with the grace you have given me. Amen.

Wisdom Calls

Whoever finds me finds life and receives favor from the LORD.
(Proverbs 8:35)

A FEW CHRISTIAN BUSINESSPEOPLE started a Bible study at their office but didn't present it as a Bible study or even as a religious group at all. They simply discussed profound truths—the importance of integrity, the value of hard work, the effectiveness of a disciplined mind—and applied them to their work setting. Eventually, participants in the discussion group asked where this great material was coming from. When the leaders explained that all of these truths were drawn from the Bible, and primarily from the book of Proverbs, some of the inquirers gave their lives to Christ. Truth had drawn them to God even when it had not been presented in spiritual terms.

Proverbs 8 is written in the voice of Wisdom, and it calls all who need understanding to enter in. Wisdom was formed before the foundation of the world and was woven into creation as its underlying principle (Proverbs 8:22-31). It flows from the mind of the Creator. So when people encounter true wisdom, they are encountering something from God. Wisdom draws people to him, whether they know it or not.

You don't have to quote chapter and verse to speak God's Word into people's lives. You don't even need to identify your counsel as biblical. You do, however, need to soak in the Holy Spirit's presence and receive insight from him. A person who saturates him- or herself in truth will find it flowing freely in moments when wisdom is needed. When you bask in the light of God's counsel and listen for his voice, you begin to think his thoughts, walk in his power, exude his love, and develop his attitudes. You represent his nature.

You have the potential to bless those around you with the wisdom of God, even if you don't think you're particularly wise. Ground yourself in truth and offer it freely—but never forcefully—to those who seek advice. Don't worry about citing your source; that time will come. Let people be drawn to the logic that founded this world.

Holy Spirit, the entire universe rests on your reasoning, your logic, your truth. Let it permeate my being. Immerse my mind in your counsel. Use my thoughts and words to bless, encourage, and advise those who seek you. Amen.

A New Mind

Repent, for the kingdom of heaven has come near. (Matthew 3:2, NIV)

IN *THE EMPIRE STRIKES BACK*, Luke Skywalker landed on a swampy planet in search of a master teacher. The first creature he met turned out to be Yoda, the teacher he was looking for, but Luke didn't know that at first. Instead, he saw a small, odd character who was getting on his nerves. Once he learned Yoda's identity and submitted to his teaching, Luke had to go through a change in mind-set to access the power of the Force. He needed a whole new way of thinking.

The Force is not God, of course, and we won't be working on any telekinetic powers in our discipleship. But like Luke, we will need to transform our minds in order to walk in the power of God's Kingdom. The Greek word for repentance, *metanoia*, emphasizes this change in thinking, and though the Gospels certainly urge us to repent of our sins, the call goes deeper than that. It includes a renewed mind, a radically different perspective, a revolutionized way of seeing the world. It involves stepping into God's counterintuitive ways and learning to think his thoughts. If we don't embrace that change of thought, we will not be able to see the Kingdom or experience its ways.

The implications are varied and enormous, but they include no longer seeing ourselves as victims of the world, feeling like life and circumstances are conspiring against us, and always being under problems instead of over them. It means taking God's promises seriously, even when they don't seem realistic. It means actually believing that, in Christ, we walk in God's favor, are worthy to receive his blessings, and can expect victories over the kingdom of darkness and the ways of the world. It means we have to learn to live by faith and not by sight.

You will need a new mind for that, but the good news is God has promised to transform your thoughts if you will let him (Romans 12:2). With a renewed mind you will not only be able to walk in the power of God's Kingdom but also see what the world needs. And you will be equipped to give it freely.

Jesus, you are my master Teacher, and I want to think like you. Change how I see, teach me your ways, and fill me with the gift of faith. Let my repentance transform everything. Amen.

The Whole Body

This will continue until we all come to such unity in our faith
and knowledge of God's Son that we will be mature in the
Lord, measuring up to the full and complete standard of Christ.
(Ephesians 4:13)

ONE OF THE MAJOR THEMES woven throughout church history is the mystery of
"all saints"—how the *church triumphant* (those already in heaven) and the *church
militant* (those still on earth) fulfill their function as the body of Christ. The theme
was particularly emphasized in medieval Christianity and the artistic works that came
out of it, but it has been recognized in some manner or other in every era of church
history. The church has never been just a movement, or just a denomination, or even
just the Christians living at any particular time. It is the collective body of believers
that includes the crowds of heaven, the great cloud of witnesses that now surrounds
us (Hebrews 12:1), every believer living on earth, and, from God's perspective, every
believer yet to come. It is an enormous mosaic of faith and gifts and life stories that
will one day compose the story of God's redemptive and restorative work.

We are part of this epic story, and we need to live with that awareness. We are not
just individuals trying to make our way in this world. We are members of an organic
representation of the body of Christ, never on a solo mission, but always connected
by our relationships with other believers and the Spirit who orchestrates the Father's
work. We are compelled to conform to the image of the Son, carry out his mission,
and depend on his power. We are not alone; we receive encouragement and inspiration from those who have gone before us and those who are walking alongside us.
We are even encouraged by the awareness that we are laying a foundation for those
to come—that our ceiling will be their floor, and what we have done will set them
up for greater works.

Live with that perspective, and you will rarely feel discouraged. Your fruitfulness
does not depend on you. It is an investment, part of a whole, and God is bringing
it forth in time.

*Father, help me think in terms of "we" far more often than "me." Open my eyes to the
majesty of your work throughout the ages. I am grateful to be a part of it. Amen.*

Past the Pain

*It is impossible to please God without faith. Anyone who
wants to come to him must believe that God exists and that
he rewards those who sincerely seek him. (Hebrews 11:6)*

IS GOD GOOD? THAT'S THE QUESTION underlying our lives and really underlying all of
human history. The superficial response to the problem of pain is that God cannot
be simultaneously all-powerful, all-knowing, and all-loving because if all three of
these attributes were operating, he would not let the extreme suffering of this world
continue. His knowledge would allow him to see the problems and come up with
solutions, his love would compel him to intervene, and his power would enable him
to succeed. But this mind-set maximizes our own experience and minimizes how
God is revealing himself on a cosmic scale for all eternity. And it is blind to the end
of the story.

You will deal with this problem not only on a philosophical level but also in
your personal life. You have experienced pain, and you have probably been tempted
either to suppress it or let it overwhelm you. As a believer in the goodness of God,
you need to refuse both. Otherwise, your pain will color your perception of God,
and your perception of God will color your relationships, your work, your attitude
toward life, and your influence in this world.

In other words, the way you see God is enormously important. Pastor and author
A. W. Tozer called it the most important thing about you, and he has been quoted
on that point innumerable times. You have to be *relentless* in believing God is good
because you will see contradictions to his goodness all around you, often in your own
experiences. But between the lines of your circumstances and behind the pain of your
losses, he is working on a story that ends extremely well for you, if you will hold fast
in faith. Trials are for a moment, but his goodness is forever. To experience it, you
will have to choose to believe in his true nature. When you do, his nature grows in
you, and many hurting people will be drawn to it.

*Lord, you have promised that our earthly trials are momentary and greatly overshadowed
by future glory. Let me live with that perspective—healed, whole, and a testimony for
others to see. Amen.*

Know Your Heart

May he produce in you, through the power of Jesus Christ,
every good thing that is pleasing to him. (Hebrews 13:21)

WHEN YOU SURVEY THE WORLD, something likely gets your passions going—some cause, some injustice, some spiritual condition that plagues your society, some group of people that arouses the sympathies of your heart. It may be in public spheres of government, media, or education, or perhaps in more personal spheres of family life and private devotion. Maybe it involves a particular institution or behavior or attitude. It may get you excited, make you frustrated, or motivate you for change. Whatever it is, it strikes at your core, and you respond to it emotionally, intellectually, and spiritually. Somewhere embedded in your visceral reaction to this need is a call from God, a connection with his purposes that is not designed to frustrate you but to pull you forward. This is very possibly where your spiritual assignment is directed.

Look for those connections and magnetic pulls into the world around you, even if they look like revulsions at first. If they are broad and diverse—a general hatred for unfairness can show up in fields as varied as politics, health care, taxes, or the school playground, for example—look for the common characteristics, the places they might intersect, as well as how those intersections line up with your gifts. Your search and your questions may be a lifelong process, but God uses them to move you strategically into his plans. That's because he rarely directs us with an audible voice or clearly orchestrated signs. He far more often directs us through the Spirit's work on our minds and hearts.

God cares about this world, and he is extremely interested in working his way into parts of it that have kept him at a distance. But he generally does that *through* his people, not *in spite of* them. Sensitize yourself to the burdens and passions he has stirred within you. Let him move you wherever he wills. He will go with you and meet the world at its points of need.

Lord, you are closer to me than I can imagine, moving and shaping me, speaking through my thoughts and activating my interests and desires. Give me the discernment to sort out your will, and move me with your Spirit to meet the world's needs. Amen.

Everything Matters

*Since we are receiving a Kingdom that is unshakable, let us be
thankful and please God by worshiping him with holy fear and awe.
(Hebrews 12:28)*

"THERE IS PROPERLY NO HISTORY; only biography," wrote Ralph Waldo Emerson, and it's true. Sure, there have been events, movements, and statistics throughout the centuries. But all of those events, movements, and statistics exist because of the people who formed them and participated in them. Perhaps that's why God gave us not an overview of salvation history but a life-by-life personal account of its major events and themes. The story of his people is the story of . . . well, actual people. It's all about his work in the real world—not only in the body as a whole but in the lives of individuals who love, worship, and follow him. It is deeply personal.

That's true for your story too. You may tend to see God's Kingdom as a global movement or a some-day prophecy, but it's much more personal than that. It's not an abstract principle. It's the story of lives, including yours. That makes every person significant, every choice meaningful, every job important, and every relationship lasting. Every encounter with another human being holds the potential for a brush with truth and meaning. We aren't dealing simply in theories and beliefs. We're building lives.

Never lose sight of that. The Kingdom of God is about lives, not principles. It changes hearts, not groups. Yes, there are collective elements; the body of Christ has many members who are meant to live and move as parts of the whole. But the whole doesn't exist without the parts, and every part is significant. Your story and the stories of those around you are vital elements in human history and the eternal Kingdom. They are made up of critical moments, each of which has the capacity to prompt growth and change. Live with the awareness that everything—every aspect of the story, even on this particular day—is sacred. Today and every day, you walk on holy ground.

Lord, you have given me a sacred gift of life and a holy calling to enjoy it, share it, and invite others into it. Teach me how to treat all of my moments, whether at work or at rest, as meaningful and lasting. Amen.

Into the Depths

I have come to call not those who think they are righteous,
but those who know they are sinners. (Matthew 9:13)

JESUS ACCEPTED AN INVITATION to dinner, and the guest list included a lot of unsavory characters—"disreputable sinners," the text calls them (Matthew 9:10). The Pharisees, like most well-behaved people, had been taught for most of their lives to avoid bad company, and Jesus' casual disregard for his associations and his own reputation irked them. "Why does your teacher eat with such scum?" they asked his disciples (9:11). We don't know how the disciples answered, but Jesus' response is recorded for us. He pointed out that healthy people don't need a doctor and that the Good News is for those who have fallen short and recognize their need.

That focus has compelled many believers to go into the unsavory places of this world—brothels, bars, drug-infested tenements and alleys—to rescue those who know their need. The work is hard and dangerous, and not always fruitful. But sometimes it results in remarkable testimonies of deliverance and restoration, of addictions that are broken and painful lives that get a fresh start. Many Christians advise against such work—usually not with the same objections the Pharisees had toward Jesus, but out of concern for the well-being of the one who ministers there. But for those who do not struggle with or have overcome the temptations of a particular environment, the calling is worthwhile. It takes the power of the gospel into the places where it is needed most.

Don't be afraid to go into challenging places with the power of the Good News. Avoid situations that are a temptation for you, of course; don't expose your weaknesses to unnecessary pressures. But don't stand back, either. Far too many Christians wait for the world to come to their churches like a hospital stands ready for the sick. In a society that assumes the church will judge and reject—or that doesn't even understand its own sickness—that approach won't work. Go where you are needed; serve wherever you can; take God's grace on the road to reach a grace-hungry world.

Jesus, you saw the hurts and needs behind people's sins while the "righteous" around you focused on self-preservation. Give me a heart like yours. Let me carry grace far outside the walls of the church to bless those who need it most. Amen.

Pictures of Heaven

*Whatever you say or whatever you do, remember that you
will be judged by the law that sets you free. (James 2:12)*

IN HIS ACCOUNT OF THE destruction of the newly discovered Indies, Bartolomé de las
Casas told of Hatuey, a chief who was tied to a stake by the Spaniards for resisting
colonial advances. A Franciscan friar who questioned Hatuey explained the way of
salvation so the chief could be saved before his execution and avoid eternal torment.
Hatuey asked if all Christians went to heaven, and when told that they did, he said
he would prefer to go to hell. De las Casas lamented, "Such is the fame and honor
that God and our faith have earned through the Christians who have gone out to
the Indies."[13]

Even today, this rationale is not uncommon. A popular song in the seventies
suggested it would be better to laugh with the sinners than cry with the saints, and
a prominent activist said he would prefer hell because that's where his people are. If
Christians are any reflection of what heaven is like and it isn't an appealing picture
to outsiders, we have a problem. That's why it's so important for us to be an embodiment of eternal truth—to reflect our Father and his Kingdom well. Some people
will hold their impressions of Christians tightly because they want to, and there's
nothing we can do to change their minds. But some simply have a false impression
that is based on cultural or nominal Christianity and not on Jesus as he really is. We
can change that.

How? By *representing* Jesus as he really is. It is often said that we are the only Bible
many people will ever read, and there's a lot of truth in that statement. Few people
go searching for truth in the pages of Scripture without first being prompted by an
encounter, a conversation, a crisis, or an example. Much more than giving a gospel
presentation, we are called to be a gospel demonstration. Live the character of Jesus,
and hearts will long for the promise he gives.

*Jesus, you must be grieved by every false testimony of your true nature and by the souls
who turned away because of it. May I have the opposite effect by revealing the depths of
your grace and mercy. Amen.*

The Template

Those who say they live in God should live their lives as Jesus did.
(1 John 2:6)

THIS VERSE IS SOBERING, filled with words that almost everyone can agree with but few will actually fulfill. Jesus had harsh words for hypocrites and once asked his followers pointedly why they called him Lord but didn't do what he said (Luke 6:46). Of course, there's a significant difference between falling short of a standard and being a hypocrite who claims something but ignores it. We can forgive ourselves for our imperfection. But for claiming to be followers of Jesus without actually following him? That's a problem. We are called to live as Jesus lived.

That's a very high standard, and it begs for interpretation. We are not called to preach in an ancient agrarian society, challenge corrupt religious leaders, and die on a cross to save the world. But we are told to live and preach the message of the Kingdom, challenge injustices and deception, and take up our cross daily. We are also told to live with humility, be generous to the poor, love and serve those around us, walk in the power of the Spirit, be wise, and demonstrate the character of Jesus in all that we do. There's a reason Scripture repeatedly lifts Jesus up as our example. He is the model we are expected to follow.

That's why Jesus called both himself and his followers the light of the world (John 8:12; Matthew 5:14), why he told them they would do greater works than he did (John 14:12), why he said they would be persecuted as he was (John 15:20), and why he presented himself as an example to follow (John 13:15, 34). Students are to look a lot like their teachers, servants like their masters, and disciples like the one who trains them. We are being made into an image of original design and divine restoration—nothing short of the exact representation of God (Hebrews 1:3). It's a high calling but a necessary one. There is grace for falling short but encouragement never to give up. If Jesus is to be seen in this world, it will be through those who follow him.

Jesus, I have done a poor job of living as you lived, and while your mercy is immense, your calling remains. May I step closer into your image every day, ever increasing in your likeness. Amen.

Your Sweet Spot

Commit your actions to the LORD, and your plans will succeed.
(Proverbs 16:3)

"I'VE DECIDED. I'M GOING BACK TO CHINA. The missionary service has accepted me," Eric Liddell informed his sister. "But I've got a lot of running to do first. Jennie, you've got to understand. I believe that God made me for a purpose. For China. But he also made me fast. And when I run I feel his pleasure. To give it up would be to hold him in contempt. You were right. It's not just fun. To win is to honor him." Those famous words from *Chariots of Fire* have been quoted often because they resonate with those of us who have been trained to think that the best, most spiritual ways of serving God involve professional ministry and missions. While lives fully dedicated to God often do find expression in those fields, many people in other areas of life are just as fully dedicated and fruitful. We were made with all sorts of gifts and interests, and all of them have the potential to reflect something of God's nature. When we are living in our sweet spot, we feel his pleasure and honor him.

God may have a specific calling for many of us, but he is far more interested in commitment and devotion in the work we do than in the position we hold. When we delight in him and commit our ways to him, he leads us through our desires and interests, opportunities and circumstances, gifts and talents, and counsel and convictions. He has been known to put his people on unexpected platforms in the least likely venues—an imprisoned Israelite named Joseph who became a ruler in Egypt, a shepherd named David who became king of Israel, a fig farmer named Amos who became a prophet, a Jewish girl named Esther who became queen of a pagan land, and more. Some of our platforms are beyond our control; some are given when we follow our interests and convictions. In any case, God thinks far more creatively about the ways we serve him than we do. Commit your ways to him in whatever you do, and see what he does in return.

Lord, you created me the way I am for a purpose. Use my gifts, interests, and activities for your glory. Let everything I do honor you, and let me feel your pleasure. Amen.

Reconcilers

God has given us this task of reconciling people to him.
(2 Corinthians 5:18)

JESUS WALKED FROM TOWN TO town in Galilee and Judea, and sometimes beyond, teaching the truths of God's Kingdom and demonstrating its true nature. Crowds knew him as a healer and deliverer, a man of profound words, the one who quite possibly would deliver Israel and restore it to its former glory. But from a God's-eye view, Jesus was doing more than blessing those around him. He was reconciling them to the Father. In fact, "God was in Christ, reconciling the world to himself, no longer counting people's sins against them" (2 Corinthians 5:19). And according to Paul, God has given his servants exactly the same mission.

That's a claim loaded with meaning and enormous implications for how we live our lives. If we are reconcilers—calling the world back to the Father, refusing to count people's sins against them because the mercy of God is pursuing them—then that calling will flavor all of our relationships. We are compelled by the love of God—not to fill every conversation with a gospel appeal, though at times that appeal will come up, but to live and talk in a way that makes that appeal inviting and understood. We are to live with open arms that welcome people into the Kingdom of God.

That makes you something of a doorway into a restored relationship with the Father. You'll have to be secure in your own relationship with him, of course, but you'll also need to live in the reality of that relationship. You are a new person in Christ, a new creation (2 Corinthians 5:17), no longer relating to God on the terms of your old nature but as one clothed in Jesus and bearing his identity and name. The old life is gone; you are now moved by his love to bless, reconcile, restore, and embrace. Wear your role as reconciler with joy, placing it above all other roles at home, work, school, church, in the community—wherever. Be the bridge that points to an even greater Bridge between the world and the Father who loves it.

Father, let your love fill me. May I know it deeply and be moved by it to love others deeply and to connect them with your love. Let my open arms welcome many into yours. Amen.

A Window to God

He gave us this wonderful message of reconciliation.
(2 Corinthians 5:19)

PEOPLE WHO HEARD HUDSON TAYLOR pray used to remark how familiar he seemed with God, talking with the Father as with a friend in the room. The same is true for people who overheard the prayers of George Müller, John Hyde, and many other missionaries and ministers whose most significant works were bathed in a rich life of prayer. There was something about the nature of these relationships with God that made people realize how accessible he is and how real he could be in their daily lives. They were moved simply by the awareness that a human being could genuinely, tangibly walk with the Father.

That kind of relationship is visible not only in prayer; it shows up in conversation, in attitudes, and in a person's responses to adversity or opportunity. When a life is truly reconciled to God, it takes on a different nature. It is seasoned with comfort, assurance, gratitude, and faith. It radiates a certain quality that seems to come from another world. It makes an impression.

This is the message of reconciliation we carry. Sometimes that message will be explicitly stated when we recognize opportunities to spell out how a person can be reconciled with God. Sometimes it will simply be implied in the way we live and the attitudes we have, with those around us asking us to explain why we are hopeful or wondering how we can be so calm in the midst of hardships. In every case, the message of reconciliation goes way beyond words to communicate the ways of the Spirit. It draws people into a relationship with God because they suddenly realize a relationship with him is possible.

Make it your goal to live a reconciled life—a life that is rooted in faith, confident in your Father's goodness, at peace with his will, and as intimate and familiar as a relationship can be. Don't force opportunities to share this reconciliation with others, but do look for them and take advantage of them when they open. Some things are better caught before they are taught, and this is one of them. Your life is a window that reveals what a partnership with God looks like.

Father, my life preaches a message, whether I want it to or not. Help me make it a good one. Let me live the kind of relationship you want everyone to have with you. Amen.

The Unoffended Life

Jesus said, "Father, forgive them, for they don't know what they are doing." And the soldiers gambled for his clothes by throwing dice.
(Luke 23:34)

IF ANYONE EVER HAD A RIGHT to be offended, it was Jesus. A perfectly righteous man was condemned, tortured, ridiculed, and executed by a host of unsavory characters who had no idea what and whom they were dealing with. They were rulers and citizens of a rebellious world, abusing the Son of God who created it. Yet Jesus refused to live or die with an offense. He forgave his tormentors for what appears to us to be almost unforgivable. His ministry of reconciliation took priority over his personal wounds.

That's a great model for us to follow. Most of us have plenty of personal wounds—some self-inflicted or well-deserved, others quite undeserved at the hands of abusive or ignorant people. Yet we have been called to a ministry of reconciliation in which we seek the highest good for the greatest number of people around us, which includes those who have hurt us. Yes, we are victimized at times by cruel and destructive words and actions; and yes, we have every right to be angry. But ultimately we find ourselves in the position of having been reconciled to God in spite of our own offenses, and we have to seek the reconciliation of others in spite of theirs. We are called to live unoffended lives.

That's hard to do. The only way we can is to see into eternity and know the grace we've been given, the inheritance we've been promised, and the love that surrounds us even now. When we do—when we're immersed in the glories of heaven—earthly offenses become minor issues, much smaller than the spiritual and emotional needs of those who offend us. We no longer have to zealously guard our own interests because we know God is zealously guarding them for us. We no longer have to lick our wounds or protect our hearts because we've been healed and are protected. We are free to love and forgive—and to demonstrate what it's like to be so free.

Jesus, your grace is always greater than anyone's sin. You have an infinite capacity to absorb and deflect the insults of this world. Let me be like you—overwhelmed with heaven's glory and unconcerned with earth's affronts. Amen.

Across Divides

You know it is against our laws for a Jewish man to enter a Gentile home like this or to associate with you. But God has shown me that I should no longer think of anyone as impure or unclean. (Acts 10:28)

BY THE EARLY 1600s, more than 100,000 Japanese men and women had converted to Christianity. But some Japanese leaders feared that the growing number of Christians was a precursor to the threat of European colonial influence, and their fears prompted a wave of brutal persecution. Many Japanese Christians died; others fled to various parts of Asia or Europe. Few actually revoked their faith. These seventeenth-century Christians were seen as dangerous to Japanese customs—and from what we know of the transforming power of the gospel, perhaps they were. But the true gospel should never threaten cultural expressions and styles; instead, it should transform humanity's desire to build their own kingdoms apart from God.

In one respect, Christianity is a threat to every culture, seeking to redeem, restore, and transform. In another sense, it doesn't threaten any culture but honors a diversity of appearances, languages, and ways of thinking, exemplified by the multitude of distinguishable nations around God's throne. This was one of the themes of the New Testament era, when the barriers between Jews and Gentiles were being broken down. Peter went to a centurion's home and ate with him, and Paul tried to find common ground with everyone he met (1 Corinthians 9:22). The Jewish Messiah was going global, and it took some time to sort out the interaction between human cultures and the Kingdom of God. It was often a contentious process.

That's why we have to be careful. We are often perceived as a threat in areas we should never threaten—as promoters of an American or European gospel, advocates for our cultural assumptions about our faith, imperialists cloaked in religion. We need to be able to break down fear of the "foreign," whether cultural or spiritual, with kindness and selfless agendas. Like Peter, learn to consider no one inferior. Adapt, honor, and communicate truth—unconcerned by diverse expressions and unhindered by false divides.

Lord, your gospel was once foreign to all of us—culturally and spiritually. It crossed many barriers to get to me; let me take it across barriers into the lives of others. Give me discernment to know what is absolute, what is relative, and how to honor both. Amen.

The Bread of Life

I am the bread of life. Whoever comes to me will never be hungry again. Whoever believes in me will never be thirsty. (John 6:35)

ONE OF THE PROMINENT FEATURES of John's gospel is Jesus' "I am" statements. The climax of those statements is the one that is least defined, when Jesus simply hinted at the divine name of God and applied it to himself: I AM (John 8:58). The others are all metaphors that are loaded with meaning—not only for how we understand Jesus' identity but also for our mission in the world. If Jesus offered the resources of divine life to his followers and then sent his followers into the world with the same mission, we need to know what we are offering. The "I am" statements give us a series of pictures of our message.

When crowds asked Jesus for a miraculous sign like their ancestors experienced when manna fell from heaven, Jesus identified himself as the true bread from heaven. Earthly bread nourishes for a moment but doesn't sustain the spirit, and it doesn't last longer than a day. Jesus, however—not just his words or his power, but his life within us—nourishes forever. To have him is life; not to have him is death. We may live in natural bodies for a time, but only with Jesus can we enter into eternal life. Only the bread of heaven enables us to thrive.

Is the life you are living qualitatively different from the life of those who are not in a relationship with Jesus? If not, you are not living from the nourishment the Bread of Life gives you, even if it has already been made available to you by faith. Salvation by grace through faith gives us access to the life of Jesus; only ongoing faith and dependence allow us to experience it each day. Receive that gift constantly, and you will grow in confidence in offering it to others. It will feed your spirit and, like one beggar telling another where to find bread, you will fill other mouths with its nourishment. The bread of life will satisfy your hunger forever.

Jesus, like many others, I have tried to satisfy my hunger with other breads in this world, and not one has filled me up. You offer to strengthen me forever. Let me experience you fully and share your life with many. Amen.

The Light of the World

I am the light of the world. If you follow me, you won't have to walk in darkness, because you will have the light that leads to life. (John 8:12)

JESUS TOLD HIS FOLLOWERS THEY were the light of the world (Matthew 5:14). Of course, we don't generate our own light; we were drawn to his light when we came out of darkness by responding to him by faith. We hardly knew how to shine on our own. But somewhere along the way, if we were observant, we learned a valuable truth: that we grow brighter simply by being around him. Like the glow-in-the-dark stickers many of us used to play with as children, we absorb the real source of light by being close to it. Our exposure to the light develops a shine in us that lasts even when darkness comes.

That's why Isaiah foretold the people of God rising with his light shining on them (Isaiah 60:1-3) and Peter wrote of the Morning Star shining in our hearts (2 Peter 1:19). Something profound happens to us when we allow ourselves to soak in the presence of God. We become reflectors of the true source, like a moon glowing from its sun and illuminating the way for those in the darkest nights. We receive vision in the light of God, and we are sent out to share our vision with the rest of the world. We become carriers of hope, ambassadors of the promises of God, signs of the wonders he is working. Jesus, the Light of the World, replicated himself in the lives of those who believe. The Light ignited millions of lights to follow him.

Live as a light—not as the source, but as a reflector of the true image of God. Shine with hope, promise, and purpose, always pointing the way into eternal truth. Radiate the nature of the Son, who in turn radiated the nature of the Father and the Spirit. Fill the lives of those around you with glimmers of eternity, sparks of anticipation of the goodness of God. Let your words, actions, and attitudes shine with life.

Jesus, your light has flooded my soul, and I'm not sure others see it in me. Let me live with the hope of your promise and the radiance of your glory. Brighten the flame in this very earthen lamp for many to see. Amen.

The Gate

I am the gate. Those who come in through me will be saved.
They will come and go freely and will find good pastures. (John 10:9)

JESUS TOLD HIS FOLLOWERS that the gateway into the life of God's Kingdom was very narrow, and only a few would ever find it (Matthew 7:14). And it's true; our entrance into the Kingdom is as narrow as a single Savior. But many people throughout the centuries have assumed that the narrow way leads to a narrow life, with hardly any room to enjoy the journey. But Jesus was just as clear that as the gateway for his sheep, he leads to good pastures—pleasant spaces with plenty of greenery and scenery and openness. He encloses us in safety but frees us to enjoy his fields. He is the entryway into a life of fruitfulness and joy.

A lot of people don't know that. Some think they can only experience freedom by entering the gate and then keeping their distance from him. Others who are used to following principles enter willfully into a new captivity just as confining as the old one, but call it freedom just to line up with Scripture. The truth is something else—a realization that freedom comes simply by entering the gate, by drawing close to the Son who sets us free and keeps us safe. There is no other way to enter into good pastures.

Make sure you represent that picture in your relationships with others. Don't offer alternative ways to freedom because there aren't any. But don't disguise the freedom you've been given with false restrictions and demands. Jesus doesn't give you a list of requirements to fulfill; he empowers you to overcome the things that weigh you down. While much of the world has sought its freedom independently of God—and gotten further enslaved to their own passions in the process—you seek your freedom *in* him. Demonstrate the unexpected paradox that freedom from God leads to captivity, but captivity to God leads to freedom. You've found the narrow gate; make it as inviting as you can by pointing to it as the source of your wide-open adventure.

Jesus, you led me to the end of my own fruitless life, guiding me through your narrow opening into eternity. Show me how to make the most of it. You have set me free; use me to lead many more captives into your spacious Kingdom. Amen.

The Good Shepherd

I am the good shepherd. The good shepherd
sacrifices his life for the sheep. (John 10:11)

SHEPHERDING IS NOT AN EASY BUSINESS. The hours and the walks are long, the conditions are often dirty, and attention to detail is a must. Sheep are not the brightest of animals, and they have strong tendencies to wander off, get stuck, or leave themselves vulnerable to predators. When David wrote that the Lord was his shepherd, he was making a profound statement about God's watchful eye over his people and his attentiveness to our needs. When the prophets wrote of shepherds who misled God's people, they were issuing strong indictments against neglectful and dangerous leaders. And when Jesus compared a shepherd's desire to leave ninety-nine safe sheep behind to go after the one that was lost, he was painting a powerful picture of the heart of heaven toward those who have strayed. The task of shepherding is constant, demanding, and based on the shepherd's compassion and care.

So when Jesus identified himself as the Good Shepherd who sacrifices his life for the sheep, he took shepherding characteristics to their ultimate extreme to assure his followers that they were under the best of care. His words remind us that our tendency to live in fear, anxiety, worry, insecurity, and mistrust—our unfounded belief that we are on our own and subject to random forces of harm—is completely unwarranted. Though we can be certain we will face trials and hardships, we can also be certain that God governs our lives and guards us from ultimate dangers. He is leading us safely and securely to very pleasant places.

It is vital, both for your own sake and the sake of those who look to you for a connection with eternal truth, to live with that assurance. It will keep you calm in crises and anchor your attitudes in the invisible realm of the Spirit. It will become a signpost to your world that there is value in living by faith and not by sight. And it will serve as an open invitation for others to enter into the watchful care of their Shepherd.

Jesus, you are my shepherd, and you impart your shepherding heart to your people. Give me the kind of compassion and care others need in order to get a glimpse of your love for them. May I shepherd those you have put into my care as you have shepherded me. Amen.

The Resurrection and the Life

I am the resurrection and the life. Anyone who believes
in me will live, even after dying. (John 11:25)

"IF ONLY YOU HAD BEEN HERE." Those words, uttered by both Martha and Mary when Jesus arrived after their brother's death (John 11:21, 32), capture the sentiment many of us have felt toward God in our disappointments. We know God was there, of course; we just don't understand why he didn't intervene and why he seems so involved in some aspects of our lives and so aloof in others. If we're honest, we have to acknowledge that a significant portion of our inward lives is aimed at disappointment management—rationalizing past pains and guarding our hearts against more of them in the future. We long for lives made new.

That's the Good News of the Kingdom, and its ultimate expression is in Jesus' emphatic statement that resurrection and life are found in him. He wasn't just raised from the dead to impress us; he was resurrected on our behalf, as the firstfruits of what God is doing with all of creation, the reversal of an age-old curse that subjected us to futility and decay. We serve a God who makes all things new (Isaiah 43:18-19; 65:17; 2 Corinthians 5:17; Revelation 21:5) and is doing so in our lives even now. You may not notice the renewal in some seasons, but it is carrying on anyway. God is redeeming, restoring, and renovating, even while we wait for the ultimate fulfillment of our resurrection at the end of the age. We have every right—even the responsibility—to live in anticipation of renewal.

Let that anticipation be contagious. Live with wonder, as though all things are fresh and new, inviting and drawing you into an adventure with God. The promise of resurrection is meant to jolt us out of apathy and tedium. Nothing is "the same old thing" anymore. Ask God to fill your heart with anticipation of his goodness—to surprise you with his blessings. A life of expectation is beautifully infectious, and it opens eyes to possibilities and a God who specializes in them. Living in the resurrection awakens others to its life-changing power.

Jesus, you don't just give me life; you are my life. I was crucified and raised with you, and I live in constant newness now and forever. May I and many others be drawn into thrilling adventures with you. Amen.

The Way, the Truth, and the Life

I am the way, the truth, and the life. No one can
come to the Father except through me. (John 14:6)

MODERN CULTURES HAVE gradually lost their sense of absolutes over the last few centuries, and we can see the signs of relativism all around us. In some respects, the change is good; not everything claimed as an absolute in the past—the earth as the physical center of the universe, for instance—actually was one. But some things still are, including God and his Word. We may grow in our understanding and interpretation of truth, but truth itself doesn't evolve. We were given insights into the eternal realm of God's Kingdom for a reason, and we are compelled to hang on to them. Reality is not a fashion, and it doesn't change with the times.

We are told, "Jesus Christ is the same yesterday, today, and forever" (Hebrews 13:8), so his words about being the way, the truth, and the life still apply. He did not present himself as one way among many, as one truth to consider among others, or as one opportunity for life among the many other things people pursue to feel alive. He is the gateway, the entry point, the door into the eternal Kingdom of God, and no one can experience real, lasting life without him. We may look around us and see people who don't believe in Jesus enjoying their natural existence, but they are building their lives on shifting sands, not lasting bedrock. Those of us who have entered into the Kingdom by faith are empowered by the powerful energy of divine life within us. Those who haven't aren't.

You are called to be a living, breathing example of what it means for a person to anchor his or her life in eternity and follow the way of true life. While others sample the buffets of earthly experience, you cling to a single guide who leads you along his unique way into real life according to absolute truth. Your path, your gifts, and your personality are not identical to anyone else's, but your Savior is universal. Do not waver from your calling; do not compromise your convictions; and do not draw life from any other source. You already have the best there is.

Jesus, you are incomparable, and your ways are unequaled. In a world full of options, focus my life on the only one that matters. Let me be seen as a personification of your way, your truth, and your life. Amen.

The Vine

I am the vine; you are the branches. Those who remain in me, and I in them, will produce much fruit. For apart from me you can do nothing.
(John 15:5)

WHEN ISAIAH WROTE OF a beloved vineyard that produced nothing but bitter grapes, he was making a pointed statement about the fruitlessness he was seeing from the kingdom of Israel in his day. The song of the vineyard (Isaiah 5:1-7) became an emblematic theme in Israel's history, not only in Isaiah but in other writings too. These writings raised the question of whether God's people were being fruitful and fulfilling their calling or falling short and turning bitter. The implication was the latter and often at critical moments in the redemptive story.

Jesus and his disciples were well aware of this theme, and Jesus' reference to himself as the true vine (John 15:1) was understood as a loaded statement. He was claiming to be the true Israel and the Son of the true vinedresser. *He* would bring the harvest his Father had always sought, and his followers would fulfill ancient promises of fruitfulness. The picture of the vinedresser hoping for a great vintage in Isaiah 5 was to be completed in all those who live as a branch on the true vine. But we are warned that those who don't produce fruit will not participate in the harvest. The good news for believers who have lived through futile, frustrating seasons is that the time of fullness has come. All we have to do is hang on as a branch and draw our nutrition and strength from the vine. The fruit will inevitably grow.

If you've been striving to produce fruit and make a difference in this world, be at rest. Lean back into the strength of the vine, and let his life flow through you. Branches don't battle for their fruit; they simply grow. In your growth, you will become a testimony of God's means for growth, a principle that works in both the natural and supernatural realms. You will demonstrate the secret for being both relaxed and productive, a vessel for the work of a power beyond yourself.

{ *Jesus, you modeled fruitfulness by doing what you saw the Father doing and being empowered by the Spirit. May your life likewise flow through me. Let me be abundantly fruitful with your works. Amen.*

"I AM"

Jesus answered, "I tell you the truth, before Abraham was even born,
I AM!" (John 8:58)

JESUS USED A RANGE OF metaphors to illustrate who he is because he serves a number of roles in our lives. He is the gateway into life, but also life itself; he is the shepherd of his people, but also the embodiment of God's people as a whole; he is the bread that comes from heaven to earth, but also the only way to get from earth to heaven. He is all that and more, and only illustrations can begin to give us a glimpse of his true nature.

But when it came time for Jesus to identify his essence, he drew from ancient Scriptures and the story of Moses. Moses had encountered God at a burning bush, where he received his calling to go back to Egypt as a deliverer of God's people. But in his insecurity, Moses asked God for his name. After all, if you're being sent on a divine mission, it's important to know who's sending you. So God gave Moses an enigmatic answer, an almost unpronounceable form of the expression "I am" that implied self-existence with no further explanation. It became known as the divine name of God.

Jesus used this name or a variation of it to identify himself before a crowd of critics. Predictably, they picked up stones to throw at him for this apparent blasphemy. Whether Jesus used the exact name is unclear, but the reaction of his opponents makes it clear that he at least referenced it. He was no mere teacher and certainly more than a metaphor. He was—and is—the embodiment of the God who created the universe.

Remember that in your life of following Jesus. You are not modeling yourself after a great teacher or embracing a philosophy. You are connecting with the source of life himself, the author of all that is. His words are nonnegotiable, though you will grow in your understanding of them. His power is uncompromising, though you will grow in your experience of it. Your testimony is not just a point of view; it is a testament to truth. You are being made in the image of wisdom, power, and love in their purest form.

Jesus, you are infinite power, light, love, truth, and joy. Let me embody your nature and overflow with it—and receive your nature overflowing from others. May I live a supernatural life worthy of your calling. Amen.

You in Christ

All who have been united with Christ in baptism have put on Christ,
like putting on new clothes. (Galatians 3:27)

PERKIN WARBECK POSITIONED himself in the late 1400s as the Duke of York, a son of the deceased King Edward IV and rightful heir to the English throne. He dressed the part, spoke the language, and had coins minted in his name. Many believed him, and he gained somewhat of a following until King Henry VII declared him to be an impostor. Warbeck was never quite able to pull off his alternate identity and eventually confessed to being a Fleming unrelated to the royal family.

Followers of Jesus also dress the part of royalty, speak the royal language, and have some currency in God's Kingdom. The difference between us and Warbeck, of course, is that we are not illegitimate pretenders at all. We have been given an invitation to adopt the identity of Jesus and a promise that we will be accepted in his name. We have to conform to a standard that's different from the one we grew up with, to be sure, and it may take some time to learn our role. But it remains an open invitation, and we have every right to step into an entirely new self and enjoy royal privileges.

Paul often referred to this image of putting on new clothes to look and act like Jesus (Romans 13:14; Ephesians 4:24; Colossians 3:10, 12). Like learning a new culture, we wear Jesus' identity until it fits, until we become acclimatized to our spiritual environment. When you wear him like a new set of clothes, he has the effect of changing you both internally and externally. Your inner and outer environments are transformed, and the change is palpable. You live and move in him, as though you are trying on a new persona or playing a part, but the role is permanent, not temporary. Over time, it fits, and sometimes you hardly know how to distinguish between Jesus and the new you. You are growing into the image of another, fully accepted as part of the royal family, and equipped to influence the world around you.

Jesus, my past behaviors and attitudes have made you an odd fit at times, but you are always able to grow me into your image. Alter me to fit my new clothes, and enable me to wear them well. Amen.

Christ in You

I feel as if I'm going through labor pains for you again, and they will continue until Christ is fully developed in your lives. (Galatians 4:19)

JESUS CAME INTO THIS WORLD as the incarnation of God—the perfect image of the Father. That alone is not a novel concept, as many religions embrace incarnations (or reincarnations) of a deity or divine figure. But the New Testament is clear about the uniqueness of Jesus as the exact image of the one true God. The Word of God was made flesh and lived among us.

We celebrate that astonishing event every Christmas, but we often forget to take the celebration a step further. We focus so intently on the incarnation of God in Christ that we neglect the incarnation of Christ in us. Not only was the Word made flesh to live among us; the Spirit was sent to inhabit our flesh and continue the phenomenon of incarnation through God's people. We have been sent into the world in the same way the Son was sent into it (John 20:21); Christ within us is the hope of glory and an age-old mystery now revealed (Colossians 1:26-27); it is no longer we who live but Christ who lives in us (Galatians 2:20); we are earthen vessels carrying an unimaginable treasure (2 Corinthians 4:7); and both collectively and individually, our bodies are described as a temple (1 Corinthians 3:16; 6:19). One of the most astounding truths of the Bible is that God not only incarnated himself in Jesus but continues to do so in Jesus' followers.

Not perfectly, of course. We begin as flawed, contaminated rebels, lumps of common clay needing to be shaped in our growth into the image of God. But that's where we are headed, and it's also how we are called to live right now. The Christ-centered purposes of God always involve his people. The promise of Christ in us means we are to live as incarnations for a world that needs to see him. It sounds both presumptuous and impossible, but it's true—and it's God's mission for redeeming this world.

Jesus, I can't possibly even begin to live as an incarnation of you apart from the power of your Spirit. But may I never dismiss my calling to do so as impossible. Send me into my family, my work, my church, my city, and my world as your image. Amen.

In His Name

*I tell you the truth, you will ask the Father directly, and he will grant
your request because you use my name. . . . Ask, using my name, and
you will receive, and you will have abundant joy. (John 16:23-24)*

JESUS PROMISED ANSWERS to prayer, and we often experience them in delightful ways.
But sometimes we don't, and we begin to wonder why. If prayer is our means for
bearing fruit that lasts and glorifies God (John 14:13-14; 15:16), and if Jesus was so
emphatic about his followers using his name, how do we explain the lack of answers
in some seasons of life? Why is he not as responsive as he suggested? Our minds
begin to answer these questions in all sorts of ways, many of them self-incriminating:
I didn't have enough faith; I haven't been living very faithfully. We point the finger at
ourselves for falling short of the promise.

Your thoughts about not being worthy, forfeiting the promises, not having
enough faith, and so on, are probably all true. You can go ahead and accept the reality. But those accusations, as true as they may be, are not relevant at all. They would
be relevant if you were praying in your own name, but you aren't. You're praying
in Jesus' name—from his worthiness, his credentials, his status with the Father. His
repeated admonitions to use his name in prayer were given to us to take the focus
and burden off ourselves. Instead of praying from our own identity, we pray from
his. What answers to prayer does the Son deserve? What does he stand to inherit?
How much faith does he have in the Father's wisdom, power, and love? The answers
to those questions are all that matter, and they are extremely encouraging. We don't
come to the Father on our own merits; we come on the merits of Jesus. That puts
us on very solid footing.

Pray from that identity. You'll need to align yourself with Jesus' purposes, of
course, but that isn't difficult. It's empowering. Pray from the position of the Son,
and you will experience his promises in increasing measure.

*Jesus, thank you for the privilege of praying in your name, on your account, and from
your identity. Align me with your purposes and bear fruit in my life. Use my prayers to
accomplish your will on earth. Amen.*

Influence by Prayer

What do you want me to do for you? (Mark 10:51)

PEOPLE WILL TELL YOU their problems, especially if you are known for having a listening ear. You will hear the laments of those who are struggling through tough times, the ailments of those with physical challenges, and the conundrums of people in dysfunctional relationships. You will hear of hopes and dreams, but also of dashed hopes and dreams. And while you may feel helpless to change their situation, there is something you can do. You can ask, "May I pray for you?"

It's a powerful question. Sometimes you'll hear no, but pray anyway, silently. Usually, however, the person you ask will be more than willing to have you pray, touched that you care, and perhaps a little surprised when an answer to the prayer comes. You may choose to pray out loud on the spot, or you may resolve to do so on your own at a later time, as an addition to your prayer list. Either way, a ministry of prayer makes a statement without actually making a statement. It creates a platform for sharing the goodness of God. It awakens a heart to the possibility that God might intervene.

Jesus asked this question, even when the answer was obvious. You should too, at least on occasion when the opportunity arises. Some bolder souls approach every person in a wheelchair at the mall and offer to pray; while most of us are more comfortable doing so within established relationships. We should feel free to connect our family, friends, and associates with the God who loves them through prayer. A simple "I'll be praying about that" is often enough to reveal the heart of God and give him an occasion to work in a life that needs him. At the very least, it demonstrates what a relationship with God looks like. Even better, it sometimes prompts a person to seek one. In any case, it offers a glimmer of hope to someone going through a hard time and reminds them there's a God who cares.

Father, you are longing to reach into the hearts of people who need you, but you choose to use your people to do so. Let me provide occasions for your touch. Draw me close in prayer, show your power, and heal hearts in need. Amen.

Friend of Sinners

*The Son of Man . . . feasts and drinks, and you say, "He's a glutton
and a drunkard, and a friend of tax collectors and other sinners!"*
(Matthew 11:19)

PULPITS HAVE OFTEN BEEN used as platforms for condemning sin and, by implication, condemning the sinners involved. As a result, Christianity is sometimes known for its hard line against the excesses of indulgence. While the desire to uphold standards of righteousness is admirable, violating Jesus' clear warnings against being judgmental is not. Our diatribes against sin are often illogical. We express shock when people who aren't Christians don't act like Christians—a thoroughly unsurprising condition—and then separate ourselves from "corrupting influences," insisting that we must not be blemished by them. After all, we want to present the right image.

Meanwhile, Jesus—our perfect example—had such reckless disregard for his own reputation that he let his love, rather than a carefully crafted image, prove his character. He seemed unconcerned that the judgmental critics around him could legitimately call him a friend of sinners and point to evidence of his many associations with them. He feasted and drank with people on the margins of religious acceptability because those were the people who wanted and needed what he offered. He justified his friendships by comparing himself to a doctor who treats the sick. He entered into the mix of fallen humanity in order to show people the Father's love.

Far too many people who follow Jesus don't follow him on this point. That's tragic for a number of reasons. For one thing, if we don't know how to be friends of sinners, we won't have any friends, since sin has infected everyone, including ourselves. But we also won't have any influence or be influenced by people who could teach us a lot about the human experience. We are called to separate ourselves from certain behaviors and attitudes—*not* to separate ourselves from people who have them. Wisdom tells us to surround ourselves with the wise; compassion tells us to have a heart for everyone. We cannot be like Jesus without loving the way he loves.

Jesus, let me love the way you love. Help me develop genuine friendships with people from all kinds of backgrounds and all walks of life. May I learn from others, and may they learn from me—especially about the power of your love. Amen.

Kingdom Friendships

As iron sharpens iron, so a friend sharpens a friend. (Proverbs 27:17)

DAVID RECEIVED SOME BAD NEWS. Saul, the king of Israel, was searching for him to kill him and had gotten word of where David was hiding. It was a critical moment—one where David could have lost heart or forgotten his God-given purpose. Fortunately, Saul's son Jonathan found David before Saul did and reassured him. Jonathan reminded David of his calling and promised to remain a loyal friend. They renewed their bond, and David was strengthened. Jonathan represented God's nature and spoke God's words during David's time of need.

That's how friendships work. Your relationship with God changes everything about you, but you don't know God in isolation. You know him through the people who personify his nature, who show you what it looks like to experience his love, compassion, wisdom, grace, and so much more. That means that to encounter God as fully as you can, you will need to connect yourself to friends, some of whom will know him already and some of whom will still be seeking him. Jesus is not a method, a principle, or a belief; he calls his followers friends. Your personal relationship with him is important, but it is not enough. In a very real sense, you can only experience him in the context of human relationships.

Seek friends who make you better by encouraging and affirming you but also by challenging you and telling you hard truths. Make sure you are that kind of friend to others as well. Throughout your life, you will need to be both someone who can be sharpened and a sharpener, someone who can be influenced and an influencer of the people around you. The Kingdom of God is built on relationships—first and foremost with God himself, but by extension with the people he has called or is calling into life with him. It is a fellowship of the Spirit, a body of believers, a community focused on one Lord and a common cause. Our influence in the world begins there, in relationships, seeking and experiencing God together.

Jesus, it's astonishing that you would call me a friend. But you do more than that; you invite me into a global network of friends who love you and serve you faithfully. Bring me into that fellowship of salt and light, and transform your world through our love for one another. Amen.

Jesus, Our Model

*It was our weaknesses he carried; it was our sorrows
that weighed him down. (Isaiah 53:4)*

THE GOSPEL OF JESUS IS COMPREHENSIVE—spiritual salvation from the penalty of sin, but also holistic salvation that includes every aspect of our lives. Here on earth we wrestle with many hardships: relationship issues, health problems, unemployment, income and debt imbalances, emotional wounds, worries about the future, and so much more. God is concerned for all of them. He even promises the eventual restoration of his material creation—bodily resurrection and new heavens and a new earth. While seeing the gospel as a legal decree may cover our ultimate concerns about eternity, seeing it as a comprehensive promise brings it into here-and-now life. And we need God for every inch of it.

Jesus knew this. He carried our weaknesses and sorrows and spent much of his ministry dealing with people's physical bodies, emotional needs, and immediate spiritual concerns. He promised eternal life, but he demonstrated the goodness of God in everyday circumstances.

That's our calling too. No aspect of life is off limits to God's mercy and grace, so no aspect should be off limits to ours. He carries our sorrows and pain, so we must carry the sorrows and pain of others. He stepped into the daily lives of the people around him, so we must step into the daily lives of those around us. Every consequence of the Fall was his concern, so every consequence is our concern too. We are ministers in the broken places and dark shadows of this world.

But we are also more than that. We are carriers of hope and glory. We cannot solve every problem, but we can point people to the one who can. While many Christians look toward a day of escaping this life, we must remember to spend our days bringing God into it. Like our divine template, we live sacrificially, expectantly, and purposefully to bring healing to the hurts of this world.

{ *Lord, I cannot thank you enough for carrying my weaknesses and bearing my sorrows. Thank you for all that salvation includes and the fullness of life it brings. Help me give others a taste of what you've given me. Amen.*

Freely Give

He was beaten so we could be whole. He was
whipped so we could be healed. (Isaiah 53:5)

WE MAY NEVER UNDERSTAND HOW Jesus' beatings heal our wounds. But the prophet Isaiah was clear when he said they do. We are also never told we won't have wounds—experience assures us that we do. But we are promised a remedy. All of our afflictions and brokenness are a result of our rebellion at the Fall, and Jesus took the torment of that rebellion upon himself. His wounds heal and restore us. He offers mercy and grace, powerfully demonstrated on the cross. Through his sacrifice, we receive from him all good things.

Jesus told his followers to freely give what they have received (Matthew 10:8), and he framed that instruction in the context of healing and deliverance. Just as our wounds have been healed, we are to go out and heal the wounds of others. If we're at all like our Savior, we may be berated or beaten from time to time in the process. But we are to heal anyway. Whatever healing and deliverance we have experienced from him qualifies us to be ministers of healing and deliverance for others. Regardless of our spiritual gifts, our station in life, our career path, or any other sense of calling, we are called to this.

Every human being is carrying wounds from the past—insecurities, fears, anxieties, shame, condemnation, disappointments, and more. People are having a tough time; we can see it in their pained expressions or even their annoying behavior. If God has forgiven our own pains and annoying behaviors, we can certainly live with the same kind of grace toward others. Everyone needs a minister of mercy in his or her life. Be one as often as you can.

Like Jesus, you will need to see past the walls and offenses people put up around them to guard themselves from further wounds. A minister of grace needs to develop eyes for such things. But when you do, you are powerfully equipped to deliver grace to those who need it most. Let the wounds of Jesus do their work in others as they have done in you.

Jesus, give me the patience, endurance, and vision to be a minister of grace, even when it costs me something. May I cover the wounds of others as you have covered mine. Give me opportunities to help others heal. Amen.

The Power of Silence

He was led like a lamb to the slaughter. And as a sheep is silent
before the shearers, he did not open his mouth. (Isaiah 53:7)

THE LAMB WAS LED TO THE SLAUGHTER. He never opened his mouth, expressing dignity and majesty in his wordless demeanor. He had lived for this moment. There was no need for legal defenses, scathing rebuttals, or statements of innocence. He simply declared who he was and let the repercussions erupt around him. In everything he did—and in what he chose not to say—he demonstrated the character of the Kingdom, even while the anti-Kingdom raged against him.

Why didn't Jesus fight back? Why didn't he call armies of angels to his defense, as he insisted he could do? Why didn't he prove his deity with a flourish of stunning miracles that would silence his attackers? Why did he silence himself instead?

Because in his silence, Jesus exposed the true battle between a depraved world and a righteous God. He put evil on display against the innocence of its victim. He demonstrated humility in the face of pride, wisdom in the face of earthly power, truth and love in the face of distortion and hate. This could not turn into a battle of wits or an exchange of ideas. This went deeper. It was a conflict of spiritual realms, light versus darkness, the Kingdom of God versus its ancient rebels, the antidote to a pandemic of pride. In this case, silence was the winning argument.

If you want to know how to conduct yourself in this world, take your cues from Jesus' behavior at his most intense moment of conflict. Our mission of reconciliation is not served by a war of words. There is a time for words, but only when they are backed by dignity, character, and peace. We are far more effective when we live the Kingdom than when we argue it. Embrace it, wear it, and demonstrate it. Refuse to fuel the fires that rage against God's purposes. Your winning argument is very often the unspoken one.

Lord, may I always reflect your Kingdom values and the power of your ways. Make my words powerful when I speak them. Make my silence even more powerful when words are not enough. Amen.

Builders of the Common Good

Let us think of ways to motivate one another to acts of love and good works. And let us not neglect our meeting together, as some people do, but encourage one another. (Hebrews 10:24-25)

IN GRECO-ROMAN CULTURE, you would have been admired for building yourself up. Self-adulation, or at least self-promotion, was considered a virtue. By contrast, it was considered a virtue in the early church to build others up. Mutual strengthening, encouragement, and comfort supported the work God was doing and drew others into it (1 Corinthians 14:3). Like a massive construction project, God's people were to be busy at reinforcing the building's whole structure, not just themselves or their own corner of it.

Paul used this metaphor in Ephesians 2:19-22, where he emphasized the unity between Jews and Gentiles as a dwelling place for the Spirit. Peter did the same when he compared believers to living stones being built into a spiritual house (1 Peter 2:5). This construction of a flesh-and-blood temple was exemplified by hybrid congregations made up of different ethnicities and religious backgrounds. But it was also displayed through encouragers like Barnabas, who introduced Saul the persecutor to the apostles and changed history by helping integrate his ministry into the church (Acts 9:26-31). Relational construction is a vital activity among the people of God.

Why is this so important? Because Jesus both tore down and built up. God is on a mission to deconstruct anything in you that doesn't fit his character and Kingdom, but he is also on a mission to reconstruct anything that does. The fellowship of believers is one of his primary tools for that. Christians who tear each other down are missing their mission, confusing "[speaking] the truth in love" (Ephesians 4:15) with biting, wounding words. Some who grew up in families or schools where people felt like it was their job to put you in your place will have to learn a new culture. We no longer bring people down to put them in their place; we lift them up to put them in their place. We are ministers of edification, and we have the power to change the world one life at a time.

Holy Spirit, give me healing, encouraging, strengthening words to build up fellow believers and draw in those who seek to believe. Make me a builder of the common good. Amen.

A Ministry of Favor

The Spirit of the LORD is upon me, for he has anointed me to bring
Good News to the poor. He has sent me to proclaim that captives will
be released, that the blind will see, that the oppressed will be set free,
and that the time of the LORD's favor has come. (Luke 4:18-19)

ONE SABBATH IN NAZARETH, Jesus went to the synagogue and was invited to read aloud from the Scriptures. Whether that day's reading fell to this particular passage or Jesus chose it himself, it perfectly described the Messiah's mission statement. Jesus faithfully read this section of the Isaiah scroll and then abruptly stopped—right after the year of God's favor and before the day of vengeance (see Isaiah 61:1-2). What did he mean by this strategic editing? Judgment would come later; now was a time for blessing. History was entering a new season.

We love the idea of living under God's favor, often without understanding exactly what it means. It is much more than the idea of all things going smoothly in our lives, though God often orchestrates situations to our advantage. Divine favor is an invitation into God's *shalom*, the fullness of his Kingdom. It's an anointing to fulfill our assignment, to accomplish his purposes, and to live under his kind and watchful eye. It is the assurance that his promises are "yes" and "amen" (2 Corinthians 1:20) and that the God of glory is on our side. It's a guarantee that even the hard things will work out for our advancement.

Savor whatever God is doing in your life, even if it isn't particularly easy. Know that you are being drawn into his purposes. You are a captive being released, a blind person being given sight, an oppressed person coming out from under the oppression. More than that, you align with his mission to become a deliverer, a sight-giver, a freedom fighter in the truest sense. You are being invited into a place of glory, whether you see it right now or not. The Son's mission of showing favor is yours. So are his inheritance, his promises, and his love. Live as though the time of God's favor has come, because it has—for you and those you touch with the power of his Spirit.

Holy Spirit, you are upon Jesus in this time of favor, and I am in him. You have invited me into his mission. Fill me with your wisdom, power, and love to proclaim light, freedom, and blessing. Amen.

Instruments of Peace

*To all who mourn in Israel, he will give a crown of beauty for ashes,
a joyous blessing instead of mourning, festive praise instead of despair.*
(Isaiah 61:3)

AN ANONYMOUS PRAYER ATTRIBUTED to Francis of Assisi asks God to make the supplicant an instrument of his peace—to sow love in place of hatred, pardon in place of injury, faith in place of doubt, hope in place of despair, and so on. It echoes the thoughts of Jesus' mission statement in Luke 4, when he read a messianic passage from the scroll of Isaiah. And it takes seriously the idea that the messianic mission was not uniquely applied to Jesus, but that it carries over into the lives of his followers. After all, Jesus sent his disciples out to do what he had demonstrated for them. The mission was meant to continue.

That means we are to become ambassadors of *shalom*, carriers of the climate of God's Kingdom, instruments of God's peace, just as the "Prayer of Saint Francis" requests. We take light into dark places, joy into situations of sadness, and life into every environment that reeks of death. It isn't an easy mission, but it's at the cutting edge of God's Kingdom in a world that long ago rebelled and attempted to secede. It's the only way to invest our lives in eternity rather than spending them on the moment. It's how we partner with God in his redemptive work.

In the verses following the messianic mission that Jesus quoted, Isaiah writes that God gives beauty instead of ashes, joy instead of mourning, praise instead of despair. We long for him to rebuild our lives from the devastations and disappointments we've experienced, and these promises assure us that he will. But they also call us into the rebuilding work to be agents of beauty, joy, and praise. When we realize that, everything changes. We have a dramatic impact on the lives around us and bear the eternal fruit of God's Kingdom. And we become the answer to our own prayer—and to the prayers of others who long for their redemption.

Lord, I do pray that you would make me an instrument of your peace—and your light, your beauty, your joy, your forgiveness, and so much more. Fill me with the blessings of your Kingdom and use me to bless many others. Amen.

Enduring Faith

You will follow the example of those who are going to inherit God's promises because of their faith and endurance. (Hebrews 6:12)

"THERE'S NO SUCH THING AS BAD WEATHER, only bad clothing." That Scandinavian maxim reminds us that we have a better chance of enduring storms than calming them, though we see both approaches in Scripture. Jesus demonstrated the latter when he slept in the back of a boat while the surrounding winds and waves raged. The disciples on the boat questioned his concern for them, and after Jesus calmed the storm, he questioned their faith. The *shalom* inside of him—his peace, calm, and rest—was stronger than the chaos outside of him, and clearly his condition won. The Prince of *Shalom* brings the environment of God's Kingdom into every situation.

But sometimes difficult situations persist, even when we are conformed to the image of Jesus and filled with his presence. The prayers, attitudes, and actions we bring to our trials don't always change them right away. That isn't unusual; Scripture is full of stories of endurance. Often people waited for a promise and received it after many years, or even watched as the promise was passed on to future generations. The book of Hebrews tells us of faithful people who saw God's promise from a distance and died without having entered into its fulfillment—but were still honored and rewarded in God's Kingdom for investing their lives in his purposes. Again and again, faith and endurance go hand in hand for God's people, with faith making endurance possible and endurance making faith last. From our point of view, the need for endurance is a sign of things gone wrong. From God's point of view, it's a normal part of our journey.

Bring that sense of patient, faith-filled endurance into every area of your life—your relationships, work, goals, and certainly your spiritual growth. It will not only strengthen you for the long haul; it will serve as a sign of eternity in your heart, an example of what it means to be anchored in another realm. Your patience makes a profound statement about the character and ways of God, and it clothes you to weather any storm.

{ *Lord, I don't always understand your ways, but I know they are extremely thorough and lasting. Build into me that character—the values of your Kingdom and the testimony of eternal truth. Amen.*

The Language of Heaven

Whenever Aaron and his sons bless the people of Israel in my name,
I myself will bless them. (Numbers 6:27)

IF SOMEONE OFFERED YOU a method for reconstructing your world—not simply changing it, but building it into something completely new—what would you do with that information? As a citizen of heaven who is called to bring heaven's culture into earthly realms, you can probably imagine a lot of problems to address and opportunities to create. You are, after all, seated with Jesus in heavenly places (Ephesians 2:6) and told to pray that things on earth would reflect his Kingdom (Matthew 6:10). You've likely envisioned how that might look in the lives of those around you. What if the master key to your vision turned out to be the words you speak?

In fact, it is—at least in part. We are called to learn the language of heaven and speak it into people's hearts. That means replacing all complaining, gossip, frustration, and attention to problems with encouragement, affirmation, blessing, and attention to solutions. Instead of crying out for help, which always begins with a problem, we praise the majesty of God, which always begins with the answer. As holders of the truths of God's Kingdom, we have an amazing opportunity to shape our environment with them—if we are intentional about putting a Kingdom angle on everything we see.

God gave Israel's priests a tool to accomplish this task: the blessing Aaron was to speak over the people, which God said he would honor. It's a simple blessing, but with powerful effect: "May the LORD bless you and protect you. May the LORD smile on you and be gracious to you. May the LORD show you his favor and give you his peace" (Numbers 6:24-26). This is the culture of heaven being spoken into earth, an expression of the heart of God, and it's remarkably easy to do. It will require putting biases and judgments aside, but those are heavy burdens to carry anyway. Learn the language of heaven, and speak it freely. God is a blesser by nature; you are called to be one too.

Father, give me grace to set aside my criticisms and complaints, and fill my mouth with words of blessing. May my words be a vehicle for your goodness. Amen.

Like an Architect's Pencil

He is our father in the sight of God, in whom he believed—the God
who gives life to the dead and calls into being things that were not.
(Romans 4:17, NIV)

GOD CREATED THE WORLD with words. He spoke, and things happened. The Creator can do whatever he wants, of course, and he has every right to give his speech such power and privilege. His voice is an expression of who he is, and it carries his authority. He used it as his chosen means of creation.

The fact that we are created in this Creator's image ought to tell us something. Our words are powerful too. They don't create worlds—at least not in the same way—but they carry authority that we derive from our Father. His Son gave us the keys of the Kingdom, and his Word tells us to be careful about what we say. When our voices spill out the thoughts and intentions of our spirit, things happen.

According to Paul's words in Romans, Abraham became our father in faith by believing in the God who calls things into being that did not exist. In a sense, we have that opportunity too—first to believe in the words of God over what our natural eyes see (or don't see), but also to declare what we know to be true, even when it is not yet visible in this world. Like our Father, we are creators too.

That doesn't mean we can expect the natural world to conform to our every spoken word, but it does mean our voices carry the power to build up or destroy lives (James 3:1-12). They can be used as dangerous weapons or powerful cures—and we get to choose which they will be. By faith, we can speak things that are not yet manifested—the will of God in a particular situation, the light of heaven in dark places, the work of healing in broken and hurting lives—and expect them to come to pass. In fact, this is why we were endowed with the power of blessing. Use it often, and use it well.

Father, if you will let my words work like an architect's pencil, I will use them to draw up blueprints of glorious things. May I speak with wisdom and power over the lives around me. Amen.

Speaking the Language of Hope

Let everything you say be good and helpful, so that your words will be an encouragement to those who hear them. (Ephesians 4:29)

THE LANGUAGE OF HEAVEN IS a language of hope. As with any language, it requires some rewiring in our brains and some training in the way we think to be able to speak it well. And though we speak it for the benefit of other people, we also need to understand that we speak it for ourselves. Why? Because we are just as in need of hope as anyone else. Our thought processes are just as in need of reform. We need an inner renaissance working within us, a manifestation of our new birth, just as certainly as we long to see new birth coming into the hearts and lives of others. We need to immerse ourselves in an entirely new way to see.

Language has that power. The language of hope is revolutionary in the way we see, the words we speak, and the lives we encourage and change. It comforts those who need comforting (2 Corinthians 1:3-4), unites those who are divided (John 17:20-23), brings life to those who are dying (Romans 10:13-15), blesses those who are full of curses (Romans 12:14), and builds up those who have been torn down far too many times (Ephesians 4:29). It captures the essence of heaven and brings glimpses of it to earth. It aligns the environment of this world to the room temperature of God's Kingdom. It changes the culture.

That's good to know. Missiologists have been working on the challenges of cultural change for a long time, and they have a lot of wonderful insights. But real change begins one mouth at a time, one new vision voiced into the lives of those who need a fresh breath from God. It begins at street level with those who carry the culture of the Kingdom within them and know how to express it well. It begins with people like you.

Holy Spirit, may my vision, words, attitudes—everything—reflect the essence of who you are. Align my thoughts with yours. Fill my mind, heart, and voice with hope. Amen.

Hope in God's Greatness

I am the LORD, the God of all the peoples of the world.
Is anything too hard for me? (Jeremiah 32:27)

THE HUMAN MIND TENDS TO enlarge the problems it sees. We envision the possibilities—what *might* go wrong grows into what really *very likely* could go wrong, which then grows into the enormous threat of what *actually will* go wrong. A molehill can grow into a mountain in a remarkably short time, but usually only in our heads. When we express our anxieties out loud, they get even larger. We are experts at cultivating our worries.

But when we speak the language of hope, problems are small and God is big. We see this dynamic again and again in Scripture, whether it's God reminding Abraham and Sarah, in spite of their laughing and skepticism, that he can accomplish anything (Genesis 18:14); God telling Moses that his arm has never been too short to save (Numbers 11:23, NIV); Isaiah declaring that God's arm is still strong and his ears still hear (Isaiah 59:1); Jeremiah hearing the certainty of God's plans (Jeremiah 32:27); or Gabriel assuring Mary that nothing is impossible with God (Luke 1:37). In spite of such assurances, we have a disease that sociologists and psychologists call "negativity bias"; we lean toward the negative in our expectations. But God pulls us the other way. We and the people around us desperately need to hear the language of hope.

You can't learn this language by studying grammar, vocabulary, and syntax; but you can immerse yourself in it by gazing at God, worshiping and magnifying him in your own heart and mind, and being fully preoccupied with him rather than the troubling situation at hand. When trials come, we have a choice: stare at them or stare at God. One choice results in futility and despair; the other in hope and faith. One turns molehills into ominous mountains, the other proves mountains to be less than the size of God's palm. As is often said, what we focus on gets bigger. You and those around you need someone to change the focus and turn the narrative. You can do that by speaking the language of hope.

Father, my mind cannot afford to be preoccupied with anything other than you. Remind me of your greatness—that you are mighty to save, and nothing is hopeless with you. Amen.

Hope in God's Blessings

Our present troubles are small and won't last very long. Yet they produce for us a glory that vastly outweighs them and will last forever! (2 Corinthians 4:17)

BY NOW, YOU ARE PROBABLY WELL acquainted with the weight of this world. You know how it pulls you into a narrow focus—the excruciating details of a painful moment or the long seasons of discontentment that still cause us to guard our hearts from heartache. Distorted minds—which we all have to some degree—magnify the negative. When we get into a difficult situation, it begins to look permanent. We project the present into the future and assume, "It's always going to be this way," even when we know it isn't. Our hearts are far too easily resigned to disappointment.

When we speak the language of hope, trials are short and blessings are long. Paul spoke this language and was able to assure his readers that his imprisonment was working out for good, that vicious rivalries were actually advancing the gospel, and that whether he lived or died, the outcome would be a blessing (Philippians 1:12-24). He managed to put a positive spin on the most negative situations—not because that "spin" was a false narrative but because he knew that God always turns distressing problems and the weapons of the enemy into blessings and glory. Paul wrote that *everything* works out "for the good of those who love God and are called according to his purpose for them" (Romans 8:28). Even more specifically, he insisted that "what we suffer now is nothing compared to the glory he will reveal to us later" (Romans 8:18), and that "our present troubles are small and won't last very long" (2 Corinthians 4:17). In other words, the glory always outweighs the suffering for a believer in Christ. Always.

Whatever trials you go through, they are a blip on the screen of eternity. The same is true for the people around you. Your language can magnify that blip into alarming proportions, or it can tell the truth. In God's Kingdom, hope is reality. Speak it always.

Lord, my mind tells me my trials are long and your blessings are fleeting. Your Word says otherwise. Teach me that foreign tongue so that it becomes my first language—for my good, others' benefit, and your glory. Amen.

Hope in God's Truth

We demolish arguments and every pretension that sets itself up
against the knowledge of God, and we take captive every thought
to make it obedient to Christ. (2 Corinthians 10:5, NIV)

IN THE MARKET OF IDEAS, truth should beat the competition every time. But it doesn't. That's because in spite of all our claims of objectivity, we are all inevitably subjective. We can arrive at something approaching unbiased truth, but we ultimately choose which facts to consider and which facts to ignore. This is true in the public discourse about faith, to be sure; but it's even more true inside our own minds. We don't always have a balanced perspective. We assume things about other people's motives and thoughts. We imagine the worst. We let our fears, worries, resentments, wounds, and judgments carry far too much weight. In other words, we listen to lies.

When we speak the language of hope, lies become laughable and truth becomes clear. The language of hope assumes the best and is not ashamed to be proven wrong on occasion. Why? Because much more often in the Kingdom of God, it will be proven right. Paul wrote that we are able to demolish arguments and pretensions that set themselves against God and that we are able to take thoughts captive and align them with the mind of Christ. Quite a few Christians are not taking advantage of those possibilities, whether in their conversations with others or the thoughts in their own heads. But that doesn't nullify the promise. When our hearts are filled with the culture of God's Kingdom, we are able to see truth and dismiss deception.

One of the rarest commodities in the world right now is a healthy perspective. Have one. Look at falsehoods, deceptions, the language of animosity, and arguments against God that are rampant in social media and other public forums, and laugh at their futility. Don't get caught up in such thinking; you speak a different language. Your words and your attitude—your refusals to buy into empty disputes and debates—strip lies of their power. Your hope overcomes. It is a precious commodity. Offer it freely to everyone.

Jesus, you never got sucked into a futile debate. You spoke truth—often pointedly—but you refused to treat it as if it were up for grabs. May I do the same, and may the truth I speak always bring life. Amen.

Psalm 105:16-22

Hope in God's Promises

Until what he had said came to pass, the word of
the LORD tested him. (Psalm 105:19, ESV)

JOSEPH COULD HAVE DESPAIRED. He had God-given dreams of glory, of being used for God's purposes in unusual and powerful ways. But as soon as he voiced those dreams to his brothers, every step he took seemed to go in the opposite direction of God's promise. Joseph's brothers sold him into slavery; his Egyptian master had him imprisoned under false accusations; his one link to the outside world forgot him. He could have wallowed in disillusionment or disappointment. He could have assumed he had forfeited the promise and beat himself up for broadcasting it. He could have feared that God had forgotten him. But every step he took away from the promise actually brought him closer to it. After much time, in the course of a single day, he was elevated into a position of power and influence. God fulfilled what he had said.

We have promises from God too, but we often assume that they come with fine print, that the conditions are greater than the promise. When we are faced with delays and silences from God, we begin to despair. We start to wonder if God meant what he said. Joseph could have entertained such thoughts, but his story doesn't say so. Abraham and Sarah did; their promise seemed forever in the future and impossibly out of reach. David did as well; years of exile and several psalms of desperation came before he secured the throne. The gap between promise and fulfillment stretches us, tests us, and redefines our understanding of hope.

When we speak the language of hope, disappointment loses its power and promises become certain. We are called to live with expectation, even if it means looking like fools for a time. We have to understand our role. Ours are the only audible voices heaven can use to tell a disappointed world that there is a God who keeps his promises and that those who believe him will see them fulfilled. If we don't express the realities of God's Kingdom, no one will. Never let disappointment take root in your heart, even if it passes through for a time. You and your world need the reality of a God who makes promises and keeps them.

Lord, your ways are often hard to understand, and your timing tests me. Even so, may I
see the reality behind my disappointments. You have stored up only good for me and all
who seek you. May my words never express anything less. Amen.

Just Being Real

The terrible storm raged for many days, blotting out the sun and the stars, until at last all hope was gone. (Acts 27:20)

PAUL AND OTHER PRISONERS were being shipped to Rome, and the prophetic impulse in Paul sensed that trouble was ahead. Even so, the ship's captain and crew continued on with the voyage. When a violent storm threatened the ship, the crew threw cargo and gear overboard. Still, the ship was tossed on the waves for days, and "all hope was gone." Well, not *all* hope. At least one passenger spoke God's will into the situation and informed everyone else of what they could not see with their natural eyes. An angel had promised Paul that even though they would, in fact, be shipwrecked, he and his fellow passengers would survive. After all, Paul had been given a mission to preach the gospel to the empire's highest officials. That mission was not going to end at the bottom of the sea.

So Paul spoke words of truth and hope: "I believe God. It will be just as he said" (verse 25). No one would have faulted him if he had said, "I think everything will be okay, but it's all in God's hands." Or if he had said, "I'm having a really hard time with this; I'm carrying an important message, but bad things happen to good people. Oh well, God has ways of accomplishing his purposes, with me or without me." Paul had seen Christians, even apostles, die. He could have become discouraged. He made a choice to listen to God and then speak the language of hope.

We're well familiar with the tendency to express our disappointments and frustrations with the claim of "just being real." But is our "real" actually real? What if our perspective doesn't align with God's? Whose reality is real—his or ours? It's one thing to be honest about our feelings; it's another to be true. God understands our ups and downs, but we need to understand the culture of his Kingdom. It always skews toward hope, blessing, and glory. May our hearts, minds, and words align fully with his.

Lord, you do not judge disappointment harshly, but you do call me into truth. If I could see with your eyes, I would never be discouraged. Give me the gift of anticipation for all the goodness you have planned. Amen.

The Master Architect

*We are carefully joined together in him, becoming
a holy temple for the Lord. (Ephesians 2:21)*

THE CONSTRUCTION OF Canterbury Cathedral began in 597 and did not reach its final form until 1510—more than nine centuries later. In fact, many medieval cathedrals were built with timelines that were centuries long. Sometimes they were built in stages, with long periods in between, and sometimes the next stage wasn't planned until it was deemed necessary. But many workers on such massive projects knew they would never see the finished form in their own lifetimes. One generation built foundations that would be necessary for the work of generations to come.

God's work is like that, but on an even greater scale. For a long time, his blueprints were hidden to all but a few key leaders. In fact, they were not visible until the revelation of Jesus. But now they are an open record, and the project is stunning in scope. It no longer includes only the parties to the first covenant; it has expanded to the entire human race. Any who enter into it by faith become part of the grand construction that has been in the works since before time began.

As you learn to envision the master builder's enormous construction project, you enter into your daily interactions a bit differently—with patience, wisdom, a discerning eye toward the gifts and roles of the people around you, an understanding of where you fit in the entire scheme, an appreciation of the diversity of materials he is using, and a sense of unity with every other participant in the plan. This is not just a beautiful building; it's a holy temple, designed and fitted to host the presence of God himself. It's a visible expression of who he is in this world. Live with that perspective—the long one, full of grace and gratitude. Your sense of destiny for others will draw them into God's grand enterprise on earth.

Father, you are the master architect, and your work is amazing. Let me see glimpses not only of the blueprint but of the finished project. Captivate my vision with what you are building. Use me to draw many into it. Amen.

The Divine Nature

These are the promises that enable you to share his divine nature and
escape the world's corruption caused by human desires. (2 Peter 1:4)

MANY PEOPLE COMPARE Christians and non-Christians and don't always see a difference. Believers have the advantage of experiencing inward transformations, and sometimes we wonder how people who don't know God function in a world that is discouraging and meaningless without him. Our hope and quality of life seems infinitely better, but our day-to-day actions and behavior don't always show it. That's because many of us are not living from our divine nature. Some of us may not even believe it's possible.

But it is. It seems like an outrageous claim to suggest that once-fallen but now-redeemed human beings can have the divine nature within themselves, but Scripture assures us that we can. It is part of our new birth and the inheritance we have through the Son. It lies latent within us if we do not claim God's promises and live by faith in him, and it remains useless to us if we don't know who we really are in him. But for those who have the faith and courage to step into his promises—the reality of who we are, what he has done, and what he has purposed—the divine nature begins to emerge. We really do find ourselves living a different sort of life than we once lived. Life becomes supernatural, wondrous, and new.

For your sake and the sake of those around you, make it a point to embrace everything the New Testament says about you—the fact of your new heart (whether you see it or not), the fact that you are now a saint rather than a sinner (whether you are experiencing that or not), the fact that you have been given all sorts of assurances about prayer and faith and doing the works of God (whether you have stepped into their fullness or not). You are who he says you are, not who you think or feel yourself to be. You are new. And the divine nature is yours to experience.

Father, may the reality of what you say become infinitely more real to me than what I
think, feel, or experience. Give me Kingdom eyes, thoughts, and words. May your divine
nature flourish in me. Amen.

Pursuing the Treasure

In view of all this, make every effort to respond to God's promises.
(2 Peter 1:5)

SPANISH DISCOVERY OF THE many silver and gold deposits in the New World upped the intensity of world exploration and fueled European economies for centuries to come. The realization that precious metals were waiting to be found and exploited by first-comers resulted in enormous changes in the wealth of kingdoms and the balance of world power. Why? Because no one ignores a treasure. People drop everything to pursue it (Matthew 13:44-46). The search becomes their focus.

Redemption is a vast treasure, yet many people who say they believe in it don't explore its depths or take advantage of its promise. It's an odd situation in light of what God has said about us. The act of redeeming includes the divine nature, a calling into astounding glory and excellence, a provision for every situation of need (2 Peter 1:3). We have been promised the fullness of an entirely new way of living and being, yet we slip into old patterns and expectations with ease. Far too often, the treasure does not compel us. We are not captivated by the vision of new worlds. Having been promised the presence and power of God, we far too often fail to see it.

Every problem in life and every obstacle you face may appear to be a hindrance to you, but it is not. Each one is an opportunity, the wind that lifts your wings, the moment to seek God's face *and find it.* The eyes of faith ask the right questions and expect the answers: *Who does God want to be for me in this situation? What aspect of his nature does he want to reveal? In what ways does he want me to experience him in the trial or trouble I'm going through?* Every moment of need is a potential moment of experiencing God in some way.

Fix your eyes on that treasure. Or in today's vernacular, bring it all to the table. In your quest to experience his fullness, never leave God's promises sitting there. Let the divine nature, already given, rise up in you.

Lord, give me the faith to believe and receive. May I not miss one step of the purposes you have set before me. May I grow fully into your promises of divine nature. Amen.

Repairing the World

You will be known as a rebuilder of walls and a restorer of homes.
(Isaiah 58:12)

TIKKUN OLAM IS A PHRASE from rabbinic Judaism, traceable back to the Mishnah, that has become a synonym for social justice. It means "repairing the world," and it includes the acts of charity and social reform common among today's activists. But its original sense involves not only works of justice but the reason behind them—human participation in the divine work of restoration. While many of us look to God to see what he will do to fix things, he often throws the question back at his people. He involves us in his plans.

Many Christians are unfamiliar with this *tikkun olam* concept, but it fits the heart of God. It recognizes not only that God saves us *from* the world, but he also saves us *in* the world. He has not called his creation a lost cause and abandoned it for something better down the road. He is fully into restoring what he made (Acts 3:21).

Christians have a distinguished history of preaching the gospel of redemption, but the gospel of restoration has gotten lost along the way. In truth, they are two sides of the same coin. God does not flee from problems; he fixes them. He does not give up; he is bent on making all things new. The good news of salvation is not just an escape; it's a renovation of life and the world around you.

That's why Jesus told his followers to ask for God's Kingdom to come on earth *just as it is in heaven.* Yes, it will come in its fullness one day, but that doesn't mean it's *only* for later. God is not biding his time. He's at work today, in your life and in the lives of those around you. And he's calling his people to embrace the business of restoration.

If you want to be like God, be a restorer. He repairs broken walls and restores streets (Isaiah 58:12, NIV), and he makes all things new (Revelation 21:5). He loved the world so much that he sent his only Son to it. And his Son sends each of us into the same world with the same mind-set and mission.

Jesus, let me be your hands and feet on earth. You have restored my life; make me a restorer in my corner of this world. Amen.

Freedom Fighters

Let the oppressed go free, and remove the chains that bind people.
(Isaiah 58:6)

JESUS CAME FOR FREEDOM. He said so, and so did Paul (John 8:36; 2 Corinthians 3:17). The messianic manifesto long foretold in Isaiah (61:1-2) and claimed by Jesus in Luke 4 signals a keen interest on God's part to see the human race delivered from the forces that hold it captive. Whether by spiritual, emotional, relational, political, physical, or any other kind of oppression, we were never meant to be caged. We were created to live unbound.

That does not mean we can live lives of independence or amoral behavior, which lead to all sorts of unintended captivities. It does, however, mean we can loose ourselves from false restraints, false expectations, and false images that distort our original design. Our spirits were meant to soar as freely as the Spirit who captivates us with his love. Seeking that kind of freedom is much higher on God's list of priorities for us than the religious formalities many of us use to become "holy" or "spiritual." That's what God's words through Isaiah mean—the "fasting" he prefers is for us to deal ruthlessly with oppression in all its forms, both for ourselves and others. Jesus made that kind of freedom part of his mission, and he makes it part of the mission of all who follow him. In many respects, his calling is our calling (John 20:21). We are freedom fighters in the truest sense of the term.

What does that look like in your life? Where many Christians emphasize a concern for either spiritual or physical captivity, you become concerned for all that and more. You begin to see every form of oppression as a distortion of the original design and an enemy of the life God has given us. Oppression is anti-gospel, which means God has a solution for it. Seek that solution for yourself and for others wherever you see the ravages of oppression. Speak words of life that free spirits, minds, and bodies from their chains. In every relationship, become a messenger of the heart set free.

Jesus, let your mission become my mission. Let my heart beat with yours when I see oppression in all its forms. Give me the wisdom, power, and love to be free and help others find freedom too. Amen.

A Heart for the Hungry

Share your food with the hungry, and give shelter to the homeless.
(Isaiah 58:7)

ONE OF THE PITFALLS OF Christian theology over the centuries is that it has tended to spiritualize everything in the Old Testament. Not that events like the Exodus, the entrance into the Promised Land, and the feasts of Israel didn't actually happen, of course, but they have become valued merely as symbols of deeper, more lasting truths. Israel's battles have become metaphors for our spiritual battles; literal hunger and thirst have become pictures of our spiritual hunger and thirst. We are right to emphasize the spiritual, but in doing so, we have often neglected the material. God is still concerned for actual captives and hungry people. He still wants to meet the needs of those who hurt.

We see this tension even in the New Testament. Where Luke quotes Jesus saying, "Blessed are you who are poor" (Luke 6:20, NIV), Matthew quotes him saying, "Blessed are the poor *in spirit*" (Matthew 5:3, NIV, emphasis added). Both are promised the Kingdom of Heaven. We can be reasonably sure that Jesus said it both ways at various times and meant it both ways each time. Why? Because God has made his concerns clear throughout the written Word. His heart is drawn to the hurting, the needy, the sick, the helpless, and the brokenhearted. And if our hearts aren't . . . that's a problem.

God wants to meet these deep human needs, and he very often does—but usually he meets them through his people, just as he does virtually everything else in this world. He has chosen human agency for a reason, which means each of us has a role in accomplishing his purposes on earth. When we see needs around us, something in our spirits should feel compelled to meet them. None of us can address all of them, but many of us can do something more. When we do, we reflect the heart of our Father in tangible, memorable ways. We put material clothes on an eternal gospel. And we show people who God really is.

{ *Jesus, you are a comprehensive Savior, and I want to be a comprehensive follower. Show me what I can do. I can't change everyone's life, but I can change some. Draw my heart toward the hungry and hurting, and let me fill them with daily and everlasting food. Amen.*

Like the Dawn

*Then your salvation will come like the dawn, and your wounds
will quickly heal. . . . Then when you call, the LORD will answer.
"Yes, I am here," he will quickly reply. (Isaiah 58:8-9)*

GOD MADE AN EXTRAORDINARY promise to his people. If they would turn from faith in their own religiosity to faith in God's true nature, he would enter into their lives in powerful ways, healing their wounds and rescuing them from their troubles. Where once their prayers had seemed to bounce off heaven's walls, they would now win his immediate response. The people's responsiveness to God's concerns would make him responsive to theirs.

Why did God set these conditions? Because he wants his people to relate to him as he *really* is—to connect with him on the issues that matter most to him, to recognize what he is doing, to become his allies in spirit and in purpose. Isaiah wrote to people who had done what most human beings inevitably do. They had turned their relationship with God into false standards of holiness and rituals of performance, focusing their attention on the principles and practices that "make life work." They dressed up their sins in clothes of penance and piety. They missed the core of their faith and forgot its central truth: that recognizing God's heart and aligning with it gives us access to him.

Jesus put it another way: Those who clothe themselves in the manner of a servant, with a genuine love for those around them, become great in his Kingdom (Matthew 20:25-28). Those who express the heart of God in meeting real needs tap into the power he designed us to have. Those who have God's compassion within them will look at others with a heart of compassion and be compelled to act (1 John 3:17). That's what it looks like to be connected with God, and that's what prompts him to act. Those who pursue his interests find him zealously pursuing theirs, and answers to their prayers break through like the dawn.

Father, show me what's on your heart today. Whose lives do you want to touch? Whose needs do you want to meet? How can I help? Guide me in compassionate directions, and let me experience your compassion toward me. Amen.

A Spring of Life

The LORD will guide you continually, giving you water when you are dry and restoring your strength. You will be like a well-watered garden, like an ever-flowing spring. (Isaiah 58:11)

ISRAEL HAD EXPERIENCED its share of deserts, and so have you. We live in a world of wildernesses, and sometimes we begin to think they are normal—that there is no Promised Land, no destiny overflowing with fruitfulness, no place of fulfillment and joy. But those who align their hearts with God find that there is. It doesn't come without a journey, but it does come. God promises to be your source, the wellspring that makes the garden of your life flourish, the nourishment you need in any season. His watering first comes *in* you; then it comes *through* you into the lives of others; and then fruitfulness comes *for* you—usually in that order. We receive him as a gift, then share what we've been given, then receive an abundance of his blessings.

How do you water others' lives and bear fruit? By choosing not to do what most people do: take their encounters with others at face value. Natural eyes see the outward demeanor of the people around them, and they react to what they see. We, however, are called to see past the surface and be sensitive. Deep inside, everyone is insecure, everyone is carrying disappointments, and everyone is trying their best to make life work. Some are still bearing the open wounds of an abusive childhood or the rejection of a loved one from long ago. Some are just going through a really hard time. Our job is to be like Jesus—to soften those who are hardened, to love the difficult-to-love, to show compassion to those who hurt, even when none of those things are on the surface. When we can't see the pain behind the pose, we miss an opportunity to be an ever-flowing spring that waters the lives around us.

Don't miss the opportunity. You have been refreshed with living waters; pour them out. You have been given nourishment; be fruitful by nourishing others. Let your own wounds be healed so you can be a healing salve to the wounded all around you. Become an ever-flowing stream.

Lord, I've been far too focused on my own fulfillment, yet it comes most fully when I nourish and bless those around me. Turn my vision outward; let me see the wounded hearts that need your touch. Amen.

The Highest Mountain

*In the last days, the mountain of the LORD's house will be
the highest of all—the most important place on earth. It will
be raised above the other hills, and people from all over the
world will stream there to worship. (Isaiah 2:2)*

H. RICHARD NIEBUHR'S SEMINAL book in the 1950s, *Christ and Culture*, explores the question of how our position of being *in* the world but not *of* the world plays out. Is following Jesus and participating in the world an either-or choice (Christ *against* culture)? Are Christians to make the world a better place (Christ *of* culture)? Is the Kingdom of God above the world but working with it (Christ *above* culture)? Do we live in two realms at the same time, giving to God what is God's and to Caesar what is Caesar's (Christ and culture in paradox)? Or can cultures be converted to resemble the Kingdom of God (Christ the transformer of culture)?

Each of these has its advocates and biblical support; each has its detractors and biblical counterpoints. Whatever the answer, as "salt and light" in this world, we have to believe in the possibility of transformation—that Jesus really can make a difference in people's lives. He saves spiritually, but he also redeems and restores. We have a significant role in his restoration project.

Isaiah envisioned a transformation of the world's response to God—not after the last days but in the midst of them. However literally you take his vision, it also represents God's desire for his people in general—that he would be exalted in the earth and that his people would be influencers of a world that needs him. Ultimate fulfillment of that vision will come. In the meantime, we are to be moving in that direction—pointing to God's "mountain," his way of doing things, his promises and purposes, his own glory at the center of the universe. We are to offer the promise of transformed hearts, minds, relationships, and experiences, even in our own age. We are to present the mountain of the Lord as the highest, best, most satisfying and fulfilling of all worlds.

Father, your ways are best, not only for me but for all the endeavors of this world. May I never shrink back from the excellence of your plans, and may I demonstrate them well to others. Amen.

Known by Love

Your love for one another will prove to the world
that you are my disciples. (John 13:35)

CHRISTIANITY HAS EXPERIENCED its share of reformations, one of which began radically transforming the church five centuries ago. One of the strengths of that reformation was its emphasis on God's Word as the reliable foundation of all truth. One of its drawbacks was that Christians began defining themselves by how they interpret that truth. The result is that we have, by some estimates, at least 35,000 denominations (and multiple streams of thought within them) in the world today, with virtually all believing they have cornered the market on doctrine and understanding. Our dedication to the Word of God has divided us in countless ways.

Scripture itself never defines us by our doctrinal understanding, and we can be grateful for that. It comes closer to defining us by our love for God and for each other—in truth, of course, not in hair-splitting, fellowship-breaking distinctions. God never changes, but his people are constantly learning, experiencing new challenges, growing in understanding, gaining insights, and being led in various ways. We will never get to the point of having exhausted all possible experiences with his infinite being. Even in eternity, we will be seeing him from new angles and marveling at his works forever. We need to have the humility today to understand that our glimpse of his glory does not define who he is but contributes to the whole picture.

What we really need is another reformation that allows the body of Christ to see and experience unity in the Spirit. In some ways, this is already happening, but much of the world doesn't recognize it yet. We are not known for our love but for being uptight, divisive, condemning, and argumentative. Love undoes such things. It doesn't ignore truth; it simply bridges the gaps in our understanding of it. It reaches into lives with real compassion and grace. When we step into that kind of love, we will change not only the image of the church but the lives of the people within and outside of it.

Jesus, we have fallen short of your purposes, but the calling you've given us remains.
Above all else, fill us with love. Overwhelm my heart with your compassion for people,
and give me opportunities to show it. Amen.

A New Way

I will put my laws in their minds, and I will write them on their hearts. I will be their God, and they will be my people. (Hebrews 8:10)

IMAGINE A WORLD IN WHICH those who know their God simply act according to his character because it comes naturally to them. They are guided by revelation rather than ambition. They are not disciplined to live by principles and rituals; they just are who they have been created to be. In every area of society, they become influencers who have divine ideas and offer solutions that are inspired by his Spirit. They bear light and carry hope, creativity, mercy, servanthood, integrity, and purity into every corner of the world. They manifest God's presence because it is with them, on them, even in them. They are, in essence, connecting points between heaven and earth that bridge the gap for a fallen world.

Does that seem unrealistic? Perhaps it is, based on our own experience, but not according to God's promise. And when our experience doesn't match his promise, one of them needs to bend to align with the other. It can't be God's Word; we have to adjust our expectations. The goal for God's people really is to rise and shine his light upon them. It really is for us to have his laws—his will and his ways—so thoroughly written into our hearts that we are guided by our new nature rather than the disciplines and habits we have will-powered onto our fallen nature. We are to be people shaped not by external demands but by an internal presence, the Spirit of God himself. We influence this world by *being*. Only then can we do what we are led to do.

You are an ambassador of the new way. That doesn't mean you have to become perfect in order to influence your world. But it does mean you have to embrace a new nature, to focus not on performing well but on carrying the presence of God into every situation you face. He changes lives through encounters with his Spirit, and his Spirit is in his people. Experience his presence, then let others experience it through you.

Holy Spirit, fill me to overflowing. Manifest your presence in me and through me. Make me a catalyst for change in every situation you take me through. Amen.

The Stories of Our Lives

Let everything that breathes sing praises to the LORD! (Psalm 150:6)

EVERYONE LOVES A GOOD STORY. In fact, the human brain is wired to learn through storytelling. We remember stories, images, and illustrations far better than we remember quotes, facts, and propositional truth—which explains why Jesus told parables and God gave us a book full of visual imagery, life stories, and profound metaphors. We grasp what we experience with our senses more easily and deeply than we process information. We are captivated by good plots and memorable scenes.

If we want to communicate the gospel to the world, then we will have to do so through stories—lives lived, situations experienced, and creative arts displayed for all to see. That doesn't mean every work of Christian literature, every piece of Christian art, and every Christian movie needs to present the plan of salvation or include a John 3:16 quote. It does, however, mean that the grand themes of redemption and restoration need to echo throughout. Hope is the property of God; we are to use it to reach a world that needs him.

The entertainment industry has come a long way toward that end, even when it hasn't intended to. Books and movies incorporating redemptive themes from Christian authors and artists—the works of a Tolkien or Lewis, the biographies of a Wilberforce or Bonhoeffer, the efforts at capturing biblical storylines—have touched hearts and drawn people toward the beauty of ultimate restoration. But even more compelling than the stories of the big screen are the stories of our lives. The ways we navigate difficult challenges, the ways we orient our entire lives toward God, and the ways we see redemptive threads in everything we go through can profoundly shape others' lives. We don't just experience the gospel. We live it. And in living it, we preach it, with and without words.

Be creative—in every form of real life and in artistic expression. The world needs living, breathing examples of humility, affirmation, redemption, integrity, inspiration, and hope. Tell those stories often. Even better, be one.

Lord, my story is full of bad turns, apparent plot holes, and missteps—but also full of hope and promises of restoration. Use it as you will. May every story I tell, idea I have, and work I accomplish point to themes of glory. Amen.

Making Friends of Enemies

*The king talked with them, and no one impressed him
as much as Daniel, Hananiah, Mishael, and Azariah.
So they entered the royal service. (Daniel 1:19)*

GOVERNMENTS ARE PRONE TO CORRUPTION. It would be hard to miss that fact in any era of history, including ours. Frustration and outrage over human governments dominate headlines and motivate thousands upon thousands of promises of "change." But real change is rare. The ways of the world infiltrate systems and sway human hearts, even those with the best of intentions. We long for a well-run society.

Imagine, then, how drastically noticeable it would be for God's people to enter into the institutions of this world without being corrupted by its age-old ills. What if those in power consulted with the Spirit of God and his people for guidance, direction, prayer, and a sense of God's voice for the moment? What if Christians in influential places prayed for God's solutions to social problems that no one has yet been able to solve—and received his answers? What if the people of God instituted a new culture of politics that invites cooperation and healthy compromise, even with people at opposite ends of the ideological spectrum? What if we became known as the people on earth most likely to be supportive and cooperate with one another—not to compromise truth but to reach common ground?

These utopian ideals may be out of reach in this age, but the intent and the character behind them are not. Far more lives have been changed by demonstrations of goodwill than by unmovable attitudes. People like Daniel and his friends, and Joseph before them, served ungodly kings and softened hard hearts in the process. They were put in a position of honoring selfish royal agendas while maintaining their integrity and doing good for kingdoms that often exploited their people. They understood a vital truth: Befriending adversaries is far more fruitful in the long run than overpowering them. If you want to influence your world, remember that. Seek the welfare even of people you disagree with and don't like. Love changes corrupt societies and even the most hardened hearts.

Lord, you have called us to a new culture. We do not conform to the ways of the world; we transform them. Show us how. Give me grace to love the unlovable and, like you, seek the welfare of all. Amen.

Beautiful Feet

How beautiful on the mountains are the feet of the
messenger who brings good news. (Isaiah 52:7)

IT IS OFTEN SAID THAT YOU will be remembered not for what you say but by how people feel when they are around you. That's a sobering and profound truth for anyone who wants to influence this world, but it also represents an extraordinary opportunity. You can build meaningful, lasting relationships by expressing the warmth, security, and joy of the Kingdom of God.

Complaining, bitterness, discouragement, and negativity leave a lasting impression, and not a good one. The good news, however, is that we always have good news. As believers in a compassionate, loving, wise, all-powerful Father, we have wonderfully encouraging stories to tell. We have promises to declare, hopes to proclaim, silver linings to point out, and so much more. No situation in this world is hopeless; even the worst events have threads of redemption running through them. God has told us so, and we have seen it ourselves. We have no reason to despair.

Even so, people around us will despair. That's where we come in as bearers of good news. Clearly the message of salvation is the core of that good news, but it is a comprehensive, all-of-life salvation. When we point others to the hope we have been given despite what we experience on earth and put a positive light on today's headlines, we are bearers of good news. The media will give us a constant stream of tragic circumstances, but we see the bigger picture. God is at work in this world, amazing things are happening, and we get to participate in and tell the story.

That's what it means to be a giver of hope and a bearer of good news. People are drawn to God through such words and begin to feel his presence. Soon, many are asking how they can know him. The message becomes simple, and responses become deep. The good news of every aspect of salvation, not only in its ultimate sense but also in its relevance to here-and-now situations, creates a heavenly environment. And the bearer of good news is beautiful in the eyes of God.

Lord, put beautiful words in my mouth. Give me the grace to speak profound, truthful words of hope in every situation. Draw people to the promise of your Kingdom. Let me voice the nature of your goodness always. Amen.

For the Common Good

Don't be concerned for your own good but for the good of others.
(1 Corinthians 10:24)

IN A FALLEN WORLD, human nature turns toward self. Self-focused people look out for their own interests above the interests of others, which means that the way of the world naturally leans toward exploitation. People generally want to make a sale for their benefit, not yours; they want to promote an idea for their sake, not yours; and they want to attain a certain status to boost their self-esteem, even at the expense of others. We call it human nature, and sometimes it shows up only in mild forms. But we also know the ugly side of exploitation in conquests, enslavements, oppression, and scams. The world is full of self-promoters.

Sadly, this tendency can infiltrate the church too, but it shouldn't. We are called to an entirely different culture. As people of a new life, the way we do business should look different from the way the rest of the world does it. Imagine the possibilities: economic policies that don't exploit anyone yet produce healthy growth and prosperity; consumer-focused capitalism that serves buyers before sellers; businesses that consider ethics an asset rather than a liability. Some have discovered the benefit of such attitudes and practices; others will realize them later. In any case, the people of God should be blazing new trails and leading the way. The marketplace is not irrelevant to the Kingdom of God; it can be a platform for demonstrating his character.

If you are in business, consider how you might apply Kingdom principles to your business practices. If you play a role in the marketplace, think of how you can contribute to changing the culture. Historically, Christians have often accommodated the ways of the world in their trade and lived a somewhat distinct life at home and church. But the gospel transforms everywhere. Even in a competitive environment, it bears fruit. God honors those who go against the grain to follow his ways. Let every area of your life, even your business and finances, become a platform for the wisdom and love he gives you.

Lord, you are selfless by nature. Show me how to live according to your nature even in areas of this world that resist it. By the power of your Spirit, may I instinctively seek the welfare of others in every situation. Amen.

Wisdom from Above

Intelligent people are always ready to learn.
Their ears are open for knowledge. (Proverbs 18:15)

IN THE LAST COUPLE OF CENTURIES, many Christians have lamented the trends in education that have marginalized biblical revelation and emphasized empirical or quantifiable knowledge to the exclusion of all else. One response to those trends has been to withdraw from "secular" organizations and create our own schools. Many great institutions have been developed as a result, but the absence of Christian voices in the public sector has also been noticeable for decades. Now, in spite of the best efforts of many, reintegrating biblical truth has been difficult. We still come across as marginal voices.

To a degree, that will always be true. Our message will always be controversial and rejected by some. But our influence in this world will always be harmed by the impulse to flee whatever we perceive as "godless" and cling to our own subculture. It makes little sense to withdraw our influence from huge sectors of society and then lament how little influence we have in them. We made choices. Now we need to remedy them.

God is calling many people in our day to go to the places we left behind and be reasonable voices of truth. There are times to isolate and become grounded in our own understanding, but even greater opportunities are found in a world that seeks understanding. We need to get past the fear of threatening influences that could change us and live as influencers out to change the world. And we can, with confidence, because he who is in us is greater than any alternative version of truth the world declares (1 John 4:4). If we go with humility, a desire to learn, a sensitivity to other viewpoints, a rock-solid conviction that we know the God of the universe, and a willingness to ask the Holy Spirit for unusual wisdom and insights, we can add light and truth to conversations that have long excluded us. We can, like Jesus confronting the educated of his day, offer perspectives from beyond this world.

Lord, I can never know everything I need to know to confront every false teaching in this world. I can, however, know your truth and hear your voice. Give me a hunger to learn, extraordinary wisdom, and spiritual insights to share with many. Amen.

The Family of God

The human body has many parts, but the many parts make up one whole body. So it is with the body of Christ. (1 Corinthians 12:12)

"LORD, LET ME REFLECT YOUR NATURE." This is a common prayer among those who want to make a difference in this world. It (or something like it) shows up often even in the pages of this book. But when we pray these words, we often think of them in terms of our internal character, our desires and motivations, our spiritual maturity, and the condition of our heart. We tend to forget that the only contexts in which these attributes appear, the only situations in which anyone might see the Spirit and the nature of God working within us, are in our relationships—especially the everyday ones. Our character is noticeable in our interactions with others as we go about our business, but it is especially noticeable in our natural families and in the family of God. We are most observably like Jesus—or not—when we are least aware of the need to be like Jesus.

The attributes of God we tend to value most are social in nature. We praise him for his love, his compassion, his kindness and gentleness, his forgiveness, his patience with us, and so on. We are impressed by things like his majesty and glory, but we aren't always likely to embrace these attributes for ourselves. But God's relational attributes—the ways he deals with each of us individually—are the ones we desire to reflect. The problem is that we are most conscious of reflecting them for outsiders to the faith. But our true level of maturity comes out when we display them at home or in fellowship with the body of Christ.

Treasure those relationships as opportunities to demonstrate the nature of God. The world notices how well we love one another, how we handle the normal tensions and frictions of everyday life. Even more important, living with generous spirits toward each other builds up an army of potential influencers. Reflectors of God's nature brighten other reflectors and shine his light in this world.

Lord, may I never take for granted the relationships in my natural and spiritual family. There, more than anywhere, let me reflect your nature—to build others up and demonstrate your goodness for all to see. Amen.

Our First Pursuit

Seek the Kingdom of God above all else, and live righteously,
and he will give you everything you need. (Matthew 6:33)

"THE BEST LAID PLANS OF mice and men go oft awry." So wrote Scottish poet Robert Burns (albeit in more archaic language), and his words have been quoted ever since because their message rings true. The best laid plans of God, however, are always on point. The question for us, then, is how we get from "awry" to "on point" as often as possible, both at the practical level of our daily lives and in the big picture of our future. In other words, how do we align ourselves with God's plans rather than spinning our wheels trying to follow our own?

The answer is counterintuitive, but it is vital for being salt and light in this world. The best way to reorient our plans to align with God's ways is to cultivate face-to-face intimacy with him—profound fellowship that involves regular feasting on his Word, two-way conversations with him, and worship at the deepest levels of the heart. That sort of relationship will take a significant chunk out of our daily schedules and perhaps leave some items on our to-do lists unchecked, but it will streamline the rest of our lives, make our paths more efficient (at least by God's definition), create opportunities we could not have created on our own, and cultivate fruitfulness in whatever we do. It will not mean a trouble-free life, but it will mean a life in sync with God. And that is worth sacrificing whatever plans we hold tightly.

When you spend time in God's presence, you tend to get much more done "coincidentally" than you ever used to accomplish when you were trying your best. As the orchestrator of faithful lives, he calls us into the kind of relationship in which we can abandon ourselves to him and expect him to work on our behalf. We do our part, to be sure, but we do it following his lead and with his backing. There is no better laid plan than that, and there is nothing with greater potential to influence the world.

Father, you tell me to seek your Kingdom above all else—and the first part of seeking the Kingdom is to seek the King. My spirit hungers and thirsts for fellowship with you; all else, I leave in your hands. Amen.

Intimacy with God

You satisfy me more than the richest feast. I will
praise you with songs of joy. (Psalm 63:5)

THE FAMILIAR SAFETY SPEECH OF flight attendants always seems to encourage selfishness in cases of emergency. They tell you that if the oxygen masks drop, you should put yours on first before attempting to help your children or anyone else. That goes against a parent's instinct, of course, but it makes perfect sense. If you are incapacitated, you won't be of help to those around you. In order to give, you actually have to be in a position to give.

That familiar illustration points to an important spiritual truth that most believers know but few practice: If we aren't being nourished by the Spirit of God, we will not be able to nourish others with anything of spiritual value. We see this from time to time when vocational pastors are so busy with ministry activities that they burn out or begin to show the cracks in their foundation that have been left untended. Maintaining a balance between intimacy with God (nourishment) and ministry with God (nourishing) is vital. Those who receive without ever pouring out become glutted and inwardly focused; those who pour out without ever receiving have no supernatural wisdom, power, or love to offer. Having a proper balance makes us both fruitful and fulfilled.

The old expression about being too heavenly minded to be of any earthly good is wrong. The world needs people who are heavenly minded—who have spent time experiencing God's presence and communing with him. A heart that embraces the attitude David expressed at the beginning of Psalm 63—a thirst and longing for God himself—will eventually be satisfied, and in being satisfied, will be well positioned to help others find the satisfaction they crave too. Fulfillment is contagious; people are drawn to those who know their God and are satisfied in him. There is no greater testimony, no matter how selfless any other attitude appears. Let your soul be filled with the power and presence of God; then pour him out on those around you. Your fulfillment reflects him well.

Lord, I do long for you; my soul cries out for your presence. Satisfy me with your embrace. Give me the faith to know in the depths of my heart how thoroughly loved and valued I am—and then to love others as I have been loved. As extravagantly as I've received, let me extravagantly give. Amen.

Minding Your Mind

Let the message about Christ, in all its richness, fill your lives.
Teach and counsel each other with all the wisdom he gives. Sing
psalms and hymns and spiritual songs to God with thankful hearts.
(Colossians 3:16)

YOU MIGHT THINK YOU KNOW who you are, but do you really? The subconscious narrative running in your head can be awfully convincing, even when it is telling a less-than-flattering story. At various times, it may portray you as a fool, a misfit, or a problem. It will rarely hesitate to point out your flaws and mistakes. And most convincing of all, it will remind you that you are "only human." It will hardly ever picture you in the fullness of your redemption.

But as God's child, a participant in the divine nature, you have to know who you are and overcome years of false narratives telling a contrary story. Tell a different one—even speak it out loud when you're alone. According to God's revelation and the calling you have been given in Christ, you are redeemed and restored, raised to new life and seated with Christ in heavenly places (Romans 6:4; Colossians 2:12; Ephesians 2:6), destined to rule with him on his throne (Revelation 3:21; 5:10), a minister of power and reconciliation (Ephesians 1:19-20; 2 Corinthians 5:20), and capable by faith of doing the kinds of works that Jesus himself once did (John 14:12). Even more importantly, you are loved extravagantly (1 John 3:1-3). If you are ever going to have the influence and impact God designed you to have, you must know these things in the depths of your spirit.

That's why it is vital to pay close attention to your internal dialogue, the thoughts you are absorbing from your world, the contagious feelings you may have caught from others, and the inner vows you have made about your own identity. You cannot afford to live from an assumption of fear, rejection, shame, doubt, resignation, or confusion. These things war against your faith, and your faith is the only currency you have at your disposal to accomplish things in God's Kingdom. You were born for greater things, and the world needs them today.

Father, you have blessed me extravagantly with a new identity, a new calling, and a new destiny as a coheir with Jesus. I repent of letting my thoughts fall short of those gifts. May I always know the fullness of who I am in you and live in the wisdom, power, and love you have given me. Amen.

A Place of Growth

Answer me when I call, O God of my righteousness! You have given me relief when I was in distress. (Psalm 4:1, ESV)

EARLY CHRISTIANS FOUND themselves in a lot of tight spots. From time to time in various places, they were persecuted harshly. In the marketplace of ideas, they were often shouted down. They came from all social strata but were often dismissed as outsiders or fools. Though there were certainly exceptions—in some cities and times they were accepted or even admired—for the most part, life as a Christian wasn't easy in the first three centuries after Jesus' death and resurrection. God allowed his people to endure quite a bit of distress.

That was nothing new for his people, of course. Hebrew Scripture describes God's people enduring numerous difficult and dangerous situations. But as this psalm of David attests, God is with his people in those places. In fact, the literal meaning of the Hebrew words translated as "you have given me relief" takes the concept a step further and suggests that God actually widens the places or enlarges the influence of his people in their most difficult times. We may not feel as if God is strengthening us, positioning us, or expanding our potential for influence in such times, but he is. He allows us to be in situations of dependence on him, knowing that if we learn dependence well, we can manage anything. Like exercise that tears muscles apart in order to rebuild them even stronger, God pulls our spirits in uncomfortable ways in order to strengthen our capacity to love and believe. We receive the substance of life in life's most trying times.

Don't resist the process. God is preparing you for greater fruitfulness. His work in you will not always be comfortable, but it will be purposeful. He is laying foundations to build on in your future. You need what he is accomplishing now. Nothing in your life is being wasted; you are not spinning your wheels or losing ground. God is enlarging your place.

Father, you have never abandoned me. You are not ignoring my needs. Give me eyes of faith to see how you are preparing me for greater fruitfulness. May I never give up, always endure, and see the fullness of your blessings in time. Amen.

Piercing the Darkness

The people who walk in darkness will see a great light. For those who
live in a land of deep darkness, a light will shine. (Isaiah 9:2)

JUST AS ISAIAH PROPHESIED, a light did come out of Galilee, and the region was filled with glory. Early Christians recognized the brilliance of the Messiah's ministry, even though it came from such an obscure place. If Galilee was nearly irrelevant from the perspective of Judeans, it was even further removed from the eyes of Rome, its empire, and the Hellenistic world. But the Messiah was made known, his works were made visible for many to see, and his message spread far and wide. Light is always most dramatically displayed in dark places.

That's true for you as well. You have been called in the same spirit of the Messiah's ministry (John 20:21), and that includes your capacity to shine in dark places. While many people lament the hardships they are facing and the difficult circumstances they are having to endure, you can rest in the knowledge that God is positioning you purposefully. You don't have to wonder why he isn't "blessing" you with the things most people define as blessings. If you are going to live a supernatural life, it will have to be in places where the light of God is not already on display. Miracles happen best in places of lack or need.

God may allow you to go through dark places for one of two reasons: (1) so you can learn who he is and strengthen your faith in him, or (2) so you can actually be positioned for greater influence. Joseph was sent away from his hometown and family to Egypt, and Daniel and his friends were sent to Babylon in the most traumatic of circumstances because God wanted to send light into dark places. If you shine with his light, you should not be surprised to go to dark places too. Wherever you are, your calling is to reflect him, to glow with his brilliance, and to display his nature where darkness has reigned. You have seen a great light in your darkness; do not miss your opportunity to be one now.

Lord, forgive me for focusing so intently on my own hardships. You have raised me to life,
empowered me to live, and called me to offer life to others. Let me shine brightly—at any
moment, wherever I happen to be. Amen.

In the Midst of Your Enemies

*The LORD will extend your powerful kingdom from Jerusalem;
you will rule over your enemies. (Psalm 110:2)*

PSALM 110:1 IS PERHAPS THE most often quoted Old Testament verse in the New
Testament. It's a messianic prophecy about the future reign of God's anointed. The
psalm continues into a somewhat surprising picture not only of the King extending
his Kingdom and ruling over enemies, but as the original language implies, "in the
midst of them." The enemies haven't disappeared; they have simply become subor-
dinate. God's purpose is for his Son to reign in his Kingdom of goodness even over
those who had opposed him.

For those who get to participate in the Messiah's rule (Revelation 3:21; 5:10),
this is a startling picture. It shows us the nature of his Kingdom even as it is growing
now. It is also a wake-up call for believers who think they should be granted immunity from the opposition of this world. Some branches of the church have spent
decades, even centuries, developing a culture of avoidance, suggesting that freedom
from enemies is part of our inheritance. But the Kingdom of God exerts the blessings of its power in the midst of enemies. That means our challenge in this age is
not to be good, faithful representatives of Jesus in a vacuum, but to be good, faithful
representatives of Jesus in the Babylons and Romes of the modern world. We are not
undone by the opposition of our enemies; we thrive in it. It gives us a platform to
show who our Messiah really is.

Far too many Christians talk about returning to the power of the early church
and then lament the conditions in which the early church thrived. If we really wanted
those times again, we would rejoice over being marginalized, dismissed, opposed, and
mocked—all signs of those times. Our opposition actually gives us opportunities to
reflect the nature of the Messiah—to return love for hate, blessing for curses, and
goodness for evil. It enables us to learn what it means to rule in the midst of enemies.

*Jesus, you endured blistering opposition and yet ruled with grace. And your rule will
continue, even in the midst of those who reject you. Give me that spirit of overcoming,
that measure of grace, as your Kingdom grows and arrives in full. Amen.*

When Victory Comes

Jesus, full of the Holy Spirit, returned from the Jordan River.
He was led by the Spirit in the wilderness, where he was
tempted by the devil for forty days. (Luke 4:1-2)

YOU ARE BEING SENT INTO a world that may or may not like the salt and light you offer. Jesus described it as sending lambs among wolves (Luke 10:3), but you have no need to worry. God does a good job of caring for his lambs. Even so, you will not always find the terrain easy and may face adversity. Some of it may even come from within yourself.

Perhaps that surprises you, but if you know yourself well, it probably doesn't. You likely have enough experience to know that certain situations can stretch you seemingly beyond your limits, some may make you prone to compromise, and some will awaken temptations you thought you had long overcome. If you're still waiting for a time of victory in these things, however, you will need to understand the dynamics of the battle. You will not overcome the wolves—either those howling inside you or those lashing out at you on the outside—if your commitment to God is still up in the air. Your real battles are won before you get onto the battlefield.

We see this in the ministry of Jesus, both in his temptation after his baptism and his excruciating night in the garden of Gethsemane before his crucifixion. We see it in Israel's entry into the Promised Land but before its first battle at Jericho, and after David's anointing but before his reign. These times of trial, testing, and temptation were intense but necessary, significant statements of commitment in which the purity of faith was tried by fire. Jesus and many of God's faithful servants won their battles before human eyes ever saw them. We need to do the same.

Prepare your heart for what's to come. The victory of Jesus has already empowered you, but you will need to win your battles before the heat of combat ever approaches. Know who you are and the nature of the world you are going into, and walk in the power you've been given.

Jesus, you won your victories long before the Cross, even before the messages and miracles that still amaze us. May I win battles today that will let me take territory for your Kingdom tomorrow. Strengthen me like steel to serve in wisdom, power, and love. Amen.

Moved by Passion

One of the things I always pray for is the opportunity,
God willing, to come at last to see you. (Romans 1:10)

PAUL OFTEN CALLED HIMSELF a slave or bondservant of Christ, perhaps in reference to the chains and walls that sometimes held him captive, but more symbolically in reference to his complete devotion to his Master's will. We aspire to such devotion, too, often asking the question a servant would ask: "Lord, what do you want me to do for you?" We want to be available to him and align ourselves with his will. But sometimes we find that his answer turns the question back to us: "What do you want to do for me?" He wants us to follow the dreams and desires he has put inside our hearts.

We don't follow every whim, of course, or even every deep, long-term passion. Sometimes our desires are just ours. But when we've cultivated a relationship with God, been saturated in his Spirit, prayed about direction, and offered ourselves up to him, we may find passions growing within us that we suspect may not have originally been ours. That's the nature of intimate relationships—hearts align. And when our hearts align with his, figuring out the origin of the desire isn't important. We know it fits his purposes.

Spend time enjoying the presence of God, and let him shape your dreams and desires as he wills. Examine your passions. Notice what breaks your heart and inspires your hope. David longed to build a temple, and God said yes to the temple but no to the timing. Paul longed to visit Rome, and God said yes to the desire but arranged it in an unexpected way. Jesus went to the cross for the joy set before him—a desire—and went through excruciating pain to have it fulfilled. God-given desires are often the motor that moves us, even when obstacles get in the way. Follow those dreams he breathes on, and let him bring them into reality.

Lord, you know my longings. You have given many of them to me yourself. Help me sort out which ones to follow and to fulfill them in your timing. Let my heart sync with yours and be fully satisfied in your will. May my dreams, and yours in me, delight us both. Amen.

Moved by Gifts

*I long to visit you so I can bring you some spiritual gift that
will help you grow strong in the Lord. (Romans 1:11)*

THE EARLY CHURCH HAD a strong sense of giftedness—being equipped with a special ability given by God through the Spirit. Paul seemed to assume that gifts could be imparted to and received from others, though he did not clarify how. He implies, however, that they were meant to be shared for the benefit of the entire body. The same can be said of our natural gifts, talents, and creativity; they are designed for mutual benefit. We can go a long way toward discovering our purpose and our areas of fruitfulness in this world by looking at the gifts God has given us.

Our passions tell us a lot about where we're going in life, but our spiritual and natural gifts show us how we are going to get there. They are the tools God uses to meet the needs of his people and cause his body to grow. Whatever geographical area, church situation, and vocational field you are called to, your gifts will give you opportunities to serve the people around you. For many of those people, the expression of God's nature coming through you will be one of the few encounters with him they have. They may not recognize the source of your giftedness, and they almost certainly won't be able to explain what they experience of him through you. But something deep inside them will resonate with the Creator who is calling them to himself. Somehow they will be drawn closer.

Cultivate the gifts God has given you. Stir them up just as Paul encouraged Timothy to do (2 Timothy 1:6). Use them not only to serve the body of Christ but to bless people in other areas of your life. You may never be able to name those gifts precisely, and it's probably best if you don't even try to explain the process, but you'll enjoy the fact that God is using you to reach hearts and minds. The Creator continues to create, often through his people. You are a vessel for him to impart his blessings to those who need him.

Lord, I'm often much more focused on your gifts for me than on your gifts through me. Thank you for the privilege of being a vehicle of your nature. Please demonstrate your power through me. Amen.

Moved by Personality

When we get together, I want to encourage you in your faith,
but I also want to be encouraged by yours. (Romans 1:12)

PAUL WASN'T KNOWN FOR his encouragement, at least not in the same way Barnabas was. In fact, he could be quite direct and demanding at times. He was more focused on theological precision. But Paul did have an encouraging side, mainly because his theological focus emphasized the ultimate value of knowing Jesus. For that, he urged and encouraged the all-out pursuit of a personal relationship with Christ. And in light of how many young churches were persuaded by contrary doctrines and pushed off track, his need to encourage moved him often.

You will find that your gifts and calling somehow fit the personality God has given you—that he rarely calls introverts into highly extroverted ministries, for example, and rarely calls strong extroverts into deeply reflective endeavors (though there are exceptions on both counts). Those who like to see results are generally not called to a life of laying foundations for future generations, but those whose patience is unshakable often are. Some communication styles fit a shepherding heart particularly well, while others fit an evangelistic bent better. Some love to go deep into his Word day after day; others love to spread it far and wide. The issue is not which approach is right or wrong, or which personality is best suited to God's purposes. They all fit in his Kingdom. The issue is how you are going to use yours to be salt and light in this world.

Understand your temperament, your degree of emotional volatility, your preference for making peace or provoking a controversial discussion, your preference for formality or just being casual, and so on. Know what kinds of situations will enhance your effectiveness in serving God. Don't be afraid to go beyond them at times; he will stretch you and use you "out of place" at strategic moments. But much more often, he will guide you into your sweet spot of usefulness. Seek that place, and make the most of it. Whatever your personality, let it serve his purposes and glorify him well.

Father, you have made me for a purpose—different from all others, but perfectly suited for service in your Kingdom. Help me find the niche that fits my personality. Lead me into my sweet spot and further into your plans. Amen.

Moved by Opportunity

I planned many times to visit you, but I was prevented until now.
(Romans 1:13)

WE KNOW GOD CAN OPEN doors no one can shut and shut doors no one can open. We also know he sometimes calls his people to move forward even when doors appear closed (like at the edge of the Red Sea). Somewhere between those two facts, we try to serve him by negotiating the open doors he puts in front of us—discerning which ones to pass through and which ones to pass by. We live by measuring our opportunities.

If we're discerning, our passions, gifts, and personalities can move us in the right direction. But only God is sovereign over the open doors in our lives. Many of us lament the lack of opportunity we have at the moment, forgetting that God hemmed in Abraham, Jacob, Joseph, David, and many, many more until their season of opportunity came. We strive for better positioning, forgetting that he is the master of putting his people in the right place at the right time. When Joseph appeared to be furthest from his dreams, forgotten in a dark prison, God elevated him to Egypt's second highest position. God is never limited by our current position or the closed doors in front of us. He is the master orchestrator for those who look to him in faith to orchestrate their lives.

Trust the timing of opening and closing doors. When opportunities seem lacking, focus on preparation—honing your gifts, strengthening your character, and refining your passions. God has arranged the seasons of your life not in a hierarchy of importance—all of them are significant for where he is taking you—but in a sequence of maximum fruitfulness. Be content in times of wilderness and wandering; learn to lean on your God and develop faithfulness. Notice the patterns of his preparation, and cooperate with them. When the time has come, all the right doors, large and small, will open.

Father, give me the wisdom to know when to push through closed doors, when to pass by open ones, and when to trust your timing with those I'm unsure about. I believe you will get me where I need to go, with lots of grace for missteps and correction. Place your opportunities before me, and give me eyes to see them well. Amen.

Your Assignment

*I brought glory to you here on earth by completing
the work you gave me to do. (John 17:4)*

JESUS WAS CONFIDENT HE HAD completed everything the Father had given him to do. He had taught amazing truths. He had healed and delivered many from sickness and oppression. He had declared who he was and gathered followers who believed him. He had cultivated a select few into a traveling school of discipleship. Now, in his priestly prayer, he was submitting himself to a sacrificial death in order to reverse an age-old curse and bring a new kind of life into this world.

But there were still truths to be taught; Jesus had just informed his disciples of that a few verses earlier (John 16:12-15). There were still sick and oppressed people throughout the region; the early chapters of Acts give us quite a few examples of apostles ministering to ongoing needs. There was still a message to tell, not only in the places where Jesus ministered most often, but also to the ends of the earth (Matthew 28:19-20; Acts 1:8). There were still people to be convinced, disciples to be trained, and entire populations in need of new life. Jesus did a lot, but he didn't do everything.

That's implied in Jesus' prayer. He did everything the Father had given him to do, which means he had not done what the Father had not given him to do. And if Jesus had a specific assignment that was limited in scope—not in its global implications, but within the framework of his earthly life span—you can assume your assignment is limited in scope too. You don't have to carry responsibility for everything, to feel the weight of the world on your shoulders, to jump into action every time you see a need. Instead, you need to listen to the Father's voice and follow it. He will lead you into situations that bring your gifts and character into the right context to maximize your fruitfulness. He will align you with his purposes. You are free to follow them—without guilt for not having done enough, and with confidence you have done what your Father has given you to do.

Father, I want to fulfill my assignment. Streamline my life to maximize my effectiveness. Align my gifts with specific situations and needs. Give me a strong sense of direction and freedom within it. Make me fruitful. Amen.

A Lamb's Nature

*Now go, and remember that I am sending you
out as lambs among wolves. (Luke 10:3)*

WHEN JESUS SENT HIS DISCIPLES into the towns he planned to visit, his commission was not entirely reassuring. It was confident and aligned with God's will, of course, but it did not promise comfort. Neither did the Great Commission that Jesus gave at the end of his earthly ministry, when he sent his followers to the ends of the earth. By following his lead, his disciples would inevitably experience a clash of kingdoms, in one form or another. They were to situate themselves on the front lines of a cosmic battle between God's purposes and the kingdom of darkness. In other words, Jesus often sent them to places they would not otherwise want to go.

That commission continues today, and we are part of it. While some isolate themselves in Christian communities and do business only in Christian circles, most of us are aware that we live and work in an environment that may at times be hostile to what we believe. There's no reason for paranoia; it's simply the reality of our calling. But we have to be extremely careful in that reality to avoid taking on the character of the environment we have entered. As sheep among wolves, we have to guard against becoming wolves ourselves.

Many Christians have not succeeded on this point, and the results have been tragic. Wars and inquisitions are prominent examples, but for most of us the temptations are much subtler—greed in the marketplace, the jealousy and selfishness of a competitive spirit, the reorientation of our values toward decidedly earthly things. The growl and the scowl of a wolf are awfully unbecoming on sheep, even when we remain sheep at heart.

Never forget your sheeply identity. Do not conform to wolfly dispositions. Discern the environment around you, and refuse to honor its allure. Your greatest influence comes when you step into an unhealthy environment without taking on its nature. Remember that this world of wolves really belongs to your shepherd, and he is taking it back for his sheep.

Jesus, you are the Good Shepherd, and this world does not belong to wolves. It is your inheritance—and mine. Give me grace to live in it without compromise, as a gentle lamb with fearless resolve. May my gentleness tame the wildness around me. Amen.

A Vulnerable Nature

Don't take any money with you, nor a traveler's bag, nor an extra pair of sandals. And don't stop to greet anyone on the road. (Luke 10:4)

THE OPENING TO THE 1986 FILM *The Mission* shows scenes of early missionaries to South American jungles. Some are crucified according to their own message, while others simply disappear. Father Gabriel, who ends up being central to the story, goes into the depths of the jungle with little more than his oboe. In each case, the people who work toward making a difference in the lives of indigenous peoples make themselves vulnerable. Later in the movie, misguided leaders who ruin the reputation of the church and destroy the work of the missions go in with weapons and decrees. The difference between the church as a humble spiritual movement and the church as an overbearing worldly institution is startling—and devastating.

Times have changed since the historical circumstances depicted in that movie, but the nature of the gospel has not. God did not send us into the world as know-it-all, holier-than-thou, ready-to-rumble, my-way-or-the-highway kinds of people. He sent us into the world with vulnerability. His commission to the seventy-two followers (or seventy in some versions) stressed simplicity: no purse, no extra shoes, no distractions on the road. Those instructions would take on a different tone later (see Luke 22:35-37), but at first they were based on the bare character of the gospel and the humility of its adherents. The sheep went out among wolves without recourse to anything or anyone but their Master's will.

That's still the case, even when we have money, shoes, and a network of relationships among our possessions. We still have nothing to depend on—no person or thing we can completely rely on—other than Jesus. Only he can make a difference in people's lives; all the rest is baggage. Far more important than the specific words we speak is the attitude we carry. We are called to be conversation starters, not dictators. We are called to serve people, not battle them. And we are called to appeal to human hearts, not condemn them. In your personal mission in this world, put aside all manipulation, all the trappings of worldly influence, and live the gospel. It, and it alone, changes lives.

Lord, human nature complicates things, and we live in complicated times. Always bring me back to the simplicity of the gospel and the vulnerability of your ways. Lead me in humility, compassion, and service. May I have no agenda other than to embody your true nature. Amen.

Keep Asking

Keep on asking, and you will receive what you ask for.
Keep on seeking, and you will find. Keep on knocking,
and the door will be opened to you. (Luke 11:9)

JESUS EMPHASIZED PERSISTENCE. He told his followers to ask and keep on asking. He gave them illustrations of a pesky neighbor at midnight (Luke 11:5-8) and a tenacious widow playing the squeaky wheel (Luke 18:1-8). He promised the disciples repeatedly that if they were united with him in identity and purpose, they could ask anything, and it would be done for them (John 14:13-14; 15:7, 16; 16:23-24). His repeated promises come across as a plea to pester the Father with requests. Jesus gave them the impression that God's work in this world hinged on their willingness to requisition his help in fulfilling their mission.

These promises have not expired. Each of us is in partnership with God, standing between heaven and earth to requisition his provision for a world in need. He gave the first human beings dominion over the world, but they lost it (or at least a healthy version of it), and Jesus won it back. He now hands the keys of the Kingdom over to his followers, promising again and again to answer their prayers. For whatever reason, God has arranged his work in this world to be accomplished through human agency. When no worthy human could be found, God clothed himself in flesh to reinstitute the calling (Isaiah 59:16; 63:5). He accomplished the role we were originally designed to fulfill, then handed us the keys to continue fulfilling it. And he insisted that we ask—and ask some more.

Don't waste this open invitation. Many people pray for a day or two, or even a month or two, and then give up because they have seen no signs of an answer. Meanwhile, those who plant seeds of prayer persistently see them growing up into fruitfulness months, years, even decades down the road. That's because prayer is a lifestyle, not a drive-thru window or an ATM transaction. It is relational, conversational, and lasting. Those who persist see his Kingdom coming and become agents of God's provision in this world.

Father, may I not grow weary in works or in the prayers I present to you. Align my heart with your purposes, and reward my persistence with fruitfulness. May your Kingdom come—today, tomorrow, and always. Amen.

Dual Immersion

Jesus often withdrew to the wilderness for prayer. (Luke 5:16)

CHRISTIAN MONASTICISM SEEMS TO have begun in the 200s in the deserts of Egypt, where hermits and ascetics retreated from the world to get closer to God. On the surface, this monastic impulse looked like a detachment from social influences, though monks created new communities of faith and often dedicated themselves to praying for the world they had left behind. They wanted to be alone with the Father, sometimes for the rest of their lives.

Most Christians throughout history have understood themselves to be "in the world" but not "of the world"—citizens of heaven who continue to live and function within the context of mainstream society. And it's true that the vast majority of believers are called to serve God among others in the routines and structures of daily life. We don't normally pull away from the world for a lifetime. But many of us do pull away mentally, retreating into our own communities of faith, forming a parallel world that functions alongside "secular" society, with our own schools, businesses, and organizations. We have a hard time finding the balance of being alone with God, fellowshiping with other believers, and influencing the non-Christian world. We aren't sure how "in the world" we are meant to be or how diligently we should avoid being "of the world."

As always, the life of Jesus is our example. He often withdrew to isolated places to be alone with the Father but then reentered the mix of daily life in order to minister to the needs of society. That's what priests do in representing humanity to God and God to humanity. We find strength in the Father's presence, but we also recognize our role in carrying the Father's presence into the world.

If you struggle with your level of involvement in the world around you—what to embrace, what to renounce, how deeply to engage—let Jesus be your guide. Get filled up in the Father's presence, then spend yourself in the presence of others. Withdraw at times, but always be ready to enter in. As a bridge between two realms, you need to be immersed in both.

Lord, teach me how to be alone with you—and how to live together with you in this world. Let my familiarity with the realm of the spirit thoroughly influence my life in the material realm. Amen.

Spiritual Authenticity

When you fast, don't make it obvious, as the hypocrites do,
for they try to look miserable and disheveled so people will
admire them for their fasting. (Matthew 6:16)

JOHN OF LYCOPOLIS, one of the early "desert fathers" who retreated to monastic life in the Egyptian desert in the 300s, used to warn visitors to the monastery about taking spiritual pride in imitating a monk's virtues. He knew, perhaps from his own experience, the dangers of taking credit for righteous behavior that looks impressive on the outside but is really just playing the part for a time. On one hand, monks and their followers faced the temptation of abandoning their vows of austerity; on the other, they faced the temptation of putting too much stock in keeping them. A focus on self-effort creates a no-win situation: Success leads to pride, failure to shame, and either way the flesh is responsible.

Non-Christians have little difficulty discerning the hypocrisies of spiritual pride, as well as of feigned humility. Many of them suspect we are playing a part, feeding our egos, and striving to impress. An effort-based spirituality is superficial religion, devoid of the power of the gospel of grace. It puts all the attention on the self—self-improvement, self-righteousness, self-discipline—and none on Christ. It misses the point of being a sinner saved by grace, redeemed by the power of God and restored by his Spirit. It aims to impress and almost always misses the mark.

Never let yourself think about impressing anyone with how spiritual you are, or even be self-conscious about the impression you are making. Some of that thinking comes from good intentions, but it is a form of independence from God. The strength of your testimony comes from being who you are—empowered beyond your own means, forgiven when you've blown it, and trusting of the work of God within you. Authenticity makes an impression that can never be orchestrated by human ingenuity. More than that, it gives God an opportunity to display what he is doing in your life. Your testimony as a Christian depends on Christ, and him alone.

Jesus, I want you to be glorified in my failures, honored in my successes, and preeminent in everything I do. Lead me into a life of dependence so you receive credit for my discipleship. Lead me into relationships, places, and situations that showcase who you are in my life. Amen.

Joy in Every Season

When troubles of any kind come your way,
consider it an opportunity for great joy. (James 1:2)

MANY OF THE DESERT FATHERS disciplined themselves harshly, embracing severe austerity in order to focus on the things of the Spirit. We would expect such deprivation to lead to cold and gloomy attitudes, and perhaps for some it did. But most emphasized cheerfulness, stressing the importance of joy in the Christian life. One monk named Apollo considered discouragement to be the lot of pagans and happiness a Christian duty. He and others felt a sense of responsibility to spread life and hope, to find some cause for joy in every situation, and to warm their world with gladness. They understood the importance of an attitude.

Many people today think they are victims of their own attitudes, as if their thoughts are independent of themselves and they can only follow their normal mental patterns. Both Scripture and experience teach us otherwise—that we can choose joy (James 1:2), tell our own souls what to remember and to rejoice in (Psalm 103:1-2), and decide for ourselves what to think about and not think about (Philippians 4:4-8). One of the reasons we so easily get discouraged or depressed is that we have developed strong mental habits, patterns of thought that grow deeper and deeper in our brains like water flowing down the side of a mountain, establishing rivulets and trails that are hard to change. But these patterns *can* be changed. As followers of Jesus called to think in new ways and influence our world with Kingdom truths, we are obliged to change them. We simply must learn the power of joy.

Make that a priority. Your happiness and joy are not dependent on your circumstances. They aren't even dependent on the things that seem so real in your own mind. They are dependent on the truths your Father has told you and that his Son has urged you to believe. His Spirit makes them available even now. Retrain your thoughts, learn how influential your attitudes really are, and embrace the possibility of joy in every season.

Father, joy is a permanent condition in your Kingdom, the prevailing climate, the "weather forecast" every single "day" of eternity. Teach me to live in it even now, and let my redeemed and restored attitudes shape the people around me for good. Amen.

Pictures of Grace

Do not judge others, and you will not be judged. Do not
condemn others, or it will all come back against you.
Forgive others, and you will be forgiven. (Luke 6:37)

IN THE BOOK *The Sayings of the Desert Fathers,* a brother in the desert community of Scetis committed a sin, and the council invited Abba Moses to come sit in judgment against him. So Abba Moses filled a leaking jug with water and carried it to the assembly. When the others asked what he was doing, he said, "My sins run out behind me, and I do not see them, and today I am coming to judge the errors of another." The council then dropped their charges against the offender.[14]

The father's visual illustration reminds us of an important biblical truth that is repeated throughout the Gospels and letters of the New Testament. God has not put us in a position of judgment. He has given us a responsibility for discernment, but that's not the same as judgment, which tends to fault others for the same sins we have committed ourselves. Jesus spoke very harshly against such condemnation, even suggesting that we will not be forgiven unless we learn how to forgive others (Matthew 6:15; 18:35). Our attitudes toward those around us are somehow related to God's attitude toward us, even when we claim the name of Christ. That's a sobering thought.

If Jesus was so emphatic and serious about our need to forgive others, it would be wise for us to be emphatic and serious about our judgments too. We have been called into a community of grace—not to ignore real issues, but to bring mercy into the midst of them. Our foremost thought in our relationship with God should center on how much we have been forgiven and how grateful we are for his mercy. When that is our relational baseline with God, it becomes our relational baseline with others. We extend to others the mercy we have received, and something of God's nature becomes visible. We become living illustrations of the picture Abba Moses gave his brothers.

Jesus, you came not to condemn but to forgive, heal, and restore. I hereby give your Spirit an open invitation to jolt my awareness anytime I let my judgments rise above your mercy. Let me embody your grace and demonstrate your nature. Amen.

A Voice in the Wilderness

*Listen! It's the voice of someone shouting, "Clear the way
through the wilderness for the LORD! Make a straight
highway through the wasteland for our God!" (Isaiah 40:3)*

JOHN THE BAPTIST WAS uniquely called and positioned in history to be a voice in a literal wilderness that prepared the way for the coming of the Lord. His ministry fulfilled the prophecy of Isaiah—at least for Christ's first coming to earth. But twelfth-century abbot Bernard of Clairvaux famously preached that Christ has three kinds of comings: his incarnation, when he was born in Bethlehem; his return at the culmination of the age; and in between, a more hidden coming into the human spirit by faith. That coming happens again and again as each human heart repents and declares him as their Savior.

Whose voices are preparing the way for those intermediate comings? Ours. Every believer is called to prepare the way for the Lord, to make straight places in the wildernesses of human societies, to raise up valleys and level out mountains so hungry hearts can find him in the midst of a rugged environment. That means you have a specific calling and anointing to speak against the things that hinder faith, to move mountains and obstacles, to reveal the glory of the Lord for those who will see it. And like the original voice in the wilderness, you may have to go against the grain of your culture to do it.

There are honorable and respectful ways to do that. It's true that the gospel is a stumbling block, but we can help people regain their balance without compromising the message. We are to clear the way, to make the highway straight, to shine a spotlight on the beauty of God's mercies, and even to demonstrate them in our own lives. We are to avoid unnecessary offenses and lavish God's goodness on those who don't deserve it, as he did with us. When we do, streams of living water flow through the rugged deserts of this world, pathways become straight and clear, and hearts open up to the Kingdom of God. The same Jesus who came, and who promised to come again one day, will come again and again through us and into the lives around us.

Jesus, how can I prepare the way for you today? How can I prepare hearts to be reconciled with you? How can I demonstrate your mercies? Show me. Give me opportunities. And make my voice a stream and a highway that leads to life. Amen.

A Time of Favor

The LORD was with Joseph, so he succeeded in everything he did.
(Genesis 39:2)

THE FAVOR OF GOD WAS on Joseph's life. It was on Daniel's, too (Daniel 1:9, 17-20). Even Jesus grew in wisdom, stature, and favor in the eyes of God and the people around him (Luke 2:52). This intangible blessing—the affection and endorsement of others—is hard to describe but easy to see. It opens doors of opportunity, softens relationships, and results in good things. It is a sign of God being with someone to give them unusual advantage in the circumstances of their lives.

How do you gain favor? According to examples in Scripture, it comes to those who are walking faithfully in the assignment God has given them. That's it. That doesn't mean every person walking in faithfulness will suddenly experience extravagant tangible blessings—sometimes, as with Joseph and Daniel, long seasons of hardship and struggle seem to line the road toward the opportunities and fruitfulness to come. But those seasons of opportunity and fruitfulness do come. Favor ensures them. A life of faithfulness does not go unrewarded, whether in this age or in the age to come.

Jesus declared his ministry to be an inauguration of an age of favor (Luke 4:19). We have the opportunity today to experience the favor of God. In fact, we already have experienced it in Christ, having received newness of life and a share in his inheritance. That means we can walk in the confidence that God is drawing people, opportunities, and blessings to us by the power of the Spirit in the proper time. All we have to do is steward them faithfully.

Seek God's favor. Don't make the mistake of interpreting it strictly in terms of health and wealth (though he does heal and provide), or of assuming that any hardship means you have stepped out of God's will. Biblical examples do not support such views. But they do support the promise of God giving opportunities and fruitfulness to those who love and serve him humbly and faithfully. Do that, and expect his favor today. Doors will open. Breakthroughs will come. And God will make your ways straight and true.

Lord, may I receive the favor you showed to Joseph, Daniel, and many others. In Christ, I receive the promise of a season of favor and the approval you bestowed on him. Open doors and increase my fruitfulness—for your glory. Amen.

A Universal Calling

*Select seven men who are well respected and are full of the
Spirit and wisdom. . . . Then we apostles can spend our
time in prayer and teaching the word. (Acts 6:3-4)*

As FAR BACK AS THE EARLY CHURCH, many Christians have assumed that those
with a deep desire to be of service in God's Kingdom should go into church work.
Somehow, we got the impression that "ministry" and "secular vocations" are two different spheres of influence. There have always been exceptions—people who understand the diversity of God's calling and the kinds of ministry that take place in every
area of society—but most people with a sense of calling have found themselves
encouraged to pursue full-time, vocational ministry. We've missed the fullness of
Jesus' commission.

Peter wasn't necessarily wrong in insisting that the apostles should be preaching
rather than serving widows—believers do carry out different roles—but it's gratifying
(and somewhat amusing) that the next few chapters of Acts are filled with the exploits
of the men who were assigned to be table-servers. Philip and Stephen apparently did
not carry a lesser Spirit within them than Peter and John did. We've already explored
the importance of carrying the same Spirit into businesses, schools, governments,
stores, media outlets, and more. These informal ministries are vital for reaching this
world, perhaps even more vital than positions within the church. They may be less
explicit, but they are more strategically placed. They take the character and power
of the gospel to people who are not likely to step inside of a church to see what God
is doing.

Do not dismiss the importance of marketplace ministries, even covert ones. Learn
to see yourself as a shepherd of a group of people, though you may never be called
"pastor." Help those around you learn, even if you're not a teacher. Encourage others
with God's voice, knowing you will likely never be considered a prophet. Every follower of Jesus is a minister of his message and a carrier of his Kingdom. Make the
most of your opportunities to take the Spirit and his wisdom into this world.

*Holy Spirit, you are the author of ministry, and you are extremely creative in the ways
you carry it out. Use me wherever you choose, as openly or obscurely as you choose,
whenever the need arises. May I carry your character, your message, and your Kingdom
wherever I go. Amen.*

Heads, Not Tails

*If you listen to these commands of the LORD your God that I
am giving you today, and if you carefully obey them, the LORD
will make you the head and not the tail, and you will always
be on top and never at the bottom. (Deuteronomy 28:13)*

GOD GAVE A PROMISE TO his people as they were preparing to enter the Promised
Land. He told them that if they remained faithful to him and carried out the instructions he gave them, he would give them success in all they did. They would be lenders, not borrowers; victors, not the vanquished; heads, not tails. It was a promise we
now distance ourselves from, fearful of equating the gospel with a health-and-wealth
lifestyle that focuses more on God's blessings than on God himself. We don't want
to distort the message of Jesus.

It's true that Jesus gave us a renewed covenant, and this promise was given in the
old. God's people never did live up to the standards of the law; human nature always
falls short. Even so, there is something of the heart of God in this promise, a desire
for his people to be blessed, to prosper (as he defines prospering), to experience as
much of the fullness of his Kingdom as they can, even in this age. And where human
nature falls short, Jesus does not. He fulfills the covenant on our behalf. In some real
and meaningful ways, we can step into the Kingdom even now, as it is coming. We
can experience the fullness God wants for us.

That doesn't mean we will never have problems or face challenges, or that we
will never stumble and fall. It does mean, however, that we will never actually be
defeated—and that we are not to live with a defeatist mind-set. In this age, we are
to be problem-solvers, culture-changers, leaders and innovators, heads and not tails.
We are here to receive God's blessings and share them extravagantly as harbingers
of the coming Kingdom. When we live with that outlook, we exude life and offer
transformation, things the people around us desperately need. We step into the
desires of God for his people.

*Father, I know we experience trials and tribulations in this world. But you promise the
power to overcome. We rise above to lead and to bless. May I do that well today and
influence many for your Kingdom. Amen.*

Wisdom in Words

O Lord, hear their threats, and give us, your servants,
great boldness in preaching your word. (Acts 4:29)

PETER AND JOHN HAD DRAWN the attention of the authorities and been threatened with another imprisonment. But instead of cowering in fear or going underground with their message, they and other believers in Jerusalem prayed for more boldness. They asked for an increase of the very things that had gotten them in trouble—signs and wonders that inevitably draw crowds. They were living in a moment of advance, and they knew it.

Jesus had told them not so long before to be as wise as serpents in their words and conduct, and to be careful about being lambs among wolves (Matthew 10:16; Luke 10:3). But these disciples understood the season, and they did not want to quench the Holy Spirit's miraculous works among them. There would be times in the future when giving an answer for their hope could be done more tactfully (1 Peter 3:15-16). But now was not the time. The Spirit was making waves and upsetting the status quo. Peter and John wanted to be a part of what he was doing.

You will need to use the same kind of wisdom in your demonstration of the power of God within you. There will be times when you need boldness because the moment is right for making waves and upsetting the status quo. There will be other times when a somewhat covert testimony is more effective—when you build relationships and let your life do the talking over time, adding words when the moment is ripe for them. While many Christians err on one side or the other—being a loudmouth when subtlety is needed, or being so quiet that no message is ever shared—we are called to discern the times, step into them with wisdom, and follow the Spirit's leading.

Learn to go with the flow. Adjust your lifestyle to the movements of the Spirit. Don't just blather an evangelistic message without being sensitive to the needs and the openness of those around you. Live a Kingdom message, and include words when they fit. Be bold . . . and subtle . . . and always in sync with God.

Holy Spirit, give me great discernment for each moment. Fill me with boldness when boldness is needed, with tact when tact is needed, and with insight always. Let me move with you. Amen.

Known for Excellence

*Whatever you do, work at it with all your heart, as working
for the Lord, not for human masters. (Colossians 3:23, NIV)*

IF YOU WANT TO BE SALT AND LIGHT in this world according to Jesus' promise (Matthew 5:13-16), you will want to be a higher quality than the kinds people are familiar with tasting and seeing. Contrary to the appearances Christendom has presented at times in recent history, you are not called to mediocrity. You are called to excellence. Though God gives us ample grace in every area of our lives, grace is not a license for halfhearted, lackluster work. If anyone should be known for creating and accomplishing excellent things, it should be those who are restored to the image of God.

Paul expressed this thought in a passage written to slaves—hardly the context most of us would want to apply to ourselves. Yet within these instructions is a priceless principle: All of us are servants of God. Like a good Father, he embraces us and encourages us even when we falter and stumble in our efforts. Like good children, our desire ought to be to give him our best. His Kingdom is marked by excellence; we should be pacesetters in establishing quality and completeness in this world.

You may be looking for a certain position or forum to serve as a platform for your influence for God's Kingdom, but an even greater platform is excellence in the position or forum you already have. Whether you feel like going the extra mile for your supervisors or clients, your service to them is secondary. In reality, you are serving the Lord. The quality of your work gives credibility to your testimony and your identity. When you polish your natural gifts to their maximum glow and ask God to add his supernatural favor to them, things happen. People notice. And you become the salt and light that not only testifies of heaven but is valuable to this world.

Father, make me a credible servant. Show me how to maximize the gifts and talents you've given me. Energize me to continually perfect them in the eyes of others and to serve you with them well. Draw the attentions of this world to the excellence of your Kingdom in me. Amen.

Positioned for Today

Your own ears will hear him. Right behind you a voice will say,
"This is the way you should go," whether to the right or to the left.
(Isaiah 30:21)

FROM THE EARLIEST DAYS OF the salvation story that began with Abraham, God has called his people into unknown situations and against overwhelming odds. He has never really been known for giving "doable" assignments; he is known rather for giving assignments that are beyond human capacity to accomplish. Whether crossing deep seas on foot, taking over walled cities, facing intimidating giants, or changing the world through a handful of people, the pathway is hardly ever clear to those who have to walk it. But all God asks of his people is that they move forward in faith—that they take the next step.

In some ways, that's a huge relief. We don't have to figure out the whole journey. We don't have to come up with an overarching strategy for being the kind of salt and light that transforms the world in this generation. We simply need to go out and be salt and light, to take the next step that he gives us. Still, we crave a plan. We feel insecure without one. We want to know not only the next step but where it's going to take us. We want to strategize much more of the future than God will allow us to see.

Get used to the sense of insecurity. In the hands of God, of course, we are not insecure at all; he knows exactly where we are going. But the life of faith is about positioning ourselves for God's purposes and then trusting him to provide opportunities. We have to learn to give him room to work. And we have to tune our ears to the step-by-step directions he gives us. When we do, he will lead us past giants that used to be intimidating, over walls that used to be insurmountable, through seas that used to be impassable, and into a culture that used to resist us. He will make us shine in ways we never could have figured out on our own.

Lord, lead me in ways that bring life, hope, and peace to those around me. As much as I want a lifelong plan, show me how to position myself for today. I trust you with tomorrow. Use me well. Amen.

Hinges of History

David left the sheep with another shepherd and set out early
the next morning with the gifts, as Jesse had directed him. He
arrived at the camp just as the Israelite army was leaving for
the battlefield with shouts and battle cries. (1 Samuel 17:20)

DAVID'S FATHER TOLD HIM to take some bread to his brothers on the front lines. Israel's army was at war with the Philistines, and a high-and-mighty colossus of a man kept taunting the Israelites and challenging them to a duel he assumed they wouldn't dare to accept. David's mission was simple: Deliver the food. But his simple act of obedience led to a crisis moment that changed the course of his own life and Israel's war. Massive doors of opportunity opened because David carried out his business.

That's generally how massive doors of opportunity work. You rarely find them when you go out looking for them; they open as you faithfully fulfill your normal responsibilities. Far too many people are trying to make things happen, hoping to force their way into the center of God's will. But the center of God's will is daily faithfulness, the here-and-now of serving him. It's fine to anticipate greater things, but you may not be able to arrange them. The doors of history often swing on small hinges, and if you're observant, you'll notice them when they do. Even if you don't, God will move you into them when the time is right. And the right time is very often a moment of crisis, just as it was for Israel's warriors when David arrived.

Don't fear the crisis moments of God's Kingdom. Many Christians pray to avoid them; wiser ones pray to be ready to step into them when they come. Just as the believers in Acts prayed for boldness when they were threatened and the Holy Spirit shook their surroundings; just as Paul's visit to Rome came in the context of controversy and an unfair imprisonment; just as many believers today are thrust into divine appointments that at first appear rather frightening; your circumstances will maximize your testimony and your fruitfulness if you are simply faithful today, tomorrow, and beyond. Dream big, but don't be afraid to work small. Huge doors open for servants such as these.

Lord, prepare me for divine opportunities, critical moments of service, and doors that
open suddenly. Open my eyes to the meaning in the mundane. Use my faithfulness today
for great things tomorrow. Amen.

Lions and Lambs

*After his brothers left for the festival, Jesus also went, though secretly,
staying out of public view. . . . On the last day, the climax of the
festival, Jesus stood and shouted to the crowds. (John 7:10, 37)*

JESUS KNEW HOW TO MAKE a dramatic entrance. There were times when he stood up in front of a crowd and shouted, moments when he defied the expectations of everyone around him, and occasions when people seeking his help made a scene and embarrassed the disciples—with his approval. There is no evidence of shyness in his ministry. But he also knew the hearts of human beings, measured their responses, and planned his moments of influence strategically. He knew how to gently work his way into the heart of a Samaritan woman at a well and how to single out Zacchaeus in a crowd. He understood when to preach a hard message with a prophetic edge or a soft message glistening with grace. He was—and is—a master of managing opportunities.

That's our calling too. We've seen how he identified disciples as lambs among wolves, and how they later lived out their mission in trying times. In our desire to influence our world for the Kingdom of God, we really need to ask only two questions of every situation: (1) *How is God leading me in this moment?* and, in the absence of specific directions, (2) *What approach will be most effective?* We may find that some situations call for a lamb-like approach, a demonstration of the compassionate heart of God, while others call for a lion-like entrance, a demonstration of his righteous zeal. Both are valid; neither is always right or wrong. Our God has many complementary faces to his character, and a multitude of ways of reaching multitudes of people. We have to learn how to represent him in a variety of ways.

If you are naturally a lion, get used to the ways of lambs. If you are naturally a lamb, embrace your inner lion. Half of your calling is knowing what your purpose is. The other half is knowing how to carry it out. Learn from the Lion of Judah and Lamb of God, and carry both natures within you.

Jesus, I want to be like you—to roar and to whisper, to do only what I see the Father doing, just as you said. Clothe me in your nature in every season. Amen.

All about Love

Let love be your highest goal! (1 Corinthians 14:1)

As CHRISTIANITY ENTERED its second century, believers began finding themselves in a somewhat different position than before. Yes, the sporadic, local persecutions that marked the first generations of the faith would continue. And yes, the minority status of Christians would remain for years to come. But over time, believers became a much more significant minority. Where once they were seen as strange anomalies, they now were seen by some as an attractive sect. The community of believers increasingly grew.

What was the impetus for their growth? Answers that often come to mind include boldness, faith, power in prayer, willingness to suffer without recanting their beliefs, and more. But ancient witnesses testify of a greater asset that drew people to the church: love. Christians were known for ministering to the sick when others fled the infectious disease; for displaying affection for one another even when they disagreed; for embracing the marginalized; and for loving the unlovely. Love was not unknown in any culture, of course, but it was not as highly valued in Greco-Roman society as it was in Christian fellowships. Love—at least in some places at some times—began to look like a new, authentic way of life.

If you're observant, you may notice a phenomenon in your life and culture. People who zealously pursue the gifts of the Spirit and the wisdom of God but don't have loving hearts tend to be frustrated (even when they rise higher in the church). But those whose prayers are motivated by love, whose service is driven by love, and whose lives are saturated with love experience unusual power and growth. More than that, they draw others to themselves. That's because God multiples fruitfulness when love is behind it. And when it isn't . . . well, he doesn't. At least not nearly as often.

Make love your highest priority—more than winning people to Christ, more than convincing others of your views, more than exercising the most powerful spiritual gifts. Set the course of your life by divine love, and watch your life flourish in ways you never anticipated. Miracles of faith and power come through those who love.

Jesus, you stressed love to your followers, and we have failed the ideal far too often. Bring me back to it. Ground me in this foundation. Let my life overflow with the power of your love. Amen.

The Voice of God

You should also desire the special abilities the Spirit gives—
especially the ability to prophesy. (1 Corinthians 14:1)

PERHAPS A FEW OF THE EARLY Christian leaders claimed to prophesy. We can easily imagine apostles and writers of sacred texts assuming such a role. But that claim sounds awfully presumptuous for the rest of us. *Who am I to speak for God?* our humility might compel us to wonder about ourselves. *Who are you to speak for God?* our judgments might more pointedly compel us to question others. Whether we question ourselves or others, the role hardly seems to fit—except for one uncomfortable fact: Scripture assigns it to us. Paul urged his readers—all of them, not just a select few—to seek the ability to prophesy, and Peter urged his readers to speak as though they were uttering the words of God (1 Peter 4:11). Through his Word, the Spirit of God gives us permission, even the responsibility, to express his thoughts to those around us.

Regardless of how exhilarating or uncomfortable that makes us feel, it's perfectly legitimate. There's no need to go around saying, "Thus says the Lord . . ." In fact, there's every reason *not* to do so. Even so, you are fully capable of speaking the heart of God into the lives of people around you. You may not know how to express his voice verbatim—that's hardly the point, since he often communicates in pictures and illustrations anyway—but you can express his nature and his ministry clearly enough. You are given his Spirit and his revelation for a reason.

Use those gifts wisely. You are fallible and always carry the potential to be wrong. Christians throughout history have landed on the wrong side of culture wars and issue debates. But you also have the potential to be right—to seek the mind of Christ, to synchronize with God's heartbeat, to receive wisdom from above. Sometimes you will be the only person in the room with access to heaven's perspective. Express it humbly but confidently. Bless your world with glimpses of Kingdom truths.

Lord, may I be known for walking in wisdom so that others seek my godly counsel. Give me a platform for expressing what's on your mind and the credibility to be received. Let my words overflow with the encouragement and comfort of your heart. Amen.

Undivided Hearts

I tell you the truth, you can say to this mountain, "May you be lifted up and thrown into the sea," and it will happen. But you must really believe it will happen and have no doubt in your heart. (Mark 11:23)

"AND HAVE NO DOUBT IN YOUR HEART." That's the catch for us, isn't it? We're thrilled and inspired by extravagant promises about our prayers of faith. They give us visions of mountains that move in response to seed-sized belief. And it's true; faith really is the currency of God's Kingdom. That's how we receive everything he offers, whether it's salvation, growth, or answers to prayer. But when it comes to the really big-ticket items of our desires, the things we long for deeply and ask God to accomplish, they often don't come to pass. Something in our hearts questions whether it might be too good to be true or condemns us for asking for more than the bare minimum of what we need. And the more we experience unfulfilled desires, the more we tend to ask tentatively. The more our faith—the currency of the Kingdom—shrinks to less than the size of a mustard seed.

Size is not the issue, of course. Purity is—faith that is undefiled with doubts, fears, and anxieties and that is confident with childlike assertions coming from a normal Christian life. If we are ever going to influence our temporal world with eternal truth and participate in the authentic growth of God's Kingdom, we will have to know how to exercise faith. When we believe with certainty, something happens in spiritual realms. Our desires and requests that line up with God's will have extraordinary power to shape the circumstances and situations around us. Undivided hearts move the world.

That's a huge part of your calling—to live with an undivided heart. When you partner with God to develop a vision for your life and your place in the Kingdom and then move and speak in sync with that vision, things change. Mountains move. Desires are fulfilled. And the blessings of the Kingdom begin to be displayed through you.

Jesus, may I speak words of faith in alignment with the Father's will and with the conviction you demonstrated. You have called me to do your works, move mountains, and see your Kingdom grow. Teach me the power of faith. Amen.

Expressing Honor

Take delight in honoring each other. (Romans 12:10)

BEHAVIOR IN ANCIENT SOCIETIES WAS often based on principles of honor or shame. We see this in much of the rhetoric in Middle Eastern, Greek, and Roman sources, along with many of Paul's writings. It's human nature; we tend to honor people for behaviors and attitudes we want to reinforce and shame them for behaviors and attitudes we want to eliminate. The gospel interrupts that dynamic with grace, but the human heart often clings to it by default. And when God's Word tells us to honor the Lord because he is worthy, honor our father and mother because it is commanded, and give honor where honor is due, we understand.

What we don't understand is a more radical dynamic of expressing honor even when we don't feel like it or believe it is due. But Scripture tells us to honor one another above ourselves without qualifying whether the other person is worthy. That's not far removed from Jesus' instructions to love our enemies and pray for those who persecute us. We want conditions, reasons, a foundation of worthiness to base it on. When the gospel goes further in calling for honor beyond that foundation, we resist. It doesn't fit our categories.

That should come as no surprise. God is an expert at defying our categories. People who have extended honor beyond normal expectations—to predecessors who had a part in building Christian institutions in ungodly ways, to rival religious leaders whose views are sincere but far from God's truth, to governments and hierarchies that have maintained peace even while enforcing bad policies, even to enemies—have won hearts, changed minds, and been unusually blessed by God. Why? Because they express a core value of his Kingdom. They base their honor not on people's pasts but on their potential. They see with eyes of faith and express it concretely. Such vision is rewarded by God and used by him to change relationships in powerful ways. The humble who show honor overcome the proud who withhold it. And God's Kingdom shows up in increasing measure.

Father, help me create a culture of honor around me. Draw others into it. Let me freely bless with no hints of bias, no hints of shame, and no unnecessary restraints. May my words call many out of a world of shame and into a Kingdom of honor. Amen.

The Mystery within You

God has chosen to make known among the Gentiles the glorious
riches of this mystery, which is Christ in you, the hope of glory.
(Colossians 1:27, NIV)

MANY PEOPLE ARE IN SEARCH of the presence of God, even when they aren't aware of it. They need a touch from him, a reassurance of his love, a hint of evidence that he exists and is working on their behalf. They long to experience his goodness, even when they question whether he is good—or real. They live with some faint hope that they will someday encounter the one who created them.

We often pray for such people, well aware that we have been there ourselves. We encountered God not because we were ingenious or diligent but because he came to us. He revealed himself. We pray that others would know him as we do, that he would come to them with a fresh touch or a special intervention in their lives. And he will. But while we ask God when he will show up, he often turns the question back to us, asking when we will show up. Why? Because the mystery of his presence, the core of the gospel message, is "Christ in you, the hope of glory."

Christ is in you not just for your hopes of glory but for others' hopes too. You are a carrier of Christ, a host for the divine presence, a temple of the living God. Paul made that clear on numerous occasions (1 Corinthians 3:16; 6:19; Ephesians 2:19-22), and it's true. If you carry his presence with faith and assurance, people will sense something different when you're around—that the environment has changed though the circumstances haven't. Things like love, peace, joy, and faith will come out of you because they are characteristics of God's Kingdom, and his Kingdom is in you. Know your potential, and step into it—never with arrogance, but always with faith and humility. The mystery of God's presence is revealed through those who wear it well.

Lord, you have given me a high calling to carry your presence, and there's nothing I can do to manufacture it. Be strong in me. Fill me with the glories of your Kingdom—the peace of your presence, the wisdom, power, and love of your ways. Jesus, be Jesus in me. Amen.

Carrying His Nature

All who have this eager expectation will keep themselves pure,
just as he is pure. (1 John 3:3)

JOHN, WHO HAD SEEN JESUS OFTEN throughout his earthly ministry, wrote a letter in his old age to believers who had never seen Jesus, except through eyes of faith. He assured them that we are God's extravagantly loved children and that we will be fully transformed when Jesus returns. Our eyes will see him as he really is, and that will change us. In the meantime, we live with eager expectation and a desire to be pure just as Jesus is pure. In other words, our vision of Jesus in the future has the power to begin transforming us even now.

We who personalize almost everything—especially those of us who live in highly individualistic cultures—forget the broader implications of our own lives. But the process of this transformation ought to make us think. If we are changed by seeing him as he is and we are growing into his likeness, then others can be changed by seeing him as he is *through us.*

That may seem like an absurd claim—we are not just like Jesus, even though conforming to his character is our goal—but Scripture calls us into it anyway. John already tells us a chapter earlier that "those who say they live in God should live their lives as Jesus did" (1 John 2:6), and a couple of chapters later he assures us that "we live like Jesus here in this world" (1 John 4:17). That means we can bring harmony into places of strife, purity into places of out-of-control desires, integrity into places of deceit. We do not walk in the spirit of this world; we walk against the grain in the Spirit of Jesus. We even have the potential to change the direction of the grain.

Make that your aim. You have all the spiritual power you need and the authority of Jesus behind you to embody his nature. Carry it everywhere. Live out your transformation in environments that need to be transformed, and you will often see them change.

Lord, I don't know the mechanics of how to change the world, and I can't figure out the strategies. But I can embody your nature and live in your power, and that is enough. Make me into your likeness and draw many to you. Amen.

The Influence of Salt and Light

On the day of Pentecost all the believers were
meeting together in one place. (Acts 2:1)

PERHAPS THE FIRST VERSE OF Acts 2 makes us think of an intimate worship service or a loving fellowship of like-minded people. There's something comforting in the unity we see in this gathering. But there's also something remarkably sobering: All the believers—the only followers of Jesus the world yet knew—could fit into one place. Maybe others who had followed Jesus for a time were scattered throughout Judea and Galilee, but this was the core. The movement would begin here. And it wasn't a very big start at all.

That's the nature of salt and light. A pinch of salt can season an entire dish. A glow from a single candle or a ray from a cell phone's tiny bulb can brighten a room. Jesus never told his disciples that they could only influence their world from a position of strength. They did not begin as a majority. They began small, and eventually they turned their world upside down. Today, nearly one out of every three people in the world self-identifies as a Christian. That's quite a change from one room in Jerusalem.

Far too many Christians complain about being a minority in their culture, even when they aren't. But even when their perspective is true—even in places where believers in Jesus are vastly outnumbered—the complaint rings hollow. A minority of influential people can transform the way a culture sees, for good or for bad. We have experienced such movements in our own generation, and other generations have too. The key is not to gain a majority and vote God's will into law. It's to live as people who are radically transformed by the Spirit and change hearts and minds with our lives. Anyone can do that, even when vastly outnumbered.

God reduced Gideon's army to almost nothing before sending it into battle (Judges 7). He is always the majority; his people never need to fear a loss of influence. Like salt from the shaker or a single ray of light, we can make a huge difference. Live with that attitude, and you will change your world.

Lord, make me contagious with the beauty of your Kingdom, and let my influence spread. Quiet the complaints of your people, and make us catalysts for change. May we fill the world with the savor and brilliance of your ways. Amen.

Faith and Vision

Your young men will see visions, and your old men will dream dreams.
(Acts 2:17)

THE HOLY SPIRIT FELL ON believers in Jerusalem on the day of Pentecost, and Peter saw it as a fulfillment of a prophecy from the book of Joel. Not everything in that prophecy happened that day—there was no blood and smoke, and the sun did not turn dark—but that didn't matter. The Spirit's advent was a sign of God's ultimate plans, the beginning of a new era, the dawn of the age to come. For centuries, God had given words and visions to occasional priests and prophets, even assuring his people that his works were always preceded by prophetic vision (Amos 3:7). Now prophetic vision would no longer be exclusive to those uniquely gifted to see; it was available to everyone. When the Spirit came upon God's people, the things of the Spirit came upon them too.

If God is a communicator of vision, and if vision is available to everyone who believes, then he means for us to live and move with it—to be motivated by vision, to hold it in our hearts and minds and pray it into reality, to cultivate the pictures of his Kingdom and speak them forth. In a sense, that's how all human beings live; we picture the future and think of ways to make it happen according to our desires. We are dreamers by nature. But now we do it in partnership with God—not crafting our own dreams but letting ourselves be filled with his, cultivating a vision that draws us deeper into his calling. We delight in him and let his desires mingle with ours until they reflect his Kingdom purposes. We move in sync with the Spirit.

If God calls you to live by vision, you have to have one—or many. When you pray, envision the answer. In fact, the picture can often *be* your prayer; it's worth more than a thousand words. When you love, envision its power. When you speak, envision the transformation that comes. Not everything will unfold with the specifics you see, but it will often unfold in the spirit you see it. God's Kingdom comes through the vision he gives his people.

Lord, cultivate my vision. Allow me to see the unseen, to walk by faith, to live fully in the spiritual realm. Use my dreams, desires, and visions to bring your purposes about. Amen.

Fear and Comfort

*The church throughout all Judea and Galilee and Samaria had peace
and was being built up. And walking in the fear of the Lord and
in the comfort of the Holy Spirit, it multiplied. (Acts 9:31, ESV)*

THE EARLY CHURCH WAS TERRIFIED of Saul, scarcely able to believe that this terrorist's transformation was real. But it was also amazed by the work the Spirit was doing, how he was changing lives and advancing their cause. These were days of awe, an unusual window in time and space through which eternal purposes were pouring into the visible world. God was clearly doing something new.

In a sense, that's always true. God is always moving, always doing something new, even when we don't see it. He never changes, of course, but his Kingdom never stops growing. He is accomplishing great things in our midst. We may wonder if the church is growing—so many stories of decline seem to filter through media from time to time, even when global numbers prove them false—but the issue is never whether God is at work. The greater issue is whether we have eyes to see what he is doing. When we do, we can no longer be comfortable with the status quo.

That's the message Acts gives us. The church throughout Judea, Galilee, and Samaria was walking in the fear of the Lord and the comfort of the Spirit. Those attitudes may seem contradictory to us, but they are characteristic of days of awe. When people of faith have eyes to see, we experience the sobering reality of God's work and the comforting assurance that we are part of it. We become aware that we are living in unprecedented times. Our entire lives turn Godward.

Learn to recognize the work of God—in your life, in your society, in your world. The headlines will not reveal it to you; just the opposite, in fact. But the Spirit will. God is saving, healing, and delivering people even in the most unexpected places. Cultivate your vision to see what he is doing, align your steps with his, and be amazed.

Lord, your people have longed for the presence and power early believers experienced. Surely it has never gone away; the growth of the church is phenomenal. Open our eyes, inspire our hearts, and call us ever increasingly into your work. Restore our awe. Amen.

Love

If I had such faith that I could move mountains, but didn't love others,
I would be nothing. (1 Corinthians 13:2)

SCRIPTURE TELLS US TO MAKE love our highest goal (1 Corinthians 14:1)—that if we don't have love, everything else we do is pointless (1 Corinthians 13:1-3), that love is central to Jesus' will for his followers (Matthew 22:36-40; John 15:12-17), that it is the evidence that we have passed from death to life (1 John 3:14), and that followers of Jesus will be known by this one overarching characteristic (John 13:34-35). In other words, our love is a really big deal.

If God is love (1 John 4:8, 16), that makes sense. He is our source of life and calls us to be like him, so it would be shocking if love were not central to our lives in him. All of the characteristics of God we are told about in the Bible flow out of this core attribute—this perfect, zealous, breathtaking love that burns brightly within him and, the more we experience him, within his people. If we get nothing else from Scripture, if we never progress any further in the Christian life than this, understanding and showing his love would be better than understanding all else. Nothing else puts us in sync with God's heart; all other pursuits are pointless without it. If we don't love, we are not living the Christian life.

If that's true—and every indication from Scripture and the life of Jesus says it is—then we really need to know what love looks like. Is it a feeling, an attitude, an action, or all of the above? Does it always make the other person feel good, or is it tender at some times and tough at others? Does it even have to be expressed, or is it enough just to have it? The Bible and our own experience tell us a lot of these things, giving us not only instructions but also examples and models to follow. For those who want to be influential in this world—even for those who just want to know God—this becomes priority number one. Above all else, we must be known as those who love well.

Lord, teach me love. Fill me with it, train me in it, make me a fountain of it. May I overflow with love—just like you. Amen.

What Love Is

Love is patient and kind. (1 Corinthians 13:4)

IF YOU WERE TO SURVEY THE comments made by Christians at the end of news articles and blogs today and draw conclusions about Christianity only from those sources and nowhere else, you would come away with the impression that the Christian faith is contentious, pretentious, hard-edged, superficial, and somewhat arrogant. You would certainly find some exceptions to those descriptions, but the majority of comments would be enough to convince you of them. You would have to wade through a lot of contrary evidence to find "patient and kind" in the mix.

Perhaps that's because people who tend to comment on such articles and blogs are not representative of Christianity in general or because the nature of the forum itself (anonymous argumentation) tends to bring out the worst in people. Even so, the church is full of people who demonstrate quite a few characteristics that would never be described as patient or kind. We are not known for our love.

That has to change. Love is meant to be the distinguishing characteristic of followers of Jesus, and when it isn't, people cannot see him for who he is. God wants his people, who are called not to fit in but to go against the flow, to express his kindness and patience to a cruel and impatient world. These are gifts of his Spirit (Galatians 5:22), and they are nonnegotiable.

The problem is that human nature falls short of these goals. That's okay; we are never told to continue living from our old human nature. We have options. We can choose each morning to walk in the supernatural patience and kindness of God, to lean back into his Spirit rather than to push ahead in our own tendencies. A decision each day to rely on the power within us can make a dramatic difference, even when we need to be reminded of that decision in the heat of the moment. Salt and light need to look a lot like their source. The best way to do that—really the only effective way—is to let the Spirit of kindness and patience reign in our hearts.

Father, you have been amazingly patient with me, and your kindness toward me has known no limits. May I never be so hypocritical as to withhold patience and kindness from others. Fill me, empower me, and move me with the nature of your love. Amen.

What Love Isn't

Love is not jealous or boastful or proud or rude. (1 Corinthians 13:4-5)

As you seek to live a life of love, some people may try to define it for you and dictate its terms. They may not say, "If you love me, you will . . . ," but the implication is clear. They will apply their perceptions of Christian love to you, especially as it relates to them. But your definition of love comes not from the needs and demands of others but from the love of the Father, the example of Jesus, and the leading of the Spirit. You are to love the way Jesus loves, which means meeting people's needs as *he* defines them, not as *they* do.

Even so, certain attitudes are clearly beyond the pale of genuine love, and Paul identifies some of them in this passage. They share a common feature—a focus on self—and none are characteristic of Jesus. Though we are told that God is jealous (Exodus 20:5; 34:14; Zechariah 8:2, NIV), the jealousy Paul writes of is a different kind, an envy of someone else's possessions or position. Though we see Jesus boldly making extravagant (albeit truthful) claims about his own identity, the boasting presented in this passage is unfounded self-promotion, and the pride is based on exaggerated perceptions and a desire to be better than others. Though we see Jesus saying remarkably offensive things to the religious leaders who opposed him, the rudeness mentioned in this passage is a put-down of others in order to feel better about oneself. Jesus' controversial statements and attitudes were for the benefit of others, not for the benefit of his own reputation or needs. Love focuses outward.

That's your guideline for knowing whether or not you are walking in love. If your attitude is focused on the welfare of others, it's love. If it's focused on tearing others down in order to build yourself up, it isn't. The human tendency to become self-absorbed is the root of all strife. Turn your heart outward before it develops unloving symptoms any further. Immerse your heart and mind in the love the Father has given you, and show others what he is like.

Jesus, you are my model and my mentor. Your love was tender at times, tough at others, and always just what was needed. May the goal of my life be to see others as you see them and love them well. Amen.

What Love Doesn't Do

[Love] does not demand its own way. It is not irritable, and it keeps
no record of being wronged. It does not rejoice about injustice.
(1 Corinthians 13:5-6)

LOVE IS A CHOICE. **Love is an action. Love is not a feeling. Love does.** Statements like these have become increasingly common in recent years as Christian culture responds to distortions in the culture at large. We ardently defend the true definition of love because we see so many false definitions and terrible misapplications. Unfortunately, many people are much more focused on preserving the definition than on living it out, but the definition is nevertheless important. If love is meant to be our defining characteristic, we need to know what it is. We need to treat it as more than a sentiment and put it into action. We need to know what it does—and what it doesn't do.

In keeping with the attitudes of the previous verses, Paul lists some things that love does not do. Not surprisingly, these *don'ts* are focused on self and what results from the attitudes that preceded them. They are full of self-promotion—a symptom of a normal human need for fulfillment being pursued in abnormal, counterproductive ways. Our fallen nature focuses on getting what we need emotionally, relationally, and materially, even at the expense of others, never realizing that the key to getting what we need is actually giving others what they need. Jesus made that clear in his teachings, telling his disciples they would receive according to the measure that they gave (Luke 6:38). In the ways of the world, the hungry heart thinks it only needs to feed itself. In the ways of the Kingdom, the hungry heart is wise enough to find its fullness in feeding others. The only way to find love in this world is to begin overflowing with it.

Make that your goal. The promise of Jesus is that when you do, it will come back to you in an even greater flow. The inward-focused heart destroys itself. The outward-focused heart is a blessing to itself and all others.

Lord, turn my attentions to those around me. Forgive me for being focused on myself. I choose to meet the needs of others and will trust you to meet mine. May I spend my love as freely as you do. Amen.

What Love Does

[Love] rejoices whenever the truth wins out. Love never gives up, never
loses faith, is always hopeful, and endures through every circumstance.
(1 Corinthians 13:6-7)

TRUE LOVE IS RELENTLESSLY GOOD. Perhaps that should go without saying, but in a world in which people fall in and out of love so easily and often, in which love is often nothing more than the mood of the moment, the enduring and selfless nature of genuine love ought to be highlighted, promoted, and celebrated. Even more, it needs to be taught and demonstrated. We serve an eternal God with eternal love; the fickleness of our own is far too often an unfortunate contrast to his.

God understands the weaknesses of our fallen hearts, but he has done something rather dramatic to undo the fallenness and restore us to his image. We have the potential to love as he loves. At times, that will mean rejoicing over truth, even when it does not work to our own benefit; forgiving the sins of others and covering them from shame, just as God forgave and covered us; seeing the treasure God has put in others rather than focusing on their flaws and sins; defining people by their future as it can be rather than their past as it was; assuming the best, even when the worst is possible; being enormously patient as people struggle through the difficulties of life and the consequences of their own past habits and mistakes; and never, ever giving up hope. After all, is God hopeless about any situation? Of course not. When we are, we are not in sync with him. A heart aligned with his will always focus on a person's well-being and come alongside that person to help move him or her into God's blessings and purposes.

You were created for God—to know him and love him, and to enjoy him forever. But part of that purpose is being created for others—to know them and love them, and to enjoy them forever too. That begins now, and it can only happen by demonstrating the kind of love the Father has shown each of his children. Take your cues from him and let your love endure.

Father, your love is beyond my comprehension but not beyond my experience. Let me
know it, feel it, and live it deeply, and draw others into it through me. Amen.

As He Loves

This is my commandment: Love each other in the
same way I have loved you. (John 15:12)

YOU HAVE A HISTORY WITH GOD. It is most likely a spotted history; sometimes the relationship has been richly rewarding and other times obscure or frustrating. But on the whole, you know that God loves you, that he forgives you, and that he has extended his grace into every area of your life. As a Christian, you believe these things, at least in principle, even if you have not experienced them as fully as you would like. You rest in God's love as the foundation of your belief.

Spend some time thinking about all the ways God has loved you—how he has been patient with you when you keep making the same mistakes; when you forget something he already taught you years ago; when his grace covers the things you couldn't, wouldn't, or didn't think, do, or say; how he has restored what was lost, repaired what was broken, reconciled what was out of sorts, and redeemed your past. Think about how much you depend on him to heal and forgive, even when you know you don't deserve it. Think about the mysteries of grace—always unmerited, but always enough.

Now, if that's how God has loved you, then that's how you are called to love others. Jesus said so in John 13:34 and reiterates it here, calling it a new commandment on both occasions. Love itself isn't a new commandment, of course; Jesus and quite a few other teachers had already pointed out that "love your neighbor" was a pretty important concept of the ancient law (Leviticus 19:18; Mark 12:29-31). But loving others in the same way he has loved you? That's different. It's radical, sacrificial, thoroughly imbued with grace and compassion, exactly the sort of thing he was illustrating when he put on the garments of a servant and washed his disciples' feet (John 13). Your mission in life is not merely to receive the love of God—as wonderful as that part of the gospel is—but also to demonstrate it. Love with the extravagance he has shown in loving you.

{ *Jesus, may others be able to count on my love the way I count on yours. Bathe me in your grace, and let me radiate it to those around me. Give me extraordinary, supernatural love. Amen.*

The Use of Gifts

He called together his servants and entrusted his money
to them while he was gone. (Matthew 25:14)

A YOUNG SCOTTISH PREACHER HAD tried pastoral ministry on at least a couple of occasions, but his doctrines weren't always popular and his health didn't always cooperate. He taught for a time as well, but he considered his years "in ministry" a failure. So he decided to do what he loved to do—what seemed to be placed in him as a gift and a passion—and wrote fantasy fiction. At a time when few people at all, and hardly any in his circles, wrote fantasy fiction, some thought he was wasting his time. But his works ended up influencing Lewis Carroll, W. H. Auden, C. S. Lewis, J. R. R. Tolkien, G. K. Chesterton, and many others—and, by extension, millions who have been influenced by such authors. Oswald Chambers thought it a pity that the Scot's writings had been so neglected. C. S. Lewis called him his master. That's pretty impressive fruit for a failed preacher who ended up writing stories.

The Scot's name was George MacDonald, and he represents a multitude of people who have wanted to serve God but never fit into conventional ministry roles. In many ages of church history, including his and ours, his career path was the type to draw a lot of responses like "Why would you leave the ministry to write stories? What a waste!" But his work wasn't a waste at all; it was far more influential than that of many of the other servants of God around him.

Jesus told a story of a master who went away and left his assets with his servants. Two invested their portions of the assets, and one buried his. Jesus commended the investors and said they were an example of how the Kingdom of God works. God gives gifts, and he expects his people to use them—not the gifts of others, not in the ways defined by others, but as they were given in ways unique to the person. Stewards are obligated to serve their master; they are free to decide how. And the diversity of ways only enhances the master's glory.

Lord, help me understand how you have uniquely gifted me to serve you, and give me opportunities to do it well—no matter how unconventionally, how against the grain, and how well received. You are my audience. May you be pleased with what I do. Amen.

The Path of Fools

Claiming to be wise, they instead became utter fools. (Romans 1:22)

IN OUR CULTURE, showing skepticism and cynicism can come across as intelligence. It doesn't matter if the skeptic can actually refute a position logically or if a cynic presents a coherent alternative point of view. The simple use of sarcasm and suspicion to undermine what other people say is usually enough to give the cynic an air of common sense and superiority. A few condescending jabs, a criticism written from a "knowing" perspective, a roll of the eyes—all convey superiority. And the technique is really easy to employ.

Christian beliefs have often been dismissed with such cynicism, even when the cynic doesn't understand what he or she is dismissing or have evidence to support a better alternative. In fact, that's the key to skepticism—you don't need a better alternative. You don't need to come up with a more coherent explanation for anything; you only need to criticize the ones that are out there. This pseudo-intellectual attitude is rampant in our society, and it appears to undermine the faith of simple believers like us. *Except it doesn't.*

There are legitimate questions and arguments about faith, of course, and genuine objections to discuss. Many thoughtful people have rejected the faith. Unbelief as a whole is not incoherent or empty. But much of popular skepticism is, and Paul put his finger on it in Romans 1. He was writing about the trajectory of false worship—paganism, to be specific, which has taken on much more diverse and subtle forms in recent centuries. The context doesn't apply to all mockers and unthinking skeptics, but the dynamics do. They profess to be wise, convincing many. But behind the rolled eyes and contemptuous expressions is the foolishness of minds that don't want to think too hard.

Refuse to be intimidated. Anyone can criticize, but very few in our world embrace a coherent worldview. You do. Know your beliefs, grow in faith, and most of all, live the gospel. No amount of cynicism will ever overcome a lifestyle of wisdom, power, and love in the Spirit.

Jesus, you stood strong against a storm of criticism. Your Word urges us to stand strong too. The world shows contempt for your truth, but you have overcome the world. May I overcome it in every way too. Amen.

Hypocrisy

The standard you use in judging is the standard by which you will be judged. (Matthew 7:2)

JESUS CAME INTO THIS world not to judge it, but to save it (John 3:17), and he sends his followers into the world in the same spirit. So it should be no surprise that he comes down hard on judgmental hearts and hypocritical words. His instructions are sharply pointed; we are not called to be critics of those around us.

Jesus' harshest words were directed at those who laid the heavy burden of perfection on others without acknowledging their own imperfections. His warnings about judging others are directed at our natural human tendency to judge, but that's the point; he is calling his followers to a supernatural lifestyle. It's the fallen nature that picks at the flaws of other people without being aware of its own. Far too many Christians shake their heads at adulterers and murderers without any apparent awareness that the lust and anger in their own hearts come from the very same roots. Every whisper of condemnation, every morsel of gossip, every "I can't believe he/she did that" comes from a heart that could have done the same thing. Jesus' harsh words were aimed at the upstanding citizens who wanted a moral society without addressing the sins of their own hearts.

Jesus did not rule out the need for discernment or right judgment, of course. Far from it. But even if we live an almost-perfect, supernatural lifestyle of wisdom, power, and love, we must remember where we come from. We must know what we were redeemed from. And we must know we owe it to every other human being to extend grace for where he or she is.

Be known for grace. In certain conditions, any one of us could end up where others have ended up. And when given grace, anyone can still end up thoroughly forgiven and cleansed. Refuse to cement people where they are; instead bring them toward the fountain of grace. Even more, be one.

Lord, your desire for every human being is to know who you are and receive forgiveness, cleansing, and restoration. Grant me deep conviction whenever I am not assisting that desire. Give me eyes to see what grace looks like in every situation and to embody it well. Amen.

Blessings of Fullness

God blesses those . . . (Matthew 5:3-10)

WHEN JESUS TOLD HIS followers they were the salt of the earth and the light of the world—sent with the same character and purpose he came with—he was following up a teaching on the Beatitudes, or the blessedness and happiness of his ways. He declared them salt and light right after the Beatitudes reoriented their values to align with God's Kingdom. The implication is clear: The followers of Jesus will have influence in this world to the degree that they take on his nature and embrace his attitudes. The Kingdom mission is vitally related to the Kingdom character.

If that's true, then it's important to understand what these enigmatic Beatitudes mean. The first word of every Beatitude, *makarios*, is the key, but it is hard to interpret. *Blessed* and *happy* are the two most common translations, yet neither expresses the full concept. These blessings indicate the pathway to flourishing as a human being[15] and experiencing the *shalom*—the fullness, wholeness, completeness, and satisfaction—of God's Kingdom. For everyone who has gone through seasons wondering how to make life work, how to experience God's blessing, or how to have some sense of peace, the Beatitudes are the answer. And for everyone who wants to be salt and light in this world as we are called to be, these are the foundation. If you want to be fulfilled in life, start here.

Granted, the list in Matthew 5:3-10 is counterintuitive. What Jesus says may not look like the pathway to happiness. After all, mourning, hunger, and persecution rarely make our bucket lists. Yet these are God's priorities for his children for the all-important reason that they reflect his nature and embody his purposes. If we want to fit into the culture of his Kingdom without looking like tourists, these are the clothes to wear. And if we are going to be salt and light, this is where we get our flavor and our shine. Ultimately, we are called to be like Jesus, and these are fitting descriptions. They reveal who he is to a world that is longing for his fullness.

Jesus, you have not just called me to believe you; you have called me to be like you, to take my cues from you, to step into your fullness and joy. Take me down the path of these blessings into your Kingdom ways. Amen.

Humble Hearts

God blesses those who are humble, for they will
inherit the whole earth. (Matthew 5:5)

MANY HIGH-PROFILE EXAMPLES from the worlds of sports, politics, and entertainment promote themselves and receive a lot of attention. They seem to enjoy their fame. But that sort of attitude is not highly valued in God's Kingdom. Instead, Scripture points repeatedly to the lowly in heart, the humble, the poor in spirit, those who know how to bow before their God and serve their fellow humans. God is with such people and will exalt them at the proper time. They don't have to promote themselves; they can trust God's timing.

That's one of the common themes that emerge in the Beatitudes, those statements of blessedness and flourishing that describe the Kingdom culture. And the promises are extraordinary. The poor in spirit and the humble of heart do not merely find God's favor. They inherit the Kingdom of God and the land of his promise. These are ancient themes, of course; Jesus' words draw on the psalmists and prophets of old. He not only affirms them but takes them a step further. Jesus promises the whole earth to the humble, and just a chapter later in Matthew 6:10, he tells his followers to pray for God's Kingdom to come upon it. His reign involves a restoration of all that has fallen (Acts 3:21), and humble hearts get to be at the forefront of that project. He promotes those who did not promote themselves.

That's one of the reasons Jesus was able to promise rest to those who are weary (Matthew 11:28). Forcing your own way through this world, climbing the ladder of success, and competing with everyone who is climbing the same ladder can be exhausting. Hard work and wise decisions are important, of course, but so is trust. Humble hearts are able to do that, and God opens doors for them in season. Embrace that attitude. You may not ever be surrounded by many fans, but you will find many friends. People are drawn to those who are at rest in their God. And you will be able to show them what it means to be blessed.

Lord, teach me the balance between boldness of faith and humility of heart. I put my trust in you to open doors, lift me up, and establish me where you choose. May I fit the culture of your coming Kingdom perfectly. Amen.

Justice, Mercy, and Peace

God blesses those who hunger and thirst for justice,
for they will be satisfied. (Matthew 5:6)

YOUR GOALS IN LIFE SAY a lot about you. The things you long for, the dreams you have, the forces that drive you forward—these are indications of the condition of your heart and the priorities you've embraced along the way. They may include goals of many kinds—personal, career, family, financial, relational, and more—and there's nothing wrong with any of these. But a life that flourishes and carries Kingdom influence in this world will be built on a foundation of Kingdom values. It will seek justice or "rightness" in all situations, mercy for all those who need it, and peace in all its fullness—the *shalom* of God. It will embrace the priorities of the King.

These have always been God's values, clues to his purposes in this world. Something should bother us whenever we see injustice or unrighteousness, the sharp edges of this world that wound people's hearts and destroy their lives, the fractured nature of human existence that keeps us perpetually unsatisfied. Those who have embraced the culture of God's Kingdom will hunger and thirst for resolutions, carry mercy wherever they go, and offer wholeness and healing for wounded and fragmented souls. They will be called children of God (Matthew 5:9), receive mercy (Matthew 5:7), and ultimately be satisfied (Matthew 5:6). No one embraces God's agenda and ends up disappointed.

Those who embody the Beatitudes and carry the Kingdom culture have what the world needs, even if many consider these blessings to be the opposite of what they need. Modern society is starving for resolution and restoration, and true Kingdom citizens are called to offer it. If you seek the Kingdom of God and his righteousness—justice, mercy, and peace—you will receive them and much, much more. You will bear fruit that lasts forever and taste its goodness even now. You will experience the kind of life that not only makes you flourish but helps others flourish too.

Jesus, you demonstrated rightness, mercy, and shalom *throughout your earthly ministry, and you taught your followers to display them too. Build me up in these things. Make me a catalyst for Kingdom ways. Satisfy my hunger and thirst so I might heal the brokenness of others. Amen.*

Your Inheritance

God blesses those whose hearts are pure, for they will see God.
(Matthew 5:8)

SOME PEOPLE ARE INTERESTED in building wealth in order to spend it. But the mentality of someone who understands his or her family as a multigenerational endeavor is more interested in building assets to pass down for the next generation to build on further. The point is not to burn up what was been gathered but to invest it in something great. The eyes of faith see ever-increasing possibilities. The family fortune is meant to go on and on.

That's how it works in the family of God, too, although usually with a different set of assets. God invests in his children, and like the master in the parable of the talents (Matthew 25:14-30), he expects his children to invest in others. Why? Because the Kingdom of God is an enormous building project that lasts throughout all generations to the end of time and beyond. Those who embrace the Kingdom culture—who embody the characteristics presented in the Beatitudes—receive a Kingdom inheritance. In fact, we become coheirs with Jesus. And what does he deserve to inherit? Everything. We become recipients of all that is.

That's why the Beatitudes promise that the humble will inherit the earth (Matthew 5:5) and the poor in spirit will have the Kingdom of heaven itself (5:3). Of course, the even greater inheritance is a face-to-face relationship with the Father (5:8). Those who seek only the Kingdom are just looking for what they can get from God. Those who know the King have the love and joy of the universe's most exhilarating relationship and the Kingdom too. In other words, a single-hearted focus on the King and his ways results in the ultimate fulfillment. That's the enormity of the promise Jesus gave.

Every human being longs for this, though many don't know it. All things in heaven and earth were created for the Son (Colossians 1:16), and all who have been adopted into his family by faith become joint heirs with him (Romans 8:17). Embrace the character and the promises of the family culture, and offer it to others generously. An inheritance so vast is meant to be shared.

Lord, the treasures of your Kingdom are vaster than I can imagine, yet you offer them to those who carry the right priorities and desires. Shape my vision, dreams, and heart to be pure. Let me see you and receive your Kingdom. Amen.

A Lasting Investment

God blesses those who are humble, for they will
inherit the whole earth. (Matthew 5:5)

A TREND AMONG CHRISTIAN THINKERS and writers of the seventeenth century was to emphasize solitude and separation from the world. A great many Pietists, Jansenists, Puritans, and others felt that forsaking the world was their sacred calling—that everything heavenly and spiritual was so completely "other" than life on a corrupt earth that no one could draw near to God without drawing away from the attachments of society and the vanity of fleeting pleasures. They emphasized the coming of God's Kingdom not on earth but in heaven. Some of them forgot that the meek will inherit the earth and focused on inheriting an existence far removed from it.

The devotional writers of that century, many of whom have had a profound influence on today's beliefs and practices, were right that there is great value in maintaining a spiritual separation from the influences of a fallen world. But that attitude of separation can be maintained, as many reformers had taught, even while engaging in the world's systems and institutions. God does not remain detached from the world, keeping humanity at arm's length and refusing to invest his heart in us. And neither should we.

Seek to live in balance, fully integrating into the life going on around you without giving your heart to its ways. The issue is not where you live and work but where your affections lie. God's love will draw your devotion away from the corruption of the world, but it will also compel you to go into the world with love and compassion. If you believe you are to escape from the world and abandon it, you will never influence it. If you see yourself as an inheritor of the world, you will invest in it. And if you invest what God has given you—the fruit and gifts of his Spirit—your inheritance will be all the more beautiful.

Lord, I'm not exactly sure what it means to inherit the earth, but I know you have plans for this planet that involve those who are humble and submitted to you. May I grow in true meekness daily and share in the fullness of your inheritance. Amen.

The Cost of Truth

*God blesses you when people mock you and persecute you
and lie about you and say all sorts of evil things against
you because you are my followers. (Matthew 5:11)*

THE PERKS OF BEING SALT AND LIGHT in this world include the inheritance of Jesus, which is everything. The Beatitudes promise the Kingdom of Heaven and earth to those whose hearts are humble and know God. But being salt and light also comes with a cost; it puts us at odds with a world with an opposing agenda. When those who embrace the Kingdom culture interact with those who don't, things happen. Our way doesn't look very appealing or effective, and only those with eyes of faith can understand it.

So the attitudes of the Kingdom will have a dual effect, drawing many to you and driving many away. Embracing the culture of the Kingdom will not endear you to much of the world, and the result is friction, sometimes conflict, and even persecution. As a citizen of the Kingdom with some level of influence on your environment, you should be prepared to experience something on that spectrum. And if you find yourself at the extreme end of it, as many throughout history have—when you are persecuted for nothing more than being a follower of Jesus, one who bears his character and embraces his mission—you should rejoice.

That goes against our instincts—no one likes to experience injustice—but it can be a sign that you are representing Jesus accurately. Salt burns wounds, and light blinds eyes that are used to the dark. The world is full of wounds and darkness, and your influence may not always be welcome. Nevertheless, you are chosen and called, an ambassador of Kingdom ways, a representative of Kingdom culture, and a sign of Kingdom life to those who will receive it. Do not be moved from your mission or pressured to compromise your character, even in the face of insults and offenses. These are signs of your strength, the reaction of darkness to the light. Continue to shine, just as God has done for you.

Jesus, you withstood insults, mockery, misunderstandings, offenses, and persecution with patience and grace. May I have eyes of faith and strength of character to do the same. Plant me firmly in the soil of your Kingdom and make me fruitful even in the harshest of conditions. Amen.

Powerful Prayers

*The earnest prayer of a righteous person has great power
and produces wonderful results. (James 5:16)*

IN 1857, a lay missionary named Jeremiah Lanphier started a weekday prayer meeting for businessmen in lower New York City. He thought some men might like to pray during the hour businesses were closed, so he passed out fliers and invited many in the district to come. But when the first meeting began, no one had come. Only a few straggled in during the hour. But the few agreed to try again the next week and the next, and within six months, more than 10,000 men were gathering for prayer. Revivals with hundreds of conversions began to break out nearby and then further away. A spiritual movement had begun.

Similar stories are told of other historical prayer movements—the Moravian movement, the revivals of Korea, and many more. In fact, history has been shaped by unknown prayer warriors even more profoundly than by the famous names and faces we put in our textbooks. That's because history's actors perform their scenes on a stage that is governed by a Playwright and his stagehands. When he responds to the prayers of his people, tides turn and trends give way to the currents of his Kingdom. He is building something magnificent through the prayers and faith of Kingdom citizens.

Because of your connection to the source of life, you have more influence in this world than you have yet imagined. You may never be recognized for that power; you may never even see its effects yourself. But people with eyes of faith know the potential and take advantage of it. Like Jeremiah Lanphier and many before and since, they believe that crying out to God for his purposes is much more powerful than trying to forge our own. A life devoted to prayer changes the course of history and blesses a world that resists its own Creator. It puts you in a position of authority no matter how little earthly power you hold. And it makes you a partner with God in his mission to rescue, redeem, and restore the lives of many.

Lord, fill my heart and mouth with the words of prayers you want to answer. May your will be done and your Kingdom come in my life, family, city, nation, and world through my prayers of faith. Pour out your Spirit on me, for me, and through me. Amen.

Count the Cost

*Everyone who wants to live a godly life in Christ Jesus
will suffer persecution. (2 Timothy 3:12)*

IN HIS MID-TWENTIES, William Wilberforce had already been a Member of Parliament for several years when he was faced with a huge decision. The nature of his recent conversion experience put him on the fringes of polite society. Would he continue in public life and face the same contempt some of his evangelical peers had faced? Or would he withdraw from the public eye and devote his life to evangelical work? His friends encouraged the former, and Wilberforce eventually agreed. He resolved to put all of his energy into political pursuits for the good of society. His conservative views would rankle some, but they would change his country for the better. He successfully fought for the abolition of the slave trade and then of slavery itself.

Many Christians face the same sort of conundrum today, perhaps not on so prominent a stage, but certainly in a similarly hostile environment. Biblically informed views are not always welcomed in "polite society," or, as we would put it today, the mainstream of public opinion. We find ourselves swimming against the tide in an ocean of ideas. That's normal; Jesus assured his followers many would be persecuted (John 15:18-25), and unwelcomed views fall far short of "persecution" status. Some are called to pull away from the opposition and work within the church. Others are called, like Wilberforce, to go directly into the opposition and work for social change. It's important to know the situation.

Count the costs, but know that the benefits will always exceed them. Wilberforce changed his nation directly, and much of the world indirectly. He saw some of the rewards of his labor in this life and surely considered his hardships worth the trouble. In eternity, he certainly has experienced the fruit of his labor. You will too. Anchor yourself in Kingdom values and refuse to compromise them in the ever-changing tides of human reasoning. Be sensitive to what others have learned and how they see, but also be insistent on what God has shown you and how he sees. A godly life is worth the resistance you face in living it.

Lord, strengthen my resolve and increase my fortitude to respond to your voice above all others. I live for an audience of one. Let my devotion reap lasting rewards, be a blessing to my society, and bear eternal fruit for your Kingdom. Amen.

Flip the Script

*Everything that has happened to me here has helped
to spread the Good News. (Philippians 1:12)*

NORMAL PATTERNS OF LIFE IN the hills of rural Southeast Asia are interrupted by the rainy season, and plans for travel and trade are often put on hold until the weather is more predictable. But Canadian missionary Isobel Kuhn, who worked among Lisu tribal villages in the mid-1900s, decided to take advantage of the poor weather and begin the Rainy Season Bible School, a program to teach new believers the basics of the Christian life. The project was extremely successful, and many trainees eventually became leaders in village churches. Kuhn flipped the script to turn what appeared to be an adverse situation into an opportunity.

Scripture is full of similar examples: the twelve tribes of Israel crossing into the Promised Land despite the Jordan River being at flood stage; Gideon's tiny army winning a huge battle; Jehoshaphat turning his army's vulnerability into an occasion for proving the power of praise; David defying Goliath and the Philistines; Esther turning the tables on an evil plot against her people and seeing them saved; Paul declaring that his imprisonment was actually a great platform for sharing the gospel; and especially a cross and tomb turning into the ultimate victory in a cosmic battle. God is a script-flipper by nature, and he invites his people into the same dynamics. Threats are often opportunities; defeat is never really defeat; and victories come from the unlikeliest heroes.

If that's a new pattern for you, welcome to life in God's Kingdom, where adversity is rarely what it seems. You are invited to be a living, breathing participant of unexpected turns of events; the overcomer who isn't fazed with his or her back against the wall; the weak, humble, or foolish person who proves the power and wisdom of God. Your life is a potential showcase for the exploits of your Father, who loves to make nothing into something and call things that are not as though they are (see Romans 4:17, NIV). You demonstrate his creativity just by letting him work in your life. Trust him to create opportunities for you that work out for your good and serve his purposes.

Lord, it is incredibly difficult to retrain my thinking about adversity, but faith can always turn it into opportunity. I invite you to speak to me, to remind me of adversity's opportunities, and to showcase creative victories through me. Amen.

Small Big Things

Do not despise these small beginnings, for the LORD
rejoices to see the work begin. (Zechariah 4:10)

EDWARD KIMBALL WAS a Sunday school teacher at a church in Boston—not an unimportant role, and certainly a worthwhile investment of time and energy. But Kimball is hardly known in Christian history except for one key contribution: He visited a young man named Dwight Moody, who was working at a shoe store, and led him to Christ. Moody became the best-known evangelist of the nineteenth century, preaching to as many as 100 million people, influencing numerous other ministers and evangelists who had considerable influence of their own, and founding Moody Church and Moody Bible Institute in Chicago, institutions that have trained many for Christian service. One visit to a shoe shop changed the face of evangelicalism and millions of lives.

That story is often told to encourage people who feel that they have little influence in God's Kingdom, and for understandable reasons. Kimball surely made many positive contributions to society and the people who knew him, but he is known for influencing one person who influenced millions of others. He is an example of a small catalyst that prompts a big change, the power of minor events to effect major movements, a case study in how the Kingdom of God often works. For every person who thinks he or she has nothing to offer, Kimball stands as a reminder that one conversation can change the course of history.

Do not think of your contributions to God's work as small things or dismiss their potential to change lives. You may never see significant impact this side of heaven, but that doesn't mean you haven't had any. You don't know what your faithfulness has accomplished, and it isn't your job to figure it out. God does, and he will treasure your gifts. Use them well, use them faithfully, and leave the results to him. From your perspective in eternity, you will be grateful for the things you have done. Even now, people who are being influenced by your life probably already are.

Lord, it's easy to feel like my work is never enough—that the needs are too great and my offerings are too small. Change the way I see. Give me glimpses of impact. Teach me to be grateful for the privilege of serving you, even in apparently insignificant ways. Amen.

An Age of Grace

I have come to save the world and not to judge it. (John 12:47)

MEDIEVAL CHRISTIAN THINKERS paid a lot of attention, with almost mathematical obsession, to degrees of sin—which sins resulted in certain consequences, which categories of righteousness and unrighteousness merited which levels of rewards and punishments in the afterlife hierarchy, and how long each degree of sin detained a person before he or she reached the ultimate paradise. The entire framework, however varied and fluid it was, reflected not the Kingdom of God but the world's desire for meticulous justice. Society was full of injustices; the church envisioned a system that worked, even in the afterlife.

We can understand that. Something gnaws at us when people get away with evils and injustices. We want them to pay. And we are right to expect authorities to keep the peace and establish order in society. That's the role of government in this world, and God has made it clear through the prophets that he is fully on the side of justice. But if we apply our vengeance instinct to personal relationships and spiritual adversaries—and to ourselves—we run into a problem. All are guilty of multiple offenses. We need a Savior who forgives, cleanses, and renews. None of us can bear the weight of our own flaws, weaknesses, and sins.

We are called to demonstrate another way, an alternative to a world full of payback—a Kingdom of grace. We can't live in both systems at the same time, selectively applying justice to some and grace to others and ourselves. It's all or nothing. When we enter into God's grace for us by faith, we also enter into an understanding that we are to give what we have received. That's how his Kingdom works. We have been thoroughly forgiven; we are to thoroughly forgive.

Jesus was not sent into this world on a mission of judgment. Neither are you. His mission statement at the synagogue of Nazareth declared a time of God's favor (Luke 4:18-19), and we are to declare the same. As a minister of God's search-and-recovery mission in this world, embody the culture of grace.

Jesus, you have proven that hearts grow full in a climate of love; it's the way of your Kingdom. Thank you for your grace in my life. May others experience it through me. Amen.

Prepared for Influence

*Can we find anyone else like this man so obviously
filled with the spirit of God? (Genesis 41:38)*

JOSEPH HAD WAITED YEARS FOR an opportunity to get out of prison. Maybe he longed
to return to his homeland or perhaps live without reminders of being sold into slavery by his brothers years before. Either way, the dreams God had given him—the
ones that irritated his brothers so harshly—seemed to have been left in the past. But
now Egypt's pharaoh was pleased with Joseph's wisdom and was promoting him to
an extraordinarily high position. The Spirit that inspired and informed Joseph was
clearly visible to those around him.

Many of us long for that kind of recognizable impact. We want to be endowed
with wisdom, power, and love from on high, and we want people to see the presence
of the Spirit within us. We're disappointed when our beliefs are dismissed as out of
touch, irrelevant, or simpleminded by the world and when our gifts are not appre-
ciated or valued by the body of Christ. We forget that Joseph was rejected by his
brothers, falsely accused by his master's wife, imprisoned by his master, and forgotten
by other prisoners who could have advocated for his release. He spent years in the
lower rungs of society, finding favor with God and occasionally with other people,
but still confined by unfortunate circumstances. He appeared to be stuck.

We can relate to that, but we have to remind ourselves that we are never stuck
in our circumstances, no matter how confined we feel or how long we have felt that
way. The day before Joseph was called before Pharaoh to interpret his dreams, he
had been forgotten in prison for two long years and had no prospects of getting out.
God's solution was a day away, but Joseph couldn't see it. All he could do was grow
strong in the Spirit until God's plan unfolded. Whatever dreams you have for serving God and influencing this world, make that your priority. His doors open at the
perfect time for those who have prepared their hearts for his timing.

*Lord, I don't have to see open doors to know that you are the one who opens them. I trust
your timing. Prepare my heart to carry the weight of my calling, and make me strong in
the Spirit for the works you've prepared. Amen.*

Sent

*Thus it is written, that the Christ should suffer and on the
third day rise from the dead, and that repentance for the
forgiveness of sins should be proclaimed in his name to
all nations, beginning from Jerusalem. (Luke 24:46-47, ESV)*

HINTS THROUGHOUT THE Old Testament make it clear that Israel's God was interested in more than just Israel—that his Word would be a light for Gentiles, that Israel would be the firstborn (not the only-born) of nations, that God's glory would eventually cover the earth, and that many would be drawn to God through the Jews. Before Jesus, that global mission was more of a centripetal force than a centrifugal one; it was focused on the center, with nations being drawn in toward the work God was doing. People like the queen of Sheba came to Jerusalem to see the marvels of its Temple, the wisdom of its king, and the blessings its God had bestowed on it. Prophets declared that God would make Jerusalem a cause for praise in all the earth. Even when God's people were scattered in exile, their hearts still turned toward the Holy City as the center of God's work.

In the New Testament, that centripetal force shifted into a centrifugal one, moving believers outward, driving the message into all nations. Jesus told his disciples to go into all the world, and persecution, trade, and missionary trips took the gospel far away from its geographic origins. Instead of drawing people in, the church focused on sending people out. The global mission became truly global.

We still live in this outward-moving age, when the geographic center of the gospel has moved locations several times, when missionaries are being sent to distant countries (and others are being sent to us), and when the Bible is still being translated into the languages of remote people groups. But the mission is more than geographic. It takes us outside the walls of our local church into the workplace, the marketplace, community organizations, and everywhere else we go. Our mission is integrated into every aspect of our lives, sometimes subtly and creatively, to draw in, reach out, and lift up until God's glory really does cover the earth—through us.

Lord, work your mission into my identity. Open my eyes to see myself as a vital, integral part of your global redemption. May I carry your presence—your wisdom, power, and love—into every area of life. Amen.

Foreigners by Design

*A great wave of persecution began that day, sweeping over the church
in Jerusalem; and all the believers except the apostles were scattered
through the regions of Judea and Samaria. (Acts 8:1)*

SCRIPTURE DEPICTS CITIZENS of heaven as foreigners, strangers, aliens, nomads, and other descriptions to distinguish us from a purely earthly existence. Such words are at times comforting and other times unsettling. They remind us that we are rooted in eternity, but they also remind us that we don't quite fit in here. And sometimes our foreign status is pressed upon us in extreme ways; persecutions have broken out since the earliest days of the church and continue in many countries today. Millions of martyrs testify to the incompatibility between the Kingdom of Heaven and earthly agendas.

As discomforting as that is, our alien status is by design. We see in Scripture and history that virtually every time God has scattered his people (or rather allowed an oppressor to scatter them), it has somehow advanced his Kingdom. This is one of the ways God gets his salt and light into the farthest reaches of the world. He is not the author of persecution, of course; but he has always demonstrated an ability to incorporate even the worst of human decisions into his overarching purposes, planning for them and compensating for them ahead of time. The dysfunction of patriarchal families, the decisions of evil kings, the persecutions of his people—all have served his purposes. He knows how to accomplish his plan in spite of—even in conjunction with—the tragedies of life.

Don't despise your alien status in this world. There will be times when you feel at home, when things are going well and you seem to fit in. Thank God for them. But thank him also for the ways he accomplishes his purposes through the hard rejections and subtle exclusions you may experience. They will ultimately serve his purposes, as well as yours. Your mission in life should never be compromised by the world's resistance to it.

Lord, give me the endurance to persevere through hard times and injustices and the perspective to see your higher purposes in them. Make me fruitful regardless of the condition of the soil I'm planted in. Accomplish your purposes in me and through me. Amen.

Higher Truth

*They spread this bad report about the land among the Israelites: "The
land we traveled through and explored will devour anyone who goes
to live there. All the people we saw were huge." (Numbers 13:32)*

MOSES HAD SENT TWELVE SCOUTS into the Promised Land—not to figure out whether
the land could be taken but to develop some strategies for the best way to do it—and
most of them came back completely paralyzed by fear. All they could see was how
overwhelming the task was. From their perspective, there were giants and obstacles
and all sorts of opposing forces. But two of the scouts had a better perspective, one
that lined up with what God had already spoken. The obstacles and opposition were
real, they said, but so was God's promise. After all, this was the *Promised* Land. But
the critics outnumbered the men of faith, and the listening crowd panicked. The
nation was consigned to wander for another generation.

Critics have that kind of power, unfortunately. What they say may be true, but
they rarely emphasize the higher truth of what God has said. They limit themselves
to a human perspective and ignore the possibility of a divine one. And the world is
full of such voices.

Sadly, so is the church. "It won't work" is a convincing statement, and it has
shot down numerous God-given visions throughout history. Plans should be cau-
tious and well considered, and appropriate objections should be raised, but when
God has guided, when his words are at stake, objections pale in comparison. When
God has spoken, the voices of critics need to fade away. With God, no obstacle is
insurmountable.

Criticism is easy, but faith and vision actually make things happen. Don't be one
of those people who point out all the problems without ever offering any solutions.
God tends to satisfy visionaries, not critics. Even when visions falter, they still get
us further than any lack of vision ever will. Choose to see from a God-centered perspective, and then step into the vision you've been given. He will lead you faithfully
into lands of promise.

*Lord, give me vision that comes from your perspective and fits your purposes, and make
me resistant to all who would poke holes in it. Give me the discernment to know the
difference between constructive advice and destructive criticism. May my faith endure
through all opposition. Amen.*

OCTOBER 24

Luke 6:46-49

If Jesus Were Lord

Why do you keep calling me "Lord, Lord!"
when you don't do what I say? (Luke 6:46)

IMAGINE JESUS APPEARING TO YOU and saying, "I appreciate your efforts, but I'll be making all the decisions in your life now. I'm going to rearrange some things. I'll teach you the values, impart the gifts, and lead you in the purposes of my Kingdom. You will have a different perspective soon, but I think you'll like it. You're going to love your new life."

What do you think your life would look like if Jesus were given free rein in it? It's an interesting question that should guide us daily already. After all, he *is* Lord, and he is supposed to be leading us and shaping us even now. But the fact that we can imagine what it *would* be like if he were truly Lord over our lives, and that in doing so we picture something different from what we are experiencing now, suggests that we are not completely submitted to his lordship. We call him Lord without actually treating him as Lord.

One of the best things you can do in your growth as a follower of Jesus is to ask yourself the question, *What would life look like if . . . ?* The question works for your personal life, your family, your work, and any other area of life. If Jesus were in charge of the situation, how would he rearrange it? The exercise of asking and envisioning the answer goes a long way toward developing a Kingdom perspective in your heart. At some point, the perspective leads to action. You may even find out that Jesus *is* rearranging your life to be more consistent with his nature and his plans. The question can lead to significant change.

In language very similar to today's verse, Jesus gave a pretty specific example of his rearranging tendencies. He washed his disciples' feet and told them to follow his example by doing the same for each other (John 13:13-15). But that's just the beginning. Ask him to redesign your personal world, inside and out. Let him rearrange your perspective. Experience what it means for him to truly be Lord of your life.

Jesus, I may never follow you perfectly, but I don't want to follow you halfheartedly. Answer my question of what life would look like with you as Lord with real experiences. Rearrange my life as you see fit. Amen.

If Jesus Were King

Blessings on the King who comes in the name of the LORD!
Peace in heaven, and glory in highest heaven! (Luke 19:38)

MUCH OF HISTORY IS THE STORY of contentious politics. In today's age of democracies, we see cycles of debates and disputes over policies and candidates. Similar debates filled the age of monarchies and empires, not over who would rule but how well they were ruling. Some governments have been good, others have been bad, and by no means have any been flawless. The fundamental question in all arguments and discussions regarding political ideology is what good government looks like, and from there springs a multitude of others: What degree of control should it have? To whom is it accountable? What policies should it implement? And on and on and on.

What if Jesus were king? He *is* King of the universe, of course, but if the living Jesus showed up in the flesh and ran one of our governments, what would it look like? What issues would be important to him? How active would he expect his subjects or citizens to be? Which kinds of authority would he delegate, and which kinds would he exercise himself? Would he seek to control or to influence? Enforce legislation or change hearts? These questions could go on and on too, but even a few are enough to spark your imagination. If Jesus were in charge of your country, what kind of environment would he create?

The answer to that question ought to guide not only your political choices but also your sense of civic responsibility. In some very real ways, Jesus has the opportunity to change society for good through his faithful people who are strategically placed in neighborhoods, cities, counties, states, and the nation. If you want to be salt and light in a democracy, you will need to have some understanding of how Jesus would be—and actually is, through his people—salt and light in a democracy. Ask him for that understanding, and don't be surprised if he gives you unexpected answers. Then live as a Jesus follower with a Kingdom perspective wherever he places you in society.

Jesus, it's hard to imagine you getting mixed up in politics but also hard to imagine you avoiding real issues that affect lives. Show me that balance. Lead me into positions of influence. Let me be part of the change you desire. Amen.

If Jesus Were CEO

Even the Son of Man came not to be served but to serve others
and to give his life as a ransom for many. (Matthew 20:28)

BUSINESS MODELS COME AND GO. Some have stressed strong, nearly authoritarian leadership. Others have emphasized leading by example or even by serving. All have their pros and cons, and examples of every kind are to be found in nearly every economic sector. But if Jesus were the CEO of a company today, how would he run it? What values would his company stress? How would he balance making enough profit to pay his employees and provide excellent service with giving charitable donations that bless the larger society? In what ways would he care for his staff and give them opportunities to grow? What would he expect from them in terms of excellence, attitude, work ethic, character, and work relationships? If he managed the business, what environment would he create there?

This may come across as a frivolous hypothetical situation—Jesus never showed any interest in running a business, did he?—but it has significant implications for everyone in business leadership or on a company's staff. With a little rewording, those implications could easily be applied to nonprofit organizations too. The point is that Jesus is alive and active, not only as our intercessor at the right hand of the Father, but also as the living presence among us. His Spirit lives in us, guides us, and implements the Father's will through us—at least ideally—in this world. So for those in any sort of business, what is the Father's will?

Spend some time imagining what the salt and light of God looks like at a practical level in the overall organization and day-to-day operations of our enterprises today. From his words to his disciples, we know Jesus would lead by serving; he made that clear. But what would his service look like? How would it bless everyone involved? How would it serve society as a whole? Answering those questions will move you closer to a Kingdom perspective in your work, and that perspective might just change the world—or at least your corner of it—in profound ways.

Jesus, you insisted that the way to greatness was to serve, not to gain power and command others. Give me a heart for service. Show me how to live a Kingdom life in the institutions of this world. Amen.

If Jesus Were a Teacher

Three days later they finally discovered him in the Temple,
sitting among the religious teachers, listening to them and
asking questions. All who heard him were amazed at his
understanding and his answers. (Luke 2:46-47)

WHAT WOULD A CLASSROOM led by the Son of God look like? We get a glimpse in the Gospels of the answer to that question in an ancient context—Jesus taught his disciples for more than three years in a format common to the time. But if he were a teacher in our society today, what would he be like? If he were the president, principal, or headmaster of a school—any kind of modern educator—what kind of environment would he create?

These questions are relevant for every follower of Jesus whose life connects with a school, whether that connection is with a public or private school, a college or university, as a student or a parent of a student, and certainly as a teacher or administrator. Pedagogical techniques have gone through enormous changes over the years, and we know a lot more about the learning process than we used to. But if what we know at a professional level is allowed to merge with the nature and character of Christ—his patience, his value for those who are learning, his creative ways of making a point— we could transform society one student at a time. We could bring the influence of the Kingdom into the classrooms of life.

This is not a question of bringing God into the classroom through words and prayers, nor is it about curriculum and the current philosophies of human experts. The environment of God's Kingdom does not depend on the kinds of things our societies have debated in recent decades. People with Jesus in them can change the atmosphere regardless of policies and curricula just by being like Jesus. Hardly anyone would resist his kindness or the creativity of his ways. If he is in you, and you are in a classroom, he is there. Let him transform your heart and the heart of others through you simply by expressing his nature.

Jesus, we have been much more concerned about our education policies than about our educators' hearts. Change our perspective. Let me influence hearts the way you did— to learn as you learned, teach as you taught, and live as you lived. Amen.

If Jesus Were a Parent

Because we are his children, God has sent the Spirit of his Son into our hearts, prompting us to call out, "Abba, Father." (Galatians 4:6)

GOD IS OUR FATHER. That is the privilege of everyone who believes (John 1:12). God planned it this way before he even made the foundation of the world (Ephesians 1:4-5), and our relationship with him leads to an experience of being unimaginably loved (1 John 3:1). If we acknowledge him as our Father, we can learn a lot about parenting from him. In fact, we can learn quite a bit about the nature of families. As believers, we have been adopted into the divine family and are being loved into a fuller awareness of the extraordinary relationships we have with Christ—in him and through him. We are living in the middle of the divine template.

But in keeping with our theme of being like Jesus, let's ask how he might govern a home. If Jesus were the parent in our family today—not the spiritual family of God as a whole, but the natural family living in our current household or that we interact with regularly—what environment would he set? What kind of values would this family express? How would he communicate, correct his children, express his love, nurture our faithfulness, and make daily life work? How would he influence his loved ones—and want us to influence each other? What would he rearrange?

These questions we've been asking over the last few days about how to create a Jesus-like environment apply to every area of your life, but nowhere are they more important than in your family. When the home is not a reflection of the Kingdom—with its warmth, its fullness, its value for the people nurtured there—the pain of a fallen world is more evident than ever. Sometimes you are not in complete control of that environment; others shape it too. But you do have influence. Your prayers, your faith, and your attitude, even under stress, can become spiritual catalysts for real change. Over time, you may see the Kingdom growing in your home in surprising ways. And when it does, it flows outward into every other area of life too.

Jesus, I want my home to look a lot like your Kingdom—every relationship, every expression, every moment of every day. Show me how. Whatever it takes, teach me to rearrange life so that my family begins to look like yours. Amen.

The Family Estate

Through him [Christ] God created everything in the heavenly
realms and on earth. He made the things we can see and the things
we can't see. . . . Everything was created through him and for him.
(Colossians 1:16)

YOU HAVE BEEN ADOPTED into the divine family, and there's something you need to know. It is the wealthiest family in the universe; your Father owns everything, and your elder brother is the heir of it all. But he has made you a coheir with him. That means you stand to inherit everything; in fact, it's already yours. You get to live on this royal estate even now. If there's anything you want to do, any portion of the inheritance you want to spend (in keeping with family purposes, of course), all you need to do is submit a proposal to the Father in the name of the Son. It may take some refining, but it is not an illegitimate request. You have access to the family fortune.

When you learn to pray from that perspective—not as an outsider trying to pull blessings down from heaven, but as a son or daughter already written into the family's inheritance—your prayers begin to take on a different tone. You don't beg; you ask. You don't wonder if your unworthiness disqualifies you; you are clothed in Christ, and his worthiness is enough. You don't ask for selfish purposes; you ask because the family is on a mission and has a plan to flourish and expand. When prayers come from that perspective and take on that tone, they begin to be filled with faith. And faith is what God says will prompt him to respond.

Learn to pray as a son or daughter who already has a share in the inheritance. See the world as your family's estate, and submit requests that will make right whatever has gone wrong in it. Know the Father's purposes, and line up with them. His Kingdom came in the Son, it is now coming through his sons and daughters, and it will come in fullness when the Son returns. Live—and ask—as an heir who longs for the restoration of all good things.

Father, teach me our family's ways so I can use our inheritance for your purposes. Let me live in its abundance and ask as a child—from a position of privilege. May I bless the world with all you have given. Amen.

The Family Plan

*God in all his fullness was pleased to live in Christ, and through him
God reconciled everything to himself. He made peace with everything
in heaven and on earth by means of Christ's blood on the cross.*
(Colossians 1:19-20)

MUCH OF YOUR DISCIPLESHIP, and therefore your mission as salt and light in this world, will be to learn the royal family's ways and understand its purposes. You are not given your shares of the inheritance to go off on your own tangent and live apart from God's ways, though you will certainly benefit from them. You are being nurtured and trained, just as every child in his or her natural family is conditioned to adopt the family's ways and adapt to its environment. The more you exhibit an understanding of family interests, the more the Father and the Son entrust their resources to you. The gifts they give are already yours, of course; you are simply learning how to use them. You are called to leverage the enormous wealth of this Kingdom, all the resources granted for your use, to reconcile the world to your Father the King and restore people to its blessings.

Kingdom wealth does not look like worldly wealth, of course, though finances certainly fall within the royal estate. The fact that your Father owns the cattle on a thousand hills (Psalm 50:10) and offers good and perfect gifts (James 1:17) tells us that he is King of both the visible and invisible worlds. The most powerful resources you are given come from the invisible realm, which explains why you are in lifelong training. They are not easy gifts to understand. They have the potential to redeem, regenerate, reconcile, and restore. They are supernatural, and only those with eyes of faith can even see them, much less learn how to use them.

Devote yourself to this mission. All the fullness of God dwells in Christ, and Christ dwells in you. The family inheritance is in that relationship, and its wealth is available now. Explore the estate, adopt the character of the royal family, and ask to learn how to use its resources well. Take up its plans and live to fulfill them.

Jesus, you know the Father's estate better than anyone; teach me its character, its assets, and its plans. Let me see its gifts with eyes of faith and use them with supernatural wisdom, power, and love. Amen.

A True Image

"The whole city is in an uproar because of these Jews!"
they shouted to the city officials. "They are teaching customs
that are illegal for us Romans to practice." (Acts 16:20-21)

AN INTERESTING SUBTHEME throughout the book of Acts is misperceptions non-believers had about Christians—that Christians believed Jesus would destroy the Temple (Acts 6:14), or that they were rebelling against Caesar (Acts 17:7), or that one of their most prominent leaders was taking Greeks into the inner courts of the Temple to defile it (Acts 21:28). Christians were said elsewhere to have orgies and partake in cannibalism (misunderstandings about the Lord's Supper) and to be disruptive to the public peace. Of course, negative perceptions are not limited to New Testament times; they have continued throughout history and are widespread today. Sometimes Christians do things to earn negative reputations, but sometimes those reputations are wild distortions. Our image has passed through all sorts of unfriendly hands and come out twisted.

One of your jobs in this life is to enhance the reputation of Christians wherever you go. Whether your strengths are intellectual, relational, character-related, artistic, financial, physical, or some combination of these assets, you have an opportunity and even a responsibility to use them well and defy stereotypes. If you think you've already blown your reputation through past mistakes, you're actually in a great position to demonstrate humility and the power of redemption and restoration now. Whatever your situation, the people you encounter need to see some semblance of Jesus clothed in flesh and blood. You have an opportunity to show them that with the gifts, faith, and attitudes he has given you.

Don't strive and strain to force the issue, and don't feel responsible for other people's impressions of Christians. Some people will choose to have a bias against people of faith, regardless of what you do. But for those who have been fed a false impression—or even a true but negative one—you can make a difference. Live with wisdom, power, and love, with lots of grace and understanding added in, and make it clear that the image that is often presented to the world does not look like the image of God in you.

Jesus, you are the exact image of God, and I want to be the exact image of you—as much as my personality and gifts can reflect you. Let your reputation be enhanced in me. Amen.

The Way of Sheep

I was hungry, and you fed me. I was thirsty, and you gave me a drink. I was a stranger, and you invited me into your home. I was naked, and you gave me clothing. I was sick, and you cared for me. I was in prison, and you visited me. (Matthew 25:35-36)

THE PARABLE OF THE SHEEP and the goats at the Last Judgment is a powerful picture. It's also a controversial one. For centuries, interpreters have gotten hung up in its details. Is Jesus referring to everyone who is poor, oppressed, and forgotten, regardless of their beliefs? When he mentions the least of "my brothers and sisters," is he referring to the neglected in general or the neglected among the Jews (his kinsmen)—and therefore making a statement about our level of concern for the chosen nation? Is Jesus actually supporting a doctrine of salvation by works—it is clear, for example, that the only difference between the sheep and the goats is not in beliefs but in actions—or implying that real faith always results in works? All of these are legitimate questions, yet sometimes lost in the midst of them is a much bigger picture: the values of God.

God's compassion is uniquely directed toward people who are hurting, even when their wounds are self-inflicted. He is clear throughout Scripture that he is drawn to the brokenhearted, the poor, and the oppressed. He does not categorize his compassion into false divisions between evangelism and social action or between government and individual policies. If we really lived like him, we would not fit neatly into any particular denomination or political party. We would simply care for people who are hurting. A lot.

Like Jesus, avoid political wrangling and philosophical nitpicking. Put hands and feet to your love and actually do something. Contributing to mercy ministries is one way to be salt and light in this world; getting involved at a face-to-face level is even better. If part of your mission in life is to embody God's values, take your cues from Jesus' strong words about compassion and live like sheep.

Jesus, may I never get caught up in diversions and distractions that undermine the truth of your words. You call us all to meet real physical and emotional needs. Show me how. Give me opportunities. Soften my heart with compassion like yours. Amen.

Jesus in Other Clothes

*I tell you the truth, when you did it to one of the least of these my
brothers and sisters, you were doing it to me! (Matthew 25:40)*

THERE HAVE BEEN TIMES IN Christian history, particularly when people who claimed the name of Christ were in powerful or dominant positions, that Christian institutions have oppressed the marginalized and forgotten rather than met their needs. "Christian" governments have persecuted alleged heretics, unevangelized populations, and even innocent bystanders who were perceived as potential threats or aberrations. According to Jesus' parable of the sheep and the goats in Matthew 25, these instigators of such violence and injustice will meet him in the eternal realm and be stunned to find out that he was a victim of their persecutions. In any place and in any age, Jesus is somehow connected with "the least of these"—even if "the least of these" were deemed unworthy or unimportant by the church.

Jesus identifies with the hurting, the suffering, the oppressed, and the neglected even when those people are at fault for their own troubles. An observant eye will notice that he doesn't say, "I was *unjustly* in prison," only "I was in prison" (verse 36). People seeking to avoid the responsibility of caring will find all sorts of reasons not to identify Jesus with the down-and-out. They may come up with plenty of excuses not to get their hands dirty with people in crisis and pain, assuming that Jesus only identifies with the godly and pure-hearted, but his words give us no such wiggle room. He has entered into the pain of this world, looked at the people who are filled with his Spirit, and essentially said, "What are you going to do about it?"

That's a good question to wrestle with frequently. What are you going to do about the people who are hurting? How are you going to help them? If you were convinced Jesus was behind their eyes, how would you respond? This is not just theology; Jesus is asking. Blessed are those who answer with compassion.

*Jesus, forgive me for neglecting the very people you have identified with. I don't always
know how to respond; their needs are bigger than my ability to supply and more
complicated than a lack of funds. Fill me with your compassion and your resources—
spiritual, emotional, financial, and more—to help. Amen.*

Dividing Lines

Don't imagine that I came to bring peace to the earth!
I came not to bring peace, but a sword. (Matthew 10:34)

WE ARE PEOPLE OF PEACE. That's our calling. Salt and light offer the *shalom* of God's Kingdom in many ways—spiritual, material, emotional, relational, physical, and so much more. We bless, influence for change, and represent the goodness of a very good God. But if we're honest with ourselves and true to the words of Jesus, we know our message does not always bring peace. Jesus was a huge point of contention during his earthly ministry and has been ever since. Families, cities, and nations have split over his identity. Souls have been compelled to come down on one side or the other. And the impact of the gospel rarely remains behind the scenes. The truth makes waves.

Our goal is to have a thoroughly positive influence on the world around us, but we have to be aware that sometimes our influence will be divisive. Though some Christians have a contentious nature and seem drawn to divisive words and actions, that isn't our calling. But the nature of the message of redemption and restoration through a crucified and risen Savior does divide loyalties and sometimes causes visceral reactions in people who have been wounded by the church, disappointed by God, or even just stuck in self-centered ways. The reasons vary; the nature of the message does not. And sometimes it will create a stir.

Be prepared for that, and be sensitive to the hearts of people who react negatively from their own spiritual wounds. Always lead with love, not with hard-edged truth. But in the context of love, don't let your salt lose its flavor or your light lose its brightness. God accomplished a lot among all the negative reactions in the New Testament, and he still does. Jesus continues to be a dividing line, and souls still have to choose whether to believe him or not. Sometimes they will face that choice by hearing and observing you as you live in Jesus' image. Let those moments come—and offer peace in the midst of them to all who will receive it.

Jesus, you were a question mark in the flesh, always provoking a decision, and my union with you makes me one too. Give me the wisdom to avoid unnecessary conflicts and embrace true ones. Grant me peace even when I become a dividing line. Amen.

Uncivil Discourse

*I tell you this, you must give an account on judgment
day for every idle word you speak. (Matthew 12:36)*

PERHAPS YOU'VE NOTICED A TREND. The advent of Internet culture and the public platforms it has opened up have created unprecedented levels of civil discourse that is anything but civil. Whether from the cover of anonymity or an ability to blend in with the multitude of other voices, people have gotten comfortable with filling their comments with venom and vitriol—to the point that discussions are hardly discussions anymore. They become just another contribution to the noise. And often the noise has a vicious tone.

Christians are fully capable of participating in this dialogue and taking on its destructive character too. Some go so far as to call people who disagree with them idiots and morons. Words that would never come out of the mouths of Jesus or the apostles flow freely from the fingertips of online debaters, and the same attitudes carry over much too easily into face-to-face conversations too. But the tone is only part of the problem. At a deeper level, people seem to be losing the ability to enter into another person's worldview and see an issue from his or her point of view. We argue past each other, with words that fit our own worldview but hardly make any sense in another. Hammering away with biblical logic has little effect on someone who doesn't believe the Bible. What would matter much more is being able to see through his or her eyes and then applying genuinely helpful biblical principles to very real concerns. We forget that the point is not to convince people of our opinions; it's to open up hearts to the influence of God's Spirit. Contentious debating and arguing rarely, if ever, accomplish that goal.

Learn to empathize with others and see from their perspective before spouting your opinions. Let your words be edifying, encouraging, and seasoned with salt (Ephesians 4:29; Colossians 4:6, NIV). If the tongue has the power to set the course of a life (James 3:3-6), use yours to direct your life and the lives of others into blessing and peace.

Lord, forgive me for idle words. Use my tongue to express your thoughts, your love, and your praise. May I learn never to attack opinions at the expense of loving hearts. Amen.

Putting a Face on God

You must be holy in everything you do,
just as God who chose you is holy. (1 Peter 1:15)

TERRORISM IN RECENT DECADES has put a disturbing face on Islam. The vast majority of Muslims would say that terrorist acts have nothing to do with their religion, and we can understand the objection. We use a similar logic when we say the Crusades, the Inquisition, and the KKK's burning of crosses have nothing to do with real Christianity. You can't define a religion by everyone who claims it. Nevertheless, outsiders do. We all tend to judge a system of beliefs by its most visible representatives, even when those representatives are visible for all the wrong reasons. Whether they intend to or not, they put a face on their God.

Think about that. People who do violence are making a statement about the nature of their God and driving people away from him. So are people who go around expressing judgment on everyone else's shortcomings and blind spots, who talk about how much they love God's Word though they haven't ever found time to read the whole thing, who say they love others without actually being interested in them, and so on. The same dynamic applies, although to different extremes. Whether rightly or wrongly, people will judge your faith by your actions and attitudes. For better or for worse, you put a face on the God you claim.

Be careful about how you reflect God's nature. You are called to be like him, not to claim his name and then act in a different spirit. If people out there are judging Christianity by your representation of Jesus, then represent him well. We were created in his image for just that purpose in the first place, and it's the reason Jesus came as the exact image of God and expression of his nature (Hebrews 1:3). Through him, we are to be transformed back into the image we were first given so we can represent him accurately. Whatever face you put on him, let it reveal the truth of who he is.

Father, forgive me for being a fallen, distorted representation of who you are. Restore me to your true image, and let me reflect you well. May I wear your true face always. Amen.

Until the Day Dawns

We have even greater confidence in the message proclaimed by the
prophets. You must pay close attention to what they wrote, for their
words are like a lamp shining in a dark place—until the Day dawns,
and Christ the Morning Star shines in your hearts. (2 Peter 1:19)

FOR ALL ITS BENEFITS, the Reformation marked the beginnings of a turn inward, a move toward a very personalized faith in which each individual would take responsibility for his or her own spiritual growth. That took a long time—quite a few Reformation-era churches and communities of faith saw religion as a corporate affair and imposed church discipline on individuals for the sake of the group—but today we consider such approaches nosy or intrusive. Faith has become a private matter, a personal concern, nobody's business but our own. We want to be treated like spiritual grown-ups who can make decisions for ourselves.

In making our decisions, however, it's important to remember that other people have a stake in our spiritual growth. It isn't just a private matter, regardless of how personal it seems. As our faith grows, Christ is being formed in our hearts—the Morning Star is arising, the Day is dawning, and the reality of the Spirit is making himself manifest through us. We experience enormous personal benefits in that process, but it's much bigger than ourselves. The world *needs* this dawning of the new day. The Morning Star does not arise in us in order to be kept secret. As expressed in Isaiah—one of the prophets we are urged to pay close attention to in the first half of today's verse—"the glory of the LORD rises to shine on you" (Isaiah 60:1). The Jesus in us is a corporate matter. He arises for the sake of the world.

We can be glad that the days of the spiritual community controlling its members are not as common as they once were. But the days of its members offering their spiritual growth and gifts to the community continue. Jesus works in us for our sake, but not ours alone. His light is rising in order to shine. His glory is to be made visible. Your growth in him—and his in you—is a blessing to the world.

Lord, it's hard to imagine the words of prophets being fulfilled in your people today—
and specifically in me. Be fully formed in me for the glory of your name. Let the Day
dawn for me, in me, and through me. Amen.

Uncomfortable Favor

When the queen of Sheba heard of Solomon's fame,
which brought honor to the name of the LORD,
she came to test him with hard questions. (1 Kings 10:1)

"THEY WILL HONOR THE LORD your God . . . for he has filled you with splendor" (Isaiah 60:9). These words were prophesied to the captive people of Judah as a promise of future glory, but one reason they were so powerful was that they evoked images of past glory. The era of David and Solomon was Israel's golden age, the time when the kingdom's borders had expanded farther than ever before, and when God had established peace on every side (1 Kings 5:4). Many kingdoms had heard of Solomon's fame, including the queen of Sheba, an Arab kingdom. They not only marveled at Solomon's glory; they recognized that the favor given to him was a reflection of his God. People honored Israel's God because of what they saw in his people. They recognized where success and prosperity had come from.

Solomon's wisdom, wealth, power, and accomplishments were evidence of favor, material symbols of much richer blessings that adorned all of God's people in a time of fruitfulness. A time would soon come when this glory was marred by division and distorted worship, but for the moment, the grandeur of Israel was a shining testimony of the glory of God. His people were in the very desirable position of reflecting God's goodness simply by experiencing it.

Those seasons do come, even today, and even though we can be very uncomfortable with them. (Perhaps you've noticed how so many of us apologize for any hint of the "above and beyond" in our lives.) In your mission to honor God and reflect his glory, you will sometimes take center stage. There's nothing wrong with that; you don't need to cover every success with the awkward disclaimer that it's because of him, not you. Your devotion to him will come through, and many people will make the connection that you are living in a season of his visible, tangible favor. If you haven't been reluctant to glorify him in times of lack, don't be afraid to ask him for times of abundance too. You have the privilege of honoring him in every season—no matter how good.

Lord, so much of my experience has trained me to honor you in hard times and feel a little guilty about the good times. Let me grow comfortable in every form of your favor. May I honor you with complete contentment in every situation and reflect your goodness always. Amen.

Beyond Competence

*Do you see any truly competent workers? They will serve kings
rather than working for ordinary people. (Proverbs 22:29)*

WE ARE CALLED TO STAND OUT. Many of us are pretty uncomfortable with the spot-light, and some have experienced the pain of standing out for the wrong reasons. But we are given the light of God for the purpose of shining, and that means we will be noticeable. It does not mean everyone is called to be a vocal evangelist or preacher. But when we apply ourselves diligently to the work God has given us, whether the church looks at it as sacred or secular, he will put us in positions of influence. We will stand out because we have something worthwhile to offer.

We've seen that principle at work often in Scripture, whether in the example of Joseph before the king of Egypt, Daniel and his friends before the king of Babylon, or the call all believers have been given to serve their earthly masters and bosses as though they were serving the Lord. We have seen that mediocrity is not a testimony to the nature of our God, but excellence is. We have every reason to become thoroughly accomplished in the gifts and talents we have been given, and to strive for the kind of knowledge that contributes to the world while also pointing to God. We are designed not only to represent his wisdom, power, and love, but to represent them as fully and completely as we can. And given the promise of his Spirit, that's a lot.

Make it your aim as a believer to lead the way in whatever field you work in. Whether that aim results in a leadership position or not—and it certainly doesn't have to—you can become known for innovation, creativity, and high standards. The wisdom of Proverbs suggests that when you do so, you will eventually enter into places of influence. There, and every step along the way, you serve as a testimony to the quality of God's ways. Your gifts open doors—to positions, possibly, but even more importantly, to hearts.

Lord, I can only imagine that Jesus had excellent carpentry skills and a commendable work ethic. May I follow in his footsteps even in these qualities. May my works testify of your nature, open doors of influence, and glorify your name. Amen.

Satisfied

You open your hand and satisfy the desires of every living thing.
(Psalm 145:16, NIV)

MONKS AND NUNS WHO SOUGHT an ascetic lifestyle in the late Middle Ages often went to extraordinary lengths to quench their impulses. The purpose was not just self-deprivation. Their goal was to subdue every physical sense in order to cultivate their spiritual senses. Most aimed for simplicity and austerity, but some went far beyond these ideals. They made their food as bland as possible and ate as little as they could; endured the extremes of cold and heat without trying to modify their conditions; avoided sleep in order to devote themselves to prayer; and inflicted penalties on themselves by punishing their bodies. This hardly accomplished the goal—pain tends to heighten senses, not subdue them—but it did reflect a genuine desire. The human heart is desperate to get beyond earthly limitations and experience something of the blessings of heaven.

The good news is that we can have a taste of heaven on earth without denying the senses God has given us. Self-discipline is never a bad thing, but it is not capable of leading us into divine experiences. Jesus is, however, and his Spirit offers us encounters with the Father that can transform us from within. The fact that Jesus' first recorded miracle was at a wedding, where there was dancing and drink and a joyful celebration, should tell us something about his purposes for us. He wants us to be satisfied with life—not superficially happy, not self-indulgent in satiating our senses, but to have fullness of joy. That is possible whether circumstances line up with our desires or not. But he often satisfies our desires just to show us how good he can be.

The heart that is always longing for something else does not reflect on our Father well. God is honored when we are satisfied in him—when we recognize what he gives, thank him for it, and enjoy it to the full. We become a testimony to his goodness when we let ourselves experience it. Enjoy whatever abundance he gives, and live with gratitude. Let the world see a good Father in you.

Lord, forgive me for what my discontentment implies—that you don't provide enough, aren't good enough, or somehow withhold your blessings from me. Delight my heart with good things, and remind me to celebrate them. May I overflow with fullness of joy. Amen.

Words That Bless

Blessing and cursing come pouring out of the same mouth. Surely,
my brothers and sisters, this is not right! (James 3:10)

THE TONGUE IS A POWERFUL THING. James spoke of it mostly in negative terms, but he mentioned its positives too—that it can bless others and praise God. In fact, as we have seen, God used words to create the world (Genesis 1), and if our Father can speak new things into being from nothing (Romans 4:17) and has made us in his image, there's at least some sense in which we can do the same. Some people suggest that we can create our own reality with our thoughts and words, which gives us quite a bit of sovereignty over our lives that should rightfully belong to God. But even if they exaggerate this point, there is a kernel of truth in it. Our words are expressions of our faith—what we really believe deep down in our hearts—and our faith shapes our lives (Matthew 9:29).

That means we need to be really careful about what we say. More importantly, we need to be careful about what we believe, which eventually comes out in what we say. What if, for example, our words and attitudes have created the very world we criticize? What if, in our constant insistence that "things are getting worse and worse," God has honored our faith—that negative, hopeless faith—and said, "Okay, here's what you envisioned"? What if our words, instead of being salt and light, have had the effect of poison and darkness? Or to put it more simply, what if our words are opposed to the hope of the gospel and the joy of the Kingdom?

Many times, they are. We have all been guilty of such things. Still, God gives us a remarkable opportunity to bless others without discrimination—to pronounce blessings on our world, peace to every heart and mind, fullness of joy to every soul that longs for it. He never tells us to wait until people deserve it or to measure it out carefully. He gives abundant grace—and mouths to speak it far and wide.

Lord, may I be liberal with your grace, forgiveness, blessing, and favor. You gave such things freely to me; may I give them freely to others. Fill my mouth with the peace, love, and joy of your Kingdom. Amen.

See the Treasure

*The Kingdom of Heaven is like a treasure that a man discovered
hidden in a field. (Matthew 13:44)*

THE KINGDOM OF HEAVEN IS like a treasure. When God conceived it, he knew it was worth the sacrifice of his Son. When you see it, you realize it's worth everything you have. So what happens when you see it growing within you? Is it a casual matter, or does it command all of your attention? Or to take it a step further, what happens when you see it—or even its potential—in the lives of people around you? Does it capture your heart?

Far more often, we look at other people and see their flaws. We admire some, to be sure, but we also realize that every human being has the ability to disappoint us. When they do, we begin to define them differently—by their mistakes or by our own misperceptions. We tend to focus on the earthly vessels of human nature. We miss the treasures the vessels hold.

God doesn't see us that way. He is well aware of our earthen nature, but he also tells us we have an unimaginable treasure inside (2 Corinthians 4:7). We are carriers of his Kingdom, hosts of his presence, incarnations of the divine nature he has given us (2 Peter 1:4). He sees us according to our future, not according to our past, always calling us into our potential rather than focusing on the ways we've fallen short. He knows our destiny in Christ, and it's a magnificent image.

Learn to align your vision with God's—to see priceless treasure not only in yourself but also in others. It will change your relationships. You will cease measuring people by their shortcomings and be amazed instead at the image of Christ being formed in them. You will see them not for their earthen humanity but by the divine nature promised to them. They may look like products of their past, but they aren't. Neither are you. In Christ, by faith, we are all vessels of glory. Let your eyes of faith see the hidden treasure—the Kingdom buried in human hearts—and celebrate it like God does.

Lord, give me a vision of the fullness of Jesus in every person, whether they claim him yet or not. Show me the glory of our future. Then move me to treat everyone I meet according to that vision. Amen.

Call Out the Treasure

Encourage each other and build each other up,
just as you are already doing. (1 Thessalonians 5:11)

IF WE ASK, God will give us eyes to see the treasure he has put within other people—the samples of his Kingdom character and gifts that have either already been given or are potential gifts in their future. When we learn to see people according to their future, whether it's a certainty or only a possibility, we treat them differently. But seeing is not the end of our responsibility. Something happens when we take a step beyond observation and actually call out the Kingdom glory in another person. When we put words to what we've seen, we build each other up and accelerate the transformation into our true, God-given selves.

Scripture urges us to do that, whether through some prophetic insight (1 Corinthians 14:3) or the natural encouragement that comes when people care about each other (1 Thessalonians 5:11; Hebrews 10:24-25). We may still notice others' sins—both fallen and redeemed human nature can be quite observant—but we are never told to focus on them. No, we are told to comfort one another, to forgive and restore where necessary, and to build each other up whenever we can. We are to notice the glory within our fellow earthen vessels and be vocal about reminding them that it's there. And they will need the reminder; people can be extremely forgetful about the blessings of redemption.

Many people know Christians as people who tear each other down. We need to develop the opposite reputation by reconstructing our true calling. Every believer is a living stone in the temple of God, the place where his glory dwells. You may not see that in yourself, but that's exactly why you need fellow believers to recognize the treasure and call it forth, and why they need you to do the same. The more we focus on the treasures in each other, the more they grow. The more we encourage, the stronger both the encouragers and the ones encouraged become. And the stronger we become, the more the body of Christ begins to look like the Kingdom of God and the community of love it was designed to be.

Lord, forgive me for focusing on the shortcomings of others and for neglecting the ministry of encouragement. Give me timely words that build others up and strengthen both them and me. Amen.

Hearts on Fire

We are God's masterpiece. He has created us anew in Christ
Jesus, so we can do the good things he planned for us long ago.
(Ephesians 2:10)

"BE WHO GOD MEANT YOU to be and you will set the world on fire." Those words, in one variation or another, are said to come from Catherine of Siena, a fourteenth-century visionary known for challenging a complacent and conflicted church. The thought is comforting to us because it does not suggest that we must behave like someone else, serve someone else's agenda, or adopt someone else's talents and gifts in order to do what we were called to do. It is challenging to us because it suggests that we were designed for the kind of influence we may not have yet. It strikes a balance between who we are now and who we were designed to be.

You will live much of your life in that tension. You are created for no other reason than to be who you were originally intended to be. The true you, the person deep inside who has not been distorted by your own sins or the sins of others, has been redeemed and is now being restored. While many people adopt false identities to cope with their fallenness, you can rest in your Father's purposes. You are not called to any image other than that of Christ as he is being formed in you. Neither are you to embrace your fallenness by making your flaws and mistakes part of your identity, as so many have done. Scripture never urges us to accept the fact that we were born this way; it compels us to grow into a new identity we were reborn to live. We are in search of our true selves, which can only be found in Christ, as he is leading us, today and every day.

Do that, and you will set the world—or at least your corner of it—on fire. The world is in great need of people who know who they truly are and live that identity to the full. Be one of them today.

Lord, set my heart—my true self—on fire with the power of your truth and love, and may that flame spread far beyond me. In every way, let me be all you meant for me to be. Amen.

Catalysts for Grace

Receive the Holy Spirit. If you forgive anyone's sins, they are forgiven.
If you do not forgive them, they are not forgiven. (John 20:22-23)

JUDGES AND INQUISITORS throughout the ages have often gotten a peculiar sense of pleasure in their power to proclaim guilt or innocence, particularly in their capacity to condemn. Perhaps that should not surprise us; in a world full of wrongs, there ought to be something satisfying in correcting them. Of course, the effort to rid the world of evil can easily lead to its own kind of evil—literal or figurative witch hunts that turn a misguided quest for justice into a pattern of injustice. The power to condemn is awfully dangerous in the hands of people who seem to enjoy it.

As people called to be priests (1 Peter 2:9; Revelation 1:6), we are given a similar power. Being unmerciful shouldn't appeal to anyone with a compassionate heart, but what really ought to excite us is the first half of Jesus' statement. As soon as he breathed the Holy Spirit into his disciples, he told them they had the privilege of declaring the forgiveness of sins. He phrased it in a way that suggests a more active role than merely declaring what the Father has already done. He implied that their forgiveness actually meant something in heavenly realms, that the decision to forgive or not to forgive lies to some degree in human hands in partnership with the Spirit they had just received. As much as we might want to defer to God alone for matters of grace and mercy, he includes us in the process. We are ministers of his pardon.

Enjoy that gift and use it liberally. With a heart of compassion and eyes of faith, learn to see the weight of guilt and shame pressing down on every human heart, even those that wear it in offensive ways. Pray forgiveness upon those who are ready to receive it and even those who aren't. See your compassion and your words as catalysts for God's work in their lives. Use your priestly privileges to connect unforgiven offenders with the mercy of their God.

Jesus, surely you would not trust your followers to implement divine forgiveness unless you trusted the work of your Spirit in them even more. Fill me with spiritual wisdom and mercy that matches yours. Turn my attitudes and my mouth into expressions of your boundless grace. Amen.

Priestly Prayers

I pray that your hearts will be flooded with light so that you
can understand the confident hope he has given to those he
called—his holy people who are his rich and glorious inheritance.
(Ephesians 1:18)

IN MOST RELIGIOUS CULTURES, certain people are designated to carry out priestly functions, whether they are called priests or not. They are mediators between the human and divine realms, representing humanity to God and God to humanity, and making appeals for harmony between the two. Old Testament priests performed that role in Temple worship and sacrifices; New Testament priests—all believers—have been given similar roles in more subtle forms, appealing only to the sacrifice of Christ and, through him, being ministers of reconciliation between God and his world (2 Corinthians 5:18-21). We stand between heaven and earth with a message of peace and restoration.

One of our greatest privileges as priests is the power of prayer. Sometimes we pray for the needs of this world without clear knowledge of which requests fit God's will, but we can be certain that he longs to show his compassion and grace. And if we want specific examples of what those kinds of prayer look like, we have several: the apostolic prayers of the New Testament. They are scattered throughout—Paul recorded his prayers in some of his letters (for examples, see Ephesians 1:16-20; 3:14-21; Philippians 1:9-11; Colossians 1:9-12)—and they are there for us to use. When we pray Spirit-inspired, apostolic prayers for the people around us, we can be certain we are asking according to God's will. And we can be certain he will answer them.

For starters, try the prayer in Ephesians 1:16-20. Substitute the pronouns with specific names, including your own, if you'd like. Envision God filling his people with the radiance of his glory, the hope of his calling, and the riches of his inheritance. See him empowering them to believe. Pray intensely and repeatedly, day after day, and see what he does. Search Scripture for other prayers and use them liberally. The Kingdom comes through the prayers of God's people in the name of his Son. Take advantage of the opportunity daily.

Father, you have lavished your love on your people, and there is more to give. May my prayers open the floodgates of your love and all its blessings on the people around me. Fill my mouth with apostolic, priestly words of faith that change lives. Amen.

Your Certain Calling

You can ask for anything in my name, and I will do it, so
that the Son can bring glory to the Father. (John 14:13)

MAYBE YOU'VE ALREADY discovered God's will for your life and are living it out. Or perhaps you're still searching for it, wondering where he might be leading you. Wherever you are on that journey, you can be sure that your calling includes interceding for this world. In your position as a priest standing between heaven and earth to present the needs of the world to God and the will of God to the world, you have been urged repeatedly by Jesus and his Word to pray. It's one of the few callings you can be certain of even when you don't know what else to do.

Jesus repeated his promises about prayer often in the long discourse of John 13–16 (see 14:13-14; 15:7, 16-17; 16:23-24). In some statements, the purpose is for the Son to glorify the Father. In others, it's so the disciples can be fruitful. These purposes flow together, giving us a picture of the Father, the Son, and the Son's followers partnering together to accomplish God's plans in this world. We've seen how the apostolic prayers describe those plans, and they are far reaching—from the redeemed and restored spirits of individual human beings to the big-picture fulfillment of all of God's purposes coming together in Christ. From the repetition of Jesus' promises in these chapters—not to mention the many promises about prayer elsewhere in Scripture—we get a clear picture of how God accomplishes his will. It's through the prayers of his people. The more we pray, the more he accomplishes through us.

That's worth getting up for every morning. The God of the universe invites us into his throne room to strategize his purposes, notice the places where they most need to be accomplished, and call them forth by faith through prayer. We may not always conceive our prayers perfectly, but even when we don't, he responds to the heart behind them. Accept that invitation, and step into the opportunity fully. Our prayers further his purposes and implement his will in the world around us.

Holy Spirit, fuel my prayers, and let my prayers fuel your work in this world. Give me glimpses of their power. Motivate me. May I see your glory and my fruitfulness in your answers. Amen.

Impartial Intercession

*Pray this way for kings and all who are in authority so that we
can live peaceful and quiet lives marked by godliness and dignity.*
(1 Timothy 2:2)

ONE OF THE MOST REFRESHING benefits of a liberal democracy is the freedom of
its citizens to criticize their leaders. Gone are the days when a negative comment
resulted in a fine, imprisonment, or even death. The majority in a democracy rules,
and, at least in theory, the leaders serve. But while that freedom to criticize has its
place in holding leaders accountable, it can also undermine an important spiritual
principle: that Christians are to pray for their government, even when they don't like
the people at the head of it.

Paul's instructions to Timothy were written long before modern liberal democracies, of course. Greece and Rome had some degree of democratic representation at
times, but the New Testament was written in an age of imperial rule. Emperors and
local rulers had quite a bit of autonomy. Some were good, some were bad, and some
were downright evil. Still, we are told to pray for them—to intercede on their behalf,
to seek their welfare, to even give thanks for them (verse 1). In praying for the welfare
of our leaders, we are also praying for the welfare of the church. When society goes
well, the benefits tend to apply to almost everyone. When it goes badly at the top,
the ill effects are passed down. Our prayers are critical in seeking God's blessing in
our communities, our cities, and our nations.

Far too many Christians spend more time complaining about the ways of the
world than asking God to intervene in them. This may be a democratic response, but
it is not at all a priestly one. You do not want to be the kind of salt that's unneces-
sarily rubbed in wounds or the light that needlessly blinds. Your mission is to bless
in truth but also in love. Use your prayers generously, applying them even to leaders
you didn't vote for. Seek God's goodness for all—the church, secular society, and the
people in positions to strengthen both.

*Lord, give me the courage to express my opinion and the humility to bless those who
disagree with it. Give our leaders wisdom to do good things, even when they don't know
you. Strengthen the church by strengthening the society we live in. Amen.*

Prayers of Faith

You can pray for anything, and if you have faith, you will receive it.
(Matthew 21:22)

J. O. FRASER, a British missionary to the Lisu people of Southeast Asia in the early 1900s, developed an interesting illustration for prayers of faith. At the time, the Canadian government was offering land incentives for British citizens to move to Canada. The western territories were wide open, and the government wanted people to cultivate it. Immigrants could claim up to 160 acres of land, but only if they would commit to care for it, accept the government's conditions, and live on it productively. It was an open invitation to spread out and steward resources for the benefit of the realm.

Fraser believed Christians have been given the same opportunity in the Kingdom of Heaven. That's what Jesus' prayer promises are about. There is plenty of territory waiting to be occupied by faith and cultivated by responsible stewards. But there are conditions. We must ask specifically, commit to tend the land faithfully, get up and move into the promise, and then cultivate what we've been given. God has chosen to expand his Kingdom through the prayers and works of those who represent him faithfully. By understanding the dynamics of prayer and acting on them, we receive the answers that were promised.

A lot of "territory" in this world remains outside of God's Kingdom, and we are given extravagant promises for expanding into it. Some Christians see the situation and retreat into their own communities to defend their faith, but the compassionate heart of a priest recognizes a deeper opportunity and steps into it. The prayer of faith is the catalyst that lays claim to unclaimed land and embraces the burden of stewarding it well.

Learn to pray with the kind of definition and commitment a land claimant has for his or her new property. Understand that God's gifts are free but still must be handled with care and faithfulness. Develop a vision for the territory of your calling, and then ask God for it in faith and take decisive, definite steps to enter in.

Jesus, fill me with the kind of faith that receives your promises decisively and completely. Give me spiritual territory to steward and cultivate. Teach me to ask according to your will, and grow your Kingdom through the faith and prayers of your people. Amen.

The News Is Good

How will anyone go and tell them without being sent?
That is why the Scriptures say, "How beautiful are the feet
of messengers who bring good news!" (Romans 10:15)

PAUL WAS PASSIONATE ABOUT the message of salvation, and he recognized its implications for both Jews and Gentiles. He shared that salvation came through faith in Christ but realized that the vast majority of people outside of Jewish circles had never heard of Jesus. So he quoted a passage from Isaiah about messengers who bring the good news of God's deliverance—how he defends his people and accomplishes salvation for them. In Isaiah, the prophecy leads to a remarkable description of a suffering servant who would come in the future. In Romans, Paul points to the same suffering servant whose work was now done.

It's a beautiful and often-quoted passage about the urgency of the gospel and the importance of faith in Christ, and it serves those purposes well. But sometimes lost in the discussion is the nature of the news itself. The Good News doesn't place a higher demand on us than the law did, though its standards are much higher. It doesn't promise a life of hardship and discipline, though things won't always be easy, and discipline is rarely a bad thing. It doesn't promise us impossibilities that it can't deliver. And it was never, ever designed to frustrate us.

That's good to know, because a lot of Christians are frustrated by the demands of righteousness, their fear that the gospel's promises might be false, the drudgery of trying to be like Jesus without the power to actually be like him, and the burdens they were never meant to bear. And a lot of non-Christians see the frustration, along with the Christians who have not lived up to what they claim, and assume the Good News isn't all that good.

But it is. It is full of freedom and hope. In your own life and in conversations with others, remember that the gospel, which literally means "good news," is actually good news. Refuse to be burdened by false versions, and live with peace and joy. That's a message today's world needs to hear.

Lord, please never cease to remind me that if the gospel I'm living isn't setting me free, it isn't the gospel. Fill me with life, hope, peace, joy, and love, and draw many into the Good News of salvation through your people. Amen.

Only Jesus

I decided that while I was with you I would forget everything except
Jesus Christ, the one who was crucified. (1 Corinthians 2:2)

PAUL'S VISIT TO CORINTH came right after his sermon at the Areopagus in Athens, where he touched on Greek religion and philosophy to introduce his message of hope (Acts 17:22-31). Though he had preached about Jesus earlier in Athens (Acts 17:16-18), he didn't mention Jesus' name in this sermon. When Paul mentioned the resurrection of the dead, those listening laughed at him and cut him short, and ultimately Paul left Athens with few converts. He arrived in Corinth with a different approach: to focus entirely on Christ crucified.

Nothing in Paul's message in Athens was misguided, and God used it to win some hearts to the truth. But in Corinth, Paul spurned lofty words and came back to the simplicity of the gospel: that the crucifixion of Jesus was a necessary sacrifice for our redemption and our cleansing from sin. He felt no need to impress his listeners (1 Corinthians 2:1); he embraced weakness and humility (verse 3); and he relied only on the Holy Spirit to change minds and hearts. He recognized that eloquence, regardless of how helpful it might be at times, is not the key to the gospel. Supernatural intervention is.

That's important for us to remember too. Presenting the gospel with eloquent words, clear evidence, logical reasoning, winsome attitudes, and everything else we put into it can be helpful and effective, but the real power of the message comes from God and centers on the simplicity of the death and resurrection of Jesus. In a culture that emphasizes what-if scenarios, to-each-his-own relativity, and sorting out intricate explanations and ramifications, all of which can be important at times, the message of a Savior who died for sins and was raised to life is still powerful. Always come back to that—in your own devotional life and in your spiritual conversations with others. Fill your life with humility, prayer, and dependence on God, and give him room to work. Ultimately, your message is not dependent on you. Its fruitfulness is fully in his hands.

Lord, you know how to inspire powerful rhetoric, brilliant reasoning, and effective
conversations, yet you have put the power of the gospel in its simplicity. Draw many
to the message of Jesus—crucified, risen, and alive in every believer today. Amen.

Genuine Devotion

Pure and genuine religion in the sight of God the Father means caring for orphans and widows in their distress and refusing to let the world corrupt you. (James 1:27)

IN THE 1200S, a spiritual movement began in the Low Countries of northern Europe. Certain women called Beguines chose a lifestyle of devotion in which they lived together, wore humble clothing, worked to support themselves, and sought to imitate Jesus in their care for the poor and simple lifestyle. They were somewhat like nuns but not cloistered away in separation from the world, not permanently bound by any vows, and not under any official authority or structure. They remained integrated into society while maintaining a sense of distinction from it.

That's a hard balance to maintain, but it's one every Christian must try to sort out. We are called to live distinctive lives but also to remain in the world as influencers of it. The Beguines managed to mark themselves for Christ and live with devotion while continuing in their normal patterns of work and community relationships. Their devotion affected the way they earned and spent money, related to others, developed a sense of community and fellowship, and participated in the larger religious life of the town. They let their commitment shape every area of their lives. In other words, they did what Christians are supposed to do.

Christians today may not dress in distinctive ways or be recognizable purely by our work and spending habits (though we seem to have developed our own vocabulary and subculture). But we are nevertheless urged to live distinctly from the world while remaining in the middle of it. We are ministers of healing who must carry the responsibility of meeting needs and solving social ills. We are servants of the common good who love the world but not worldliness, striving to remain unstained by its corruptions. We live as salt and light by demonstrating what we support rather than focusing on what we don't. We must always remember that we are devoted to a Savior who is devoted to saving people in their fallenness, brokenness, and pain.

Jesus, my commitment to you always has implications for how I live. Transform me thoroughly to distinguish me from the world around me — and to love the world around me as you do. Grant me pure and genuine devotion. Amen.

In a Foreign Land

How can we sing the songs of the LORD while in a pagan land?
(Psalm 137:4)

WHAT DO YOU DO WHEN your society makes it impossible to live a biblical lifestyle? Jews who had been taken captive to Babylon and then Persia found it virtually impossible to follow all the commands from the law of Moses. With difficulty, they could keep dietary laws, as Daniel and his friends did, but keeping laws of sacrifice at the Tabernacle or Temple (both of which no longer existed), observing certain elements of feast celebrations, and maintaining a viable priesthood were often beyond their circumstances. The heart of their worship was centered in Jerusalem, and Jerusalem was in ruins. They were far from home geographically, spiritually, and emotionally. They had to learn new ways without compromising their faith.

We experience something similar today, often without realizing how far from home we have been taken. God's instructions are written on our hearts, but our hearts have to live in a world that complicates his instructions. It is extremely difficult to live in a culture of credit without charging or paying interest, both of which are strongly discouraged by biblical teaching. It is quite a challenge to strive for biblical simplicity in a society that practically demands expensive transportation, high-tech communications, and almost constant availability. It often goes beyond our thinking to care for widows and orphans when we have public and private programs that do that. Our culture shifts our mind-set away from biblical purity.

So what do we do? Like the scattered Jews, we adapt to our circumstances while preserving our distinctions wherever we can. We recognize the heart of God's instructions even when the details are culturally far removed from us. We sing songs of the Lord, even in a spiritually distant land. We ask hard questions about absolutes and cultural relativity, and we negotiate between them the best we can.

Our calling as Christians in the midst of non-Christian (or historically Christian) cultures makes us feel like aliens in a foreign land. In fact, Scripture uses the same metaphor. Embrace your foreignness. See yourself as a traveler passing through this world. And fix your heart on eternal truth. The Lord's songs go wherever you take them.

Lord, my discomfort in this world is by design. I'm a citizen of heaven living in a foreign land. Make the most of my involvements here, but keep me anchored in your Kingdom. Amen.

Without Hypocrisy

*You Pharisees are so careful to clean the outside of the cup
and the dish, but inside you are filthy. (Luke 11:39)*

MANY LATE MEDIEVAL CLERGY and high ecclesiastical authorities preached the virtues of renunciation, but they exemplified extravagance in their own lives. Many of them preached morality and celibacy while having common-law wives or concubines on the side. Many preached the virtues of honesty and integrity while manipulating the processes that put them in their positions. They are just one example among many—in all ages—of spiritual hypocrisy.

We have no business condemning them, since hypocrisy is common to our age as well. We preach biblical morality while loosening the standards of what we expect of ourselves and those around us. We condemn greed while many around us take advantage of capitalist values to exploit others for personal gain. We condemn governments for taking on too much responsibility for people's welfare while neglecting to take on such responsibilities for ourselves. Like preachers and teachers of ages past, we violate our own standards, often without noticing the contradiction.

Jesus had harsh words for hypocrites, who taught one message outwardly and lived another one inwardly. And while we each have our inconsistencies—none of us have fully recovered from our fallen nature, after all—we are not as diligent about eliminating them as we ought to be. As a result, much of the world is convinced that Christians are no different from anyone else and have simply learned to clean ourselves up (sometimes) on the outside. They do not always see clear examples of transformed hearts and lives of integrity.

Give them one. Live with a transformed heart, and do whatever you can to live with integrity in every area of life. Be honest about your faults but also about how God is redeeming and restoring you into his image. Admit your inconsistencies, but also aim to eradicate them. Let the world around you see spiritual authenticity, genuine depth, and a life consistent with its love and commitment. God has made you into a new creation; depend on his Spirit and live like one always.

Jesus, you see right through me, and I want you to be pleased with what you see. I'm covered by your forgiveness and declared new; let my experience line up with my new nature. Make me an example the world needs to see. Amen.

Colossians 1:11-14

The Great Transfer

He has enabled you to share in the inheritance that belongs to his
people, who live in the light. For he has rescued us from the kingdom
of darkness and transferred us into the Kingdom of his dear Son.
(Colossians 1:12-13)

ONE OF THE MOST PROMINENT themes in John's Gospel is the contrast between darkness and light. "The light shines in the darkness," he wrote, "and the darkness can never extinguish it" (John 1:5). Jesus' words and works highlighted the interaction between darkness and light. Paul wrote about this theme too, reminding the Colossians that they had been transferred from one kingdom to another, rescued from a world of darkness and transplanted into the Kingdom of light. It's a dramatic picture, and it appeals to all of us who love clear distinctions and black-and-white issues. It reminds us we are not living in the gray.

In our daily experience, however, we encounter a lot of gray. Sometimes it confronts us and confuses us; sometimes we go looking for it on our own. For all of the glorious promises of our transfer into the Kingdom of light, we still choose to dabble in darkness every once in a while. Even when we don't, we find shadows on the edge of truth, borderlines between right and wrong, with no clear answers to be found. Ethicists are adept at pointing out moral dilemmas that leave us without clear choices, and life presents us with many such examples. Over time, we may forget which kingdom we live in, or at least forget the luster of the one we've chosen. The light becomes much less visible.

That's why it can be a healthy exercise from time to time to go back to the beginning—mentally, emotionally, and spiritually—not to revert to any earlier immaturity, but to remember who we were and what we were rescued from. When we rehearse our first love—those times when we were captivated by the gospel of light and transformed by its brilliance—something happens inside. Things become clearer. The light within us shines brighter once again, God reminds us of our priorities, and the gray begins to recede.

Jesus, may I never forget the amazing rescue you accomplished on my behalf or the inheritance you have given me as a citizen of the Kingdom of light. Rekindle the fire within me; remind me of my love; and distance me from the darkness once again. Amen.

Seeing God

He lives in light so brilliant that no human can approach him.
No human eye has ever seen him, nor ever will. (1 Timothy 6:16)

MEDIEVAL CHRISTIANS THOUGHT a lot about the beatific vision: the possibility of seeing God directly, particularly in the highest places of heaven after we die. This vision is a prominent theme in the theology of Thomas Aquinas, the climax of Dante's *Divine Comedy*, and the hope of many believers as their final state of bliss. It taps into the longing every human heart has to encounter the divine presence visibly and completely. It gives us a sense of purpose.

We don't have to wait for the afterlife to begin experiencing God, however. On one hand, Scripture tells us no one can see God (Exodus 33:20; John 1:18; 1 Timothy 6:16; 1 John 4:12). On the other hand, we are told that Moses spoke with God face to face (Exodus 33:11); God appeared to Abraham in human form (Genesis 18:1); Jacob saw his face (Genesis 32:30); Isaiah saw the Holy One sitting on his throne (Isaiah 6:1); Daniel saw the Ancient of Days on his throne (Daniel 7:9-10, NIV); Ezekiel saw God's glory (Ezekiel 1:28); John saw the one sitting on the throne (Revelation 4:3); we can see the Lord's glory (2 Corinthians 3:18); and we will see him as he really is (1 John 3:2). In some cases, these visions were physical representations of God or manifestations of his glory; in others, they seem to be direct visions of God himself. In any case, they are hints of the beatific vision—not in the afterlife but in the lives of people on earth.

Paul and John were clear that seeing God—or some true representation of him—has the power to transform us into his image. In light of that, one of our highest goals should be to see him more clearly each day, to ask him to reveal himself in increasing measure. What the medieval scholastics saw as a one-day final event, we can get a glimpse of today. And in doing so, we become what the world needs most—children of God who are truly remade in his image.

Lord, I want to see you—in whatever form and to whatever degree of intensity you will allow. Let my vision of you change me forever, and empower me to live in your image. Grant me now a glimpse of what I will experience in full one day. Amen.

Immersed in Love

His faithful love endures forever. (Psalm 136:1)

PSALM 136 MENTIONS a lot of things God did on behalf of Israel, and every phrase is punctuated by an emphatic reminder: "His faithful love endures forever." This statement appears in each of the twenty-six verses of this psalm, clearly making the point that all of God's works—even his works of judgment—are motivated by love. We see that theme often in Scripture, particularly in the New Testament writings about the work of Christ. Jesus was sent into the world because God loved it. His love has been poured out on us extravagantly, and we are urged to understand the height, width, depth, and lengths of God's love and all its power. In fact, God *is* love. It is his defining characteristic.

That means that if you want to know God, and if you want the world to know him, you will have to saturate yourself in this love. It may seem uncomfortably self-ish at times to bathe in the love of God so thoroughly and personally, but it's the only way you can become the vessel of love he is creating you to be. You will be able to love others only to the extent that you experience his love for yourself. You will forgive others only to the extent that you experience his forgiveness for yourself. You will bless others only to the extent that you have understood blessing in your own life. Your capacity to give love depends entirely on your capacity to receive it. It will shape your life more than any other force.

That's a powerful rebuke to many of us who once assumed that God's love is just basic Christianity and then pursued higher things. According to Scripture, there is no higher thing. This is it. After all his years of following Jesus, John the disciple wrote of little else in the letters of his old age. The Christian life is a matter of going deeper in experiencing the love of God and going further in expressing it. Our life of faith begins and ends with the love of God. So does our testimony and influence in this world. Immerse yourself in it completely.

Lord, make my walk with you a story of ever-increasing encounters with your love. Immerse me in it. Let it transform me. May it so fill me that I overflow with it into the lives of all around me. Amen.

Visible Faith

Suppose you see a brother or sister who has no food or clothing,
and you say, "Good-bye and have a good day; stay warm and
eat well"—but then you don't give that person any food or clothing.
What good does that do? (James 2:15-16)

SALVATION COMES BY grace through faith. So does sanctification—our growth process into spiritual maturity. Scripture makes that clear, especially in Paul's letters, which emphasize the free gift of eternal life given to all who believe. But even with that clear doctrine, questions arise. What is faith? What does it look like? Is it simply a matter of intellectual assent, or does it actually do something? Does real faith always work its way outward into our external lives? These were contentious points during the Reformation as well as before it, and have been ever since. Inward belief produces some sort of outward sign, even when that sign is merely a by-product.

James emphasizes that side of faith, probably intentionally contrasting the teaching of Paul. It isn't that these two apostolic writers were in conflict, necessarily, but they did differ in their focus. And James's point, just as biblical, is clear: If inward faith is genuine, it produces external results. The person who claims to have faith but experiences no practical change in lifestyle or values does not actually have faith. Faith is the key to all things in God's Kingdom. But faith always works.

Be intentional about that as you seek to make your faith relevant to the world around you. If you really believe God cares for the poor, for example, let his care for the poor prompt your action on their behalf. If you really believe God answers prayer, pray your heart out. If you really believe God protects and provides for his people in all circumstances, refuse to let pessimistic words come out of your mouth. And if you really believe all your possessions come from God and ultimately belong to him, use them in keeping with his purposes. If your faith is invisible, it will have no influence in your life or any others. If it becomes visible, it will transform the world around you.

Lord, let my beliefs reach into every area of life. Make them powerful, visible, and transforming. May others see into my heart because I wear it in my actions. Help me put feet and hands to my faith today. Amen.

Visible Love

"You must love the LORD your God with all your heart, all your soul, all your mind, and all your strength." . . . "Love your neighbor as yourself." No other commandment is greater than these.
(Mark 12:30-31)

IN A FAMILIAR PASSAGE written in three of the four biblical Gospels, Jesus answered a question about the greatest commandment. The most important, he said, is to love God with everything in us, and a second equally as important is to love others. All of God's Word could be summed up in these two commandments, with all other commandments falling into one of the two categories—our vertical love toward God or our horizontal love toward others. They are part of the same package, all wrapped up in their Source.

But what does this love look like? Is it an attitude, an action, or some of both? Is it something that happens to us or a choice we make? These are common questions, usually answered with an emphasis on tangible expressions. While we often internalize faith and resist talking about its works, we do the opposite with love, externalizing it and minimizing its internal, emotional senses. We instinctively know that it has to have some sort of practical effect.

It does. The most transforming power on earth is divine love. But people rarely experience God's love in an unmediated way—directly from him in some type of individual spiritual experience. The only way for most people to experience his love is through those who carry it. God's normal means for expressing his love in this world is for those who have experienced it to spread it, demonstrate it, and display it as though he were displaying himself through them.

You may not feel qualified to share that kind of love, but that isn't the point. You *are* qualified whether you feel so or not, simply by virtue of having experienced God. In fact, because God's love is by nature given to those who are undeserving of it, it is best expressed through those who are undeserving of it. That includes all of us. We are all in a position to manifest the love, compassion, and affection of our Father, and we have everything to gain by doing so.

Lord, make my love visible. Give me opportunities to express it—to you and to others. Let it overwhelm me and overflow from within, affecting those around me with the compassion and affection of your heart. Amen.

Carpe Aeternum

*I'll sit back and say to myself, "My friend, you have enough stored
away for years to come. Now take it easy! Eat, drink, and be merry!"*
(Luke 12:19)

CARPE DIEM. SEIZE THE DAY. You only live once. Eat, drink, and be merry, for tomorrow you die. Each of these maxims, the last of which was expressed in the disillusioned reflections of Ecclesiastes, expresses the same thought: that it's important to live life to its fullest because the future is so uncertain. There's truth in these sayings; we all want to make the most of the time we've been given. But the sentiment behind them often includes hints of desperation, hopelessness, melancholy, and doubt about what life really means. They suggest that the here-and-now is most important because it may be all we have.

It isn't, of course. Scripture is clear that creation has direction and purpose and that death is not final for any of us. But the *carpe diem* mentality shapes the ways of the world. Without being grounded in eternity, human beings adopt a package of attitudes by default: We seek after comfort and ease instead of hard and painful truth; we minimize brokenness and sin rather than acknowledging it and receiving redemption and restoration; we emphasize human potential, power, and accomplishments rather than the acceptance and destiny God has given us; and we frantically seek temporal experiences now, before death comes, rather than trying to maximize our experience of eternity. In other words, we put all our energy into getting the most out of "life," forgetting that life here and now is just a fraction of life as it really is.

Don't make that mistake. *Carpe aeternum*—seize eternity, not just the day. It's easy to slip into a temporal approach to life, especially when everyone else around us sees that approach as normal and natural. There's a tremendous difference between living under the clock in a panic and patiently waiting for endless time to begin. Many people, even many of those who claim to follow Jesus, seek immediate returns on their investments of time, energy, and resources. But we should seek eternal returns on much more farsighted investments—and become models of patience, peace, and eternal truth.

Lord, help me find the balance between making the most of the time you have given me and living with an eternal perspective. I'd rather invest my life than spend it. May I always seize the Kingdom, not just the day. Amen.

Which Path?

Seek his will in all you do, and he will show you which path to take.
(Proverbs 3:6)

ROBERT FROST WROTE of two roads diverging in a yellow wood, and sorry that he could not travel both, chose the one less traveled.[16] Many who have followed Jesus throughout the centuries have felt the same way—that the road less traveled has made all the difference—though in a sense, the path of discipleship has been well traveled because of them. In any case, we face choices in this life, decisions about which road to take, which stream to drift in, and how much resistance we are willing to face in the process. Some of us will find the way of Jesus to fit nicely into our culture; others will find his direction for our lives to go against the forces surrounding us. The right road isn't the one more or less traveled; it's the one God leads us to follow. Finding it is rarely an easy process.

Martin Luther was one of those who followed his convictions and found them assaulted at every turn. He remained resolute when standing before the imperial assembly. Dietrich Bonhoeffer and the Confessing Church movement felt compelled to choose a direction that would put their lives in danger. Whichever way God leads you, it will go against your culture at some point, even if only in apparently minor ways. Your resistance against the streams of travelers along the world's ways may never be as dramatic as that of Luther or Bonhoeffer, but it is important anyway—not for the sake of playing the role of antagonist, which no one appreciates, but for the sake of demonstrating the true course of the Kingdom. It flows against the world's ways, and it's easy for many believers to get caught up in the wrong movement. Your job is to get caught up in the right one and to invite others into it, in love. God is far more interested in your path than you are. He will help you find it, and that will make all the difference.

Lord, direct my steps, even when I'm not confident in the direction I've received. Whether looking forward or reflecting on the past, help me recognize your guidance. Make my path one of lasting influence and impact. Amen.

Signposts for Eternity

*If our hope in Christ is only for this life, we are more to
be pitied than anyone in the world. (1 Corinthians 15:19)*

OVER THE COURSE OF the twentieth century, several of Christianity's most prominent theologians decided that the idea of life after death did not fit the modern mind and could not be sustained in light of current philosophies and scientific understanding. Still, they continued to commend the ethical implications of our faith, retaining some amorphous concept of God, and some even suggested they found it worthwhile to live as a Christian only for the sake of this life. In that perspective, they disagreed with Paul, who considered our faith pitiable if our hope was only for this age. After all, our entire faith rests on Jesus' resurrection. But for these theologians, Christianity had become a philosophy, not a concrete faith.

That approach does not satisfy the human heart, of course, which was created for eternity and longs for lasting hope. It will not feed the hungry of our age. Our message is much more life-changing and has much greater implications. It opens the spirit to invisible realities and anchors lives in eternal truth. It gives people a reason to live that goes much deeper than a nice idea.

As you live out your faith in the eyes of others, make sure that it goes beyond an ethical system or a religious philosophy. It should certainly shape your ethics and your worldview, of course, but it should also fill you with a palpable hope that others can sense. Every relationship you have is with someone who will live after death; every trial you face will be overshadowed by glories to come; every decision you make has the potential to be invested with meaning. The Resurrection is true, whether it fits modern understanding or not, and it is our message of hope for people desperately searching for something to base their hopes on. You become Exhibit A in the case for eternity, simply by living out your faith and remaining anchored in the spiritual realm. Never lose that focus. You are living in the Resurrection, both now and in the age to come.

Jesus, your resurrection is the gateway to life for all who fear death, the hope of eternity for all who feel trapped in time. Let me embody that life and hope and be a standing signpost to the reality of your Kingdom. Amen.

Unyielding Devotion

*Even though the people were afraid of the local residents, they rebuilt
the altar at its old site. Then they began to sacrifice burnt offerings
on the altar to the Lord each morning and evening. (Ezra 3:3)*

THE PEOPLE OF JUDAH spent years resettling the land after it had been devastated by
the Babylonians, and it wasn't an easy process. Local populations had continued to
live there in the captives' absence, and they understandably resented the exiles' return
more than a century later. To Ezra and his peers, their project of rebuilding Jerusalem
and its Temple was the work of God. To the locals, it was an intrusion.

Ezra and his fellow returnees encountered a lot of opposition, and they could
have cowered under the threats of attack. Instead, they pushed through their fear,
rebuilt the altar on the Temple site, and reinstituted daily sacrifices. They lived under
the conviction that God was on their side, that trials and challenges did not represent
a lack of his favor, and that they would eventually succeed in reestablishing their
worship in Jerusalem. They valued their faith over their reputations, their hardships,
and even their lives. They pressed ahead in uncertain times, enduring opposition for
the sake of their calling.

We are given the same task, even in very different circumstances. Most Christians
in many parts of the world, though certainly not all, do not face life-threatening
persecution. The worst resistance most of us will have to endure is a little harass-
ment and some negative attitudes here and there. Even so, we feel the pressure from
a culture that historically may have grown out of a Christian background but now
expresses contempt for some of Christianity's core values. We know we are not always
perceived well.

Like the returning exiles of Judah, don't let the perceptions of others influence
your devotion. Continue to worship as you normally would, in spite of negative
attitudes and cultural interference. Enduring faithfulness makes a powerful statement to a world that has lost its sense of absolutes. Your persistence is a testimony of
truth, even when some consider it a relic of a less-informed age. It honors God in a
culture that needs to see him.

*Lord, my faith does not depend on public opinion. It depends on your eternal truth.
Anchor me in the realities of your Kingdom, even when my beliefs go against the grain
of my culture. Let me honor you always. Amen.*

The Weight of a Prayer

When I heard this, I sat down and wept. In fact, for days I mourned,
fasted, and prayed to the God of heaven. (Nehemiah 1:4)

NEHEMIAH HEARD NEWS in Persia of the condition of Jerusalem, and it broke his heart. Jerusalem's disrepair, still painfully evident long after its destruction at the hands of Babylon, weighed heavily on him. So Nehemiah sat down to mourn, fast, and pray to God. Not long afterward, he became the answer to his own prayer, as God gave him an opportunity to go to Jerusalem and oversee the rebuilding process. The burden of disappointment moved Nehemiah to plead with God, which moved God to intervene, just as he had planned.

That's often how prayer works. God hears our intercession, and sometimes he prompts an emotional burden in his people to ask for things he wants to do. Nehemiah's grief fit with God's purposes; his confession on behalf of his people and petitions for God's intervention were all according to design and were vital in the restoration and fulfillment of God's promises. Nehemiah became a vital player in Israel's history because his spirit had been provoked by devastating news.

We often hear devastating news and grieve without much hope of anything being done about it. But if we learn to read the movements of God in the news—whether the headlines of the day or the personal developments in our lives—we begin to understand that the burdens we feel are more than just grief. They are promptings, provocation, and catalysts for the asking-and-answering process God instituted at the dawn of Creation. He intervenes in this world through human agency, even when that agency is nothing more than a request. He repeatedly and consistently urges us to bring our petitions to him so that he might do what he had already purposed to do.

Make that one of your missions in life—to be a human agent who prompts God's intervention, a requisitioner who brings the needs of the world and the requests of God's people into his throne room. Ask with anticipation of a response, even one that might involve you. Know that your emotional burdens can be the catalyst for a significant move of God.

Lord, remind me often to turn my concerns into prayers—to see them not as pessimistic complaints but as the beginnings of change. May my burdens invite your solutions into this world. Amen.

Armed with Love

God is love, and all who live in love live in God,
and God lives in them. (1 John 4:16)

DURING THE REFORMATION, many people contending for their understanding of the true Christian faith spent quite a bit of time and effort in arming themselves with truth. Generally, that's a good thing to do. Scripture teaches us to be grounded in truth, to contend for it and stand firm in it, and to live out the purity and simplicity of the true faith. But something tragic happened in the midst of the Reformation and counter-reformations since. As people armed themselves with truth (as they saw it), they forgot to arm themselves with love. And because the truth of God's Word emphasizes the priority of his love, that's a problem.

If you are made in God's image, and if he is love, then your inevitable purpose is to embody love. No other purpose can trump this one. All other purposes you have sought and all other prayers you have prayed are wrapped up in this overarching design. When you walk in love, you walk into the specific calling you have been given. When you increase in love, you increase in the divine power and wisdom you have been promised. You discover insights you wouldn't otherwise have seen, you experience miracles you wouldn't otherwise have experienced, and you get answers to prayer you wouldn't otherwise have received. Love is a vital key to unlocking almost all of the treasures of God's Kingdom.

You cannot manufacture this love; it has to come from the God who defines himself by it. But a prayer to be filled with his love is clearly in line with his will and certain to be answered. If you are like many Christians, this request may not be at the top of your prayer list, and you may not be nearly as diligent in cultivating love as you are in training yourself in truth. But this is God's priority for us: that we each embody his nature, which he portrays as love above all other characteristics. It's who he is—and who we are called to be with everyone we know.

Lord, help me keep first things first—to express your heart and embody your love. Your truth is always packaged in compassion, affection, and concern. May the words I say always be bathed in your love. Amen.

Behind the Annoyances

*Jesus felt sorry for them and touched their eyes. Instantly
they could see! Then they followed him. (Matthew 20:34)*

TWO BLIND MEN SHOUTED at Jesus as he was leaving Jericho, and the surrounding crowds told them to be quiet. The men were making a scene in front of the Master, apparently annoying those who were trying to listen to Jesus or make a good impression on him. That's often what happens when people who don't pick up on social cues (or are too desperate to follow them) violate normal protocol. They are quieted, marginalized, dismissed as impolite, and left to deal with their own awkwardness. Walls of separation go up between the "normal" and the "inappropriate."

Jesus often walked through those walls. In the case of these blind men, he stopped and asked what they wanted from him. We don't know whether their shouts annoyed him just as they annoyed his followers; we only know that any annoyance took a back seat to compassion. Jesus "felt sorry for them." He saw the need behind the irritating racket. He apparently was not bothered by any awkwardness, lack of dignity, or breach of etiquette. He didn't insist that they ask him nicely. They couldn't see, and he had the power to restore sight, so he acted on his compassion and opened their eyes.

You may find that a lot of people in this world make you uncomfortable. The natural reaction in such cases is to distance yourself. But don't be fooled. Behind the contentiousness, the stress, the egos, the rejection, the incivility, the anger and insults, and every other sign of human hearts gone wrong is a desperate need to encounter God's goodness. You have both the calling and the capacity to give it to them. There is always something of his nature to share with those who long for his touch. Look beyond the annoyances and see the need. You have been given insight into human nature and know the hunger behind the masks so many of us wear. When necessary, cross the boundaries that limit your compassion and show it to those who are crying out for it.

Lord, condition my heart to react with compassion rather than annoyance when people rub me the wrong way. Help me see their needs, and move me to speak and act with your compassion. Amen.

People of Celebration and Joy

Go and celebrate with a feast of rich foods and sweet drinks,
and share gifts of food with people who have nothing prepared.
This is a sacred day before our Lord. Don't be dejected and sad,
for the joy of the LORD is your strength! (Nehemiah 8:10)

WHETHER DESERVED OR NOT, Puritans had a reputation for being dour people incapable of having fun. Lutherans were known as a contentious lot, and Jesuits were known for being harsh and demanding. In fact, self-professed Christians down through the ages have had reputations, usually some form of a stereotype that, perhaps, fit in some cases but certainly not all. Even so, there is something to be said for being known as "a people of [fill in the blank]." When one particular characteristic stands out, you know you've embodied it well.

Christians are to be known for a lot of positive things—being a people of love, humility, and kindness, for example. We'll explore some of these in the next few days, but we have to admit, we often are not known for having the attributes of Jesus. We are both fairly and unfairly stereotyped, and the result is an image we may wish we didn't have. When that happens, there's only one way to change it. We have to present the true image—the real image we were given long ago and that is being restored to us even now. We are to express the nature of God in the real situations and relationships of daily life. We are to be known as a people of all things good.

One of those characteristics is joy and celebration. Nehemiah and the Levites made the point that "sacred" and sadness did not go hand in hand. Nowhere in Scripture are we told that dignity, sober-mindedness, or fiery zeal is our strength. But joy is. When we live in it, our relationships grow closer, and others are drawn to the image of God. People who don't know him get a taste of his Kingdom. We can bring the joy of heaven into the sadness of earth in almost any situation. Life doesn't get any more sacred than that.

Lord, turn my heart toward the joy of your Kingdom. Let me see beyond my own agendas, needs, and pains to celebrate the extravagance of an eternity filled with your love. And let that celebration bring heaven into earth each day. Amen.

People of Kindness

A servant of the Lord must not quarrel but must be kind to
everyone, be able to teach, and be patient with difficult people.
(2 Timothy 2:24)

WHEN CRITICS PULL ARGUMENTS against Christianity out of history, they inevitably point to worst-case scenarios: the Crusades, the Inquisition, the Salem witch trials, and all kinds of other examples of aggression and judgment. The fact that these events don't actually reflect true Christianity and the teachings of Jesus is ignored; they are "Christian" behaviors because people who called themselves Christians did them. And the overarching theme that strings together these various acts of violence, aggression, and hate is that they are *not* expressions of love. They are presented as evidence that we are not a people of kindness.

But we are. Perhaps we don't show it on every occasion, but real Christianity and the work of the Holy Spirit in a person's heart produces kindness over time. It's one of the fruits of the Spirit and a frequent instruction in his Word. Some Christians forget that, reserving kindness for those they like and unleashing unkindness on those they don't, just as everyone in the world is prone to do. But when the Spirit really grips a person's heart and does a profound work in them, kindness grows. That person begins to see people through lenses of compassion and grace, aware that we are all recovering from the trauma of living in a fallen world and healing from wounds we have received here. Kindness, patience, and grace flow from eyes that have learned to see and a heart that has learned to love.

Remember that. We are to be known as a people of kindness, both toward each other and to those who do not believe as we do. When we treat each other this way, others are drawn to the Christian community. When we treat outsiders this way, they get to experience something of God's nature. The passage above acknowledges difficult people, assumes our kindness will be tested, and urges kindness anyway. Take that seriously. Being kind is an underestimated means of demonstrating the kindness of God in a way that reaches people wherever they are. It is a remarkably simple way to change lives.

Lord, in seeking after the dramatic fruits of your Spirit, I've often neglected the "easy" ones. Make me a person of kindness. Fill my vision, my thoughts, and my words with grace. Let my kindness awaken hearts to your goodness. Amen.

People of Humility

Always be humble and gentle. Be patient with each other, making
allowance for each other's faults because of your love. (Ephesians 4:2)

IN SIXTEENTH- AND seventeenth-century England, seating in churches was often categorized for attendees in terms of their rank, age, property holdings, and gender. Where you sat depended on who you were. Pew disputes were not only a social phenomenon; they could become a legal one, too, as parishioners sometimes ended up in court over violations of "their space" at Sunday services. Somehow, the focus of the church service turned from the worship of God to a defense of personal status. For many, it was far less important to learn and pray than to be seen and respected.

Our desire for status today may manifest in subtler ways, but we are still prone to have it, and it can still affect our relationships with other people. Many Christians get offended much too easily. Whether the offense is justified isn't the point; we are designed to be full of grace even (or especially) when grace, in keeping with its definition, is clearly undeserved. An offended Christian, as most of us have experienced in ourselves and others, is not a pretty picture—or a compelling portrayal of our faith. And being offended almost always comes out of an attack on our pride.

We are told quite often in Scripture to be people of humility. God is drawn to the humble and lifts them up (1 Peter 5:5-6). He blesses the poor in spirit and offers an enormous inheritance to the humble or meek (Matthew 5:3, 5). He urges us to think of others before ourselves, just as Jesus humbled himself in taking the form of a servant and suffering on our behalf (Philippians 2:3-11). Humility leads to gentleness, patience, and grace toward others' faults, as Ephesians 4:2 suggests. It is one of our most appealing distinguishing marks.

If we have it, that is. If we don't, we become as unpleasing as those who vied for pews in old churches or ignored the feelings and needs of others in order to serve themselves. Humility makes us like God, and pride makes us . . . well, not. Choose which you will be known for, and live it to the full.

Jesus, you are the perfect example of human and divine humility—of infinite worth yet focused on others. Work that into my heart. May I become a pure reflection of your selflessness. Amen.

People of Generosity

God loves a person who gives cheerfully. (2 Corinthians 9:7)

JOHN WESLEY WAS KNOWN for urging people to earn all the money they could, save all they could, and give all they could. His philosophy grew out of his experience with an expanding income. Instead of limiting himself to a 10 percent tithe, he ultimately gave away the vast majority of his wealth. He preached often on the blessings of generosity—how the one who gives is actually the one who receives—and took Jesus' saying to heart: "It is more blessed to give than to receive" (Acts 20:35). A lifestyle of generosity comes with its own rewards.

Generosity is about more than money, of course. We are called to live with generous spirits—what used to be known more commonly as magnanimity: a wideness and openness of heart that is eager to share, to give the benefit of the doubt, and to offer grace by default. Such a heart is not inclined toward condemnation or competition but toward kindness and favor. It overlooks offenses and looks instead for reasons to affirm and encourage. It seeks the well-being of all.

If that description looks at all familiar, it's because it describes God. He has been generous with us, and we have the amazing privilege of being generous with others and with him in return. Paul's words in 2 Corinthians about giving describe a cycle of generosity—God giving generously to his children, who in turn give generously back to him and to those in need, and in turn are given more so they might share even more. This act of giving looks to many like it will lead to emptiness, but it leads to fullness instead. The magnanimous life overflows with good things.

It also looks like the Father. It makes us apples that have fallen not far from the tree, the spitting image of the one who created us in his image, generous children of a generous God. And when people see the goodness of God in his people, they are drawn to him. Our generosity—of spirit, of material resources, of kind words, and more—serves as an invitation for people to experience his.

Father, you have been so generous with me, even in ways I have hardly noticed. Make me aware. More than that, make me open-hearted and open-handed. May I give to others as you have given to me. Amen.

People of Restoration

Heaven must receive him until the time comes for God to restore
everything, as he promised long ago through his holy prophets.
(Acts 3:21, NIV)

GOD PROMISES RESTORATION. We may debate about how much of it we are meant to experience in this age, but we cannot argue with Scripture's insistence that God's ultimate purpose is a restoration, a restitution, and a renovation of all things. The prophets pointed to new heavens and a new earth (Isaiah 65:17); Jesus said Elijah would come and restore "all things" (Matthew 17:11, NIV); Peter mentioned the restoration in his sermon in Acts 3; Paul said creation would be liberated from its decay and restored to freedom (Romans 8:21); and Revelation 21:5 tells us God will make all things new. The miracles we see in the Gospels and Acts, as well as in much of church history, suggest that tastes of the Kingdom are available now; yet we know the fullness of the Kingdom comes only when the King himself returns. In any case, as people who have been called as ambassadors of Kingdom realities, we are to live as pictures of what's to come. We are to be a people of restoration.

What does that look like in this world? We reconcile relationships; we encourage people to pray for healing, deliverance, and abundant life; we point to the work God is doing in hearts, societies, and cultures; and we insist that history is headed in a certain direction and toward a return of the King. Because we remember our sinful past and the restoration we were freely given, we refuse to blame, accuse, put down, or criticize. Instead, we encourage, strengthen, and build up. As far as possible, we live out the future we have been promised.

Remember your role as a restorer. Refuse to blend in with a critical, destructive, deteriorating world. Your words, actions, and attitudes have the power to reflect the restoration God has promised and give people a taste of it. When they do, the Kingdom grows stronger, and so do you. The restoration of all things—including you—is promised now and in the days to come.

Lord, forgive me for any part I've had in tearing down—with my words, attitudes, or actions. Make me known as a builder and restorer, a reflection of life in your Kingdom. Heal, encourage, and strengthen many through me. Amen.

People of Love

Most important of all, continue to show deep love for each other,
for love covers a multitude of sins. (1 Peter 4:8)

JESUS MADE IT CLEAR THAT his followers would be known by their love (John 13:35). Unfortunately, when we don't show it, we become known for our lack of it. That's why it's so important to see love as our distinguishing characteristic, our mark of discipleship, our "brand" as believers. All other godly attributes flow out of this one. Humility comes from esteeming others; kindness comes from compassion toward others; generosity and restoration come from desiring the best for others; and on and on. When we love well—both God and others—all other godly characteristics grow strong. When we don't, they don't. It really is that simple.

Peter and James both tell us that love covers a multitude of sins (1 Peter 4:8; James 5:20, NIV). Does that mean that when we love, our own sins are covered? No, they have already been covered by the blood of Jesus. When we love, we cover the sins of others in forgiveness, quietness, and grace. We refuse to bring sins to the surface because we no longer live law-based lives. We live and breathe in a culture of mercy, always minimizing the faults of others and searching for the worth and gifts God has put within them. We seek always to lift up, never to tear down. We draw people into the Kingdom of God by the warmth and kindness of his overwhelming love.

However you see your calling as salt and light in this world, it has to include love. Peter prefaced this verse with a statement of priority: "most important of all." Paul made the same statement in his great chapter on love (1 Corinthians 13), as did John in his Gospel and letters. There's a reason Jesus and the biblical writers focused on this key characteristic: It epitomizes God. It captures the climate of his Kingdom and explains why we were created and how we are to live. Show deep, genuine love, and you will grow closer to God and others. You will fulfill your calling to represent Jesus as he really is.

Lord, if you are love and I'm created in your image, my ultimate purpose is to be love.
May I center my life on this foundational truth. You are love, and you made us to be like
you. May I embody it well. Amen.

The Name You Wear

It was at Antioch that the believers were first called Christians.
(Acts 11:26)

THE TERM "CHRISTIAN" THAT was applied to early believers meant "little Christs," and it wasn't necessarily a compliment. It was a convenient label that reflected their focus on their Savior, as well as their messianic desire to save the world. Even so, Christians bore the name willingly, embracing its suggestion that they looked something like Jesus. Peter urged his readers to praise God for bearing that name even in the midst of their sufferings (1 Peter 4:16). What was a pejorative term for some became a badge of honor for others.

The name is often used with contempt today, too. For many people, the word "Christian" has a negative connotation of an entire subculture, way of thinking, political persuasion, naiveté, or even ignorance. Within the church, we use it comfortably. Outside the church, we are much more hesitant because we know the reactions it brings.

Most people today do not respond to Christian faith and teachings purely on the presentation of truths and implications. They see the truths and implications as part of a package, and you are part of it—the good, the bad, the ugly, and every other connotation or assumption that comes up in people's minds when they hear the words "Christian," "church," "Jesus," and the like. You have the opportunity, however, of defying stereotypes and changing perceptions one heart at a time, and it's important to take that opportunity seriously. Much of the world thinks we have a branding problem. They aren't wrong.

The power of Christianity comes from much more than branding, of course. Our influence in the world is not simply a matter of PR. But reputations are nevertheless important, and we all have a part in establishing the reputation of the whole. Living with love, joy, kindness, generosity, humility, integrity, and everything else honorable in this world will change the way many people see our faith. It will remind them of the truths we teach. And it will demonstrate something of the Kingdom and its King, just as the Christians who first wore the name did long ago.

{ *Jesus, it is an honor to be associated with you by both admirers and critics. One of my highest goals is to change how people see you and to bring honor to your name. May I represent it well. Amen.*

Revolution

Clothe yourself with the presence of the Lord Jesus Christ.
(Romans 13:14)

YOU'VE SEEN THE MOVIES, read the books, and know the theme well. The small but spirited band of fighters goes up against the huge, monolithic regime and somehow finds a way to break free from oppression. Sometimes the story is based on history—a legal battle, band of brothers, or grassroots movement. Sometimes it's fictional—the destruction of a Death Star or a fellowship of unlikely creatures against a world of evil. In any case, it's true. It's a picture of overcoming unthinkable odds to accomplish whatever is good, right, and beautiful. The fact that the story seems so impossible is what makes it so compelling. We love a good revolution.

That's our story too. We are part of a revolution. There really is an evil empire, though humanity has gotten so used to its ways that the culture of it seems kind of normal. But when you entered the Kingdom of God, you chose to walk contrary to the ways of the world, whether you intended to or not. You chose to defy your old nature. You joined a revolt.

Your revolt does not involve swords or guns, at least not in any material or conventional sense. It does, however, involve weapons of the Spirit and clothing yourself in a new culture that conflicts with the old. It fits our original design, even though that design seems nothing more than an ancient echo for many of us. We are called to bring that Kingdom culture into this world—not to tear down what has gone before but to transform it. The transformation begins in the depths of our hearts and works its way outward. Our mission is to be relentless agents of change.

Live with that sense of mission and invite others into it. You were created not to conform to the world but to conform to the image of God. Clothe yourself in the presence of Jesus and live a wonderfully subversive life. Season your world with truth and love—the kind of revolution it craves.

Jesus, your ways are revolutionary in this world, and I embrace them fully. Give me the courage to embody the Kingdom's culture and stand against the world's. May your Kingdom come and your will be done in me. Amen.

In This World

This world is fading away, along with everything that people crave.
But anyone who does what pleases God will live forever. (1 John 2:17)

ONE OF THE RECURRING themes throughout Christian history is a sense of detachment from the world—what the medievals called *contemptus mundi*, a rejection of temporal things paired with a focus on eternal glory. For obvious reasons, this attitude has been much easier to embrace in times of social upheaval, war, plague, and other calamities. Death and destruction tend to force the issue within the human heart. But Scripture advocates that we have some sense of this attitude all the time. Regardless of how well life is going, temporal things will come to an end, but the Kingdom of God will last. We have to choose where we will invest our lives, and given those options, the choice should be fairly obvious.

This is what John meant when he told us not to love the world. We are called to love people, to value God's creation, to enjoy his good gifts, and to experience abundant life in the here and now. Yes, we have our hearts turned toward the there and then—the glory of eternity—but we also have gifts and callings that are needed right now. We are not reminded of the fading nature of this world so that we reject it outright; we are reminded of it so that we keep our priorities straight. We still have a lot to do in this life.

Make sure to balance your perspective. Let your heart and mind envision heaven without developing an escapist attitude. Do not neglect the calling, gifts, and responsibilities God has given you to be salt and light in the systems and institutions of this world. You have an assignment to flavor the ways of the world with the values and power of the Kingdom of God—to strengthen governments, schools, businesses, arts and communications, families, and more with the Spirit God has put within you. Keep your eyes on heaven but your hands and feet on earth. You have the tremendous privilege of bearing eternal fruit in a world that is passing away.

Holy Spirit, you were given to us for life in this world. May I never lose sight of that, even as my heart longs for heaven. Give me opportunities to season this planet with your nature. Give me lasting fruit. Amen.

The Meaning of Your Gaze

We do this by keeping our eyes on Jesus, the champion
who initiates and perfects our faith. (Hebrews 12:2)

LATE MEDIEVAL AND RENAISSANCE ARTISTS often hinted at the themes of their paintings by strategically posing their subjects' gazes. Following the eyes of the people in the scene, we can often tell a lot about the message the artist wanted to convey. Sometimes those gazes were directed at a holy object or an important symbol; sometimes they pointed to a background figure whose name or identity represented an unseen truth. Rarely were eyes randomly focused. The gazes mattered. They shaped the meaning of the scene.

Your gaze performs a similar function—not in determining how people interpret you, necessarily, but in how you define meaning in your life. Faith is all about our line of sight—whether we invest our lives in the visible world around us or in the deeper meanings of the unseen world. As with the dominant figures in a Renaissance painting, our gazes may go beyond the obvious subjects; we see the important messages of God's Kingdom that are written into the scenes of our lives. The direction of our eyes determines what we will ultimately experience.

That's really important to remember in our life of faith. The gospel does not tell us to focus on our sin, our problems, or our obstacles. It does not call us to figure everything out, lament our failures, live in regret, or stare at the hardships before us. It tells us to keep our eyes on Jesus. Though some pray with an eye on the mountains, faith focuses our attention on the God who can move them. We are never told to escape our past; we are told to grow into our future. There's a tremendous difference. Being preoccupied with Jesus gives us a vision of what we are becoming. It empowers us. It fills us with truth.

Just like the meaning of a masterpiece, your life will always unfold in the direction of your gaze. Guard your vision carefully, and you will grow into it in time. You may even inspire the gazes of those around you.

Jesus, my eyes are on you. You never told your disciples to figure it all out; you told them to watch and follow. May I grow into your image increasingly, thoroughly, beautifully. Amen.

The Power of Your Focus

Bless the LORD, O my soul, and all that is within me, bless his holy name! Bless the LORD, O my soul, and forget not all his benefits.
(Psalm 103:1-2, ESV)

THE DIRECTION OF OUR GAZE is transforming; Paul has assured us of that, promising that as we look at the Lord with unveiled faces, we will become more and more like him (2 Corinthians 3:18). Just as young athletes take on the mannerisms of their favorite ballplayers and young music lovers sing the songs of their favorite stars, we will grow in the direction of our loves.

We will also grow in the direction of our preoccupations, and that's where the problems begin. Our hardships and challenges draw our attention away from God and his answers. We become sharply focused on the negatives in our lives—the missed opportunities, the problems that need to be fixed, the one discouraging comment in a chorus of encouraging voices, the one troublesome grade on a child's otherwise stellar report card, the one health or financial problem interrupting our general well-being. But few ever overcome debt by staring at it, recover from a sickness by dwelling on it, or resolve relational issues by magnifying them. Neither do we overcome sin by directing all our attention and efforts against it. No, we overcome our challenges by focusing on solutions, being grateful for the good, and, as David once wrote, gazing on the beauty of the Lord and seeking him in his temple (Psalm 27:4, NIV). A downward gaze only imprisons us; it's the upward gaze that saves us. We have to choose what to magnify in our lives.

For all our criticisms of positive thinking, the Bible encourages us to think positively by focusing on God and his goodness. (The book of Philippians is a virtual field manual in positive thinking, for example.) Why is this so? Because hope is true, and discouragement isn't. Faith is effective, and negativity is futile—and a really bad testimony. Our spiritual eyes are powerful. When they are fixed on God in his dwelling, they change our own lives and many others' as well.

Father, I've been so casual about guarding my focus, yet it can change lives, including mine. Forgive me; train me; help me turn my attention toward your goodness and your promises always. Amen.

Praying with Vision

We have stopped evaluating others from a human point of view.
(2 Corinthians 5:16)

MEDIEVAL DEVOTIONAL PRACTICES often focused on pictures rather than text. Monks and nobles could read, but many common people could not. So instead of meditating on words written on a page, people often meditated on a picture that represented the words. Images of Jesus and his sacrifice were powerful in prompting transforming thoughts. People understood the power of vision.

Not only does Scripture support this power of vision in our relationship with God (see 2 Corinthians 3:18 and Hebrews 12:2, for example), it also supports it with regard to other people. When we look at people with suspicion—as competitors for status or love or affirmation rather than as objects of God's affection—we close off our hearts and limit the depths of our relationships. When we define people by their past or even their present, we miss out on what God is doing in their lives. When we focus on people's flaws and problems, we pray for them without power and hope. We begin to define the world around us through the wounds and weaknesses of our own hearts.

What would we think of a businessperson who constantly stared at company losses but never at company vision? Or a ministry leader who was obsessed with opposition and obstacles but never the mission itself? We would have little hope for growth and advancement in such instances because we instinctively know the power of focus—that, like sunflowers turning toward the sun, our hearts always unfold toward their vision. We were designed to live by hope.

Next time you pray for a prodigal, take your eyes off the bad decisions, the negative influences, and the dangerous situations. Fill your mind instead with a picture of who that child can (and will) become in Christ. Next time you pray for a friend or colleague who needs the love of Christ, refuse to look at any hardness of heart or past mistakes. See instead the treasure within that person and the hope of his or her calling. In other words, pray positively, hopefully, expectantly, always with eyes on the power and promise of God. Cultivate your vision, and let it become a prayer that changes the world.

Lord, your Kingdom is like a treasure hidden in a field. May I always see the treasure and never the dirt around it. Empower me with heavenly visions and transforming prayers. Amen.

Glimpses of Beauty

*God has made everything beautiful for its own time. He has planted
eternity in the human heart, but even so, people cannot see the whole
scope of God's work from beginning to end. (Ecclesiastes 3:11)*

TODAY'S THEOLOGIANS ARE masters of splitting hairs and parsing doctrine, creating something of a line-item theology that could rival any accountant's ledger for specificity. Many see Scripture as a fence around a small plot of orthodoxy rather than a gateway into a wide-open field of meaning. But Scripture shows Jesus being not nearly so precise in his statements, which are often intentionally ambiguous. They point to larger things, ideas and beliefs that are bigger than the human mind and can only be evoked, not explained. In other words, they are beautiful.

That is an aspect of Christian thought that is so often missing today. From the trilogy of truth, love, and beauty, we have pursued truth above all, given lip service to love, and neglected beauty far too often. But theology and history should be told with some sense of artistry. There is ugliness in the human story, to be sure, but there are threads of meaning, too. We ought to have enough insight to bring them out, and to bring them out beautifully—just as God has done in Scripture and in revealing himself to human beings throughout history. He is far less interested in defining theology for his people than he is in captivating their hearts with his works.

Never reduce your faith to a set of propositions. It is so much more. It is a fascinatingly complex web of meaning woven throughout the human story. It is the artistry of a Creator who cannot be contained in finite minds. It is an echo of eternal and infinite things that you will never grasp fully but can nevertheless represent truly. Your beliefs do not define creation or salvation; they offer only a partial picture of both. Express yourself with that awareness; live with that humility; and always, always point toward the uncontainable majesty and artistry of your God.

Lord, captivate me with the beauty of your work. Break me of the ways I have tried to define you too narrowly. Expand my vision so I can see how small it actually is, and let my words, heart, and life reflect your artistry. Amen.

A Life of Enjoyment

I concluded there is nothing better than to be happy and enjoy
ourselves as long as we can. And people should eat and drink
and enjoy the fruits of their labor, for these are gifts from God.
(Ecclesiastes 3:12-13)

ONE OF THE FAULTS OF SOME Christian movements from the past and present has been their tendency to favor austerity and strip beauty away from the faith. Perhaps this tendency grows out of a fear of human passions, which they believed should be constrained, not unleashed. Historically, the church has tried to contain the heart far more often than it has tried to set it free. But constraining human passion comes at a cost. Like treatments that aim at killing a cancer by poisoning the entire body, spiritual treatments target the capacity to sin passionately and to believe passionately at the same time. They often quench the spirit.

Such attempts almost always result in reactionary movements toward freer expression. The human heart will always struggle for freedom, even if it has to rebel to do so. But it should not have to. Jesus' sacrifice allows us to be free not only of sin but also of the religious restrictions that try to contain it. He wants us to be neither slaves to sin and self nor slaves to law and willpower. He wants us to be conformed to his nature simply by gazing at it and stepping into it. As we do, we experience the fruits of his Spirit and of our own labor. We live in joy and satisfaction.

Many teachers will argue that it is God's purpose for us to be holy, not happy—as if the two were mutually exclusive. But God makes it clear that he has designed us for fulfillment. Jesus spoke a lot about joy and abundant life. Ecclesiastes, for all its negative statements, nevertheless urges us to enjoy life. To do less is to dishonor the gifts God has given us to enjoy (1 Timothy 6:17; James 1:17). It is to ignore our capacity for deep feeling and godly passion. It is to mistrust the image of himself within us. Honor him by seeking joy and celebrating his gifts in all their fullness.

Lord, may I never seek my own happiness selfishly. Even so, may I find it completely. May I discover my truest, deepest joy in you and all of your gifts. Amen.

Agents of the New Creation

Looking intently at Simon, Jesus said, "Your name is Simon, son of John—but you will be called Cephas" (which means "Peter").
(John 1:42)

IT'S EASY TO HAVE HARSH THOUGHTS and even unkind words for people who are not living up to our expectations. We make all sorts of judgments—some of them true, some of them not, and most of them beyond our abilities and our calling—about the behavior and attitudes of the people around us. For a people of grace, we can be awfully ungracious. We lament a world gone wrong and become its accusers. We see people for what they are doing rather than who they really are.

We are reminded in 2 Corinthians 5:16 that we are called to see people according to the Spirit, not according to a human point of view. It may be difficult for a human not to have a human point of view, but we have been given deeper vision. We are given the task of seeing like Jesus, who looked past the brash impulsiveness of Simon and called him Peter, meaning "rock." We are expected to be like our Father, who instead of seeing only a terrorist named Saul saw an apostle who would take on a Gentile name and reach the hearts of pagans. As people of a new name (Revelation 2:17), we are to see others with their new "name" too—their true identity, their potential among those who are redeemed. We are to leave behind the petty judgments of this world and speak life, hope, and truth into lives that need the newness of God. We are agents of the new creation.

When we treat people according to their potential rather than their past, we become catalysts for God's work in their lives. Something happens in the spiritual realm when a believer chooses to see the unseen and walk by faith. The past is undone and a new identity breaks through. It may take time, but the process begins. The inner life of a person of faith transforms the outer world far more effectively than we realize. People are waiting for someone to see the positive within them. Choose that vision, speak accordingly, and watch God work to change your world.

Lord, retrain my eyes to see the treasure in the people around me—even when the treasure is hidden. May my vision and words draw people into their true identity for your glory. Amen.

A Model of Values

Think about the things of heaven, not the things of earth.
(Colossians 3:2)

YOUR LIFE IS A DEMONSTRATION of your values. The things you choose to invest your time and money in, the ways you manage your relationships, the decisions you make about lifestyle and career—all of these are reflections of what is most important to you. Regardless of how you express your values verbally, your decisions in day-to-day life prove your true priorities. You are constantly expressing your deepest, truest loyalties.

That thought may be scary or sobering, or perhaps challenging or encouraging. Jesus called his followers to seek his Kingdom above all else (Matthew 6:33), and you probably sense that in some ways you have taken up that calling seriously and in other ways are falling short. He has plenty of grace for you as you grow, but the people around you may not. They may see where your heart lies, but they need to know more: Is the unseen realm real to you? Are you investing more than your words in God's Kingdom? In spite of your imperfections, are you growing in the right direction?

Paul's words in Colossians 3:2 are not an appeal to a life of escapism, in which you ignore the needs of the world and think only spiritual thoughts. It is rather an invitation to align your thoughts with God's—to see as he sees, value what he values, and prioritize what he prioritizes. They offer an opportunity to demonstrate the reality of the Kingdom of God in everything you do, even the mundane tasks of daily living. Even more, they urge you to express his heart to those around you.

Take that invitation seriously. Recognize what is most important and resolve to invest your life in those things to the full. Be a signpost to eternal realities—not only the gospel of salvation but also the goodness of God in every area of life. Become a living, breathing picture of the values of God's Kingdom.

Lord, let me see as you see, think as you think, and do and say what you do and say. My natural thoughts do not align with yours, but your Spirit changes everything and gives me the mind of Christ. May I display it in everything I do. Amen.

A Model of Redemption

You died to this life, and your real life is hidden with Christ in God.
(Colossians 3:3)

YOU MAY THINK YOUR SUCCESSES are the greatest arenas for showcasing your values. Your dependence on God, your prayer life, your loving relationships, and your commitment to truth are all testimonies to your citizenship in God's Kingdom. But another arena is just as powerful, if not more: your losses. How you respond to disappointment, to failure, and to insurmountable obstacles says a lot about your priorities and your grounding in the unseen realm. Your joy in Christ in spite of your missteps and defeats is a remarkable testimony to the reality of your faith.

Many Christians don't understand that. When their own consciences or other people bring up their past, they feel defeated and overwhelmed with regret. They don't realize that even a scarred past serves as a testimony to what God has done in their life. They see their flaws as blemishes rather than as examples of what salvation overcomes. They forget that Jesus came not for the righteous but for sinners—and that their imperfection is the only thing that qualifies them for his grace.

Go ahead and accept your imperfect record, no matter how awful it is. According to God's Word, you have died to it. It no longer has any influence over you. You can trust God either to hide any record of your sins (see Psalms 31:20; 32:1) or use it for his glory. Your real life is rooted in the soil of God's Kingdom and can bear nothing but eternal fruit. Those who feign righteousness to give the right impression to others are more transparent than they think, but those who abandon the pose and claim only to be bathed in the love of God attest to a much deeper reality. In them, righteousness grows naturally. Live with that freedom, embrace the fullness of that love, and trust that God will bury your old life and unveil your new one in time.

Father, my life in Christ is like a seed hidden in the ground, but I know you have plans for new growth. Let me flourish, unveil the real me, and let my newness surpass any hints of my old ways. Amen.

A Model of Destiny

When Christ, who is your life, is revealed to the whole world,
you will share in all his glory. (Colossians 3:4)

YOU WERE CREATED FOR GLORY. Somewhere deep in your soul you've known that, even if, like most people, you've buried the impulse beneath layers of disappointments and regrets. Even so, your original design is there, sometimes showing up in a desire to do something great and make your mark on this world. Imagining a glorious future is not arrogance or presumption; it's truth. You were made in the image of your Creator, who is nothing short of amazing. The image of glory within you is destined to be revealed with his.

Your life will be shaped to a large degree by the destiny you envision. If you carry no vision or image of glory in your mind, your life will tend to look formless and void, just as creation did before the Creator spoke light and purpose into it. But if you know where you are headed, you will tend to step into that vision. You will live as a glorious creature united with a glorious Christ. You will grow into the truth of his ultimate purposes for you.

That not only has a profound influence on how you live; it also has a profound influence on how you treat others. They, too, have the astounding potential of sharing in the glory of Christ. That's a life-changing message for a world that has embraced meaninglessness and a random existence. For people who have no idea what to do with their impulses of glory, you become a testimony of purpose. You have the power to speak purpose into formless lives around you. You become a messenger of hope and meaning.

That is a vital ministry—to your family, friends, fellow church members, coworkers, and everyone else around you. At times that ministry may be subtle and nuanced; at times it may be open and direct. In any case, it breathes life into the dead places of sleeping hearts, where the impulse for glory still lies. Live as a revelation of human destiny and speak it often.

Spirit of God, may I live not according to my broken past, others' perceptions, or unwise plans for the future, but according to the true destiny you have given me. Fill my vision— and help me fill others'—with the hope of glory. Amen.

All about Heart

God did what the law could not do. He sent his own Son in a body
like the bodies we sinners have. And in that body God declared an
end to sin's control over us by giving his Son as a sacrifice for our sins.
(Romans 8:3)

HISTORY IS FULL OF Christians who went up against prevailing laws, social structures, and systemic patterns to change the way the world works. That's important; culture is not defined by its laws, but it is often inhibited or restrained by them. When we change the framework of society to fit with God's ways, we do a good thing. But if we think that's where the real battle lies, we will spend our lives focusing on the wrong things. We will be like painters who change the face of a building without affecting what goes on inside of it. We will fight a lot of unnecessary battles.

Many Christians are fighting on political and legal fronts to make society look a bit more like the Kingdom of God, and there's nothing inherently wrong with that. But the real battle is for the hearts of human beings. If they change, the laws become unnecessary; if they don't, the laws will always be insufficient. Many of the social trends we want to reverse are better approached through winsome conversations, exemplary attitudes, and appeals to matters of the heart than they are through hard-nosed political talk and legislative threats. The Kingdom of God has never been accomplished outwardly, whether through the law of Moses or the self-discipline of our own resolutions. It has always been a transformation of the inward nature that works its way outward. If we want to see society change, we need to help individual lives change. When they do, society will follow.

Never turn your mission as salt and light in this world into a behavioral agenda. Win hearts, one by one, conversation by conversation with grace upon grace. The Kingdom is built on such things—specifically, the foundation of a Messiah who never overturned a law but has won hearts by the billions. His mission and his ways are yours.

Jesus, for a people who claim to want to be like you, we have a remarkable tendency to
resort to means you never used. Turn our hearts back to the core of our mission. Equip us
to win hearts with the wisdom, power, and love of your Kingdom. Amen.

Strength in Weakness

My grace is all you need. My power works best in weakness.
(2 Corinthians 12:9)

THE WORLD LONGS FOR a revelation of the children of God (Romans 8:19), and sometimes we think the best way to be that revelation is with our tidy lives, impressive works, or relentlessly joyful attitudes. Exemplary lifestyles, the power of the Spirit, and joy are certainly important; our lives should be marked with them consistently. But the greater revelation comes not through any immunity to life's frailties and fallenness but through the power of God in the midst of them. Like a fragile baby born in Bethlehem, we are earthen vessels containing the divine Spirit (2 Corinthians 4:7), intersections between visible and invisible realms, incarnations of the image of God. Weakness becomes strength, flaws are covered with mercy, pride bows down to humility, the decay of death gives way to life, and temporal bodies are finally clothed in the eternal. Our fragility makes us a wonderful showcase for God.

Paul stressed that point when his prayers for deliverance from a problem—we don't know whether it was physical, relational, or something else—were answered by a profound truth that God's power works best in our weakness. Paul began boasting in his frailties, rather than trying to reestablish his former strength, because he realized that his frailties were where God revealed himself. This powerful, divine light inside of us may be obscured at times, but much of the Christian life involves uncovering it. The Spirit in you may remain hidden for a while, but he is there eventually to be revealed. That's your role in this world.

Lean back into God with all your weaknesses, faults, frailties, fallenness, and brokenness. You don't need to go to great lengths to cover them up; they are platforms for the glory of God, a stage for the revelation of his nature. No one is moved when God makes a strong person strong. But when he makes a weak person strong . . . that's another story. In fact, it's your story, worth telling again and again. Don't be afraid to live it for others to see. His grace is all you—and they—will need.

Holy Spirit, let this earthen vessel burst from the power of the light within. Fill my brokenness with your restoration, my wounds with your healing, and my weakness with your power. Let me be a revelation of glory. Amen.

Your Legacy

*The one thing I ask of the LORD—the thing I seek most—is to live
in the house of the LORD all the days of my life, delighting in the
LORD's perfections and meditating in his Temple. (Psalm 27:4)*

DAVID'S DEEPEST LONGING, according to Psalm 27:4, was to spend time in the Temple of God, meditating on the Lord's perfections. It's a beautiful thought, and we can imagine him taking every opportunity to visit the Temple grounds to worship. The only problem was that when David wrote this, the Temple didn't exist yet, and it wouldn't in his generation. God had said yes to his request for a temple, but no to the possibility of David building it himself. It was a dream deferred, and it must have made David's heart sick.

Even so, David did everything he could to set up the next generation for this building project short of stacking the stones himself. He drew up blueprints, donated massive amounts of gold and building materials, wrote a psalm for the dedication of the Temple (Psalm 30), and encouraged others to give, plan, and prepare (1 Chronicles 28–29). He understood that his contributions in this world were part of a bigger picture, and he equipped the next generation to further it.

Your contributions in this world are part of a bigger picture too. God's plans began back in Genesis, and really even before the foundation of the world. You can be salt and light right now, but you are also sowing seed that will not be harvested in this generation. While governments often saddle the next generation with enormous debts and problems, Kingdom citizens are to bequeath our contributions to the Kingdom-building project to those who will come next. We are always to be mindful of the eternal scheme.

One of the greatest investments you can make in God's Kingdom is to prepare the next generation to carry it forward—to cultivate their role as salt and light just as you have cultivated your own. Take that opportunity seriously, pray for ways to expand your influence beyond your lifetime, and know that your fruitfulness in this world will continue long after you are gone.

Lord, show me ways to expand my reach chronologically and not just in current circumstances and relationships. Give me lasting influence. Sow my life as a seed that will bear fruit for generations to come. Amen.

Always New

No one puts new wine into old wineskins. For the wine would
burst the wineskins, and the wine and the skins would both be lost.
New wine calls for new wineskins. (Mark 2:22)

ONE OF THE MOST COMMON and predictable cycles in Christian history is for dynamic, Spirit-inspired movements to grow stiff and stale over time. One of the reasons for that phenomenon is our desire to preserve whatever God is doing. We want to create institutions, codify rules and structures, dissect the process, and make sure we maximize the opportunity God has given us. But our efforts are like pouring concrete into the river of life. We interrupt the flow. Many religious orders and denominations that began as powerful renewal movements have become crusty, unbending institutions that have lost their former glory. We get so stuck in what God has done that we miss what he is doing now.

Christians have a remarkable ability to fixate on the last thing God has taught them, the revelation that seemed so life-changing at the time. That's why some people are still living in the moments right after their conversion, basking in a glow of insight that is no longer glowing. They are living in days gone by, missing the ways God has tried to lead them ever since.

What's the solution? At any given moment of our lives, we need to look into the past to steward what God has done without trying to preserve it as it was. We also need to look into the future with the expectation that whatever God has done in our lives was perfect for that season but will surely grow and take new form over time, perhaps in unexpected ways. In other words, we need to live with new wineskins, always prepared to carry the freshness of the Spirit into the new situations of the future. God's Spirit moves like the wind (John 3:8); salt and light are dynamic expressions of his power; and though his character never changes, his work is always new.

Holy Spirit, you have invited me into the flow of your work. May I always flow with you, and may I keep the flow going in my corner of the world for the next generation. Let your Kingdom continue to come in fresh ways. Amen.

A Ministry of Presence

I'm not asking you to take them out of the world, but
to keep them safe from the evil one. They do not belong
to this world any more than I do. (John 17:15-16)

YOU PROBABLY REALIZED LONG ago that you were living in hostile territory. Like a defector from a communist country, you left the culture of this world and embraced the culture of God's Kingdom as your own, trading your natural homeland for a spiritual one. You belong to the world God created—you were part of his original design—but you no longer belong to the fallen world it has become. You have a citizenship in heaven, even while you walk out your days in this material realm.

When Jesus ascended into heaven, he didn't take his followers with him. The time had not yet come. There was work to be done, and he sent them on a mission—the same kind of mission he had undertaken when the Father sent him (John 17:18; 20:21). He had already told the disciples they could not go with him to heaven (John 13:36), but he had also told them that he was preparing a place for them to come (John 14:2). He left them but assured them they would not be alone. In fact, he said it was better for him to leave so his Spirit could come to inhabit them (John 16:5-15). His prayer the night before his crucifixion was that they be left right where they are, in the midst of a world of chaos and evil, but protected from the evil one.

That's where we still live. We are in the midst of a world of trouble, but we are confident that Jesus has overcome it, just as he said (John 16:33). He continues to be present in this world through his people. That's why one of the greatest things we can do for people in need of God is to be there—to be present, in the context of problems and pain, carrying the counsel and companionship of God wherever we can. As long as we live, that's our ministry, just as Jesus intended.

{ *Jesus, you left me with a mission, and I want to accomplish it well, to complete it with faithfulness and excellence. Manifest your wisdom, power, and love within me, wherever the world needs you. Lead me in a ministry of presence. Amen.*

One with Him

*I pray that they will all be one, just as you and I are one — as you
are in me, Father, and I am in you. And may they be in us so
that the world will believe you sent me. (John 17:21)*

"THE FATHER AND I ARE ONE," Jesus once said to an antagonistic crowd (John 10:30). He didn't explain exactly how they are one—whether in purpose, in personality, or in essence. But we get the sense throughout the rest of the Gospel of John that all of the above are true, that he and the Father are one in every way possible. There is no lack of unity, no hair's breadth of difference between the Father's nature and the Son's. So when Jesus prayed that his followers would be one *in the same way he and the Father are one*, we could hardly be blamed for gasping in astonishment. He saw his followers as completely united with him and with each other, just as the members of the Trinity are united.

That's a staggering thought, and we wonder if it could possibly be true. Are we really one with Jesus in the same way that he and the Father are one? And are we really united to other believers with that degree of oneness? In spiritual terms, the answers are yes. If God has united us to himself as the body of Christ, we know we are truly united. But in practical terms, we have every reason to be disappointed over our actual experience. We don't *feel* at one with Jesus, at least not all the time. And we look around at our fractured church that hardly knows how to get along and has never managed its diversity very well. Our experience falls short of the truth we have been given.

Even so, Jesus tied this unity to the world's belief. When we step into our oneness with Jesus, and when diverse Christians are able to live in unity with each other, people notice. It makes a powerful statement. We demonstrate the binding love of the Godhead when we embrace the binding love of the Son and his followers, and the world begins to see.

Jesus, I want to experience the promise of your prayer in all its fullness — complete unity with you and your people, one in spirit, for all the world to see. Bind me to yourself and make your glory seen in me. Amen.

Created for Glory

I have given them the glory you gave me, so
they may be one as we are one. (John 17:22)

ISAIAH'S WORDS WERE EMPHATIC: God does not share his glory with others (Isaiah 42:8; 48:11). The context was idolatry, and we can understand God's jealousy for the hearts of his people. No loving relationship flourishes between divided hearts, and the hearts of God's people were divided between him and false gods. He clearly would not and should not share his glory with such rivals.

But Jesus said he had given his followers the glory the Father had given him so that they might experience the oneness of divine fellowship. The only way to reconcile the statements of Isaiah and the words of Jesus are to assume that we are no longer "other"—that we are intimately bound into the love and unity of the Trinity and can share in the glory of the Father, Son, and Spirit. We were created for such glory to begin with; we were made in the image of God, and it's impossible to have his image without his glory, as the two are surely inseparable. But we shattered that image in the Fall, lost our ability to reflect the glory of God, began seeking our own glory, and set ourselves up as rivals. Jesus came in that image to restore us and to endow us with glory once again. We have been redeemed, are being restored, and are able to reflect the glory we were once given.

What does that mean in real life? It means that part of our purpose in this world is simply to be the image of God—to reflect his nature, allow him to demonstrate his strength in us, be recipients of his provision and power, and carry his wisdom and love. It means the direction of our lives should always be moving toward his likeness. It means the amazing words of his prayer are not too good to be true.

Accept them. Believe them with all your heart. Step into them daily and wear them well. The world needs you to experience what Jesus has promised and spread it far and wide.

Lord, you made me for glory. I feel it. I've even tried to get it in the wrong ways. Restore me to your true image, and let me reflect your glory well. Let me be who you long for me to be. Amen.

To the Farthest Corners

I have made you a light to the Gentiles,
to bring salvation to the farthest corners of the earth. (Acts 13:47)

IN THE EARLY TWENTIETH CENTURY, selections from Hebrew Scripture were found in the caves of Dunhuang, China, as part of a huge library of ancient documents. The biblical texts date from the first Christian millennium, perhaps as early as the 400s. They provide firm evidence that the God of Israel and his plan of salvation were made known in the East much earlier than modern missionaries once thought.

One motivation behind the modern missions movement that began among Protestants in the late 1700s and gathered momentum throughout the nineteenth century was the tragic amount of time previous generations of Christians had taken to get the message out. William Carey lamented the unreached masses of India; Hudson Taylor wept over "China's millions"; and many others expressed the same regret that the Savior of the world was still unknown to so many people around the world. But awareness of the gospel had made inroads into many of those places before: the apostle Thomas in India; Nestorians venturing into China; unknown journeys of many into the civilizations of Africa and the steppes of Asia, where vibrant churches once stood. The message of Jesus has always encountered resistance, but it has also been carried by relentless messengers. Over time—apparently God's preferred method—the word has spread into diverse cultures and language groups.

That process is still going on. The Great Commission of Jesus has not faded, though methodologies for carrying it forward have changed throughout the centuries. Today, nearly one in every three people in the world self-identifies as a Christian—a staggering number compared to just a couple of centuries ago, but still not enough. Much of Christianity's gains have come through un-Christian efforts—conquest, forced conversion, violence, and manipulation—but those carrying its true spirit have continued to be fruitful. In one way or another, you are part of that mission—wherever you are, in whatever work you do, and in whatever ways you support the overall cause. You are called both to be salt and light and to support the salt and light around you. You are always and forever a carrier of good news.

Lord, thank you for the privilege of being part of your mission—a recipient of its graces and a carrier of them as well. May your will be done in my life, in the lives of your people, and in this world now and forever. Amen.

{ Notes }

1. Frederick Buechner, *Wishful Thinking: A Theological ABC* (New York: Harper & Row, 1973).
2. Sociologist Rodney Stark has used these terms extensively in some of his books, including *God's Battalions: The Case for the Crusades* (New York: HarperCollins 2009); and *The Triumph of Christianity: How the Jesus Movement Became the World's Largest Religion* (New York: HarperCollins, 2011).
3. Though they were given in Aramaic and written to us in Greek, they come from a Hebrew context.
4. Anthony B. Bradley, "You Are the Manure of the Earth," *Christianity Today*, September 23, 2016, https://www.christianitytoday.com/ct/2016/october/you-are-manure-of-earth.html.
5. Story and theme taken from an article by Andrea Palpant Dilley, "The Surprising Discovery about Those Colonialist, Proselytizing Missionaries," *Christianity Today*, January 8, 2014, https://www.christianitytoday.com/ct/2014/january-february/world-missionaries-made.html.
6. Norman Grubb, *Rees Howells, Intercessor* (Fort Washington, PA: Christian Literature Crusade, 1987), 231.
7. John Howie, *Heroes for the Faith: Lives of the Scottish Worthies* (London: Ward, Lock and Co., 1827), 443–445.
8. Watchman Nee, *Sit, Walk, Stand* (Carol Stream, IL: Tyndale House Publishers, 1977), 32–33.
9. Bartolomé de las Casas, *The Devastation of the Indies: A Brief Account* (1542), trans. Herma Briffault (Baltimore: Johns Hopkins University Press, 1992), 29.
10. Ibid.
11. Description of Carver quoted in Andy Andrews, *The Lost Choice: A Legend of Personal Discovery* (Nashville: Thomas Nelson, 2004), 97.
12. Peter Brown, *The Ransom of the Soul: Afterlife and Wealth in Early Western Christianity* (Cambridge, MA: Harvard University Press, 2015), 90–91.
13. Bartolomé de las Casas, *Devastation of the Indies*, 45.
14. *Sayings of the Desert Fathers: The Alphabetical Collection*, trans. Benedicta Ward, SLG (Kalamazoo, MI: Cistercian Publications, 1975 [1984]), 138–39.
15. This concept is fully explored in Jonathan T. Pennington, *The Sermon on the Mount and Human Flourishing: A Theological Commentary* (Grand Rapids, MI: Baker Academic, 2017).
16. Robert Frost, "The Road Not Taken," 1916.

{ Scripture Index }

{ About the Author }

Insightful and thought-provoking, CHRIS TIEGREEN has inspired thousands of people through his popular One Year devotionals, including *The One Year Walk with God Devotional, The One Year At His Feet Devotional, The One Year Hearing His Voice Devotional,* and *The One Year Experiencing God's Presence Devotional.* He is also the author of the devotionals *The Wonder of Advent* and *The Promise of Lent* as well as *Unburdened* and numerous other books that have been translated into more than thirty languages. Tiegreen's experiences in ministry, journalism, and higher education bring a unique perspective to his writing.

REDISCOVER THE HEART & POWER OF CHRIST'S EARTHLY MISSION.

Beloved devotional author Chris Tiegreen brings readers full circle with two thought-provoking devotionals that dive deeper into the life, death, and resurrection of Christ.

THE WONDER OF ADVENT DEVOTIONAL WILL RECONNECT YOU WITH WHAT HAPPENED IN BETHLEHEM LONG AGO— AND HELP YOU EXPERIENCE IT ANEW IN YOUR LIFE RIGHT NOW.

THE PROMISE OF LENT DEVOTIONAL PREPARES YOUR HEART FOR THE IMPACT OF CHRIST'S ULTIMATE SACRIFICE— AS YOU BEGIN TO SEE THE MAGNITUDE OF GOD'S REDEMPTIVE PLAN.

AVAILABLE FROM TYNDALE MOMENTUM.   CP1302